REBUILDING CITIES

REBUILDING CITIES

•

PERCY
JOHNSON-MARSHALL
MA, DIP ARCH, ARIBA, AMTPI
Professor of
Urban Design and Regional Planning
University of Edinburgh

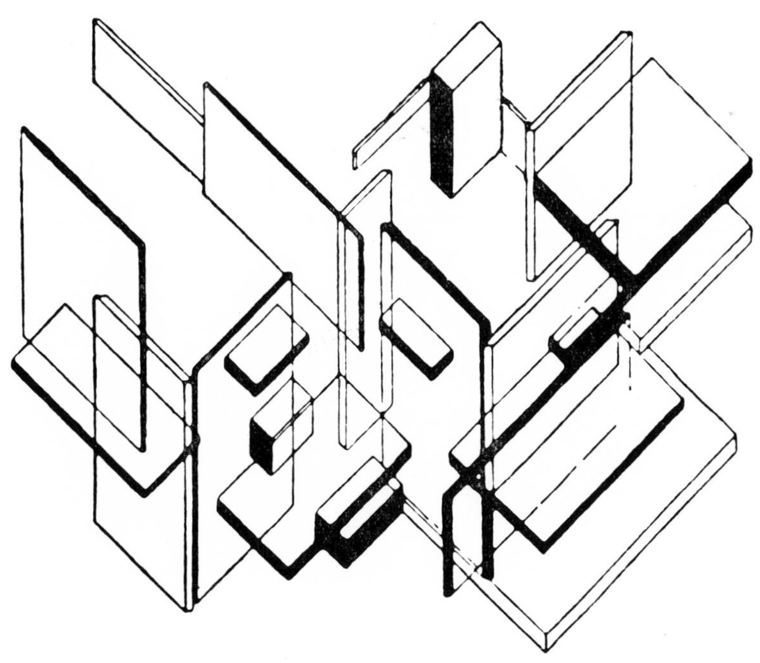

EDINBURGH
AT THE UNIVERSITY PRESS

•

EDINBURGH UNIVERSITY PRESS
George Square, Edinburgh 8
North America
Aldine Publishing Company
320 West Adams Street, Chicago
Australia and New Zealand
Hodder & Stoughton Ltd.
Africa, Oxford University Press
India, P.C. Manaktala & Sons
Far East, M. Graham Brash & Son

The drawing on the title-page, called *Space Study*, is by the Dutch architect-planner Van Doesburg

Printed in Great Britain
by T. & A. Constable Limited
Printers to the University of Edinburgh

PREFACE

The idea of writing this book began over ten years ago. By 1955 I thought that enough planning and building had been undertaken in some of the bombed cities of Western Europe to make its recording a useful exercise. My *Reconstruction Areas Group* in the London County Council Architect's Department had by then spent seven hard years on London's Comprehensive Areas with varying degrees of success, against almost every conceivable kind of difficulty. It was then that Monica Pidgeon, Editor of *Architectural Design*, asked me to report on progress. This took the form of a special number, and the idea became firmly established. Various articles and broadcasts followed, on London, Coventry, and Rotterdam, and a further impetus was given when the Royal Institute of British Architects invited me to read a Sessional Paper on Comprehensive Development in 1958. This was published in five articles in the RIBA Journal during 1959 and 1960, with the enthusiastic help of the then Editor, Noel Musgrave. Since that time the making of the book has gone ahead, changing in size and to some extent in conception as the University Press staff in Edinburgh worked steadily through the various drafts and mock-ups. In the three years since I wrote the text much has inevitably happened. Other important books on planning have been published, and I would have liked to have amended some of the contents in consequence. This, however, would have involved further delay, and have made this book less immediately useful.

A book of this kind owes a great deal to many people—to my wife and family, who always suffer on such occasions; to Lewis Mumford, for ideas and thoughts at varying depths; to Patrick Geddes; to the men in charge of these vast and complicated planning operations: my good friend Donald Gibson, first Chief Architect and Planning Officer in Coventry, who posesses humanity and sagacity in full measure, and who took me into his home after the great 1943 bombing raid on Coventry when my own was severely damaged, and on whose living-room floor the first germinal model of the future city centre was born in the early hours of a winter's morning; Robert Matthew, who was the great revitalizing force as the post-war Chief Architect and Planning Officer of the London County Council. Since 1949 I have worked with him in his new Department in the University of Edinburgh, and also on a number of planning adventures, and I continue to admire the driving force of his fine personality, and his high sense of social purpose.

To Leslie Martin, who was Deputy Chief Architect of the London County Council when I arrived, and who for too short a time was Chief Architect after Robert Matthew's departure; to Hubert Bennett, who followed him in this biggest of all architectural/planning tasks (and to whom I am extremely grateful for permission to use a large number of photographs); to Frank West, for ten years Deputy Chief Architect and Planning Officer after Leslie Martin; I give my thanks for their unfailing generosity and civilized leadership.

To Cornelius Van Traa, for twenty years Chief Planner of Rotterdam, I extend unbounded admiration. Rotterdam is not, in fact, any great distance from London or

Edinburgh, but time rather than distance is today the enemy, and my visits to him and to his dynamic city have been too few to do them both justice. In many ways Van Traa has succeeded more than almost any other Planning Chief, and Rotterdam has been implementing his plans both at the strategic and tactical levels. If some of the ideas now come under criticism today, it is partly because they are at least *there* for all to see, and partly because we have the wisdom of hindsight.

Arthur Ling, who persuaded me to join his reorganized Planning Division in the London County Council Architect's Department, who guided London's planning over the vital post war years, who then took Donald Gibson's place as Chief Architect and Planning Officer in Coventry in 1956, has been a close colleague and warm friend, and for the last ten years has guided Coventry's astonishing redevelopment. Leslie Lane who followed him as Senior Planning Officer, took over one of the world's toughest planning positions, and filled it with stature and efficiency.

To the three senior planners of my Reconstruction Areas Group, Gordon Logie, Walter Bor, and Graeme Shankland, and of these particularly Walter Bor, who was with my Group for ten years of intensely dedicated and unremitting service, my warmest thanks must go for the comradeship of journeys in exploration; and with them the large number of unselfish and devoted people who worked days and nights in the cause of humanity—for what is planning if it is not that? If I pick out for mention Ann MacEwen and Richard Bigwood, it is because, like Walter Bor, they were with me for the whole ten and a half years of my stay at the London County Council; but even this is unfair to all their colleagues, many of whom are now filling important positions in various parts of the world—some with me now in Edinburgh.

Of the original small team in Coventry, Messrs Pinion, Lycett, Powell and Burgoyne, who worked with me on the very first Coventry scheme, and also of the many good friends in the Planning Office at Rotterdam, I have warm memories in spite of the sometimes grim and even tragic experiences we went through together.

Nor must I forget those known in Britain as the 'elected members', who have the hard task of actually making the decision to plan or not to plan: Bill Hodgkinson of Coventry, Messrs Fiske and Stamp and Edmonds of London, Dr Van Walsum, Burgomaster of Rotterdam, who, although in a slightly different position, was nevertheless faced with the same order of decision-making, or decision-persuading.

Then there are so many others who have helped in various ways: numerous officials and good friends in the GLC, in Coventry, in Rotterdam, and in the City Corporation of London, who have all helped to find photographs and other material; Messrs Aerofilms, in particular, have provided a spectacular service in a comparatively new field, replacing the old bird's-eye view or balloon prospect with infinitely more accurate although less romantic airscapes. To all those who have allowed photographs and other material to be reproduced; to colleagues at the University and at my Bella Vista Studio, and especially to Miss Elsie Bryce, who did so much of the typing; and lastly to my publisher, Archie Turnbull, of the Edinburgh University Press, who became as enthusiastic as a planner over planning, and who helped in so many ways to make this book possible—to them all, many thanks.

PERCY JOHNSON-MARSHALL
Edinburgh
July, 1965

CONTENTS

This book
is dedicated to those
who suffered in the destruction
of cities

INTRODUCTION

Since 1930 there has been a plethora of books about the modern movement in architecture, but there has been a singular dearth of studies dealing in a broad historical and critical way with the similar transformation that has been going on in the design of cities. This lack of comparative information over what has actually been thought and done about the Rebuilding of Cities gives to Professor Percy Johnson-Marshall's survey a particular distinction and value.

In the main, for lack of active intercourse, the relations between the new architecture and the new planning have been perfunctory and superficial, too often actually sterile. This is perhaps because those working in one field have been indifferent to the needs and possibilities opened up by their colleagues in the other field. The notable exceptions before 1930 were achieved by Fritz Schumacher in Hamburg, Ernst May in Frankfurt-am-Main, Bruno Taut and Martin Wagner in Berlin, and above all, Le Corbusier in Paris, for all of these pioneers treated architecture and urban design as a unified process.

After the regressive Nazis empoisoned contemporary culture in Central Europe, Le Corbusier remained the chief vocal exponent of a unified approach: his immense influence is perhaps partly attributable to the fact that his new architectural designs were conceived as being finally realized within the ideal urban layouts he had projected. If his town planning principles were stated in almost exclusively biological and technical terms, with no sufficient insight into economic and social complexities, his unity of purpose nevertheless offset some of the human insufficiencies of his projections.

After half a century of experience in the building and rebuilding of cities, in an attempt to repair the damage and wanton mischief done by short-sighted builders and municipal officials, and to lay down sounder general principles for creating new urban quarters, it is time for those concerned—and who is not?—to look at the results. Toward this end the present book makes a positive contribution by assembling the great mass of relevant material needed for such an assessment. This is a task of both acceptance and rejection: of approval and dismissal. Mr Johnson-Marshall's generous array of examples does justice to the abundant creativity of our period, and shows that we have already achieved, at least in outline, the beginnings of a fresh urban form: one that connects with the best work of the past and opens up further developments for the future.

But if these examples are carefully scrutinized, we shall also find that many seemingly ideal images conjured up during the last generation have proved, on experiment, aesthetically depressing and socially valueless, despite their sanitary or technical excellence and superficial order. Among the latter, I would count many of those multiplying high-rise flats, no matter how widely spaced, whose excessive first costs and equally extravagant upkeep have no valid justification—except, perhaps, the dubious one of furnishing larger profits to the contractors and suppliers of materials, larger fees to the architect, or larger ground rents, based on excessive densities, to the land owners. Though the author's emphasis has naturally been upon positive examples of the planner's art, he has provided a sufficiently wide range of illustrations to encourage the discriminating reader to think twice about some of the current solutions. Since a large part of our municipal budgets for housing and planning now promotes high buildings at excessive densities, along with an equally costly and futile mono-transportation based on the private motor vehicle, even the richest countries cannot find sufficient money to support the educational, cultural, and social activities that justify the city's existence.

By the catholicity of his taste and the abundance of his examples, Mr Johnson-Marshall has accordingly done a special service to the reader: he has not merely provided through his prefatory essay excellent clues to the illustrations, but he has given such a wide conspectus to the movement for rebuilding cities that the reader himself can sort out in his own mind the bad from the good, the extravagant from the prudent, the purely mechanical from the organic forms which integrate mechanical functions into biological norms and human purposes.

Not the least value of this work is that it comes not from a detached observer like myself but from a professional planner who, not too long after he left the School of Architecture at the University of Liverpool, in the great days when Sir Charles Reilly was its leader, was plunged into the practice of planning. Mr Johnson-Marshall's pre-war service as planner with Donald Gibson at Coventry gave him exceptional opportunities, for even before the Blitz had ruined its centre, this dynamic industrial town's needs and opportunities were happily balanced, since, with a population of less than three hundred thousand and municipal ownership of no small part of its land, its problems were still manageable and its future growth was still plannable.

The author's response to this challenge is so well described in his own words that any further comment of mine would be gratuitous. Returning from military service, Mr Johnson-Marshall became head of the Reconstruction Areas Group in the Town Planning division of the London County Council's Architect's Department under the two architects who boldly shaped its post-war policy, Robert Matthew and Leslie Martin; and his leadership in the large-scale rehabilitation of the Stepney–Poplar Reconstruction Area, beginning with the deservedly admired Lansbury Neighbourhood, counts as one of the outstanding examples of post-war urban planning.

During this active period of planning, the author had the valuable experience, as a householder with a large family, of living at one end of the great central square at Hampstead Garden suburb; and by this enlivening contact with the intense humanism of the older generation of planners, as exemplified by Raymond Unwin and Barry Parker, he brought to his mature conception of urban building certain values that were too often lacking in Le Corbusier's early schemes. Since Unwin and Le Corbusier stand for the two diametrically opposite poles of modern planning, Mr Johnson-Marshall's reconciliation and synthesis of their approaches has been one of his happiest achievements.

To these general conceptions of planning, the author himself had added still another element that I make bold to point out. This springs from his association with Coventry, an old medieval centre that still, though inundated by modern industrialism, retains a medieval sense of civic responsibility and initiative that has proved a powerful force in rehabilitating—or perhaps one should say even regenerating—that city, as the bold initiative that produced its magnificent new Cathedral bears witness.

In the preliminary work done by the author's team, under Donald Gibson, he addressed himself to the main task of every city, that of reconstructing its centre and bringing it back to life, not just as a shopping area and office district but as a focal point in the whole civic life of the community and its region. In his present stress on the importance of the civic nucleus, Mr Johnson-Marshall, long before the C.I.A.M.'s symposium on 'The Heart of the City', brought forward functions and purposes that other contemporary theoreticians had—like the proponents of Civic Centers in the United States—either ignored or failed adequately to interpret in present-day terms.

By emphasizing the role of the pedestrian core, as an assembly place and a meeting-place, Mr Johnson-Marshall brings out the very elements that enable a city to function culturally *as* a city: the elements that pass on the cultural heritage, and ultimately give form to all its subordinate activities.

Where the civic nucleus does not exist, or where it exists only in a shrunken, vestigial form, the town, if it continues to grow, becomes an undifferentiated, urbanoid mass. Its parts often multiply rapidly, like cancer cells, because the central nucleus does not perform one of its main functions, that of holding the parts together and preventing any one part from expanding at the expense of the effective life of the whole.

The importance of this concept of the *civic nucleus* fully justifies the devotion of a whole chapter to its post-war development at Coventry in the pedestrian shopping centre, in the Cathedral Close, and in the planning of the related buildings thereabouts. At this juncture, the lesson of the historic city, continuous from Mesopotamia through Greece to the Middle Ages, and the lesson of the British New Towns in our own time, beginning with the now relatively ancient Letchworth Garden City, were successfully applied to an industrial city in order to contain its growth and both intensify and amplify the kind of social and cultural stimulus it gives to its citizens.

Here Mr Johnson-Marshall has provided an important key to anything that can be called modern town planning and city design; a key that applies equally to the planning of neighbourhoods, precincts, sectors, and the city as a whole. I emphasize this contribution because, in the wealth of illustrations that constitutes such a vital portion of this book, that central perception might too easily be passed over.

A final word about the author himself. We first met at dinner in 1946, and I remember vividly his conducting me afterward from Regent Street back to my hotel not far from Victoria Station: he threaded through the maze of intervening streets, from one devious passage to another, in a way that shamed my old pride as a lover of London, for some of these streets I had never seen even by daylight. He made me appreciate, as never before, the wonderful combination of seclusion and intensely social living that London had up to then preserved, to the secret enrichment of its daily life: a combination not analyzed or taught in town planning schools.

This intimate knowledge, not only of the form but the texture of cities, is one of Mr Johnson-Marshall's prime qualifications as a planner. To that he has added an unflagging devotion to public service, at the expense of private interests his professional qualifications could have furthered. This sense of responsibility to his public mission goes beyond even the high traditions of the British Civil Service: it is a dedication and a commitment of an even deeper sort. By sticking to his post, when many of his colleagues were being lured away to more 'creative', sometimes more lucrative tasks, he gave his Group in the L.C.C. a continuity and a sense of social duty that contributed not a little, I am sure, to the high quality of its performance.

In transferring his sphere of activity to Edinburgh University, Mr Johnson-Marshall has put at the service of the coming generation of planners not merely his skill and experience but something even more admirable: his human example. If our civilization learns to master its wanton energies and give form to its urban and regional environments, it will be through the kind of knowledge this book presents and through the passion for aesthetic and social form that it encourages.

LEWIS MUMFORD
Amenia, New York
Spring, 1965

PART ONE

1

The Historical Background of Growth

PRE-INDUSTRIAL. Most sites for European urban settlements have been established for hundreds of years. The fourteenth century saw the cores of many of our large cities already in existence, so that today we have half a millennium of urban development, redevelopment, expansion and contraction available for study. Some settlements grew from the ruins of older Roman cities, others from a straggle of stalls beyond the castle gate. Others, again, had to await the development of a mercantile system and organized trade; these, in consequence, nearly always grew up near a navigable river or inlet of the sea, and usually achieved urban form as rows of merchants' houses, the largest grouped round the high street or market-place, the more modest set side by side in the lanes leading up to it. Parish churches would be built, followed by religious buildings for the various monastic or other orders. A parish church would sometimes be enlarged to cathedral status; and, as the Church was responsible for much of what one would today call social welfare, there might follow hospitals, schools, and even homes for the aged. So there arose, among the dwellings of citizens, a hierarchy of religious and social buildings not only expressing their function in three-dimensional form but also their urban significance in the fabric of the city.

As secular society became more stable and complex, specialized crafts appeared—each keeping very much to one street or district—and organized themselves into guilds, with their attendant guildhalls; while the increasing number of travellers necessitated the building of hostelries and inns. Finally, as city government and the rule of law evolved, town halls and law courts were built.

The medieval city thus contained diverse groups of buildings for domestic, social, economic, and political purposes. Although the siting of these buildings on the ground eventually took a wide variety of forms, it probably began in a haphazard way around the original market or meeting-place, with enclosed spaces left, or cleared, facing the churches and other public buildings. There were of course regular-planned towns, such as Turin, rebuilt on its original Roman pattern, or the medieval colonial New

Towns, which were nearly always laid out in a rectangular formation. These, however, were exceptions rather than the rule.

A political factor which influenced the form and density of the late-medieval city was the need for defence. Most cities had fortifications, consisting of walls, gates, boulevards or aprons, and perhaps a moat. As the population grew, this very solid urban fence forced up the density of building *within* it, and tended to encourage an urban sprawl *beyond* it, usually in the form of temporary and easily demolished buildings. Since this overspill was liable to be destroyed from time to time little effort was made to plan or design it, and when at length greater security came, it was too late to re-form a straggling pattern of lanes, defined and fixed by buildings on either side. In some cases, however, the destruction of the fortifications themselves eventually gave an opportunity for urban development on more spacious sites, as in Vienna; in others the re-forming of walls and aprons enabled a new urban component—the tree-lined boulevard—to be laid out.

With the general increase of security and the development of certain crafts into small industries, the towns continued to increase in population. The problem of finding sites for the new workshops and for additional dwelling-places was solved at first by infilling and building over the town gardens, until sheer urban congestion forced development beyond the old fortified area.

In some cases these urban extensions just continued to straggle out along the roads, but in others landowners employed architects to lay out new residential areas for the upper-income groups. It was these groups which, finding the cheek-by-jowl living of the old towns increasingly unsatisfactory, demanded new and more open living conditions, thus initiating the separation of living places from the tight all-class living/working/shopping milieu of the old cities. This culminated in the virtual elimination from central areas of all but the poorest homes.

The decongestion resulting from this first overspill programme created the first great opportunity for urban renewal in the old core, and occasionally it was taken. There were, for instance, the striking multi-level redevelopment schemes undertaken with such boldness in Edinburgh, where the whole area to the west of the Cathedral was drastically altered, and the town provided with one of the first multi-level traffic intersections, equipped even with one arm of a clover leaf.

The most famous Renaissance achievements of planned urban redevelopment took place in Rome and Paris. In the first, a religious leader directed the creation of a number of separate urban set-pieces, and in the second, during some 300 years, a whole series of potentates worked to refashion and redesign various parts of the centre of a great capital city. This culminated in the burst of planned improvements by Haussmann, which brought the prolonged but comprehensive operations to completion with such success that the Renaissance layout of Paris was for long taken as the model for all cities to follow.

Although cities increased in size during the seventeenth and eighteenth centuries, they remained small by present-day standards. Until the end of the eighteenth century, one could walk out of even the largest cities in any direction in fifteen minutes, and since the majority of person-movements took place on foot, the whole character was attuned to this scale. Eventually, however, the rapidly increasing pace of mercantile trade, particularly in the case of seaport cities, brought additional growth of population, and eventually created exceptional opportunities, which were sometimes taken, of creating large-scale planned layouts, enabling important new planning ideas to be developed. Examples of these layouts may be seen in London, Glasgow, Edinburgh, and Bristol.

INDUSTRIALIZATION. The Industrial Revolution had drastic effects on all towns which contributed to it. Towards the end of the eighteenth century the most intense industrial activity in Britain naturally took place near the sources of iron and coal: Tyneside, Lanark, South Wales, and the Midlands. New means of communication, however, first by canal and then by railway, in time brought similar industrial expansion to most of the existing mercantile centres. This resulted not just in an increased number of small workshops but also in a new ring of urban development, muddled and unplanned, with railway yards, storage sheds and factories all mixed up with rows of low-cost housing. In the older urban cores the all-purpose merchants' houses were replaced by large specialized commercial buildings, built in such a piecemeal fashion that although the building volume, and hence the urban working population, greatly increased, the spaces between the buildings—in the form of roads and open spaces—remained as before, and therefore became relatively smaller. The net result was a deterioration in the total urban environment.

Increasingly congested conditions in the central areas caused more and more people of the upper- and middle-income groups to move out along railway lines, and this developed into a large-scale daily mass movement of commuters to and from the centre. The continual demand for building space in the centre, mainly for the new administrative and commercial uses, caused a huge rise in land speculation, so that by the beginning of the twentieth century the land in city centres was not only divided up into a large number of ownerships but was also of prohibitive cost, thus rendering even the possibility of remedial planning measures impracticable.

Then came the motor vehicle. Its ever-increasing impact on the city is only now beginning to force people into drastic measures of urban renewal. Contemporaneously with the internal-combustion engine, a number of other technological inventions were developed which, by not being considered in relation to a planned environment, merely caused an even greater intensification or urban disorder. The electric lift, for instance, enabled a much larger number of people to work on the same site, while the underground railway brought commuters flooding into the centre in thousands instead of hundreds.

These factors caused a degeneration and decay in the centres and inner rings of large cities. This was often not immediately apparent; it took many forms: one was to turn the centres into a night-time desert, because nobody lived there any more. Another was the overthrow of the older building hierarchy. Churches and other public buildings which formerly had stood high over surrounding buildings of lesser importance were now submerged visually by commercial over-building. A third was that human scale was overwhelmed, and often the sense, and the reality, of space for the cultural, recreational and even contemplative pursuits of man were diminished drastically.

Owing to this build-up of new urban conditions, with the city centre as a place for work without pleasure; where cultural activity was only just tolerated, if not entirely squeezed out of the urban core altogether; where the muddle of uses had become so great as to constitute gross inefficiency of the city as a collective machine for work; where enormous invisible financial bonds tied down every site; men despaired of ever achieving an environment worthy of our time. Somehow, the greater the possibilities, the greater were the difficulties, so that before the last war one could even find city plans which had the whole of their centres excluded from any planning proposals. The dreamers had visions, but were laughed out of town by the practical men, and it was only the sudden sharp shock of devastation wrought by air bombardment that caused a ray of light to penetrate this darkness.

TIME, SPACE AND THE URBAN PATTERN. One of the most difficult problems of town planning is that concerned with *time*. A town may be planned and built within a few years, but a city is almost inevitably a matter of generations. In Europe, and in Great Britain in particular, we are concerned almost entirely with the replanning and rebuilding of existing cities, and, as we have seen, they are often very old, with remnants of their framework reaching back centuries in time. It is often not too much to say that today's architecture is created in, and conditioned by, the urban pattern of yesterday's culture.

Owing to the absence of conscious planning and co-ordinated control over the last 150 years, as it has been described above, a series of maladjustments has taken place, to the ever-increasing detriment of the city as a *human* environment. A road pattern, for instance, which was more than generous for a small centre with horse and pedestrian circulation has become hopelessly inadequate for a large city with the fantastic increase in motor traffic which we are now experiencing. In the meantime the slow process of piecemeal renewal and increasing property values has held the old pattern in a vice-like grip which only large-scale acquisition and demolition can change.

Another problem of time in relation to the lack of planning is created by the increase in building volume which can take place in a city, without complementary changes accompanying it. The most glaring example of this is Manhattan, where the road pattern has remained more or less static but the building types, based on family residential units, have changed over a period of about 100 years to offices and commerce, and a vast increase in building volume has occurred on each site.

In this context, perhaps the most difficult lesson to learn, particularly for the architect, is that urban redevelopment may take many years to achieve, and that one has therefore to think of urban design as a *continuous* and *flexible* process. It is salutary to remember that some famous civic set-pieces, which we are accustomed to think of as comprehensive architectural unities, sometimes took centuries to complete. The *Piazza San Marco* in Venice is a good case study. Its history began in the early part of the ninth century, when the nucleus comprised the Byzantine church of St Theodore, a castle, a campanile, and an orchard. When the Venetians brought the remains of St Mark from Alexandria in AD 828, a new church was built alongside the old one. This church of St Mark was rebuilt in the tenth century, and rebuilt again in its present form about AD 1000, the Byzantine church then being demolished to stress the reality of Venetian independence. The castle was rebuilt five times, the third time marking the change from castle to palace. The Doge who was responsible for the fourth rebuilding, Sebastiano Ziani, was also the first real planner of the Piazza, the floorscape of which, incidentally, was resurfaced first in brick in 1264 and then in stone in 1723. The present Doge's Palace was built in the fourteenth century; then followed the Watch Tower (1496-1499), the Campanile, rebuilt in its present form (1513), the Procuratie Vecchie along the north flank, by Sansovino (1500-1532), the

Library by Sansovino and others (1540-1588), the Procuratie Nuove along the south flank by Scamozzi (1582-1640), and the church of St Gimignano moved from a site near the Campanile to close the west side of the Piazza. Finally Napoleon demolished the west side, including St Gimignano, and replaced it with a large dance-hall! So the time scale for the creation of St Mark's Piazza was approximately 1,000 years, its form evolving over many generations, partly by the somewhat haphazard grouping of public buildings, and partly by conscious design.

It is therefore important for us to know something of the interaction of the time factor and the social environment on the nature of the urban pattern, and we shall now take a closer look at this aspect of things.

The medieval town grew slowly, so slowly that by comparison with today it would scarcely be termed growth at all. A full sequence of plans of an old town shows how great is the difference between the rate of urban growth in the last two hundred years and all the preceding centuries. Yet as the medieval town achieved stable form and redevelopment took place, urban design of considerable quality emerged; but perhaps 'design' is not the correct word, since it is very difficult to say how many of the effects achieved were purely accidental, or how much they owed to the conscious awareness of designers. We have seen that one of the first opportunities for medieval urban design was created by the hierarchy of building types. This hierarchy, although present in every period, became characteristic of medieval towns. At first the Castle was the dominant building form, in contrast to the surrounding hovels; but when cathedrals came to be built they nearly always expressed in scale and siting their commanding role in society. There was indeed a hierarchy of religious buildings, from the cathedrals, with their great urban spaces of squares, precincts, closes and cloisters, via the parish churches with smaller places and graveyards, down to the minor chapels and friaries. A secular hierarchy of buildings evolved over the same period: each craft having a hall in the street or district appertaining to its particular activity. All the tradesmen together might have a larger, more richly designed, and more centrally placed guildhall. Thus there slowly evolved—and without much geometrical control of the road network—an informal but none the less well-integrated urban pattern which accurately, if undeliberately, reflected that central medieval concept of order, or *degree*, in which the harmony of the whole geocentric universe depended on each component, however lofty or lowly, performing its appropriate function. 'The Heavens themselves', Shakespeare wrote in a famous passage,

> Observe degree, priority, and place,
> Insisture, course, proportion, season, form,
> Office and custom, in all line of order.
> . . . How could *communities*,
> Degrees in schools, and brotherhoods in *cities*, . . .
> But by degree, stand in authentic place?
> Take but degree away, untune that string,
> And, Hark, what discord follows.

It was this sense of cognate life, of proportion and relationship, which created an urban scene of narrow winding streets leading to and opening suddenly on the greater urban spaces, enriched with public buildings of dignified scale, and soaring vertically godwards. This sense of meaningful contrast induced strong feelings of the variety, surprise and even sublimity of human life—in the suddenly experienced glory of a whole cathedral front.

SELF-CONSCIOUSNESS AND URBAN DESIGN. In the Renaissance, scientific theories and observations displaced the Earth from the centre of the Universe and the Divine scheme of things, and consequently untuned the music of the spheres. Man no longer was sure about his place in God's scheme, and there was therefore a loosening of that sense of human community existing through mutual responsibility which had characterized medieval Christendom. In its place the Renaissance put the ultimate value on the free development of individual personality; each man (within the limits of law) for himself. With this increase in self-awareness, town planning ceased to be a natural expression of the life of the community and became, much more consciously, a branch of artistic self-expression, often intended to glorify some particular prince or despot, in deliberate imitation of Roman antiquity. Since most European cities were by then in existence, however, the Renaissance urban designer had perforce to content himself with the *remodelling* of existing urban scenes, or with the development of planned town extensions.

The planners were much influenced by contemporary artistic trends: the cult of the antique, the mathematical-geometrical laws of perspective painfully worked out first by Brunelleschi and Alberti, and the expression of both trends in theatre stage-sets. Thus there was established a whole set of *rules* for the urban designer which survived until the twentieth century. Based on the concept of visual order, these rules were simple geometric formulae. Two symmetrical street façades, forming a *vista*, were to carry the eye onwards to a terminal feature, the latter preferably a completely symmetrical form which would be the central point of an open, symmetrical, but geometrically surrounded space. Later achievements, particularly in Britain, developed and enriched this vocabulary by experimenting with the various forms of geometrical enclosed spaces, so that in the New Town of Edinburgh, for instance, one may progress through formal streets and squares and on to circuses, crescents, and even a three-sided square with a crescent at one end.

The components or building types forming these urban designs were usually the dwellings of the middle classes—the rising bourgeoisie of mercantile capitalism joining forces with the older landowners, accepting in accordance with the dictates of convention a surprising degree of regimentation and similarity in their dwelling forms, so that the urban designer could play with whole streets of houses and create at times the semblance of one great palatial mansion, as at Queen Square in Bath. *Variety* was now achieved through a hierarchy, not of function, but of wealth, expressed by a graduated scale of house types in the town; but at least some formal *order*—in the narrow sense—was imposed by having entire streets of often identical houses, the street widths varying according to the scale of house types, so that in one street all the houses would be classified within a given category, which would specify the permitted height, cornice lines and other design details. For the terminal features the designer might have a new church, more occasionally a town hall or even a palace, but in some cases a large medieval building served. Often, however, no terminal feature was available and then it was left for time and the *romantic landscape* movement to complete the design with mature trees. This later landscape movement had indeed a powerful if unpremeditated effect on the design of Renaissance layouts: squares which were designed to be seen as enclosed urban spaces, with perhaps a statue or obelisk set in a simple horizontal plane of earth or paving, were radically transformed by the enclosure of a large area with railings, which was converted into a green carpet on which were planted large trees, so that 150 years later the building façades are almost impossible to distinguish behind a mass of green foliage.

Apart from the techniques of geometrical layout and the pattern-book classification of houses into first-, second-, third-, fourth- and fifth-rate types, there were yet other elements in this ordered creation of the post-Renaissance urban scene. One such was the development of regulations for controlling building, which began after the great Fire of London. These regulations affected not only building techniques in terms of stability and fire-resistant materials but also the innumerable minor objects which previously tended to encumber streets. Then there were stipulations affecting the orderly layout and surfacing of streets, roads, and pavements (*sidewalks*), and the development of a large number of standardized elements of street furniture—the railings, lamp posts, the street names, house numbers, door knockers, and so forth, all tending towards an orderly *disciplined* urban scene.

Innumerable lessons may be learned by examining the details of these layouts—the problem of the treatment of corners at the meeting of two streets, the methods of providing road access to squares while still retaining space enclosure, the masking of pitched roofs, chimney pots and other untidy but necessary appurtenances behind a great sweep of cornice—a dubious lesson, this—the common gardens shared by two terraces, as in Ladbroke Grove in London, and many others.

In fact, so intelligent, imaginative, flexible and generally excellent are these eighteenth- and early nineteenth-century town layouts that it is only now, with the full impact of the motor vehicle upon us, that their limitations are becoming apparent.

THE COLLAPSE OF URBAN DESIGN. Although orderly, planned developments continued well into the nineteenth century—indeed some of the best residential layouts were done in the first fifty years of the century—a vast change was taking place in the whole character of urban development and redevelopment. With the introduction of machinery and the factory system, the great mass of the working people was separated from the land and herded into factory town to serve the needs of cotton-spinning, coal-mining, iron-smelting, shipbuilding, and railway-making. These factory towns were the new workshops of the world, and in the great age of *laissez-faire* capitalism no one connected all this vast industrial development and its mass housing with the possibility of *planned* development. The huge increase in the productive capacity of Western man might have been used to enhance, indeed to transform, the social condition and environment of human beings, but selfish interests turned capital and labour into bitter foes, instead of partners in the new society, whose appalling *mis*management was reflected in the increasing squalor of industrial urban conditions.

The shape and quality of the factory towns was not determined by human needs. Man was regarded as subservient to the all-powerful machine. Manufacturers wanted to make things to make money, and they built their factories with that end in view; indeed, this might not have mattered greatly if all the other and different manufacturers were not at the same time doing the same thing, and if the railways were not enabling a torrent of raw materials to pour into the agglomerations, and manufactured goods to pour out. Other business men made money merely by running up acres of sub-standard terraced (*row*) houses, which were often fitted in closely among the factories, workshops and coke ovens, and too often formed a solid mass of dwellings with only a public house at each long terrace end to serve as community centre. The upper-income groups who had previously lived cheek by jowl with their less-fortunate fellows in the older settlements now followed the fashion set by Nash's *Park Village* near Regent's Park, by building individual villas in informal gardens dotted about off winding roads, located usually near a park or the new railway station.

One might say that the large industrial plants and their associated mass housing were both now—if lamentable—urban elements. So, too, were the new business centres. These usually grew out of the core of some older and attractive market town, with its attendant town hall, parish churches, merchants' houses, and shops lining a high street or market-place. As the business side of industrial capitalism developed there was an increasing demand for offices and commercial buildings—for banks, insurance offices, warehouses, and other new urban components. Retail trade, too, changed its character as shops grew larger and vastly increased in number down all the old streets leading to the centre. Since there were no effective planning controls to deal with a piecemeal situation of growth, a free-for-all took place and a whole new system of speculative property dealing grew up, with land and buildings looked on increasingly as a profitable commodity. Again it was the *scale* of development which quite changed its character and created a new situation. For after properties had changed hands several times at a higher price each time, the community as a whole could no longer raise enough money to acquire parts of the town site in order to carry out the urban planning improvements which soon became necessary. As the cities grew in size and population and as the buildings were rebuilt on the same sites, but with double or treble their bulk, the earlier road pattern which had been adequate for a small pre-industrial population became increasingly congested. Desperate attempts were made at street widening, a prolonged and expensive process which meant acquiring frontages piece by piece along a whole street; so prolonged indeed that the improvement was often obsolete before it was completed. A classic example of this street widening method is the Strand in London, which has been undergoing the process for many years but is still incomplete, and still remains inadequate for its purpose.

The free-enterprise system which brought about the redevelopment and enlargement of the new commercial buildings was thus forced to bring into existence—with however ill a grace—a new system of building controls. Large buildings tended to overshadow their neighbours, to deny them their rights of light; when built alongside, with a common linking or party wall, further problems occurred, and rights of access were often transgressed.

An extreme case which illustrates the party wall problem is that of the American woman house-owner who rebuilt a house adjacent to a vacant plot. On its completion, the property company which owned the vacant plot wrote to point out that she had rebuilt six inches over their property and would she please go back. With this expensive demand she was forced by law to comply. Not long afterwards the property company built a twenty-five-storey block of flats on the empty plot. When it was completed the lady wrote to point out that she had rebuilt her home one foot behind the property line, and would they now please move their building.

All these controls gradually evolved into a code of building by-laws. There were not only problems between neighbouring sites but also between sites and the public generally. Simple angles of light controls were instituted in some cities, so as to prevent buildings facing a street taking too much light from those on the other side, and the needs of fire fighting brought others, such as the 80-foot maximum vertical height once permitted in London.

Yet the resulting urban pattern which emerged in city centres still tended to be a congested mass of building in the central area, with narrow streets flanked by shops on the ground floor (*first floor*). Above this towered enormous piles of masonry, taking all manner of derivative architectural forms, and of varying block widths and heights, the higher ones having a series of set-backs on the upper floors. With the arrival of the motor vehicle, which was allowed to traverse almost any public street in the city, the defects of this unplanned urban pattern became too obvious to ignore.

The lack of sanitation and adequate water supply, the overcrowding and the rapid decay of the condition of the dwellings of the industrial cities of the nineteenth century forced into existence a whole system of public responsibility and enterprises. In England, then the most advanced of the industrial nations, the social conscience, although submerged, had never been stifled, and since the end of the eighteenth century social reformers such as Robert Owen had struggled to ameliorate the urban misery. By the 1840s, when Engels in Manchester was documenting his attack on the capitalist economy, Parliament was actively concerned, and Sir Edwin Chadwick's *Report on the Sanitary Condition of the Labouring Population* (1842) is a milestone in the long road towards renewing the human urban environment. Beginnings, of course, were small. First, the roads had to be paved, drained and scavenged, and gradually these tasks became almost wholly a municipal responsibility, so that 'the private street' of yesterday is almost extinct as a concept. Then municipal responsibility was accepted for all main drainage, and later for water supply. In course of time, other public utilities were interlaced right through the urban pattern—gas, electricity, and telecommunications—all using the public highways for access, and all creating new urban components, such as gas-works, electricity stations and sub-stations, post offices, telephone exchanges, and eventually large office buildings to house the administrative staffs required to run them.

For the dwellings, minimum standards of all kinds were slowly evolved, becoming very slowly minimal as living standards rose throughout the community. Early attempts to ameliorate the appalling conditions of the industrial workers were made by philanthropic societies, who built large substantial tenement dwellings for artisans, often with sanitary services and water supply shared by several families, but providing at least sanitary and reasonably healthy living conditions. The second attempt was the introduction of by-law standards for low-cost housing. Out of these there emerged a new residential pattern of minimum by-law streets and pavements, minimum garden depths, maximum building heights in relation to street widths, and so forth.

Finally, as a living environment, the nineteenth-century city was conspicuous in its omissions, its gross underprovision of public open space, educational facilities, community buildings, and indeed all those things from which no economic profit can normally be derived, but without which the good life for all does not even begin to appear as a possibility.

THE REDISCOVERY OF URBAN DESIGN. The chief urban difference between the late nineteenth and early twentieth centuries was a speeding up of peripheral growth.

To more and more of the underprivileged proletariat, the greatest hope for their children seemed to be 'elevation' to the ranks of the petty bourgeois, the white-collared workers—of which Leonard Bast in E. M. Forster's *Howard's End* is a good representative. Success in these aspirations was sealed by moving from the congested slums of the city to the newer outskirts. Thus this period saw the development of the *suburb*, following on the building of commuter railway lines and the short-lived tramway system. Mass transport stimulated the decentralizing move out of the large city, and yet another new urban form emerged—suburbia. Generally the suburb, although a greatly improved physical environment for the middle- and lower middle-income groups, left almost everything to be desired in terms of social provision and aesthetic quality. Too often the close friendly community life of the overcrowded and congested old city was destroyed in the move outwards, and this problem still remains, as the social scientists Young and Wilmot[1] have recently pointed out.

The sprawling suburb was to some extent brought under control by the early planning legislation, which dealt almost entirely with the urban periphery and gave public authorities limited powers to determine zoning and residential density; but it was only unremitting work by the planning idealists that eventually produced an acceptable form of it.

Throughout the nineteenth century, reformers from Robert Owen and Buckingham onwards had suggested starting completely anew with ideal towns fashioned round the needs of the time, but the sheer isolation of Saltaire, Bournville, and Port Sunlight showed how out of tune their efforts were in the country as a whole. William Morris, one of the most potent reformers and visionaries of the second half of the century, deemed a major *political* upheaval essential before the new environment, described in *News from Nowhere*, could be created. From the idea of suburban decentralization, however, came a more complete and autonomous theory of the *Garden City*. In a closely reasoned argument around the concept of the three magnets of town, country and town-country, Ebenezer Howard evolved a very complete idea of Garden City, and more important, he and his followers even succeeded in getting two practical examples, in Letchworth and Welwyn, on the ground. Following this very considerable achievement of the planned small town, there came eventually a real and brilliant attempt to plan the suburb, and here the dynamic efforts of a woman reformer (Dame Henrietta Barnett), coupled with the practical imagination of a notable architect-planner in Raymond Unwin, created in the famous *Hampstead Garden Suburb* the first complete *Neighbourhood* twenty years before the word was coined for planning usage. It is with a good deal of humility, almost of despair, that one has to admit that fifty-five years after its inception the Hampstead Garden suburb has hardly been bettered. With its full provision of social facilities, its provision of a wide variety of dwellings for different family types as well as income groups, its generous system of green spaces and school building, its squares, culs-de-sac, and pedestrian super-blocks, and its general atmosphere of livability, it remains an outstanding example of residential planning.

The centrifugal movement to the urban outer ring of surburbia, which too often took the form of ribbon development along railways and roads, did little to solve the increasingly pressing problem of decay inside the inner urban ring. During the first

[1] *Family and Kinship in East London*, by Michael Young and Peter Wilmot. Routledge and Kegan Paul, 1957.

half of the twentieth century a whole series of Housing Acts was passed to try to deal with slum clearance; that is, to provide immediate *ad hoc* remedies for the worst aspects of the industrial expansionist legacy, rather than to conceive a new type of environment altogether. Progress, in any case, was slow owing to the high cost to the community of the land, as well as to the large number of slum families requiring to be rehoused. In order to solve this dual problem of using the minimum amount of land and rehousing as many people as possible, increasing use was made in the large cities of multi-storey tenements, again so often built without any *social* provision, creating in some cases the same type of urban conditions as had existed for centuries in the densely built tenements of continental European towns or the Old Town of Edinburgh. This over-compression of low-income groups without adequate facilities for a full life is a serious social problem whose consequences are difficult to analyse even today, when many countries contrive to repeat the mistakes of yesterday.

Perhaps the most important lesson of this period was not directly a visual one, but was the recognition of the necessity for public authorities to provide for the housing, educational, and other basic social needs of a large part of the community. It had become increasingly clear that no private developer could replan and rebuild to the scale and degree of *comprehensiveness* that the situation demanded, and as yet the central government were not prepared to provide the money or legal sanction for the large-scale compulsory acquisition of land and buildings which would be involved, nor had any city council begun to think seriously in terms of *positive* planning for the central or inner-ring areas. In the meantime the rapid increase of motor transport was creating a new set of problems, but, like so many other causes for change, it did not at first create a sharp or intense enough condition to force drastic remedies into existence.

The British urban designers during the first half of the century were slow to appreciate the need for a *fundamentally* new approach, mainly because aesthetic thinking was dominated by a fashionable Renaissance revival led by the outstanding architectural genius of Sir Edwin Lutyens, whose layout plan and three-dimensional realization in the Renaissance manner for the new imperial city of New Delhi set the stamp on contemporary thought. The minor examples of urban improvements actually carried out in Britain, such as Kingsway in London and the Headrow at Leeds, both used a Renaissance street improvement method which followed closely that employed by Nash in Regent Street. Unfortunately their clients' needs were entirely different, and all they did was to create anew the muddled and obsolete 'corridor street' which *laissez-faire* was bringing about naturally in most city centres.

To cure this chaotic urban pattern many radical and complex solutions are necessary, which even today are only half understood.

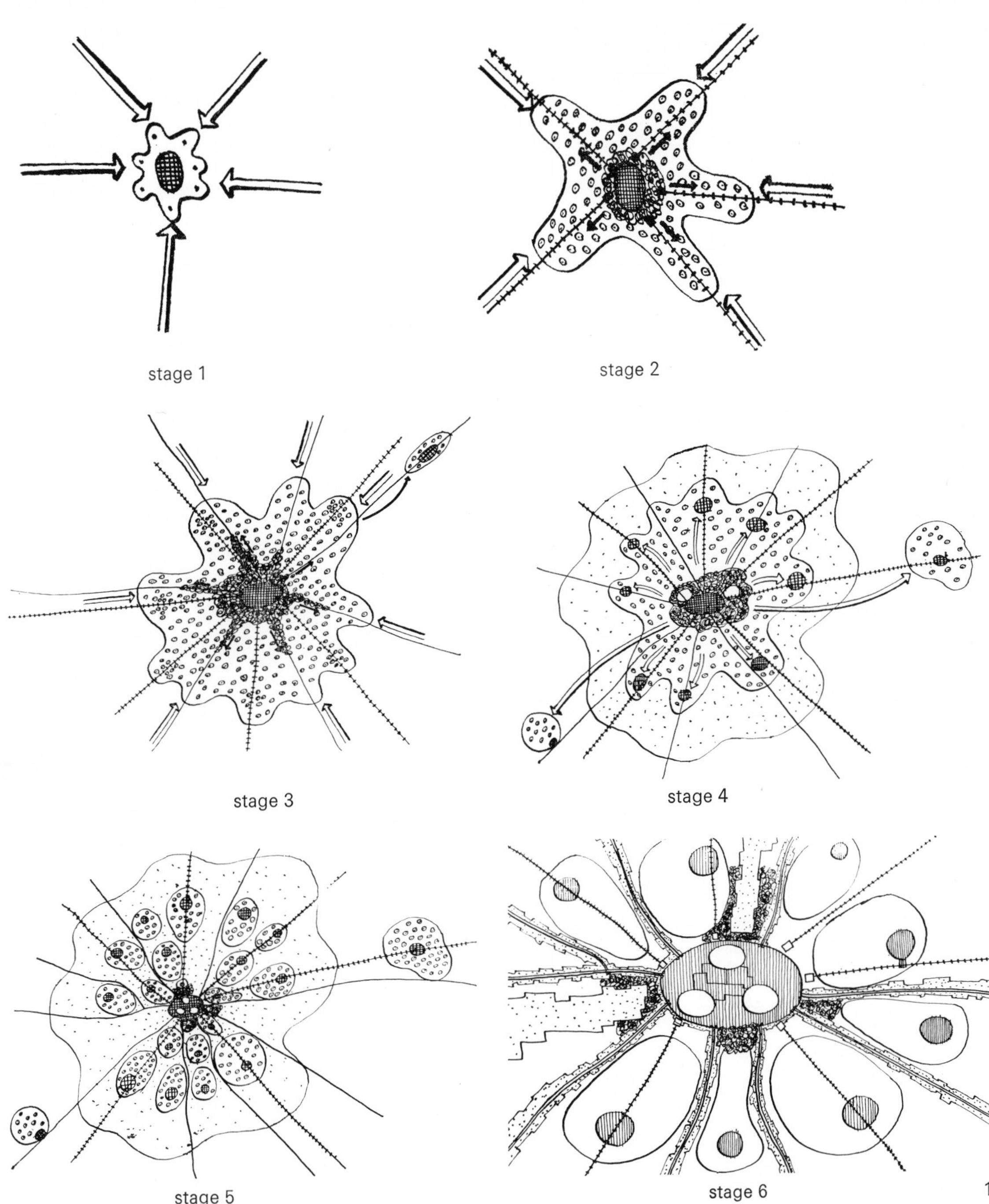

1. Urban diagnosis

Stage 1: 1770-1820
The modern city begins—industrialisation as the magnetic impulse.

Stage 2: 1820-1900
Concentration—some decentralisation along railways.

Stage 3: 1900-1939
Congestion—decay in the inner ring; unplanned decentralisation.

Stage 4: 1945-?
Post-war planned decentralisation to new and expanded towns; comprehensive redevelopment of inner areas.

Stage 5: ?-?
The city re-created.

Stage 6: ?-?
The redeveloped centre.

1 HISTORICAL BACKGROUND

2 

3 

Origins Around a Nucleus

2. The Old Town of Edinburgh

Edinburgh is a classic example in the growth of cities. Beginning with a castle on a rock, the town began to develop down the hill from the castle gates. This upper town grew around the High Street while another town developed around the Canongate, leading up the hill from the Monastery (later the Palace of Holyrood). Eventually they coalesced and formed a long ridge-top city, as seen in the drawing.

3. Castle over town, Brno

Another good example of a castle on a hill dominating the town, which is similar in many respects to Edinburgh. The cathedral is below the castle on the left, while the town hall tower is immediately to the right. Geology was obviously an important factor in the formation of both Edinburgh and Brno, affording, as it did, superb possibilities for fortification and defence.

4

4. Abbey and town, St Albans

The Roman town of Verulamium was in the valley to the south (just below the bottom of the photograph). A new settlement grew up on the top of a small hill. The High Street can be seen in the upper centre of the photograph terminated by a parish church. On the south slope below the town is the Abbey with its religious precinct. The Abbey church tower was built in Norman times, largely of bricks taken from the Roman ruins. The whole Abbey was extensively restored in the nineteenth century.

5 

6 

5. Church and village

In *Return from the Fair* Breughel depicted a medieval nucleus of church and village. In some cases such villages would grow into towns, and eventually, cities.

6. The medieval city square

This painting shows the piazza of the Signoria in Florence. The dome of the Cathedral, recently executed by Brunelleschi is in the left background, while the dark forbidding building with the campanile is the Signoria, or fortress/palace of the ruling house. Here the medieval square has reached its climax. It is still dominated by the great fortress, and the artist has taken some liberties with the dimensions of the square, but it does show a central urban space actually being used for a dramatic civic purpose; in this case the burning of Savonarola in 1498.

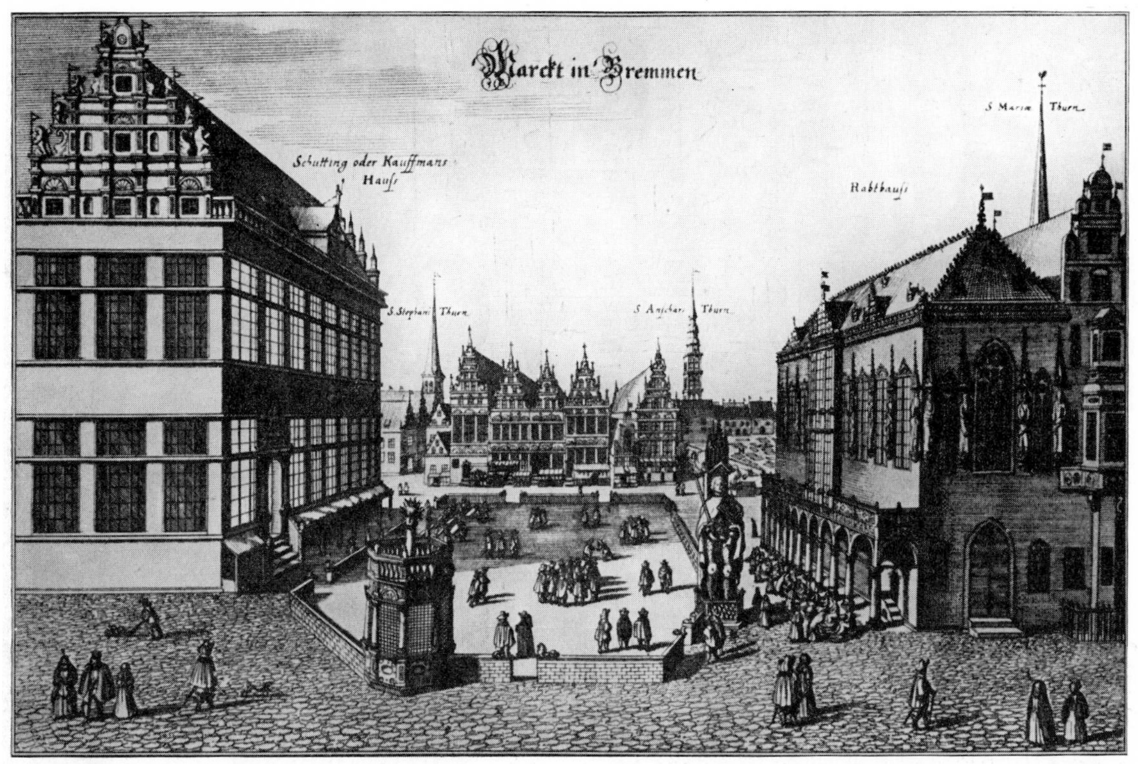

7

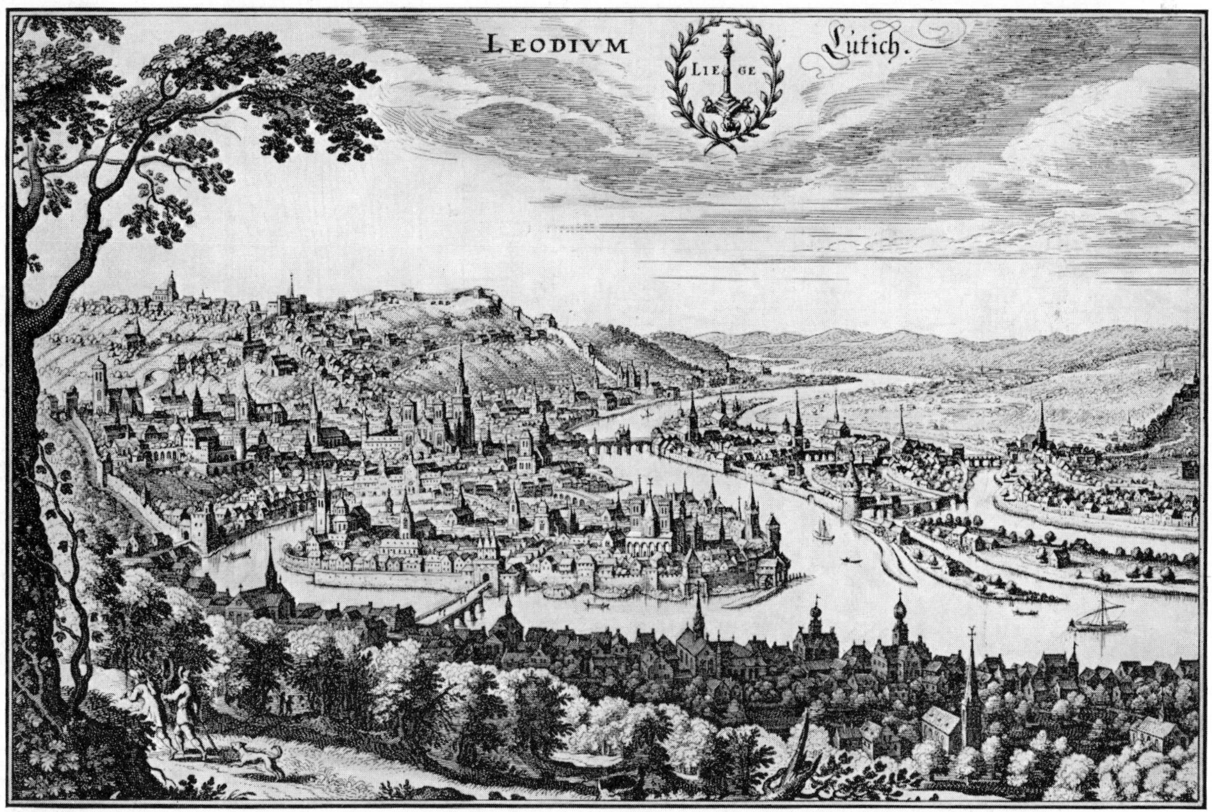

8

7. The market-place

An engraving of 1653 showing the market-place in Bremen. The Town Hall usually faced on to one side, and Bremen was no exception: the Rathaus is on the right of the picture, with a covered arcade along its front. In the background is a terrace of merchant's houses. The market-place was a nodal point, around which many medieval cities grew.

8. The river confluence town, Liége

Medieval towns grew for various reasons; sometimes at the foot of a castle, and others at the crossroads of two important routes, or else at the confluence of two rivers. This mid-seventeenth-century drawing of Liége shows the nucleus of the town on an island at the junction of the Meuse and the Ourthe rivers. The main direction of urban expansion has been on the easily defended peninsula behind, but the erection of bridges has stimulated growth on the far bank of both rivers. The many church spires dominate the urban silhouette.

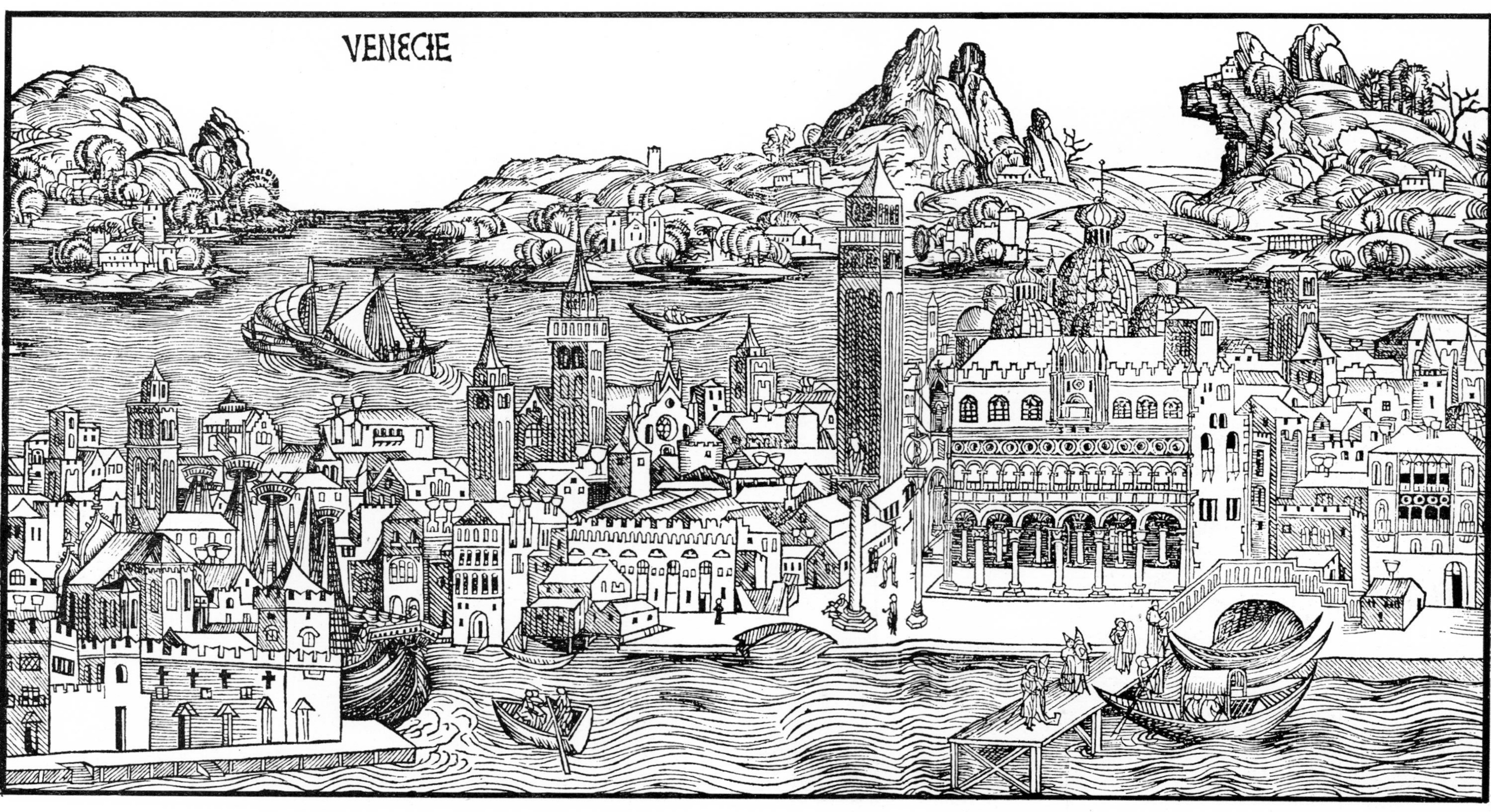

9

9. Venice

This view, drawn in the late fifteenth century, presumably from the campanile of St Maria Maggiore, shows the main water front of the civic area. In the centre is the campanile in the main square or piazza and to its right is the Doge's palace with the domes of St Marks rising up behind. The library which faces the palace has not yet been built, nor has the great church of St Maria del Salute that now stands at the entrance to the Grand Canal, which is seen on the left of the drawing. The hills in the background offer an exciting prospect, but are entirely imaginary.

Growth in Time

10

10. The piazza of St Mark: a village of the Veneti

A conjectural view of the original village with its church. The Veneti moved here from Malamocco for safety because Pippin (son of Charlemagne) was fighting the Byzantines on the mainland.

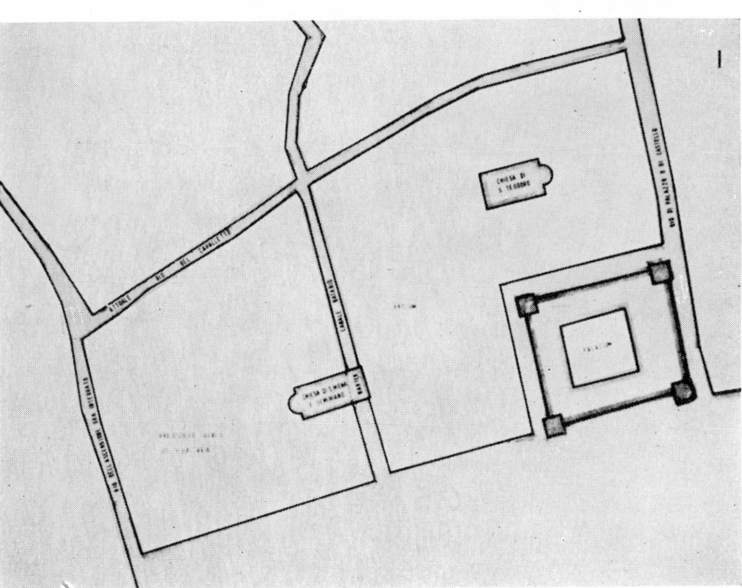

11

11. The piazza of St Mark: ninth century

In the ninth century the Castle was built on the site of the present palace, and nearby is the Byzantine church of St Theodore. Running across what is now the piazza was the Canal Batario, bisecting an orchard. This remained until 1170, when over it was built the church of St Gimignano. In 828 the Venetians sailed over to Alexandria and stole the bones of St Mark, who replaced St Theodora as the town's patron saint. The Doge Partecipazio then built the first St Mark's church to house the relics.

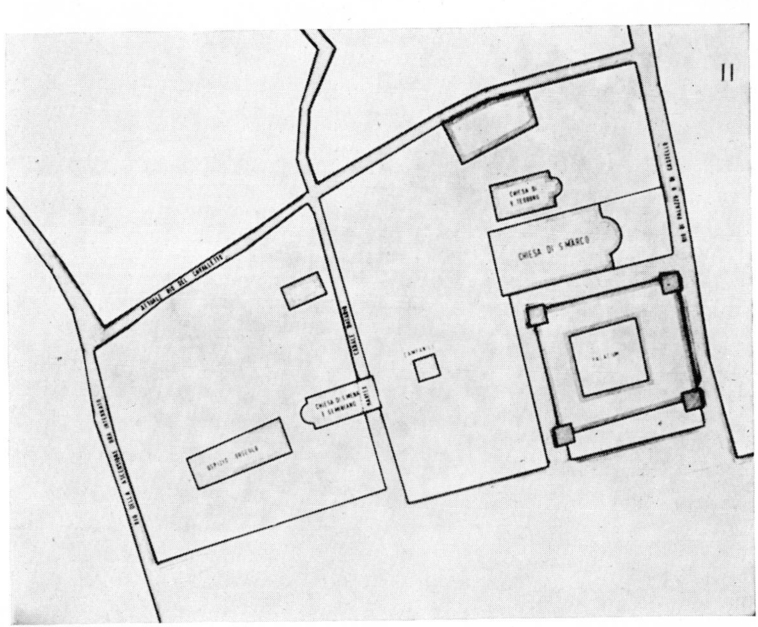

12

12. The piazza of St Mark: tenth century

Here the new church of St Mark can be seen between that of St Theodore and the Castle. Together with the castle it was destroyed in 976 in a revolt against Doge Pietro Candiano. Two years later the new Doge Pietro Orseolo rebuilt both, and also built a hospital near the church of St Gimignano. The Campanile had been rebuilt at the beginning of the century as a military watch tower.

13. The piazza of St Mark: eleventh century

During this period the Byzantine church of St Theodore was demolished and the new cathedral of St Mark was built on the site of the two churches in 1094. This marks the emergence of Venice as an independent great power, although architecturally the Cathedral was strongly influenced by Byzantine forms. In 1106 the castle was again destroyed and rebuilt, but between 1172 and 1178 Doge Sebastiano Ziani radically altered the whole scene by rebuilding the castle as a Palace, and in fact enclosing the piazza by government offices, and other buildings with arcades.

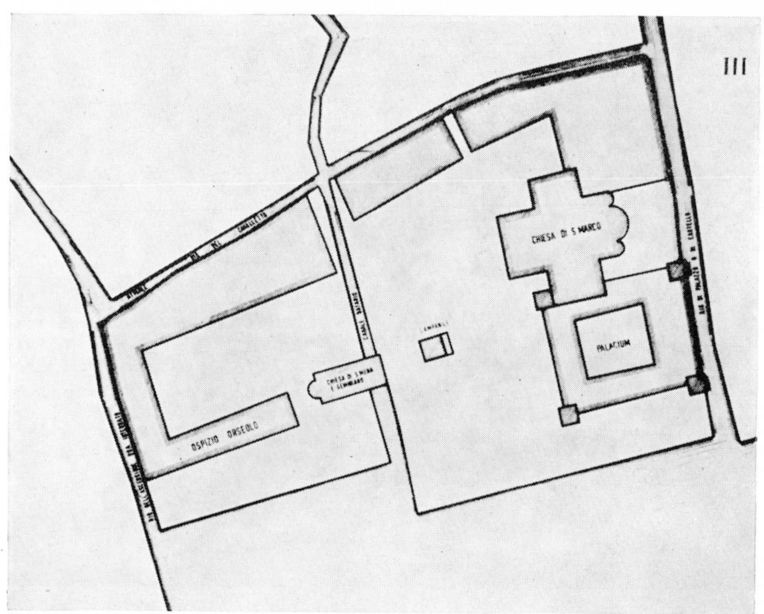

13

14. The piazza of St Mark: thirteenth century

In 1264 the piazza was given a new brick floor and a new Palace. This palace represented the efforts of the 500 leading families to form a ruling oligarchy and to house their Assembly in a new Hall; the present building is, for the most part, unchanged. At this time, when Marco Polo was relating his fabulous stories of Cathay, there was a slave market at the base of the three great flagstaffs before the Cathedral.

14

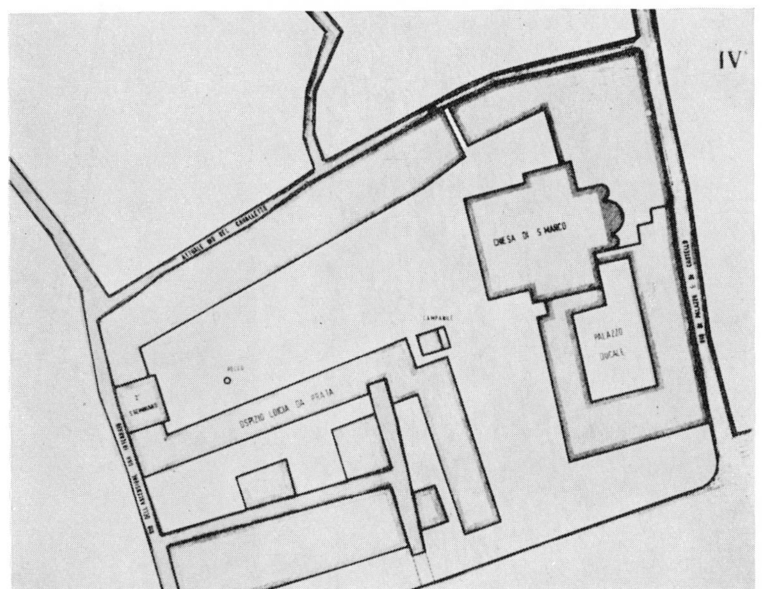

15

15. The piazza of St Mark: fifteenth century

By this time the church of St Gimignano had been moved from near the Campanile to a site at the far end of the piazza which Doge Ziani had developed in its present form.

16

16. The piazza of St Mark, 1496

This well-known painting by Gentile Bellini of the Corpus Christi Procession in the piazza of St Mark was made in 1496. By this time the great urban space was fully formed, although a number of changes were still to take place. For instance, the buildings along the south side of the piazza were then in line with the Campanile, which itself was last rebuilt in 1902. The picture shows a noble space, surrounded by magnificent buildings and being used for an important public ceremony.

17 

18 

17. The piazza of St Mark: eighteenth century

The piazza is now practically as it is today. In 1496-9 the Watch Tower (seen on the left) was built, and the Campanile finished in its present form. The houses on the north side were replaced by the Procuratie Vecchie between 1500 and 1532, partly for offices and partly residential. Between 1540 and 1588 Sansovino designed the splendid new library, demolishing some old hotels houses, and a bakery in the process. In 1582 he started to build the Procuratie Nuove on the south side of the piazza, which involved the demolition of the Hospital. He had previously in 1550 re-designed the facade of the church of St Gimignano, destined to be demolished by Napoleon to make way for a dance hall. In 1723 the floor was once again re-laid, this time in marble, as it is now.

18. The piazza of St Mark today

The piazza today, with Napoleon's finishing touch of the dance hall closing the western end, has a floorscape designed to be seen from above as well as to be used by thousands of pedestrians. The recovery of such large areas for pedestrians in the centres of our cities is a major planning task today.

19

20

Man-made Limits

19. Arles: circular fortification

Before the development of wall-smashing cannon the circular walled fortification was usually adequate for defence. At a few points heavily fortified gate houses would be built and egress strictly controlled. This view of Arles shows the circular form at its simplest; but this medieval town is really behaving like a hermit crab in that it is built into the ruins of the old Roman amphitheatre.

20. Paris: concentric urban form

Braun and Hogenberg's map of 1575 shows the fully developed medieval city. Commencing its urban life in, and on either side of, a small island on the Seine, its first form is clearly delimited by a city wall that appears in the drawing as remarkably similar to the first annular ring of a tree. Within this wall nearly all the urban space is occupied by buildings, but between this and the outer wall there are still considerable pieces of open ground and large gardens.

21 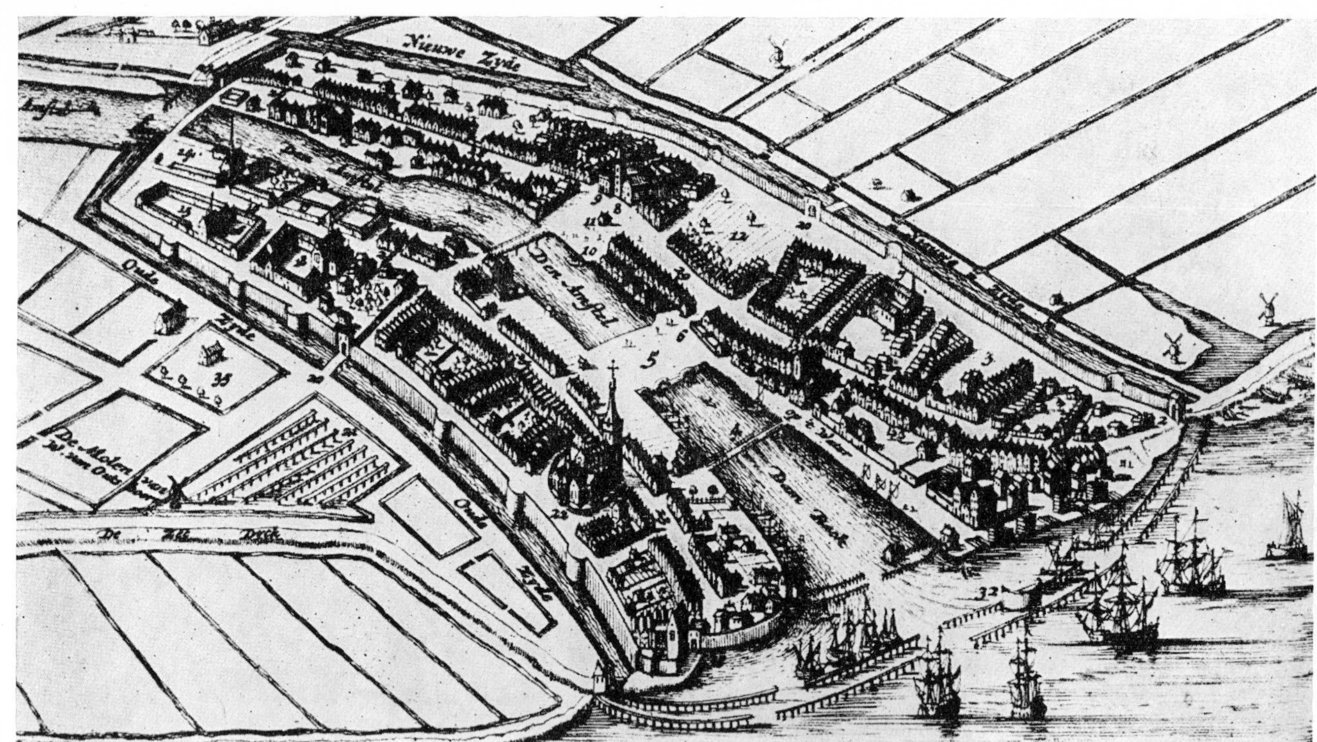

22 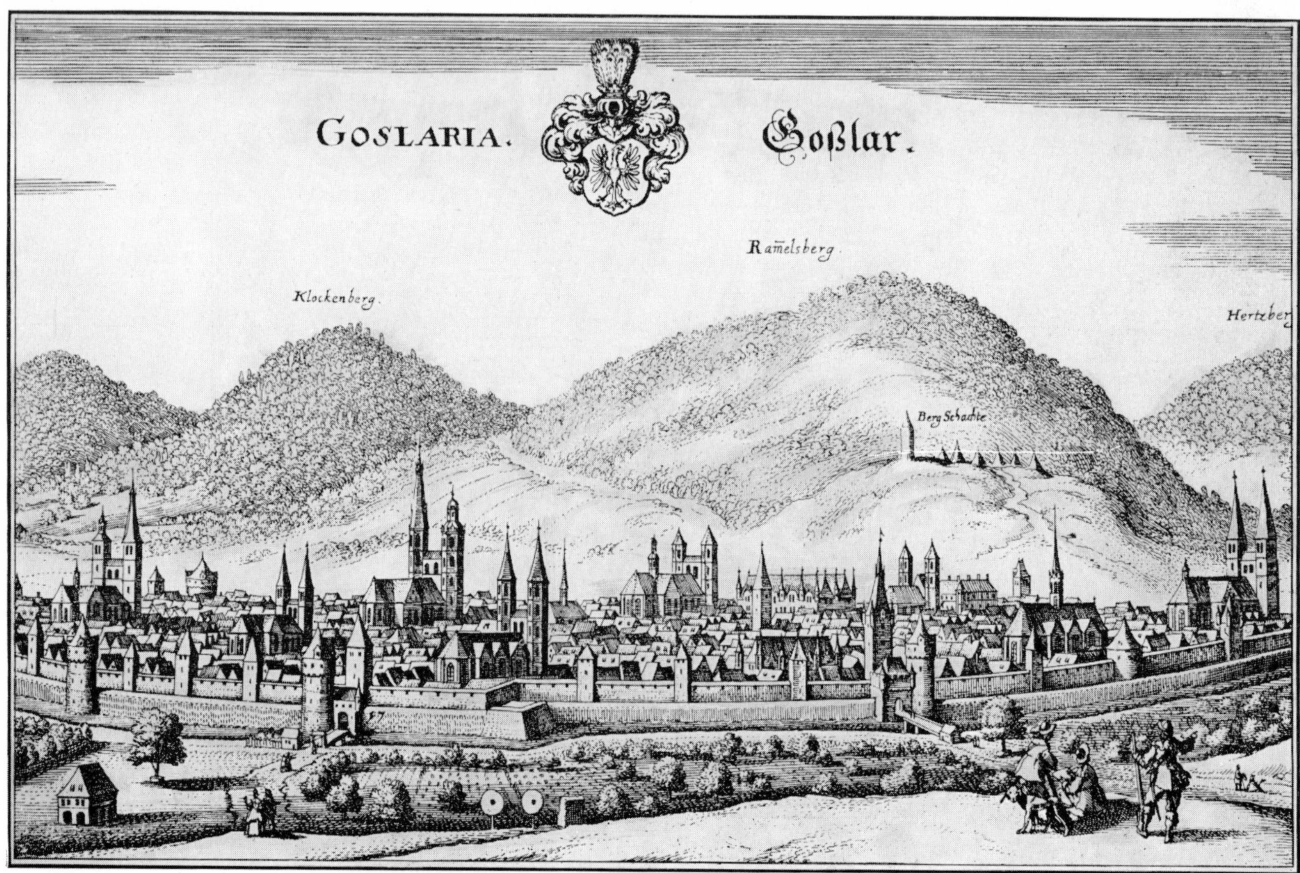

21. Amsterdam: semicircular urban form

This thirteenth-century plan of Amsterdam shows the form in its early stages, built on either side of the river Amstel. Succeeding generations enlarged it by creating a series of semicircular rings around the original core.

22. Goslar: circular fortifications

This seventeenth-century drawing shows Goslar, a medieval German town north of the Hartz mountains. It was known as the Emperor's town, and his palace can be seen below the Ramelsberg hill in the background. On this hill, incidentally, are early iron-mining shafts, the surface buildings of which can be seen as pyramids on the hillside.

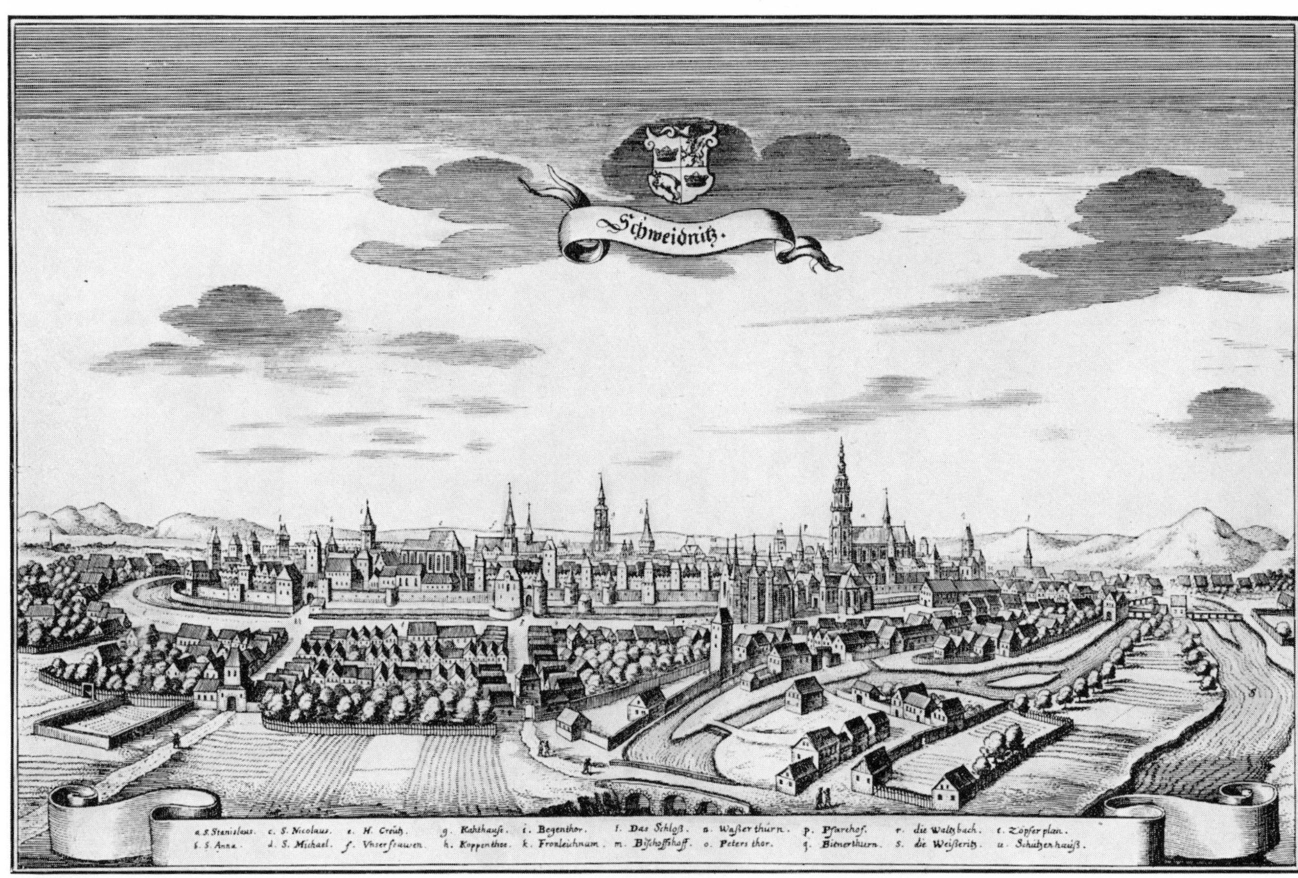

23

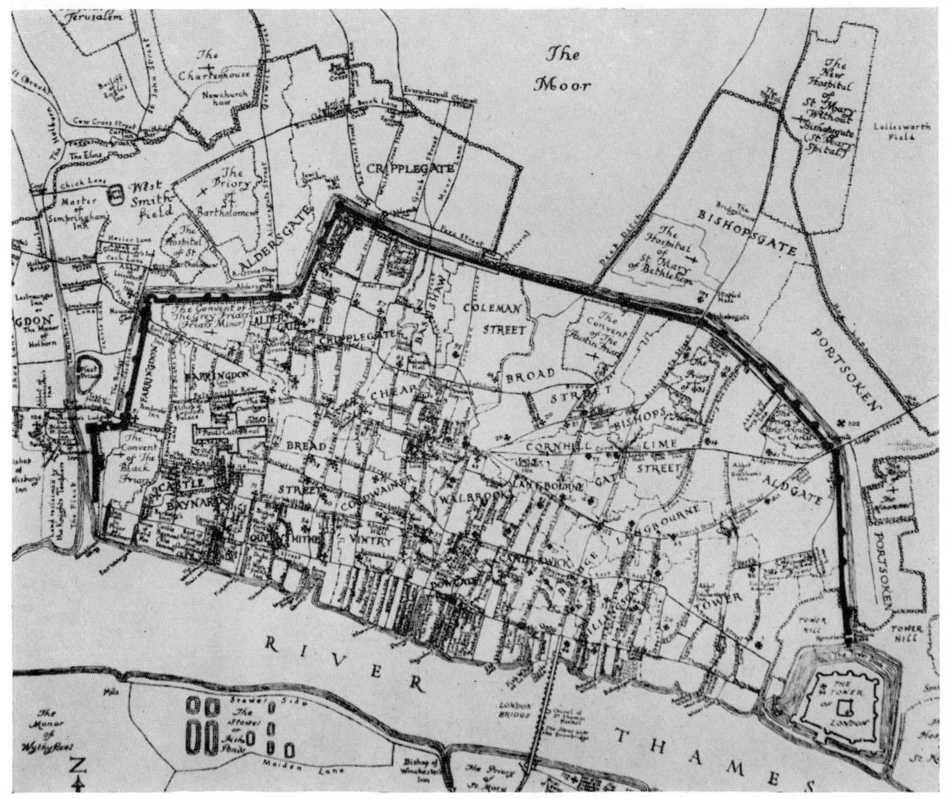

24

Expansion Outwards and Upwards

23. Schweidnitz on the Weistritz

Another seventeenth-century drawing of a German medieval town of circular form in Silesia, which shows the town beginning to overspill from its original man-made confines.

24. London: expansion and renewal

This map of medieval London shows the position of the city wall, overbuilt on the line of the earlier Roman fortification. On the right is the protecting Tower of London, in the lower middle is old London Bridge, and on the left is the Fleet ditch, separating the City from Westminster. A number of craft precincts are shown, such as that of the Cordwainers and the Vintners. Beyond the city wall are the hospitals, and the Liberties, where the new immigrants settled outside the gate houses of Aldgate, Bishopgate, Cripplegate, Aldersgate, and Ludgate.

25

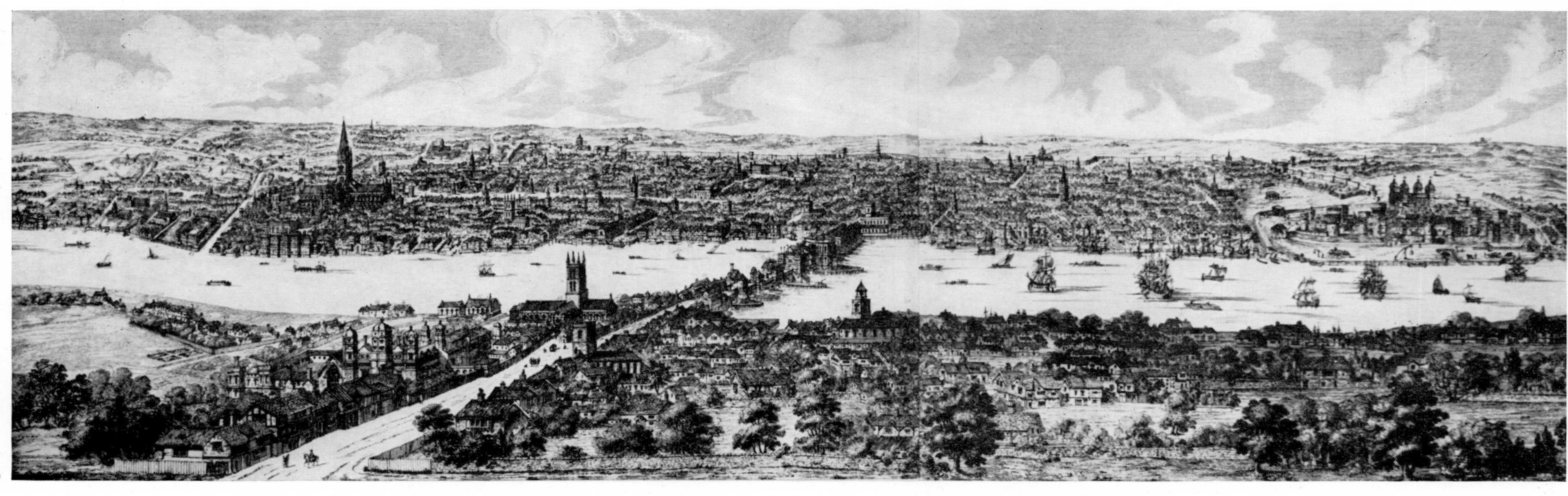

25. London: mid-sixteenth century

King Henry VIII had been on the throne for thirty-four years when this view was drawn by Wingaerde in 1543. London was now reaching its full development as a medieval city – there is always a time lag between a culture and its full expression in urban form. Old St Paul's Cathedral still has its spire (which collapsed in 1561 and was never rebuilt) and the City is adorned with a multitude of spires and towers, which must have made a striking skyline; while the immensely powerful Tower of London stands guard at its eastern end, protecting the city from attack up the river.

26

26. London, 1563

This is the London of William Dunbar's famous poem *In Honour of the City of London* and of which he sings:

> Gemme of all joy, jasper of jocunditie,
> Most myghty carbuncle of vertue and valour;
> Strong Troy in vigour and in strenuytie;
> Of Royall cities rose and geraflour;
> Empress of towns, exalt in honour;
> In beawtie berying the crowne imperiall;
>   paradise precelling in pleasure;
> London, thou art the flour of Cities all.

Any Scotsman might be forgiven today for feeling that London today was a much too 'myghty carbuncle'. In the sixteenth century it was one of the great cities in Europe. The river, too, was both an efficient means of communication and a magnificent open space.

27

28

27. London in the sixteenth century

This drawing from the second half of the sixteenth century, is a close view from the Bankside, as this part of the South Bank was called. The City presents a romantic and even dramatic skyline, in spite of the recent collapse of St Paul's Cathedral spire. The congestion and overbuilding is, however, only too evident, and Elizabeth and her administrators were so concerned about the growth of London that an Act of Parliament was passed to attempt its restraint.

28. London: Norden's Map of 1593

By the close of Elizabeth's reign, London, a rather late starter by western European standards, was reputed to have a population of some 200,000 people. It was overflowing into the Liberties beyond the City Walls, especially to the east, behind the shipping wharves, and west to join up with Westminster. Its total extent, including town gardens, was not much over one square mile, so that one could walk out of it easily in fifteen minutes in any direction.

34

35

34. London in the eighteenth century (Guardi)

The City of London has now been rebuilt in a more orderly and organized way. St Paul's is still the dominant architectural mass, although proclaiming the accepted architectural form first introduced over 200 years before in Florence. In the foreground is Westminster, where large areas were subject to planned development, making London one of the most spacious and harmonious residential cities in Europe.

35. London, 1830

St Paul's Cathedral had been completed only 120 years when this print was made. It shows the city after the first industrial revolution. The merchants' houses and wharves have been replaced by much larger brick warehouses, but the scale of building still enables the church spires to be seen and for the Cathedral to dominate the city.

36

37

36. London, 1958

Today the city is undergoing another transformation. The merchants' houses of the seventeenth and eighteenth centuries were replaced by warehouses, banks, and large office buildings in the nineteenth and early twentieth centuries, and the residential population shrank almost to nothing. Fortunately the height controls had been rigidly enforced before the last war, so that although the silhouette of St Paul's was impaired it still stood high in impressive dignity. The L.C.C. and the City Corporation, as joint planning authorities until 1965, have enforced a height control between St Paul's and the river, and they have also had a long-term plan to open up the whole river front.

37. Paris during the reign of Louis VII

At this early stage of its evolution Paris had almost nothing of the urban splendour it was later to achieve. At this time it consisted of a fortified island, with the main bulk of the urban area on the north bank of the river, enclosed by a city wall. At least five small towns added themselves to the centre outside the wall, and later necessitated another wall to encompass the whole group. The Louvre was still a castle outside the city. The origin of Paris as a meeting-place of roads at a river crossing can be clearly seen.

38

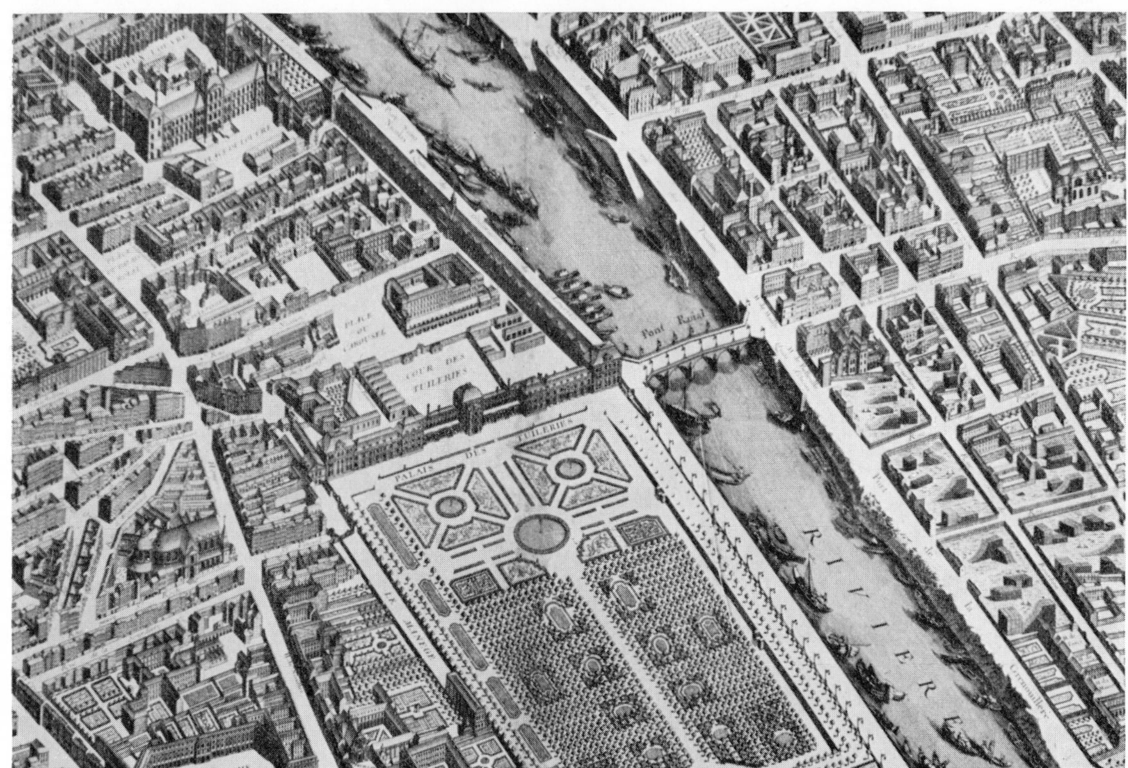

39

38. Paris: the Louvre in 1730

Already this part of the centre of Paris has achieved a fine civic form, with great squares, spacious places, and wide terraces. The integrated urban design of palace and river walls has begun a magnificent theme in which the river is made the central adornment of the whole vast urban composition.

39. Paris, 1742

Turgot's map shows the planned urban centre slowly emerging from the medieval pattern. The great core of palaces, public buildings and their formal gardens have been created, but the older pattern of buildings still huddles among the great new courts and places. The new form and scale of buildings is accompanied by a new road pattern and a new and larger arrangement of urban spaces.

40

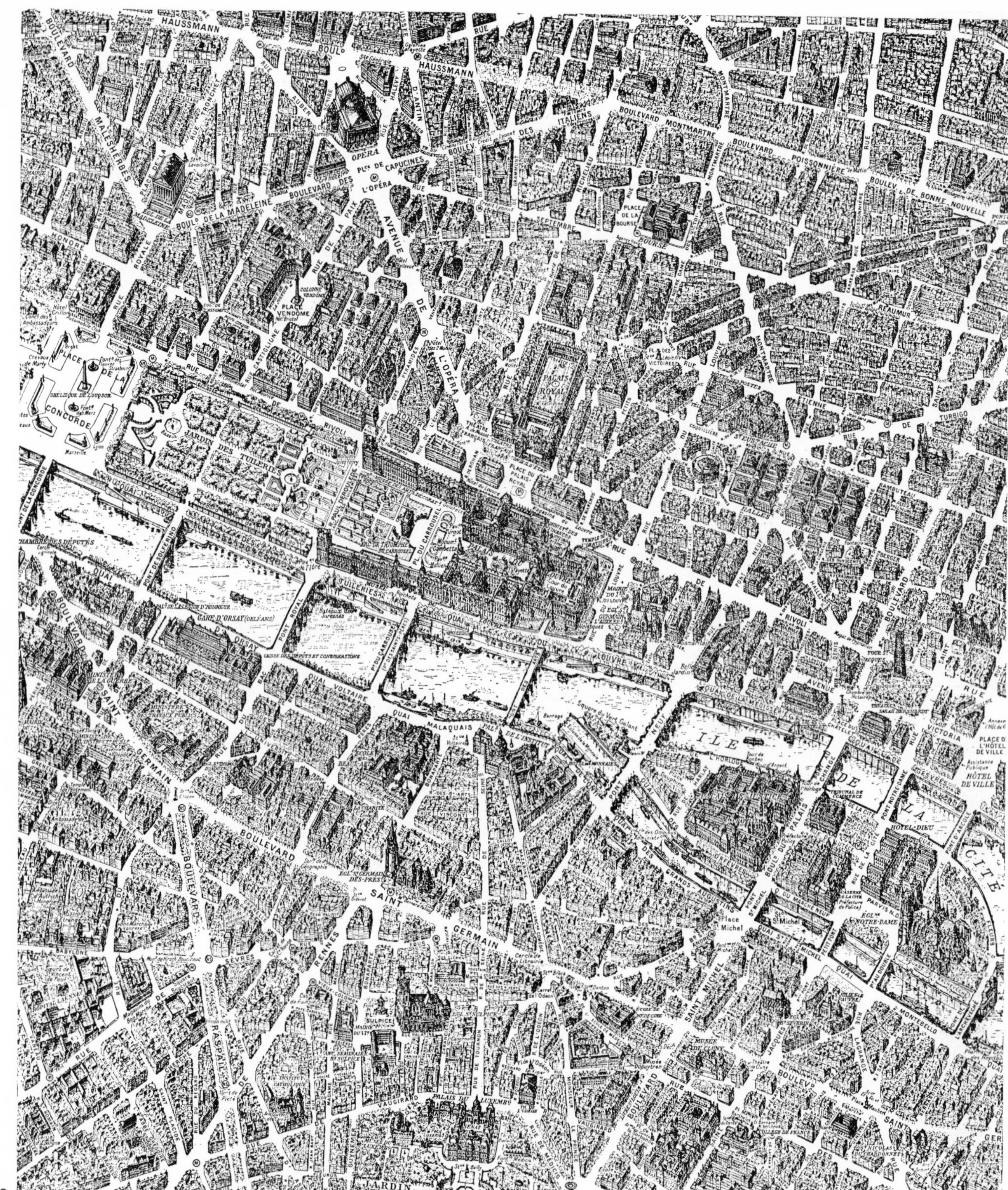

40. Paris today

This remarkable contemporary drawing shows the greatest Renaissance city of all time. It took several hundred years to create from its original medieval pattern, but the metamorphosis is now more or less complete, with its geometrical forms of places, *rond points*, and avenues, with their vistas and terminal features. This total achievement over a considerable period of time was due to the combined operations of crown, state, municipality, and wealthy citizens, all seeking a broad common goal. Only in the twentieth century are the practical limitations of such a planning theory becoming manifest, and even now, with a vastly expanded population and all the problems created by twentieth-century mechanical transport, it is still visually the world's finest and most spacious city centre.

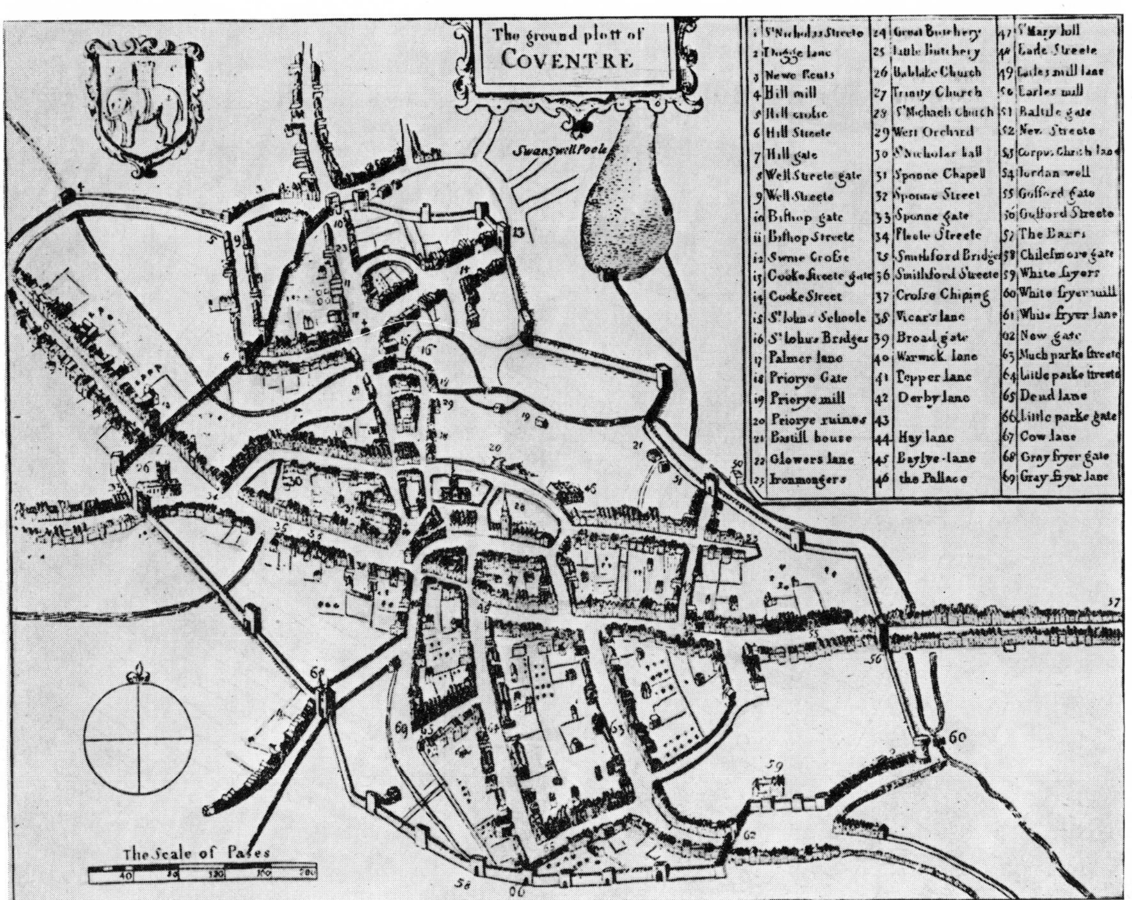

41

42

Urban in-filling

41. Coventry, 1610

This plan of 'The ground plott of Coventre' appears in Dugdale's *Antiquities of Warwickshire* (1656), but was, in fact, engraved from John Speed's map of 1610. During the Civil War, Coventry was a notable Parliamentarian stronghold. The historic phrase 'sent to Coventry' is believed to have its origin in the refusal of the citizens to fraternize with the Royalist prisoners held in St John's Church. The outline of the city wall with its Gatehouses may be seen clearly, the area within corresponding approximately to the present central area.

42. Coventry, 1748

This drawing shows part of the old medieval city of Coventry to the south of where the Council House now stands. The city walls are still there, although in ruins, and the burgher's houses were still in the general medieval pattern, with large gardens behind them.

43

43. Coventry: in the nineteenth century

This drawing should be compared with the previous one, for it shows typical infilling over the old town gardens. Much of this consisted of industrial workshops, and it was taking place on a large scale in many pleasant British towns. After a certain point the whole urban character would be changed.

Redevelopment

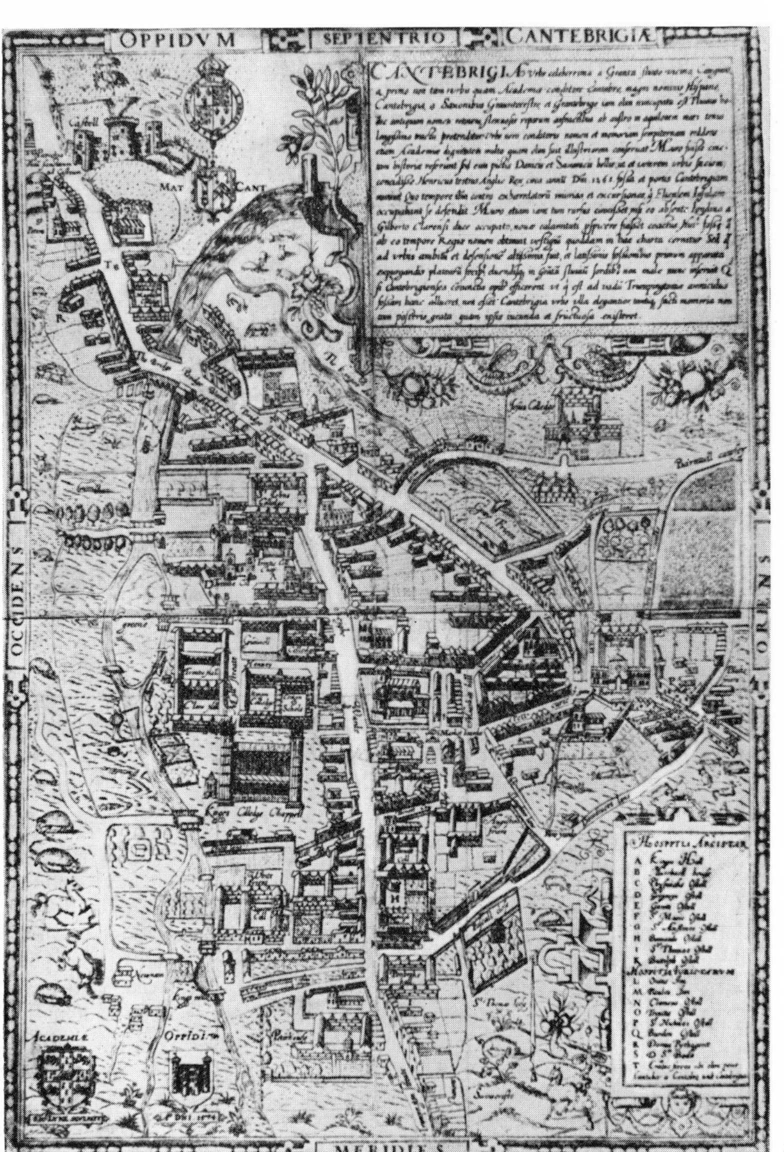

44

44. Cambridge, 1574

This map by Richard Lyne shows clearly the relationship between the University and the Town. Here King's Parade is still a normal medieval street, lined on both sides with houses and shops. The superb group of University buildings in the form of interconnected quadrangles and situated between the town and the river had long been created, while that late and wonderful flower of Gothic architecture, King's College Chapel, still awaited its present setting.

45. Cambridge today

Walking up Trumpington Street as it widens into King's Parade, the whole scene appears to be a carefully planned set piece, with the beautifully sited chestnut tree in front of King's College Chapel completing a rich composition. Only when one glances back from the Senate House is it apparent that King's Parade was originally a two-sided street, the opening up of which was not completed until the nineteenth century.

45

46 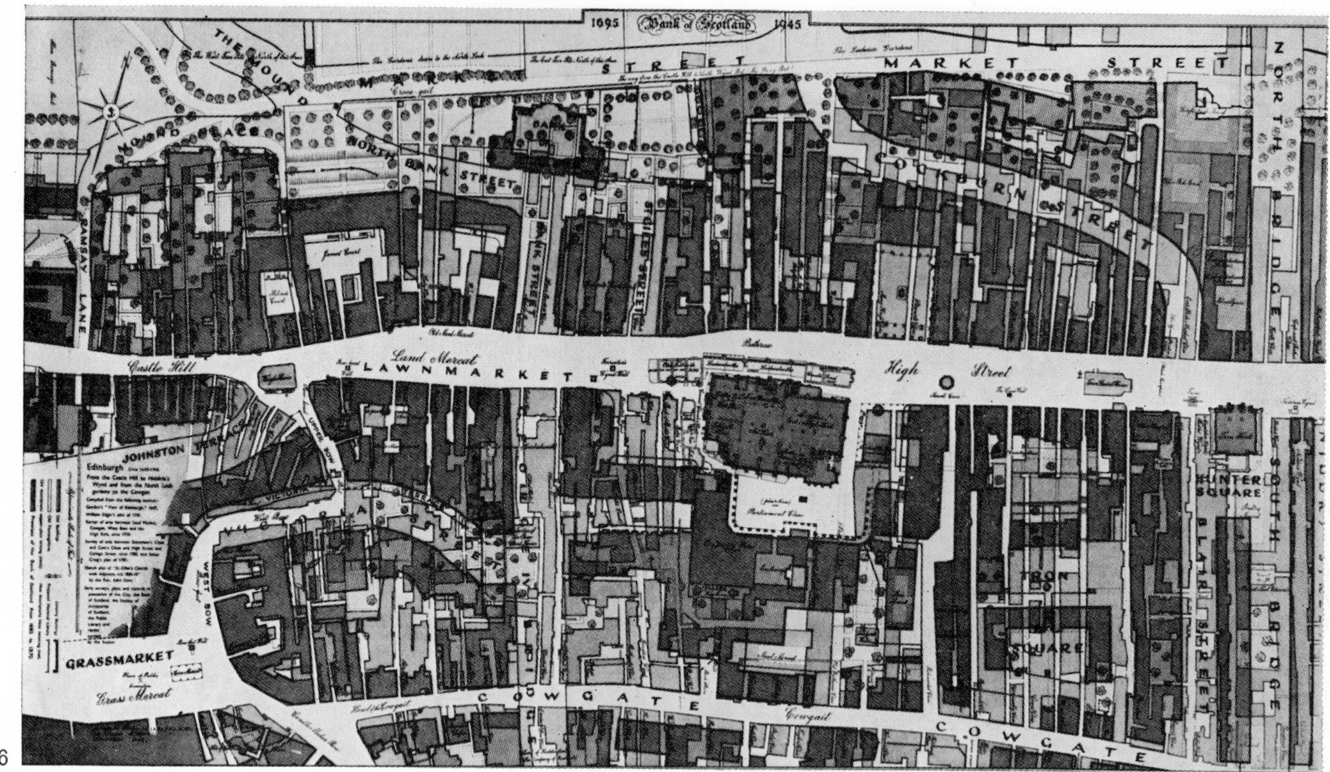

46. Edinburgh: redevelopment of the medieval core

It is difficult to realize what drastic civic improvements were carried out to the old Town of Edinburgh while the New Town was being planned and built. This overlay plan, prepared for the Bank of Scotland, shows the original layout in a light tone, and the area after rebuilding of the early nineteenth century in a dark tone. It can be seen that major urban design changes were made around St Giles' Cathedral, and that a new road was cut through the wynds from the new Bank building right across the Lawnmarket, and then by an overpass bridge (George IV Bridge) to south Edinburgh. A new street from the bridge down to the Grassmarket and thence to the Cowgate below forms the first part of an urban clover leaf. An even bolder proposal for a tunnel under the High Street did not materialize, but the scale of the operation (made easier by a great fire which caused extensive damage in the area) is very impressive. Another great improvement may be seen at the extreme right of the plan, where the North and South Bridges were constructed.

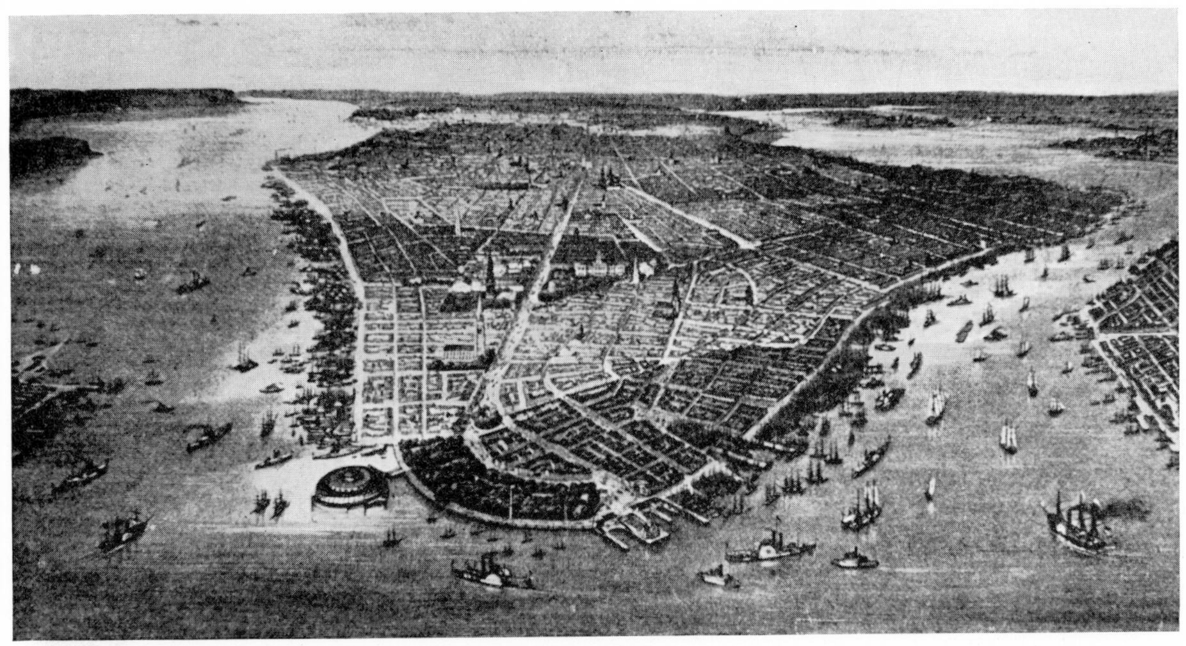

47

48

Effects of Development

47. New York, 1851

This remarkable steel engraving of Manhattan shows what was in many respects a fine and spacious city. Behind the narrow strip of docks and warehouses lining the Hudson and the East River is a city of three- and four-storey terrace row houses set in an ordered pattern of broad streets, providing adequately for the traffic of the day and giving plenty of light and air. At the southern tip is Battery Park, at this time overlooked by fashionable residences. Castle Garden, once New York's guardian fortress, is still virtually an island, although its use has changed.

48. New York, 1951

Over a comparatively short period of 100 years the urban scene has changed drastically – so much so that the city is unrecognizable. The blocks of three- and four-storey terrace houses of Lower Manhattan have disappeared and in their place is a vast jumble of towering skyscrapers, akin in scale to the Grand Canyon turned upside down. Only a few vestiges of the original city remain – Battery Park with the circular Castle Garden incorporated into it, and the roads, which are much the same as in 1851. The failure to change the road and open space pattern so as to relate with the fantastic changes in architectural design is demonstrated with startling clarity in Manhattan.

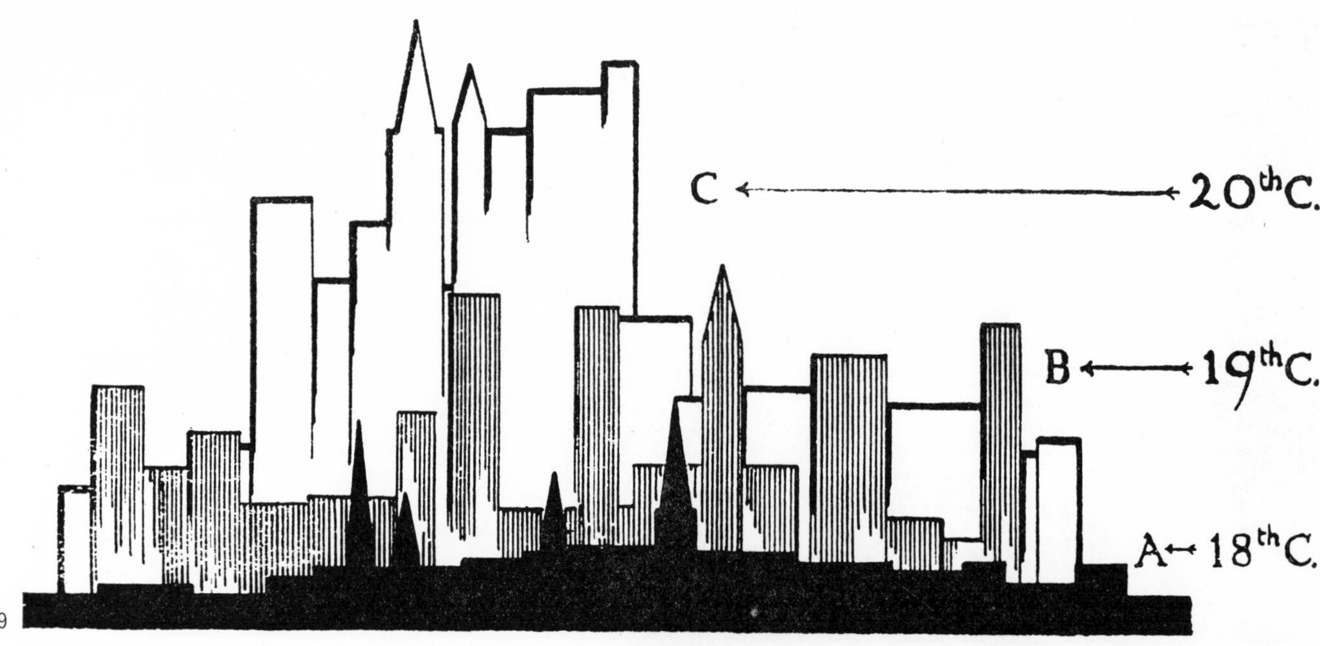

49

49. New York: three stages of growth

In this sectional diagram C. R. Ashbee, an early and highly intelligent critic of the modern city, brings out the significance of the changes of scale that have taken place over a century of upward growth.

50. New York from the docks

Here three scales of building can be seen, corresponding broadly to technological development in the eighteenth, nineteenth, and twentieth centuries. Development was essentially uncomprehensive, particularly in that the street pattern failed to change in relation to the vastly different scale of the buildings. One can also see in this photograph the effect of the attempts to achieve some daylight down at pavement level by means of municipally enforced regulations, which drew angles back from the street above a certain level, thus creating an unpremeditated and unfortunate architectural form in the series of floor by floor set-backs.

50

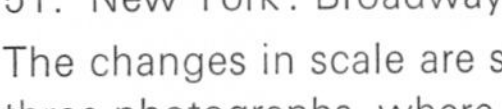

51. New York: Broadway

The changes in scale are strikingly portrayed in these three photographs, where an important public building has, comparatively speaking, disappeared in the jungle of unplanned urban growth.

51

52

52. New York: an office canyon

Here is one end of the road in urban design. It is an example of brilliant technical achievement (the sky-scraper) in one direction, almost completely nullified by failing to make a corresponding change in the basic urban pattern.

53

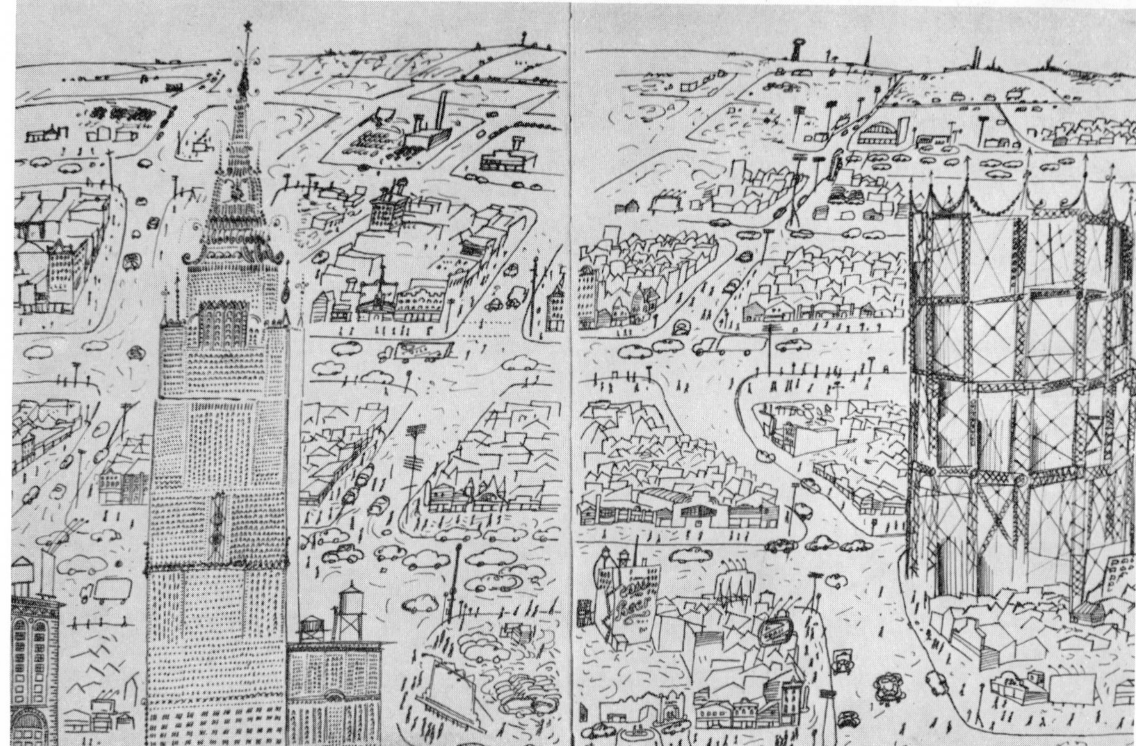

54

53. A Lancashire town, by Lowry

Laurence Lowry is a British artist who has been painting the towns of his native county of Lancashire for many years. He paints with something of the power of the French or American primitives, and his paintings make a poignant call for an environment better than the degrading muddle of the nineteenth-century industrial town. One could wish for more painters who react in this way to their environment.

54. The City, observed by Saul Steinberg

A sharp and brilliant satirist, the American artist Saul Steinberg shows, to those who have eyes to see, what too many contemporary cities look like today. We need more artists of this calibre telling everyman that the contemporary environment is substandard functionally, socially, and visually.

55

55. London: the urban scene

This view, looking east from St Paul's Cathedral, shows that the business core of London consisted largely of a medieval street pattern but with predominantly nineteenth-century buildings, most of them already too large for their sites. Through this muddle rose towers and monuments of earlier periods, while here and there were small groups of post-Great Fire dwellings. In the background are two achievements of nineteenth-century technology: the great iron railway shed of Cannon Street Station, now, alas, dismantled; and above it the Tower Bridge, a bold technical innovation camouflaged in mock medieval trappings to 'fit in' with the Tower of London itself (just visible at top left). During the last ten years a third major urban renewal has been taking place in the same area.

56

57

58

58. New York: the urban scene

Manhattan is a classic case of commercial and residential, rather than industrial, congestion. Here the highest levels of technological invention have been effectively frustrated by a lack of urban control. In the background the Mid-town skyscrapers push up, like giant sequoias, out of a street pattern designed for four- or five-storeyed buildings, while in the foreground Stuyvesant Town and Peter Cooper Village show what a too high density really means, especially when accompanied by a lack of compensating open space or other social facilities.

---

56. Birmingham: the urban scene

Birmingham is a comparatively new European city, whose only excuse for muddle was the frantic speed with which secondary industrial development (as distinct from the heavy industrial concentrations) took place, combined with an almost fanatical belief in non-planning. If only a small portion of Birmingham's wealth had been devoted to planning at an early stage it could have been one of the finest cities in Europe.

57. Delhi: contrasting urban patterns

One might describe Old Delhi as a hundred villages in search of a city. This type of urban pattern was subject to searching examination by Patrick Geddes, the great pioneer of contemporary planning ideas. He found, of course, that it was often a reflex of a complex social organization, and suggested that it might require a complicated form of conservative surgery rather than total demolition and redevelopment.

59

60

59. New York: the suburban scene

Suburban sprawl is typical of speculative man's futile answer to urban chaos – a desperate escapist operation conducted at enormous cost in money, land, convenience, and urban living.

60. Toronto: undesigned redevelopment

The fastest-growing city in Canada has been repeating many of the mistakes of large cities south of the border. A vast increase of floor space on downtown commercial sites has created what is almost a standard pattern of urban chaos, in addition to a flood of cars on a street pattern which was spacious enough in the pre-automobile era.

61

62

61. Detroit: towards a new pattern

The characteristic grid-iron pattern is clearly visible; but it is difficult to pick out the Renaissance radial pattern, designed in 1806 for the original Detroit, in the muddle of skyscrapers in the centre of the photograph. Detroit is making fine efforts to replan and redevelop itself. It has made a bold beginning in the lake shore layout, seen at the left of the photograph, with the civic buildings and Ford auditorium, and behind them the Cobo Hall and Convention Arena.

62. Phoenix: an urban mushroom

The population of Phoenix in Arizona has grown from some 40,000 to over 400,000 within thirty years; a phenomenal growth rate for a city without industrial or mineral resources, and with a rapidly diminishing water potential. This is unrestricted urban primary growth, based on the simple grid-iron road pattern, and cannot be said to have achieved much urban design quality – in fact, this form of development is only too likely to be obsolete by the time it is completed. An interesting sidelight of urban growth is that the micro-climate has been altered by the large number of suburban gardens and orchards. In the background is Camelback Mountain and the Phoenix mountains, arid and of semi-desert character.

63. São Paulo: an urban jungle
Recently São Paolo was the fastest-growing city in the world. Unfortunately the commercial free-for-all was much stronger than the somewhat tentative planning system, and São Paolo is now a typical urban jungle, with the biggest buildings pushing up above their less fortunate rivals and removing any opportunities for good urban design. The former colonial Portuguese market town has been overwhelmed by the speed and intensity of speculative development.

63

64

64. San Francisco: urban possibility
A city of great character with superb natural geographic possibilities. Over-development has to some extent been curtailed by the building of a second large business centre across the bay at Oakland, made very accessible by the Bay Bridge, seen in the background. Unfortunately there is the usual muddle of congested business buildings in the centre, and vast expressways have been forced right into the heart of the city. There is also far too little public open space. In the foreground is the monumental civic group; recently the whole piazza in front of the City Hall was excavated to provide a vast underground car park. The two symmetrical buildings on this side of the City Hall are the Veteran's Auditorium and the Opera House (site of the signing of the United Nations Charter). San Francisco is another city which is making commendable efforts towards planned renewal, particularly with the first great project, the Golden Gate Redevelopment. The site lies between the cluster of skyscrapers and the Bay at the top of the photograph.

65

65. Chicago: technological success, planning failure

Buried in the urban muddle of downtown Chicago are a number of remarkable phenomena. The superb late nineteenth-century skyscrapers by Sullivan and other architectural pioneers can be paralleled by the bold treatment of multi-level motorways along and across the Chicago River. At present, however, the urban scene is almost as unsatisfactory as the nineteenth-century urban agglomeration, with bold but piecemeal urban improvements tending to cancel each other out.

66

67

66. Cleveland: the motorway and the city

This view of Cleveland shows what damage unrelated urban components can do to a city. It is clearly more easy to travel in and out of the downtown area, but the motorways have been inserted into the urban pattern much as the nineteenth-century developers carried in the iron railroads on viaducts – regardless of everything else. The housing scheme on the left was once illustrated as a model example of its kind.

67. Los Angeles: total victory for the automobile

Los Angeles is the sad example of a city that concentrated on fulfilling the needs of the automobile. It has a great network of expressways, skyways, and motorways, together with a vast area of the city given over to parking lots. The estimates give one-third of the land each for roads, car parks, and everything else. The result is devastating in conventional urban design terms, and because it is uncomprehensive does not solve the problem. In this photograph the famous 'Stack' freeway interchange is seen in the foreground, while the Civic Centre is in the background.

2

The Components of Planning

BUILDING AND BUILDING GROUPS. It is a commonplace that, as a building is made up of numerous components which enclose its various internal spaces to form rooms, halls, corridors, ducts, etc., so a city is an aggregate of a variety of buildings which enclose or frame its external spaces to form squares, closes, roads, paths, gardens, parks, and so on. But whereas a building is normally designed, with all its elements, to be an entity in space, a city, as we have now seen, is almost invariably faced with the problem of replacing its components over a period. This creates the difficult problem of co-ordinating many components of different periods into the same visual scene.

The tasks of the architect and the urban planner may stand a further comparison in that, although the architect today is responsible for the design of the whole building, he often incorporates a large number of prefabricated elements which have been, or will be, designed by others. In the same way the planner, in preparing a comprehensive layout, may not be responsible for the design of any of the specific buildings, bridges, or landscaped spaces within it.

However, if his plan is to have significance it must comprise much more than coloured zones in two dimensions (important as zoning, as a factor in good planning, may be): it must be an imaginative study in *three* dimensions; forward looking in that it will anticipate the most advanced architectural forms, with enough flexibility so that changes in form may be made to individual buildings when they come to be built, without damaging the main principles of the overall design. To a great extent a comprehensive layout is bound to affect, and to be affected by, the design of the individual components, but one would wish neither to condemn the limitations placed on the designers of individual buildings in some of the great Renaissance compositions, nor to deny that the lack of planning in the nineteenth and early twentieth centuries did not always give building designers freedom. On the contrary, it often imposed on them an arbitrary and sometimes ridiculous set of design conditions. The central area of any large city bears this out, with its height set-backs, party wall problems, rights of light restrictions, awkward site shapes and other frustrations to good design. Such problems have created difficulties for the planner in his consideration of evolving building forms; apart from other restrictions, the shapes of individual sites were often so complex that architects spent too much ingenuity in overcoming difficulties of this sort and too little in producing significant results in terms of the purpose of the building.

For the planner another problem already referred to, which links component design and the time dimension, is caused by changes in social and economic organization which take place in society over a period. To illustrate this further I have made comparative studies of three major building types: shops, offices, and residential buildings. The most elementary study shows how fundamentally the changing social and economic structure of society has affected the building programme and hence the building form in each case.

SHOPS. Shops began as wayside stalls, were later grouped in market-places, and then occupied the ground floors in the surrounding houses and in the streets leading up to the market-place. A variant occurred in the eighteenth century with the pedestrian shopping terraces, which one finds associated with the town extensions and the Spa towns of that period. In the nineteenth century a number of new ideas were evolved, springing in some cases from new technical inventions, and in others from economic changes. Examples of the first category were the large new market halls, exploiting cast iron and sheet glass, in the up-to-date industrial cities such as Leeds and Milan, and the covered pedestrian arcades sometimes even designed on two floors, as in Birmingham. The second category introduced Department Stores, like the Bon Marché in Paris, which was really a large number of different shops combined under one ownership and in one building. In each case the main effect was to provide improved conditions in terms of weather protection for the shoppers.

The early twentieth century, however, saw a step backward with the emergence of an inferior planning component in the corridor shopping street. It consisted, usually, of shops on the ground floor, creating heavy pedestrian congestion on the narrow pavements; and, later, a dense mass of motor traffic running in two directions, separating the two pedestrian streams by an often lethal movement, especially when morning and evening rush hours bring down to these overcrowded pavements an additional mass of office and other workers from the buildings above the shops. Above the muddle, noise, and fumes created by these conflicting uses rise ever higher cliffs of building.

The shopping street was largely the result of an unplanned change of use in buildings without a change in the planning form of the group, and even reached respectable status in the Headrow at Leeds, where its anachronisms are now obvious to expert and layman alike. Moreover, in large cities the corridor shopping street tended to trail far out to the urban fringes in an effort to follow the motor car, until the Americans took it to its logical conclusion and built complete shopping centres right out in the country, surrounded, however, not by the rural sounds of lowing herds, but by the drone of a thousand revving engines. It is probable, and much to be hoped, that these new components will in fact become complete new urban centres by the decking over of their now open car-parks and by the superimposition of the full range of associated buildings. It must be emphasized, too, that neither these supermarkets, nor, incidentally, the British New Towns, render unnecessary in any way the redevelopment of central areas. Fortunately, it is still generally accepted that most of the collective activities or urban man, and particularly those concerned with the interchange of goods and ideas, should take place in urban cores, and as I describe in a later chapter, the disasters of war gave Coventry and Rotterdam the opportunity of experimenting with a new kind of shopping precinct within their city centres.

OFFICES. Offices make another interesting planning component to study in evolution. They began as accounting rooms within that early form of mixed development, the merchant's house, and evolved slowly towards specialized forms. During the eighteenth century they were regarded largely as units of the greater planning element of the street or square, as in the *Inns of Court* in London, but in the nineteenth century any advance in individual development was counteracted by the combined effects of an obsolete street pattern, the lack of planning controls and the property rights of adjacent owners. They were twisted for the most part into inconvenient and ugly shapes. As the economic units of development became larger, architects went back to Italian palaces for inspiration, and even when a striking technological invention like the skyscraper was developed, most architects could think of the forty floors below only as a means of supporting the architecture at the top. Inspiration came eventually via Chicago to the pioneer architects of *Congrès Internationaux d'Architecture Moderne*, and a more open and fundamental approach began to be adopted. One can trace a line of development from the original skyscraper offices of the *City of Tomorrow*, the *Pensions Office* in Prague, with a glance at the *Rockefeller Centre*, via the *Ministry of Education* in Rio de Janeiro (probably the most important advance of all), closely followed by the *United Nations* building in New York, to the full development achieved in the *Lever Building*, also in New York. In both the official Stockholm *Lower Norrmalm* and the joint London County Council/City Corporation *Barbican* schemes the basic Lever Building form of tall tower on a low slab is integrated with several others of similar types to make a new kind of urban planning component.

In some ways the wheel has gone full circle. The original medieval merchants' houses were composite units, consisting of residential, commercial, office, and sometimes shopping uses in the same building. Eventually, after a gradual separation of function followed by the nineteenth-century pattern of separate uses muddled together, necessitating the sanitary zoning exercise of recent planning theory, we come back to a new kind of composite planning component, embodying a number of different buildings in one co-ordinated unit which share common services, a common ground floor for vehicles and a common first floor for pedestrians. The clearest theoretical exercise of this idea was probably the Boston *Back Bay* project by Gropius and associates, although, as I describe in Chapter 3, Paul Boissevain, Colin Buchanan and I carried it very much further in our scheme for the centre of Berlin.

Such urban planning components, however, imply a radically new approach in the conception of the road pattern. The road ceases to be an isolated technical unit and becomes an integrated part of the whole scheme, so that in many cases it is no longer possible to define roads and buildings separately. Even in existing centres built in the old way, the intensity of traffic, particularly in shopping streets, will force the pavements to the first floor, which will have the effect also of forcing the design integration of building and means of communication.

RESIDENTIAL BUILDINGS. The evolution of residential components is a long and complex study, and can be outlined only very generally here. Too often history books on *the house* confuse the issue by describing castle, palace, mansion, and ending up with a semi-detached villa; ignoring the reality of the plum-stone rhyme of rich man, poor man, beggar man, thief. Any serious attempt to describe the evolution of dwellings must perforce carry through at least three if not four parallel strains in descending order of the economic condition of the dwellers. The subject is also marked by strong emotional feelings among different sections of the public, both as urban dweller and as consumer. These are expressed, for instance, in the desire of lower income-groups to fulfil upper income-group myths. Thus the average speculative house is only the reality of the 'mansion in the country' dream, and the erection of a whole garden-city planning theory around this dream does not make it universally valid.

Ideas, however, spring from unexpected places, and in the hands of an outstanding client (Henrietta Barnett) and a brilliant architect planner (Raymond Unwin) a new concept of the suburban *neighbourhood* was created empirically in the Hampstead Garden Suburb. The neighbourhood and other subdivisions of residential areas are, however, still a subject for research, and although the physical concepts of both *community* and *neighbourhood* are beginning to prove their validity, there is still a missing unit between house and neighbourhood. Here again the planning component is seen as something bigger and more complex than the individual building, especially as the dwelling unit is so small, and we are still in a world of experimental forms, from complete neighbourhoods in one building, such as le Corbusier's *Unité d'Habitation*, slab blocks, point blocks, four-storey maisonette squares, to little domestic greens, which, although they may superficially resemble the old village greens, have in fact great differences owing to the motor vehicle and many other new visible and invisible artifacts. At this stage the problem is one of experiment and research, which must include a special study of residential density, as this is intimately linked to building forms, and is in many cases one of the determining factors in the character of any residential component.

Let us look briefly, however, at the evolution in dwelling type of the largest and lowest income-group. For many centuries the poorest urban dweller lived cheek by jowl with the middle and upper income-groups, usually in the basements or the attics of large town houses, or in hovels or shacks thrown up in alleys or back gardens. As the middle and upper income-groups moved out to new segregated residential areas, the poor moved in, but in much larger numbers; so that, although there was no distinctive urban component for this group, the external shells of whole streets in the eighteenth and nineteenth centuries almost completely belied their contents. During the early nineteenth century, however, the very large increase in population forced a new type of component to emerge—the artisan's dwelling—usually arranged in long narrow streets of terrace or row houses, facing straight on to pavement or sidewalk at the front, a small garden or yard at the back, and minimum accommodation within. This grossly inferior component was thrown up in large numbers by speculators, usually without any thought of community or open-space provision, and usually formed a tight one-class residential ring round urban cores which, soon degenerated into the characteristic twilight or slum areas which are today so difficult to replace.

It should be said that even at this early stage reformers were endeavouring to improve both individual dwelling-type and community provision. These reformers were usually enlightened industrialists who provided dwellings, in the form of terrace houses or tenement blocks of flats, together with shop, school, and church. The pioneer in this type of venture was Robert Owen at *New Lanark*, early in the nineteenth century. He was followed, during the century, by Titus Salt in *Saltaire*, near Bradford, and by other less well known reformers both in Europe and America right down to the end of the century, with the Lever Brothers at *Port Sunlight*, near Birkenhead and the Cadbury Firm's *Bournville*, near Birmingham. By then the idea of the Company Town was giving way to the concept of municipal responsibility, but it was the former which had in fact germinated the idea of the component of the planned neighbourhood.

Right through the nineteenth century the appalling conditions of overcrowding and urban slums animated a whole series of reformers whose work crystallized in building forms. Prince Albert was patron of a prototype of improved artisans' dwelling, which was built for the Great Exhibition in London in 1857, and still exists in Kennington. Later came statutory regulations which improved the space and sanitary standards of the terrace house and gave rise to the name 'bye-law' housing.

This movement was largely concerned with new development on the urban fringe, but parallel to it the problem of slum redevelopment was being met by private philanthropic bodies, such as the Peabody Trust, with the erection of tenements in the form of large, solidly built blocks of flats, usually with a maximum of six storeys in height, and with slowly improving internal space and sanitary standards. These tenements, as Dickens pointed out, represented a great improvement at the time, but today, with their very high densities, and their grossly inferior space standards between blocks, they are a difficult redevelopment problem.

By the beginning of the twentieth century, when housing legislation was putting the onus of responsibility for slum clearance and the rehousing of the lowest income-group firmly on to the municipal authorities in Great Britain, the new residential component for this group had become established, more out of necessity than design. In the case of the redevelopment of the inner residential areas, the inevitably high densities required to meet the problem of replacing the same number of people in a given area necessitated the provision of dwellings either in the form of rows of houses or superimposed as blocks of flats, and later development has concentrated on variations of these two themes. The development of a larger residential component in the form of a *neighbourhood* represents, however, an important new technical and social element. Its beginnings are difficult to set out accurately, since they are drawn both from the company towns and from the self-contained village, in addition to growing out of the problem itself. Thus in the first decade of the twentieth century the L.C.C.[1], as Housing Authority, demolished a large and notorious slum area just beyond the north east boundary of the City of London, and in redeveloping it as the *Boundary Estate* included in a comprehensive design a small open space, a school, laundry, and other community faculties.

TRAFFIC. Although other forms of communication, such as the telephone, cable, wireless and television, make a considerable visual impact on our environment with their wires and struts and wirescapes, not to mention their other less obvious effects, it is the motor car which has brought about the greatest change and which today threatens to dominate our urban life.

The person/movement means of communication began with the relay runners of Persia and Peru and the travellers by foot, donkey or horse; early vehicles, such as palanquins, carts, waggons, and chariots, all required a firm and reasonably level

[1] London County Council; now replaced, in 1965, by the Greater London Council.

surface. The Romans were highly skilled in the art of building roads and streets, but in the Middle Ages town streets were minimal spaces left between buildings and the roads between towns were rough straggling tracks. The Renaissance brought formal street patterns and pedestrian pavements; but the complete methodology of street and road making, with smooth, cambered and drained surfaces, came with the Industrial Revolution, McAdam and the great engineers. The nineteenth century saw the development of the railways as a highly organized and controlled method of mass transportation.

The invention of the motor car presented new problems. At first, it seemed that cities with broad, spacious streets could deal adequately with the new vehicle, but within the last few years the inadequacy of the traditional street has become obvious and has necessitated a drastic reassessment of the urban pattern. We are now witnessing the evolution of a specialized road in the form of a motorway which, in its bold use of cuttings, tunnels, embankments, viaducts, etc., bears a close resemblance to the railroad of the nineteenth century. In the city centres, where the problem is one of local circulation and access to vehicle storage space, there will be a radical change in the conventional street/pavement component: the pedestrian surface will be moved to a different level and will be provided with moving walkways, escalators, etc., where the building density makes it economically viable. Outside the central areas multi-lane tracks with complex and space-consuming junctions are being, and will be, built, based on one-way traffic circulation, their design requirements computed as accurately as rail tracks.

1

The Urban Condition

1. New York: Lower Manhattan

This illustrates the need for the control of volume and daylight in city centres. In a sense Manhattan is a special case, as it is the core of metropolitan New York. It is also closely surrounded by a blue, instead of a green, belt; but congestion such as this is today both unnecessary and environmentally substandard. The idea that individual property owners can of right place a fifty- or sixty-storey building with 100 per cent cover on a site originally laid out for three- or four-storey residences is one that should belong to the past.

2 COMPONENTS

A city is made up of a large number of components, consisting chiefly of different building types, many of which have been constructed at different periods. The illustrations in this section show something of the complexity of the resulting urban pattern by following the evolution of four different components; shops, offices, residential buildings, and traffic.

2

2. New York: Lower Manhattan
This has the great centre of finance, known to the world as Wall Street. The original urban pattern first laid out by the Dutch settlers was pleasant enough for merchants' houses, but now it has become an untamed jungle, with each successive skyscraper reaching even higher for the sky and thereby pushing its neighbour down into the shadows. It is one of the most dramatic sights in the world from a distance, and one of the most chaotic from close up.

3. The City of nightmares
Steinberg's drawings are almost savage in their intensity. He is a ruthless critic of the contemporary city. Every city needs its Steinberg or Lowry to see its true self.

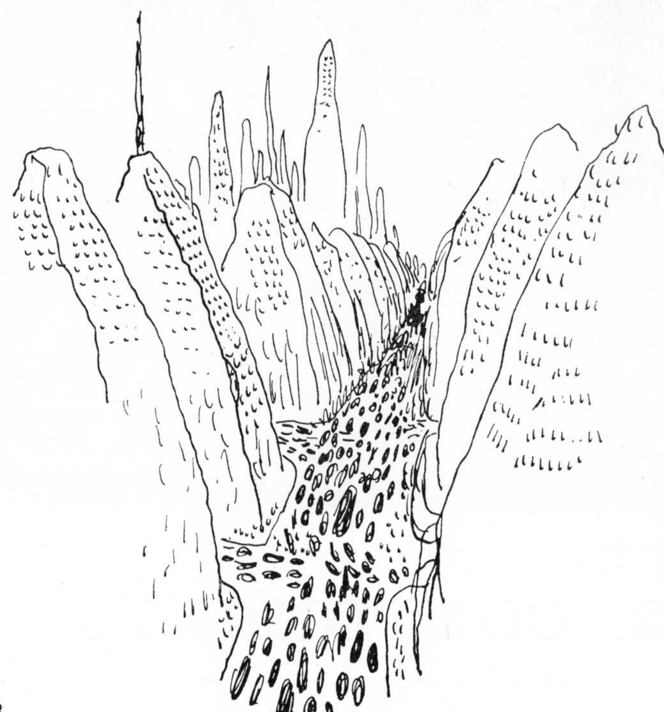

3

4

4. San Francisco

San Francisco has undoubtedly one of the most beautiful natural settings of any city in the world. It is situated on a hilly promontory almost surrounded by blue water and (usually) has warm and sunny skies above; attractive hills frame the background on all sides except the west, which has the glorious Pacific Ocean. Its problem of central area (or 'downtown') congestion has been eased by the rapid growth of Oakland across the Bay, while the wonderful bridges (the Golden Gate Bridge is in the background of the photograph) all help to enable a planned and equable distribution of urban resources to take place. Effective planning, however, as in most American cities, has been largely confined to the routing of great motorways in a manner as bold and as heedless as that of the Railway Age. In the right foreground the last span of the great and beautiful Bay Bridge ends in a massive viaduct that swirls traffic through a large and space-consuming road intersection perilously near the heart of the city.

The high viaduct (in some cases on two superimposed levels with car park below) crashes right through tightly built urban patterns, regardless of noise and fumes, and dominates the townscape. At last, however, planned urban renewal has begun to arrive. When I was in San Francisco in 1960 the result of a limited competition for the Golden Gate redevelopment area (just above the top of the Bay Bridge pylons at the right of the photograph) was announced. The scheme is progressing well and is a hopeful portent of things to come.

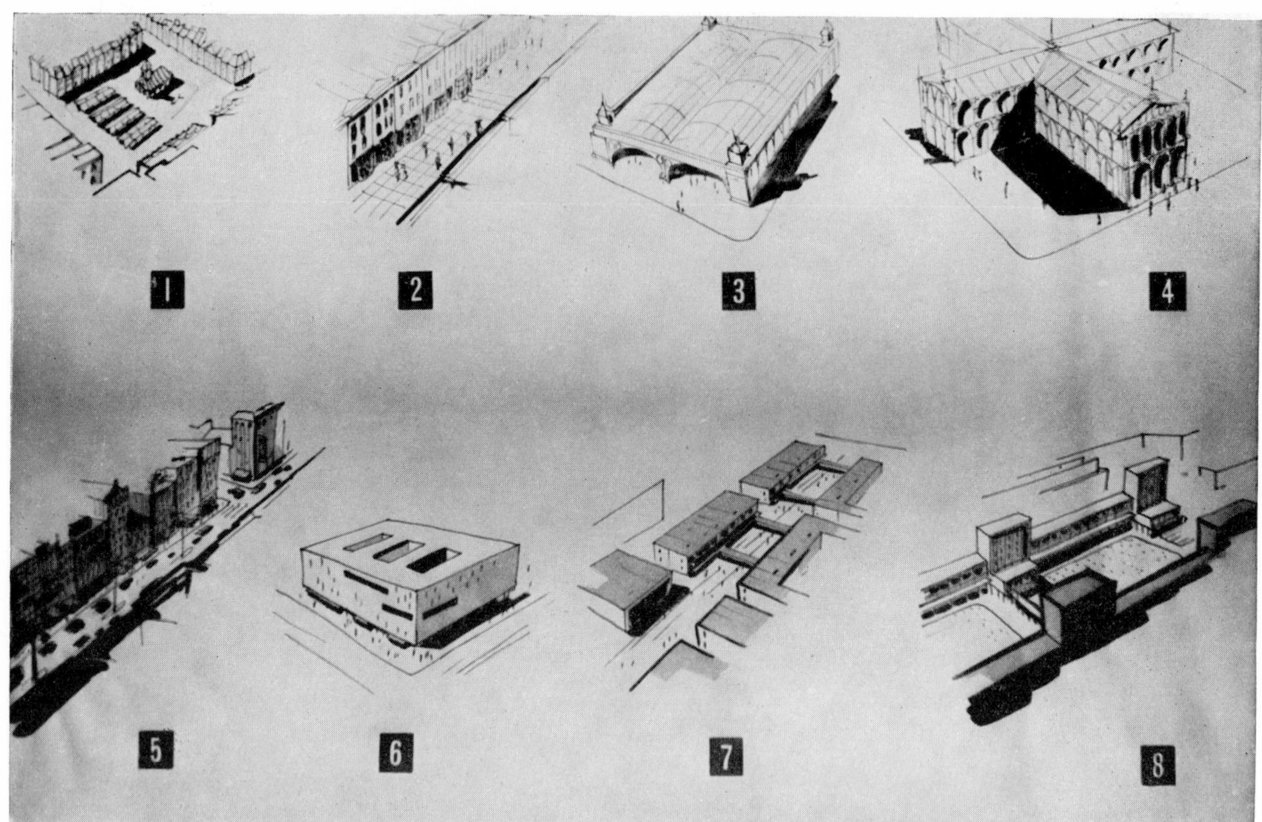

5

6

Shops

5. The evolution of shopping centres

These sketches illustrate various stages in the evolution of the shopping centre. No. 1 shows the medieval market-place, and no. 2 the Renaissance terrace; nos. 3 and 4 show nineteenth-century developments in the covered market of cast iron and glass and the shopping arcade; no. 5 illustrates the step backwards in the Corridor shopping street, and no. 6 is the Department Store; nos. 7 and 8 are the Rotterdam and Coventry versions of the shopping precinct.

6. Delft: the medieval market-place

Delft has one of the most spacious of medieval market-places, and, as with most Netherlands towns, has a regular layout, and an orderly urban form. At the north end is the New Church with its tall spire which dominates the urban space. At the south end is the Town Hall, designed by the architect Kayser in the seventeenth century. The market-place is still used for a variety of public events.

7

8

7. Chester: the Rows

One of the first multi-level pedestrian shopping centres. The Rows provided a considerable length of covered shopping walkway on two levels. The drawing shows the upper level.

8. Regent Street: the Renaissance shopping arcade

A new development in shopping was introduced with the covered arcade for shops. This was usually confined to the shopping centres of the wealthy classes, and the two most memorable examples, the Rue de Rivoli in Paris and Regent Street in London, were both in the fashionable quarters of the two capitals. The drawing is of the Quadrant, where Nash laid out Regent Street with its southern part carried round in a quarter-circle to enter Piccadilly. Sad to say, this splendid street was given a face lift in the prize-fighting tradition, and is now unrecognizable.

9

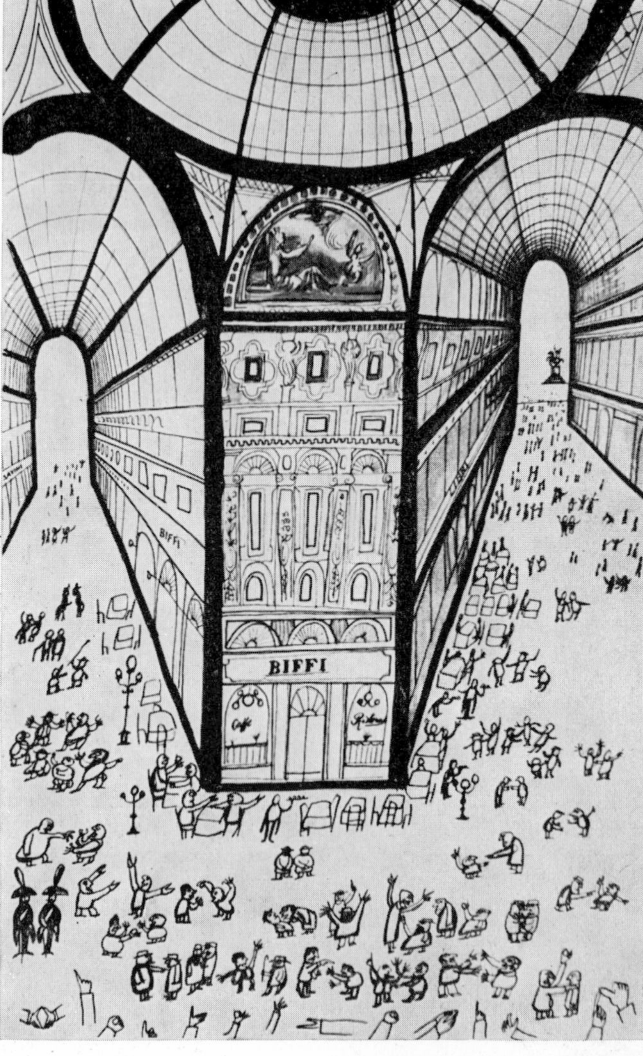

10

9. The nineteenth-century covered market

Here is technical invention in the use of the new materials, cast iron and sheet glass providing an improved standard and creating a new component.

10. Milan: the Galleria

Steinberg's drawing shows more clearly than any photograph the exciting possibilities of the arcade as a shopping component.

11

11. Leeds: the Headrow

This is a classic example of a new but out-of-date solution. A large area in the centre of Leeds was cleared and a new road was made along the lines of Nash's Regent Street. In a hundred years, however, the vehicle had changed urban requirements, and the traditional method of lining main streets with shops and offices above them no longer made sense. The saddest aspect in the case of Leeds is that near by are a number of splendid covered pedestrian arcades which are monuments of nineteenth-century technical skill and consumer convenience.

12

13

12. Los Angeles: the shopping ribbon

One of the worst features of city development in the twentieth century, and one directly due to the motor vehicle, has been the almost endless prolongation of urban streets far out into the country, lined with shops, restaurants, cafés, and petrol filling (or gas) stations. This is totally the wrong kind of shopping centre – an inferior mutation due directly to lack of planning policy and, more important, planning ideas.

13. Levittown: the out-of-town shopping centre

When the uncontrolled growth of American cities had caused congestion of a degree which only affluence could create, some American planners gave up all hope of doing anything with the downtown, or central, areas. In consequence some of the brighter speculators decided to build comprehensive new shopping centres right outside the cities. A good example is shown in this air view of Levittown, a residential community planned by private enterprise outside Philadelphia. The shopping centre covers sixty acres and has parking space for 5,000 cars. It is pedestrian throughout. The most unsatisfactory aspect is the sea of cars all round, making it very much an isolated island. If, of course, it proves to be a rational centre for the surrounding area, the car parks could be covered over with decks for public and other buildings, so that a real new town centre could be created.

These centres may end up in decongesting the existing central urban areas sufficiently to enable comprehensive redevelopment to take place. I have seen many out-of-town shopping centres in various parts of North America, and, although it is in planning terms an escapist solution, there is no doubt that nearly all were of a high standard of design, and the shopping facilities were comprehensively planned.

14

14. Rotterdam: the multiple store
The multiple store as an urban component was first developed in Paris. It rapidly became popular because it enabled the customer to see a large number of different articles under one roof. 'Under one roof' means protection from weather and from wheeled traffic. There are, however, economic disadvantages, such as the tendency towards monopoly. This multiple store is the well-known Bijenkorf in the rebuilt centre of Rotterdam.

15. Coventry: the pedestrian shopping precinct
One of the first attempts to plan a fresh type of shopping component in the heart of the city was made for Coventry's devastated centre in 1940. In a new kind of urban unit it provided for both large and small shops, restaurants, cafés, and a hotel, with broad pedestrian squares and walkways. Garaging and car parking was proposed on either side, with bus access at each end. Its root ideas came from the historic Rows of Chester and the Departmental Store.

15

16

16. Rotterdam: the pedestrian shopping centre

The second essay in new central area pedestrian shopping precincts was in Rotterdam. As in Coventry, war damage provided the opportunity, although in this case both design and execution were different. The Lijnbaan, as Rotterdam's precinct is known, is confined to small shops and practically the whole complex is designed as one component of architecture.

17

Offices

17. London: the Temple

The first group in the urban community to develop a specialized precinct and building form for offices was the legal profession. As some of them combined their place of domicile and place of work it was natural to lay out harmonious squares, which the romantic landscapers later adorned with fine trees and smooth lawns. The Temple and the two Inns of Court (Grays Inn and Lincolns Inn, seen at top left) provided legal offices, libraries, chapels, and dining-halls in a series of compact precincts around the Law Courts.

18

18. Chicago: office buildings in the urban pattern

Public ownership of the foreshore land held the eastwards movement of building in the central area of Chicago. Although expansion was possible north, west, and south, commercial development was concentrated in the 'Loop' of the Chicago River.

The photograph shows in the foreground the luxurious effect of planning a public building with a relatively adequate amount of horizontal space. Otherwise the free-for-all of nineteenth- and twentieth-century commercial private enterprise has created an urban jungle on a regular street plan, and without the physical space limitations cf Manhattan. In meeting these client demands the architects of the nineteenth century, led by Sullivan, Holabird and Root, and other less well-known but brilliant designers, developed the skyscraper, with superbly functional and well-designed steel frame and glass walls. The high buildings took various forms, depending somewhat on the size of site available. Here may be seen the hollow square of tradition extended upwards into a rectangular tube, the H form, the long slab, the solid cube, the tapering tower, and even, in the foreground, the traditional 'street frontage' type.

19

19. London: County Hall

The design for the headquarters of the great new Municipal Government in London was won in open competition by Messrs Knott and Brewer in 1911. It represents the apogee of the civic office building, housing thousands of employees, but setting out deliberately to create a feeling of civic dignity. For inspiration the architects of the day went back to the Italian Renaissance palace, with its hollow square or cortile, so well suited to the Mediterranean climate. County Hall is still a very imposing building from outside, but working in it, facing one of the inner courts, soon reveals the faults in the building form.

20. New York: Lower Manhattan

This shows what happens to a city when many commercial firms, banks, and other enterprises all try to concentrate within a small area. With no comprehensive plan, no plot ratio or daylighting control, ever higher buildings are placed on sites originally designed for three- and four-storey buildings. The result is to create extensive congestion and an effect of being at the bottom of a great canyon.

20

21

21. New York: the skyscraper as cathedral spire

The Empire State Building rises out of mid-town Manhattan. It is halfway between the rock outcrops under Wall Street and Fifth Avenue, which have been so helpful in creating the two fantastic accumulations of high buildings on this long central area surrounded by a blue, instead of a green, open space. Erected in 1929, it is 1472 feet high, and its creators deliberately set out to build the highest building in the world. Although mannered in detail, it does uplift the eye as a dramatic soaring mass tapering to the sky, and is well seen in contrast to the surrounding low buildings. This gives it that quality of light and air and space which the theoreticians advocated in support of the tower form of building.

22. Rio De Janeiro: the Ministry of Education

This building, inspired by le Corbusier but very imaginatively designed by a distinguished group of Brazilian architects in 1942, represented an important step forward in office building design. It consists of a simple tall rectangular block with a low block set at right angles to it, allowing two spacious pedestrian squares to be formed on either side.

23. Prague: the Pensions Office

An aerial view of the famous office building designed by architects Honzig and Havliçek, and built between 1932 and 1934. It is true that it was ante-dated by the London Passenger Transport Board's office in Broadway, London, in its open planning form, but it was a great advance generally in architectural design.

22

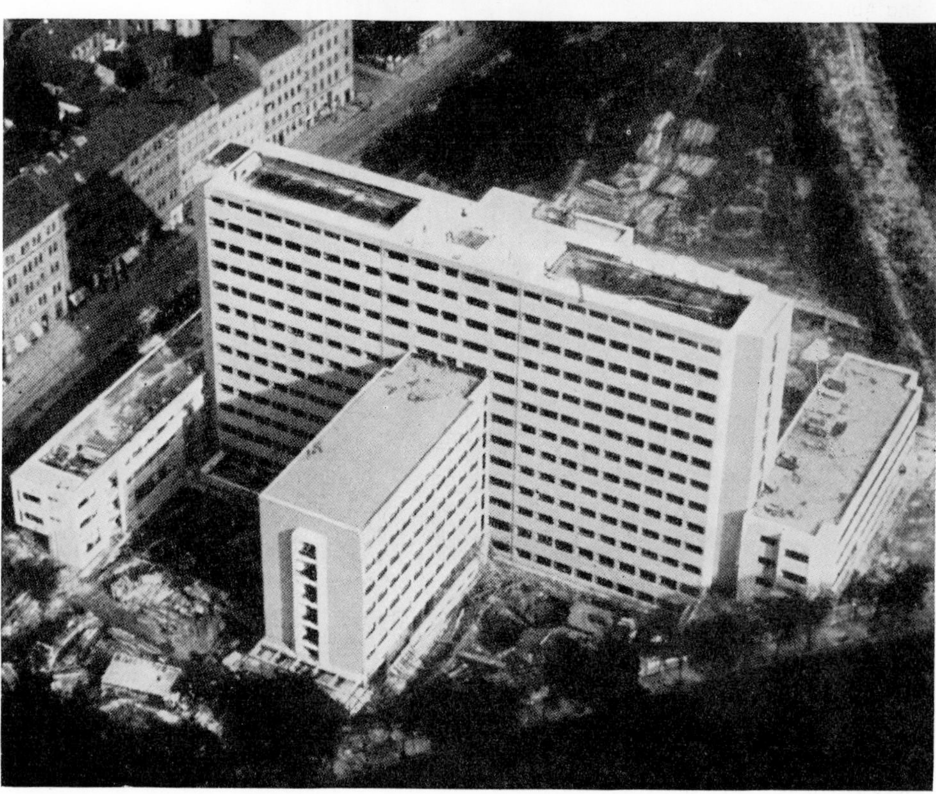

23

24

24. New York: tall slab, low block, and 'acoustic' shape
The United Nations Building is important for many reasons. It was designed after a good deal of discussion between a consortium of international architects. Credit for the final design must be given to both le Corbusier and the brilliant young Brazilian architect Oscar Niemeyer. The executive architect was Mr Harrison (of Harrison and Abramovitz) and many interesting new problems were faced, as the building includes a large lower level garage, a complex of meeting halls, and two large Council chambers (given a not very satisfactory external form). It also has a main waterside road running below its terrace. The whole group stands out, whether seen from land, sea, or air, in striking contrast to the gross overcrowding of Manhattan.

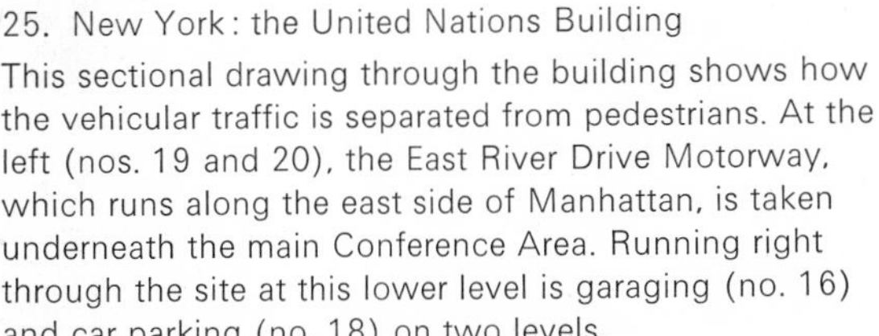

25. New York: the United Nations Building
This sectional drawing through the building shows how the vehicular traffic is separated from pedestrians. At the left (nos. 19 and 20), the East River Drive Motorway, which runs along the east side of Manhattan, is taken underneath the main Conference Area. Running right through the site at this lower level is garaging (no. 16) and car parking (no. 18) on two levels.

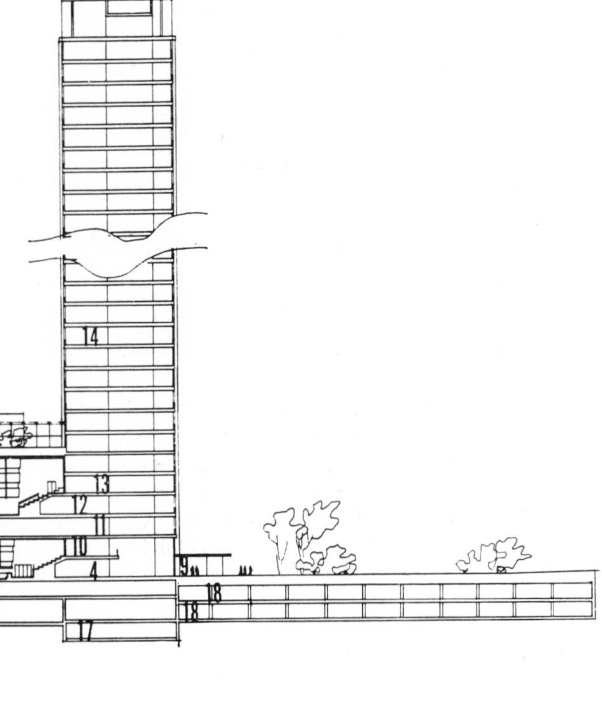

25

[80]

26 

26. New York: vertical slab on horizontal platform

This superb design by architects Skidmore, Owings, and Merrill for Messrs Lever was a pioneer in the form of commercial office buildings. Taking a corner site on the highly valuable real estate area of Park Avenue, they deliberately kept below the permissible bulk for the site, and broke radically with the traditional form which would have shielded the blank wall on the left with a perimeter frontage round the corner of the block. A simple vertical form, larger but of approximately the same shape as the Ministry of Education building at Rio, was placed over a low platform consisting of a two-storey hollow square with most of the ground floor left open.

Compared with almost any other building in Manhattan (except the U.N. Building) the public gain was very great. It was this building that we made our prototype for the Barbican scheme in London, proposing a number of tall blocks with low slabs, the latter being joined by bridges to form a complete upper level pedestrian system. Alas, the Lever Building remained a lone adventurer in Manhattan. Both north and south of the Lever Building the street has since been largely redeveloped in the old and deplorable Manhattan 'corridor' tradition.

27

27. New York: the Square tower

The Seagram Building, designed by Mies van der Rohe, rises from a small but enormously expensive (in real estate terms) piazetta on Park Avenue. Its form is in a sense a return to the earlier symmetrically planned skyscrapers, but its detailed design is very different, and consists of bronze clad steel and glass. Visually it has a powerful effect which could have had much greater significance if the building could be seen in its total form, but the lush jungle of skyscrapers frustrates the view. Behind it can be seen the earlier and equally famous Lever Building, with its tall slab and low hollow block with garden roof terrace. If only this terrace level could have been continued across and up and down Park Avenue the dreams of the New York Regional Planners of 1929 could have been realized.

28

28. Milan: the Pirelli Building

This elegantly designed skyscraper by Sr Ponti stands out in the urban chaos of modern Milan as an almost isolated example of good contemporary urban form with space around it.

Residential Buildings

29. Liverpool: housing for the working classes

For its time (1905) this was a pioneer project. It provided clean, sanitary, neat and tidy accommodation for the 'artisans'. It was such an improvement on the nineteenth-century slums that its shortcomings were not easily discernible at the time. It is interesting to compare it with some of the more recent L.C.C. schemes.

29

30. Nottingham: residential suburb

After the congestion, chaos, and slums of the nineteenth century citizens of all classes endeavoured to escape. The garden city movement made a planning theory of it, and although its aesthetic limitations are obvious enough, its social and economic consequences still remain to be studied.

30

31. New York: Knickerbocker Village

The vexed problem of slum redevelopment has been through a series of stages, motivated by cost, design, and the hard facts of having to replace as many people as possible on small sites in congested areas. The characteristic component of pre-war days was the tenement, a dreary affair at its best. Charles Dickens is on record as praising some of London's first tenements, which seem to us today almost as bad as the grim dwellings they replaced. Here in New York are some 'new tenements.'

31

32

32. Hampstead Garden Suburb

This is one of the most significant examples of a new urban component, emerging largely by client demand. In the first few years of the twentieth century Dame Henrietta Barnett, working with her husband (Canon Barnett) at Toynbee Hall in London's notorious East End, decided to create a new type of residential area, where rich and poor, young and old, could all live a Christian life. She formed a Committee and a Trust, engaged a young architect planner, Raymond Unwin, and proceeded to tell him what was required. By 1905 he had laid out the framework of a new component in the Hampstead Garden Suburb, still one of the finest residential neighbourhoods in the world. The photograph looks down on the centre of the suburb, with the Institute (a Secondary School and Community building) facing the Central Square, in which are also the Parish Church and the Free Church. Nearby is the Friends' Meeting House, and on the perimeter of the Suburb (not in the photograph) the Catholic Church and a Synagogue. The spiritual needs of the community are thus well cared for. Educationally, in addition to the Secondary School there are two Primary Schools, one just beyond the former building. Upper-income dwellings surround the Square and are located mainly between the Square and the Hampstead Heath Extension, to the right of the photograph. In the centre is Big Wood and to its left is Little Wood, two clumps of trees which were there when the area was acquired and were retained in the layout. Above them is the Mutton Brook, with its streamside walk and recreation space. Much of the residential development is in the form of squares or culs-de-sac. There are also a series of footpaths and small playgrounds within each super block. There are several blocks of flats around green closes, two of which may be seen to the right of the Primary School. Although the landscaping of the roads tends to be dull owing to the over-planting of flowering fruit trees, the whole neighbourhood is excellently maintained and is one of the most pleasant areas for family living in the London area. It was an outstanding achievement (and I say this having been a resident in it for over ten years).

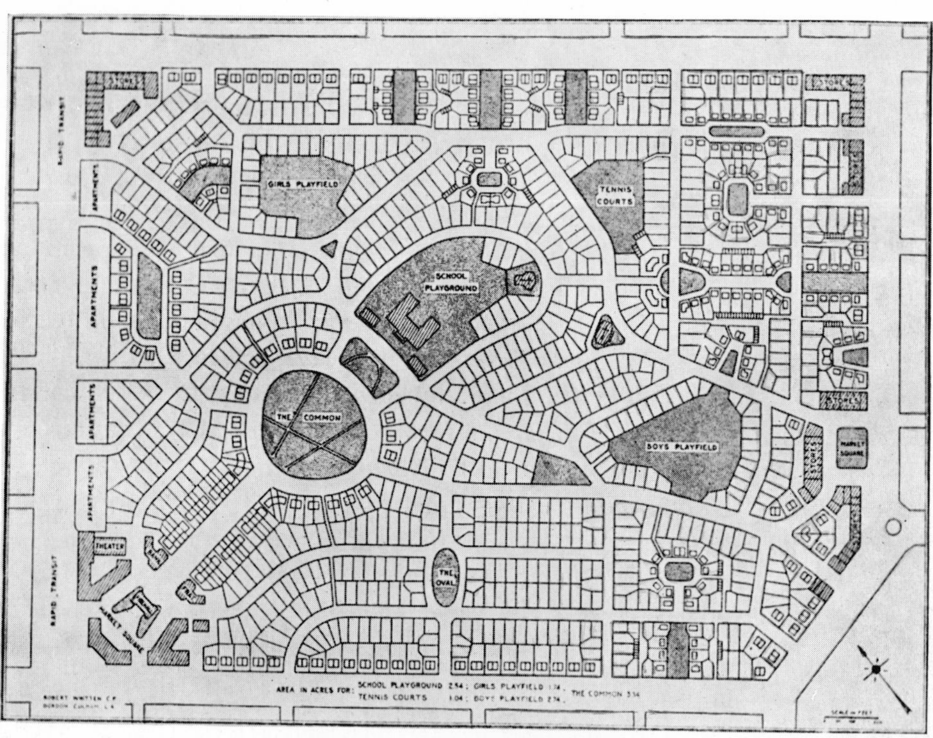

33

33. New York: Clarence Perry's Neighbourhood Plan
This was the first time that a conscious design had been prepared for a Neighbourhood. Although a residential area on similar lines had been designed and built by Sir Raymond Unwin as far back as 1907, it was then called the Hampstead Garden *Suburb*, and suburbs had a habit of spreading infinitely around large cities. Perry's famous plan was intended to show how new housing schemes should be provided with a Primary School, recreation areas, shops, and other social facilities, all integrated into the layout. This plan was originally included in the New York Regional Plan, Volume 7, 1929. It is for an area of 160 acres, with a density of 37·5 persons per acre and a population of 6,000. 16 acres was allotted to Public Open Space. (The theory behind this plan is fully described in *Housing for the Machine Age*, C. A. Perry, Russell Sage Foundation, New York, 1939.)

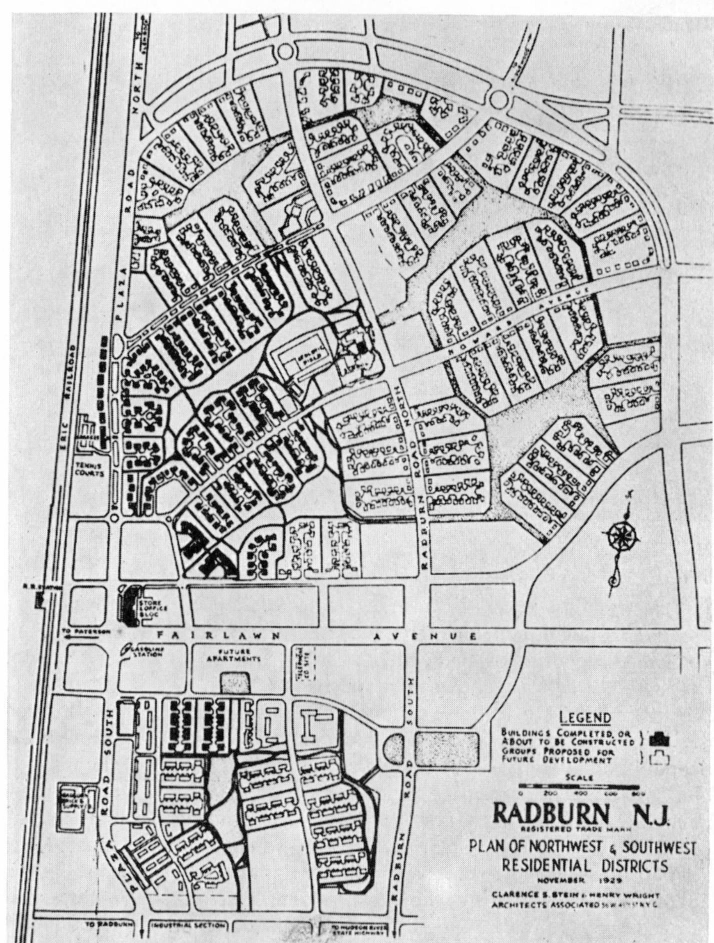

34

34. New Jersey: Radburn—a neighbourhood for pedestrians.
One of the definitive studies of the neighbourhood whose name is now a household word for planners everywhere. This project was designed by Clarence Stein and Henry Wright during 1929, the year of the great economic slump; but in spite of this, Radburn eventually became a reality, and is today a very attractive, harmonious, and safe residential family environment. The principles were simple: clusters of houses around culs-de-sac, with green parkways between the clusters affording large areas of automobile-free space. Although Radburn began without the advantages of the existing trees of Hampstead Garden Suburb, the excellent tree planting has now matured, and the effect is arcadian.

49

50

49. South-west London: five point blocks

Here at Trinity Road the L.C.C. Architect's Department extended a secondary school (seen in the background) and built five point blocks on a well wooded site of somewhat awkward shape. The visual advantages are obvious, although at this time (early 1950s) car parking had not become the problem it is now in Britain – this is one salutary lesson which could have been learnt from American experience.

50. South-west London: Roehampton I

This scheme, known at first as the Alton Estate, was designed in the early 1950s, the second of the large mixed development projects in south-west London, where the London County Council pursued a vigorous policy of acquiring large plots of land for public housing. This was a development from the earlier Ackroydon Estate, and used square point blocks with four flats per floor for small families, four-storey maisonette (duplex) slabs for medium sized families, and two-storey terrace (row) houses for large families. All three types can be seen in the photograph, and the quality of layout design on a well wooded sloping site is outstanding. The net residential density of the zone is 100 person per acre.

51

52

51. South-west London: Roehampton I

This attractive and informal group of houses is part of the Roehampton I housing scheme in south-west London. Using high point blocks for the smaller families, considerable space has been gained for the larger families at a comparatively high residential density.

52. South-west London: Roehampton II

This scheme began in 1949 as a planning exercise in the Planning Division of the L.C.C. Architect's Department. After the new Housing Division was established in 1951, and took it over as a housing project, a great many studies into different house and flat types were carried out, and eventually the final scheme emerged, using a great variety of forms. There are two groups of eleven-storey point blocks, six eleven-storey slab blocks, long rows of four-storey maisonette (duplex) blocks, two-storey terrace (row) houses, and single-storey clusters for old people. The scheme has a number of other social facilities, such as two primary schools, shops and club rooms. The density of the zone is 100 persons per acre.

53

54

53. South-west London: Roehampton II

A close view of the eleven-storey Point Blocks showing the good quality of the prefabricated wall cladding, and the space largely left open on the ground floor. To the left are parallel blocks of four-storey maisonettes (duplex) using cross-wall construction, and behind are five large eleven-storey slab blocks of maisonettes.

54. South London: high slabs and low blocks

The Loughborough Estate is part of the redevelopment of a worn-out area of housing in South London. Here the Housing Division of the L.C.C. Architect's Department experimented with eleven-storey slabs of maisonettes (duplex), with access galleries along the north side. Interspersed between these blocks are four-storey blocks of maisonettes (duplex) and two-storey terrace (row) houses. The density of the zone is 136 persons per acre.

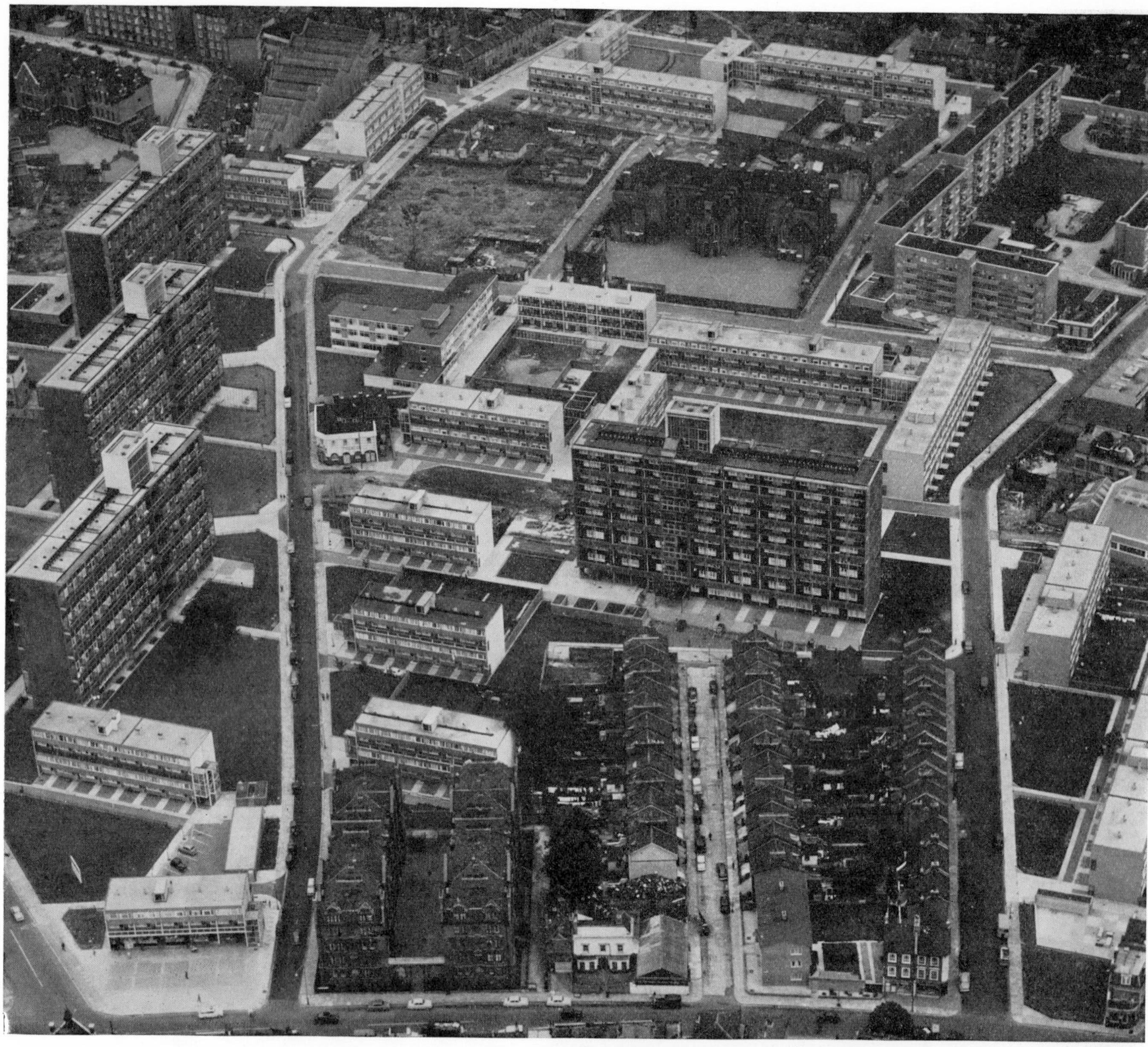

55

55. South London: high slabs and low blocks

In the Elmington Estate the Housing Division of the L.C.C. Architect's Department used the similar general form of high eleven-storey slabs of maisonettes (duplex) and low four-storey blocks of maisonettes (duplex), but experimented with a new technique of prefabrication, using aluminium and wood as facing materials. Their appearance is a great deal lighter and less sombre than those using an *in situ* concrete finish. In this area great difficulty was experienced in acquiring large enough blocks of land for redevelopment. The density of the zone is 136 persons per acre.

56. South-east London: Canada Estate

In a large city, redevelopment has to take place over a period site by site. This particular piece of land is situated in the Bermondsey Reconstruction Area, and was for many years the site of a large Thames-side warehouse, where barges would bring argosies of spices and other less attractive commodities right up to the warehouse. From it a fine view is obtained of the whole reach of the river below Tower Bridge. The small families are given full advantage of this view in the tall towers, while the larger families live in the 'T'-shaped clusters of four-storey maisonettes (duplexes). The density of the zone is 136 persons per acre.

56

57

57. South-east London: Pepys Estate

This project uses two residential components, the higher tower of twenty-four storeys, and the chain of slab blocks of eight storeys all linked together. By this means residents can proceed under cover throughout the scheme. The project is for a riverside site in Deptford that was formerly occupied by the Royal Navy as a dockyard. Here Pepys used to visit the work of fitting out the Fleet for the Dutch wars, and in fact in the foreground may be seen two of the old navy rum warehouses which are being converted into riverside flats. The density of the zone is 136 persons per acre, and garaging at a standard of 50 per cent is being provided under the eight-storey blocks.

58

58. South London: Brandon Estate

In the Brandon Estate, of which this is a model, there are six seventeen-storey point blocks of flats overlooking Lambeth Park. Next to them are long seven-storey blocks of flats with a small shopping centre, library and club rooms. Then there is a group of four-storey maisonettes and two-storey maisonettes and two-storey terraces following generally the existing pattern, part of which has been retained by rehabilitation of the old nineteenth-century terraces. The density of the zone is 136 persons per acre.

59

59. South London: Brandon Estate

Integrally planned with the housing is a small pedestrian shopping centre, marked by a low point block (left), and provided with a library and community hall (near left). In the background is one of the seven-storey slabs with the ground floor left open, and above it may be seen the top of one of the seventeen-storey point blocks.

60. South London: Brandon Estate

Here is a close up view of one of the seventeen-storey point blocks. The wide bands on the façade are there for structural reasons, while an attempt was made to provide an interesting silhouette by providing penthouses on the roof. On the right are two of the seven-storey blocks of flats. The density of the zone is 136 persons per acre.

60

61

62

61. South London

A skyline view of South London, looking north. In the foreground are typical nineteenth-century terraces of middle-income houses. Behind and right are the six seventeen-storey point blocks on the Brandon Estate, while on the skyline may be seen the new Shell Building on the South Bank, and, far right, the dome of St Paul's. The high buildings now being built all over London enable new and exciting panoramic views to be obtained, but stress the need for careful siting of these formidable urban features.

62. London: Ham Common

This scheme, by Eric Lyons, was designed for the Span Development Company and broke new ground in laying out a middle-income estate in a form which had been largely confined to eighteenth-century aristocrats or twentieth-century workers. At a density approaching 100 persons per acre Lyons designed terraces in the form of inter-connecting squares, each carefully landscaped.

63

Traffic

63. Los Angeles: the corridor street

The very affluence of Los Angeles has brought about hothouse conditions, where everything else has taken second place to the automobile. Here is a traditional street with central area buildings facing it on each side and a narrow strip of footway between them and the roadway. The enormous volume of traffic has caused this roadway to be made a one-way street, which certainly speeds up the motor traffic, but is almost the last straw for the pedestrian.

64

64. Los Angeles: the motorway

The vast scale of the new urban component of the motorway is well seen in this photograph. It is a great space eater, and should be used with the greatest discretion near the centres of cities. To the visitor, Los Angeles seems to be nearly all arteries and very little heart for human activities.

65

66

65. Chicago: the expressway

The photograph illustrates the effect of a new urban component in the ten-lane expressway carving its way through the central area of a metropolitan city. Although cut through at a low level, it has an effect more powerful than a dozen main rail lines. The New Congress Street Expressway goes on straight through the large building in the background – a prodigious technical achievement, but scarcely in harmony with a true city centre.

66. Stockholm: motorway across a park

The right way to use the motorway. This new component, highly useful and capable of dramatic and beautiful designing, nevertheless needs handling with great care. It should, wherever possible, be kept out of city centres and insulated with parkways.

67

67. New York: the George Washington Bridge

A general view of the New York City approaches to the George Washington Bridge, which spans the Hudson River, and connects the States of New York and New Jersey. This picture was taken from the bridge tower on the New York side. It illustrates the striking contrast between a great engineering achievement and the existing urban pattern.

68

68. Los Angeles: the 'Stack' Motorway intersection

This highly complex motorway intersection has no less than four levels, and is designed with generous curves so as to avoid the drastic slowing down which occurs at normal intersections. Its vast use of space, however, makes it quite unsuitable as an urban component in central areas of cities.

69. Los Angeles: the Stack; a close up

Here is the motorway intersection in full flower as an urban component. It is a great dominating feature, and apart from the problems of noise and fumes, requires a very large amount of space for it to be able to work efficiently.

69

70

71

70. Stockholm: the Slussen cloverleaf

Although an early and modest example of the cloverleaf type of road intersection, the Slussen clearly shows how much space is eaten up by a modern traffic junction. This type is normally unacceptable in central areas of cities on space grounds alone.

71. New York: bus terminal

The viaducts leading to New York bus terminal relate far more closely in scale to the skyscrapers than to the earlier urban pattern through which they cut such a swathe. Buses coast easily down the long ramps to the open highway from the city of New York. These ramps overpass the city's streets and contain central heating elements that will melt snow and ice. The terminal handles an average of 2,300 buses daily (both commuter and long distance), has four levels, and is connected with the New York subway system. Space on the roof accommodates 450 parked automobiles. This is communication building in the scale of the railway tradition.

72

72. Salt Lake City: multi-storeyed garage

Here is an attempt to create a new urban component to meet the new urban problem of the motor vehicle. It is a self-parking garage with space for 542 cars, and is clearly of great assistance in solving the off-street car parking problem. It raises, however, a question of planning principle – whether parked cars should use up valuable, light, airy and desirable space, which might far better be used by human beings. In general it is much better to keep the cars down and out of sight.

73. Washington D.C.: a multi-storey garage

Even if the multi-storey garage were the right type of urban component in a city centre, this is the wrong way to make use of it. It is a flagrant example of automobiles being rated as highly as very expensive people.

73

74

75

74. Chicago: underground garage

Another new urban component developed for the automobile is the underground garage. American experience is most valuable, since so many of these large garages have been built and their problems, including lighting, ventilating, fire-proofing and access ways, well explored.

75. Chicago: the garage escalator

Part of the new urban component of the underground garage is the problem of getting to and from it. With large numbers of people it becomes economically possible to provide escalators and moving walkways. If one could imagine that *both* garages and roads were at the lower level this escalator could really be part of the new urban environment.

76

76. San Francisco: the underground garage

The underground garage is an excellent idea, and is the right place to put cars when not in use. The wrong way to handle leafy city squares, however, is to surround them with heavily trafficked roads, remove the trees, dig out the sub-soil, insert a garage with its complicated access points and then put potted plants back. One also sees the effect of no planning control on an urban space which was obviously designed to have an orderly framework.

77. Detroit: roads and buildings

The city of Detroit is pursuing an energetic planning and development policy, although its task is hard and unenviable. In the central area by the Lakeside it has embarked on some ambitious projects. In the foreground is an enormous new Convention and Exhibition Building, completed in 1957. It has car parking space for 626 cars inside the building with an additional 1,100 on the roof, which is approached by spiral ramps, reminiscent of the New York Worlds Fair Buildings.

77

3

Visions and Designs

VISIONS IN HISTORY. In the creation of a civilized environment the vital spark of vision is of critical importance, yet it is liable to be extinguished in the complex technical and administrative processes of planning. The visionary or imaginative ideas of the planner are inevitably based on his accumulated knowledge, and it is interesting to see how planning ideas in the past have so often been conditioned and trammelled by a rigid set of traditional rules.

For centuries men have had visions of ideal cities. In the case of the early Indian philosophers, these visions were dominated by religious observance and the caste system; in the case of the Greeks, they appeared as offshoots of political studies. This also happened much later with such philosophers as Sir Thomas More, whose *Utopia* had a not very inspiring urban vision. Only with the Renaissance philosopher-architects do *speculative* ideas about the design of ideal cities really begin to proliferate. For the most part these designs took the form of geometrical patterns, assuming complete symmetry around a central feature, and providing vistas and compositions which conceived of the architecture as so many complicated stage sets or painted compositions—whence, indeed, many of the ideas had originated. In startling contrast to these somewhat stereotyped exercises were the studies of Leonardo da Vinci, whose powerful imagination and scientific curiosity broke through to more fundamental problems of town planning.

The geometrical theorists, however, held the day, and the next three centuries, too, for whenever the opportunity occurred—as it did, for instance, in Paris—thinking was concentrated on even longer vistas and ever-grander symmetrical compositions, until there arose the incredible vision of the Louvre duplicated, as part of a grandiose dream involving the Isle de la Cité and both sides of the Seine. This kind of thinking continued into the present century, where it found its realization in New Delhi or Belo Horizonte in Brazil, and in a cloudy outburst of dreams in the wartime *Royal Academy* plans for London.

In Britain, however, a number of other ideas were being slowly advanced. Of these, a series of projects for multi-level communications, so pertinent today, were probably the most valuable. Their origin went back to the two level 'Rows' at Chester, but in modern terms really began with the bold Adelphi scheme by the Adam brothers in the 1760s. Here, the gradient down to the Thames was used as a means of achieving lower level commercial circulation. These ideas were continued in the remarkable Edinburgh bridges and in the much later Holborn viaduct in London. Then came the extraordinary nineteenth-century railway developments, where the new railroads were sometimes carried through on two or more levels above the ground or, later, as a complete system below it. Here was the quality of imagination and practical application which, if only it could have been applied to city planning as a whole, might have created wonders. By this time, however, property boundaries, site values and the paraphernalia of land speculation were effectively preventing even the older dreams from being realized.

Throughout the nineteenth century urban visions seem, in fact, to have turned away from the possibility of creating a civilized environment out of the raw components of the new industrial-commercial society, as these changed the whole character of cities, and to have concentrated instead on small Ideal Towns such as Papworth imagined in Hygeia, or Buckingham in Victoria. These schemes achieved their reality in the company towns of Saltaire and Port Sunlight, and, later on, a fuller theoretical exposition by Ebenezer Howard and the Garden City movement, with practical achievements in Letchworth, Welwyn, Green Belt in America, and the post-war new towns in Britain.

THE TWENTIETH-CENTURY VISION. The new twentieth-century visions were at first limited, avoiding many of the central problems of the time. As far back as 1911, Patrick Geddes explained that *two* kinds of vision were necessary in countries such as Britain, which includes numerous urban agglomerations: one, a vision of economic activity and broad land use distribution, was regional in scale; the other, essentially visual, was a three-dimensional exploitation of the imaginative possibilities inherent in all technological inventions which had, by their misuse, tended to destroy the existing environment rather than help to create a new one.

Such concepts, frustrated at every turn by economic and social conditions in a society which had little time for any kind of planning, were even more stifled by the dominance of conventional ideas. The virtual completion of a vast urban design for the centre of the great capital city of Paris had all too successfully given planners and influential citizens throughout the world one practical example of what a city should be like. In order to replace this all-powerful conception, which fitted in so well with the whole corpus of neo-classical ideas, a very powerful momentum was needed. In environmental terms there had first to be an architectural revolution, which would permit all the components of urban design to be looked at afresh. Fortunately, by the beginning of the century, this was beginning to take place.

It took time for the revolution to have its effect on the broader panorama of urban design. The architectural pioneers, when called upon to prepare urban layouts, only too often tended to base them on the classical vocabulary in which they had been schooled. But visionaries were at work, both in Europe and America. There was, for instance, Hugh Ferriss' dream of skyscrapers. Ferriss was an American architect who was carried away by the romantic possibilities of vast height and size, and who created powerful images of tomorrow's cities. An almost direct outcome of these dreams was the Rockefeller centre in New York. Here some twelve acres of enormously expensive real-estate in a highly desirable part of mid-Manhattan was acquired by the Rockefeller interests and redeveloped as a single unit. The provision of a large, safe, pedestrian space over the whole area represented a great advance on its surrounding urban pattern, even though the pedestrian streets are almost entirely in long tunnels. Where it fails basically is in allowing far too much floor space on too small an area, in not providing sufficient car-parking space, and in fact in not being comprehensive enough to take full advantage of its technological possibilities.

In Europe, meanwhile, new ideas were beginning to proliferate. Let us consider one of these. At the very beginning of the century, between 1901 and 1904, a percipient architect, Tony Garnier, had formulated an entirely new conception for an industrial city. In his famous book, *Space, Time and Architecture*, Giedion writes of Garnier as follows:

His *Cité Industrielle* grew out of a broad understanding of social requirements. The balance of its layout is not destroyed by concentration on single issues, on the specialized problems of traffic or the more or less specialized problems of housing which absorbed the advocates of the garden city. Garnier sought for an organic inter-relationship between all the functions of his town. . . . There is a clear separation of all the different functions of the town: work, residence, leisure, and transport. Industry is cut off from the town proper by a green belt, as it was later in the Russian schemes for stratified cities. The health centre occupying a protected site on the slope of an outlying hill is oriented toward the south. The middle of Garnier's elongated town is reserved for a civic centre, a high school district, and very complete and elaborate athletic fields. This sports area adjoins open country, which gives it room to expand and a fine view as well. Main-line railway traffic enters the city terminal through a subway. (This terminal, like some other buildings in the Cité Industrielle, is extraordinarily advanced for its date: the simple and functional exterior is genuinely revolutionary.) Garnier even includes an autodrome or speedway, as well as testing grounds for *moteurs d'aviation*.

The town site is divided into long, narrow lots, running east and west to facilitate proper orientation of the rooms in the buildings which stand on them. These lots—the basic units of the Cité—are thirty by a hundred and fifty metres. These stretched-out plots give a new aspect to the town and represent an extreme departure from the centralized Renaissance type of layout.

Most of these lots are placed at right angles to the main arteries of traffic. Contemporary urbanists have adopted a similar arrangement to avoid the rue corridor and to isolate residential sections from routes of heavy traffic. Garnier was quite aware of what he was doing: "On traverse la ville indépendamment des rues". The closed blocks and light-wells of Haussmann's time are completely eliminated. There are open spaces between all Garnier's blocks, the "community blocks" on the main thoroughfares, with their roof gardens.

Each individual dwelling has a large central living-room and small but well-organized bedrooms, bath, and kitchen. The open areas between the houses are filled with greenery. The schools, low and open in their planning, are distributed throughout the town to add their lawns and shrubbery to the green areas around the houses. Later on, the newer suburbs of Amsterdam were developed along similar lines. . . . Garnier's plan clearly separated the different functions of the city: work, housing, traffic, and recreation. In allotting them their places, Garnier arranged things so that a future expansion of any one of them would leave the others undisturbed. These long blocks with their greenery are often planned to constitute neighbourhood units and have their own schools and all necessary services. The drawings for every building are complete down to the last details of construction and layout, and often foreshadow future developments in the astonishing manner. Garnier's chief material, ferroconcrete, is employed to reach unexpected solutions in his schools, railway stations, sanatoriums, and residences.'

LE CORBUSIER. The urban vision of Garnier is probably the first really important and vital new statement of urban planning of our time, although other European visionaries followed closely afterwards. They included the Italian architect St Elia—tragically killed in the First World War—who saw at a very early stage that the new architectural components should be combined with multi-level communications. But it remained for Le Corbusier, the most famous and imaginative of European architects and city planners, to take Garnier's ideas and distil them with a wide range of individual new artefacts, such as the skyscraper and the motorway, and to create therefrom the first comprehensive vision for the city of tomorrow. This visionary concept, prepared for the town-planning section of the *Salon d'automne* in Paris, was first exhibited in model and diagrammatic form in November 1922. At last an imaginative diagram for a great city was set out in three-dimensional form, embodying nearly all the technological ideas that had been pushing their way into the older urban patterns, but synthesizing them into a full contemporary vision.

This great project, entitled first *La ville contemporaine*, and later and more poetically as *La ville radieuse*, or in prosaic English *The City of Tomorrow*, was not a working drawing suitable for carrying out literally on the ground, but was a power-house of interrelated visions of urban design. Although it retained certain ideas from the Renaissance, in that it was highly symmetrical in layout, in every other way it exploded almost all the other 'traditional' planning theories, and no better diagrammatic statement of ideal cities has since been made.

During the twenties and thirties Le Corbusier and his colleagues applied this vocabulary of urban design ideas to a number of well-known visionary projects for the planning of existing cities. The *Voisin* plan for the centre of Paris, in 1925, was more or less a straight application of the original forms contained in the *City of Tomorrow*, as were plans for the *Norrmalm* area of Stockholm in 1933 (which compares very interestingly with the comprehensive scheme now being carried out for the same area); for the left-bank area of Antwerp, also 1933; and the plan called 'Marcia', for Barcelona, 1932. In this last there was a variation, in the use of Y-shaped towers instead of the original cruciform skyscrapers.

In a comprehensive scheme for Algiers, 1930, the designers made use of the natural contours to create and achieve a multi-level scheme, proposing long, sinuous, plastic forms for the flat blocks, with a high-level bridge going out to the main dockside commercial blocks.

In a first visit to South America, in 1929, Le Corbusier had produced some preliminary planning studies for both Rio de Janeiro and Buenos Aires, and on a return visit in 1938 he produced not only a highly original design scheme for a new University for Rio, but also a well-developed project for the replanning of Beunos Aires. In the latter he proposed to overcome the practical difficulties of redevelopment by siting a new group of skyscrapers far out in the shallow waters of the River Plate, made accessible by a great motorway bridge. At the end of the war he prepared town plans for the redevelopment of the small city of St Die—a bold, simple project using a series of large self-contained residential slabs of flats, with a well-designed, pedestrian town centre. The residential slabs, developed as *Unités d'Habitation*, were again suggested for the replanning of the centre of Marseilles, 1947. Although neither planning scheme was accepted, one *Unité* slab was finally built in the outskirts of Marseilles, to be followed by other examples at Nantes, Berlin, and Briey-le-Forêt.

In 1947 Le Corbusier visited New York as a member of the United Nations Building Commission, and although it is difficult to assess the relative design contributions of himself and his former Brazilian collaborator Oscar Niemeyer, there is no question that the final form of the United Nations Building owes a great deal to his vocabulary of design ideas. From New York he went to Columbia, where, with Sert and Weiner, he prepared a comprehensive plan for Bogota. This plan is particularly notable for the careful thought given to the communications pattern, and in Corbusier's plan for the new East Punjab capital of Chandigarh this pattern was further developed. In this example the original town plan had in fact already been laid out by the Polish planner Matthew Nowicki.

Unlike all the other great city plans of Le Corbusier and his associates, the plan for Chandigarh is actually being carried out, but it is as yet too early to judge its success or failure. The same may be said of Brazilia, the new capital city of Brazil. Its urban designer Lucio Costa and its main executive architect Oscar Niemeyer were both strongly influenced by Le Corbusier, and many of their ideas owe not a little to his original inspiration, although the planning and design of Brazilia is of course an entirely independent achievement.

In looking back over this great corpus of planning projects by Le Corbusier and his associates, we cannot fail to recognize the quality of imaginative effort involved in giving embodiment to a new environment, by creating new forms for all the various urban components and by the intelligent synthesis of these new forms with the many other artefacts of our time.

In some cases, of course, the word 'new' really means 'first brought to notice', for, as inventors so often find, nearly every thing 'new' has already been conceived by someone and has lain in limbo owing to a failure of communication. The Unité block at Marseilles, for instance, which is a great slab of residential apartments, comprising shops, hotel rooms, club, nursery, gymnasium, cinema, etc., was ante-dated by some seventy years by Whitehall Court in London, where a slab block of strikingly similar form, and even more romantic silhouette, included appartments, hotel, club, gymnasium, shops—a nineteenth-century Unité in nearly everything but name. But planners will always be grateful to Le Corbusier for his astonishing imagination and vitality in the use of new and varied forms for his urban components, and for the clear lead he gave in setting them within a clearly thought-out circulation pattern appropriate to our own time.

PRACTICAL DUTCH VISIONS. Among more practical solutions to twentieth-century planning-problems one should mention the fine town-extension planning in the Netherlands, particularly that for Amsterdam. In the second half of the nineteenth century a great increase in population took place in this superbly laid-out historic city: between 1875 and 1900 the population was doubled. But instead of accepting the usual unplanned suburban overspill, the Dutch acted well ahead of other countries, and in 1901 passed a Housing Act which not only facilitated public acquisition of the land but also required every town of ten thousand or more inhabitants to draw up a scheme for its future expansion, which included detailed layout plans. Another technique for development—still to be learnt in Britain—was the co-operative building society, which, instead of just lending money as do our mis-named building societies, actually raised money and employed architects to build complete housing schemes. This technique, in common use in Scandinavia as well, has done a great deal to prevent the scourge of badly designed, badly laid-out, speculatively built suburban sprawl which continues to plague our cities. Finally, and most important, the Amsterdam City Council invited one of the best Dutch architects, H. P. Berlage, to prepare the overall layout for Amsterdam South, the first large-scale town extension.

It is interesting to compare Berlage's original layout of 1902 with his second scheme of 1915, and both with the extended layout prepared by Van Eesteran and his official colleagues in 1934. Although Berlage's layouts failed to break away from Renaissance concepts, they did provide a new model of the importance of open space throughout the area, and they were combined with a high standard of architectural design. Most important of all, the second layout was actually carried out as planned. The official 1934 scheme, however, broke clean away from traditional layout planning: gone was the system of avenues, round-points and street façades. In its place was a form of layout strongly influenced by the Bauhaus and other German experiments in layout. These experiments had been largely concerned with the problem of getting as much sunlight as possible into buildings. These studies concluded that there was one optimum angle at which all living-rooms, and hence dwellings, and then whole blocks of dwellings, should be arranged on a plan. In the 1934 Amsterdam South plan, the layout was entirely rectangular in form, with a long central rectangle containing the community buildings and high blocks of flats, and nearly the whole of the rest of a large area laid out with parallel blocks on a north-south axis. This type of layout was carried to the extreme in some of the early new cities of Soviet Russia. These were the work mainly of German architects in the twenties, and they showed above all that between a diagram and a complete community plan there lay a vast gulf.

The planning of Amsterdam adds a chapter to the story that Mumford described so well in *The Culture of Cities*, and demonstrates not only that continuity of three-dimensional (as well as overall) planning is extremely important, but also that a layout plan is not a static but a *dynamic* design, to be changed from time to time, so long as the changes are in the hands of imaginative but practical urban designers.

Many other influences from the pre-1945 period are worthy of note, but there is space here for only a few. Of considerable significance was the residential layout evolved by the French architects Beaudoin and Lods in their project for *Drancy de la Muette*, near Paris, in 1934. In this large scheme, planned for 1,200 dwellings, there were two main types of building components, sixteen-storey point blocks and three-storey slabs. The project had a sad history, yet it deserves to be recorded as probably the first to combine tall towers and low slabs in one planned layout.

In Sweden, too, the point-block form was developed for residential layouts and used with great effect on hilly sites, such as in the *Danvickslippan* scheme by Backstrom and Reinius in 1943-1945; and the well-known *Reimersholme* island scheme by H.S.B. architects in 1945. The Swedes also developed, pre-war, a number of other interesting residential component forms, but their most interesting layout designs have been created since the war, culminating in such large-scale comprehensive autonomous satellites as *Vallingby* and *Farsta.*

AMERICAN VISIONS. Since the emergence of the *Ville Radieuse*, there have been a large number of visionary projects for cities in various parts of the world, and nearly all of them have owed a great deal to its thinking. In the U.S.A., however, Frank Lloyd Wright, that astonishingly fertile and individual genius from the Middle West, produced in *Broad Acre City* a vision of a city in tune with the vast open spaces. Each urban component is set well away from its neighbour, in an arcadian layout where trees and agriculture dominate the urban forms. Few countries can afford the space for such a vast horizontal spread, and it would be applicable only to certain specific types of community, such as a group of research establishments.

Walter Gropius, the famous teacher and pioneer architect of the Bauhaus, has been concerned throughout his life with visions of a new environment, always tempered by a careful regard for practical possibilities. His best known work since he went to the U.S.A. has been the project for Boston's *Back Bay.* This was one of the first schemes for a large central area redevelopment where a whole group of individual urban components, office blocks, theatre, shops, garages, etc., were unified into a single conception, forming an urban component of a new scale, and separating pedestrians from motor vehicles in a bold multi-level proposal. This scheme bore out a fact we have been slow to realize: that the scale of yesterday's town planning is that of the architecture of today.

A younger American architect, Victor Gruen, has also been prolific of ideas, and has an uncanny way of turning these ideas into practical projects. His out-of-town shopping centres, such as *Northlands*, near Detroit, were great achievements as pedestrian shopping centres, with their service access to shops served from a lower deck. They are, however, limited experiments at present, although (as I mentioned in Chapter 2) if a pedestrian deck were taken right across the vast car-parks which surround and isolate them they could form the nuclei of new town centres. Gruen's biggest dream was for *Fort Worth* in Texas. Here he faced the practical problem of converting a city centre from the usual urban muddle into a contemporary well-planned core. He proposed to make the whole central area a pedestrian precinct, surrounded with motorways and with perimeter car-parks, lower level service access, and in addition to suggesting better forms for the urban components he proposed that there should be a considerable reduction in building volume, so as to provide more urban spaces. It is sad that the project was not adopted by the city, though its value survives in its being a reasonably practical vision for today. But in America the creation of ideas goes on advancing; in the urban design theories of men like Hilberseimer and Malcolmson in Chicago, Louis Kahn in Philadelphia; of Gruen himself; in the writings of Lewis Mumford; and, in a more directly practical way, in cities such as Philadelphia and Detroit.

BRITISH VISIONS. In Britain before the last war the dead hand of academicism stifled all the bright new technological ideas that flowered so early on. We have mentioned the multi-level schemes carried out in the eighteenth century for Edinburgh and for the Adelphi in London. During the nineteenth century numerous designs for two-, three-, and even four-level solutions were put forward, but it was not until the *Modern Architectural Research Group* (*MARS*)—now alas defunct—was established as an offshoot of C.I.A.M. that new twentieth-century visions began to appear. One of the earliest was a large model for a Modern Garden City by F. R. S. Yorke and Marcel Breuer in 1936. Although only a fragment, it was enough to show several exciting new urban component for different functions, related together, and not seen, as hitherto, as isolated fragments. The next important contemporary vision was the *MARS* plan for London, completed at the outbreak of war. This plan was based on considerable study by a group of outstanding architects, and although it had no hope of being realized it contained a great deal of imaginative thinking. It set out for the first time a comprehensive regional diagram of the main elements of the metropolis and then followed this in successive stages right down to neighbourhood layouts. An unexpected pay-off from this wholly theoretical vision was that one of its leading executors, Arthur Ling, later worked as a senior planner in Sir Patrick Abercrombie's *County of London Plan* team, and, later still, as Senior Planning Officer of the London County Council. There is no doubt that the pre-war exercise was invaluable to his later outstanding official work.

Perhaps the main sources of visionary ideas in Britain were those Schools of Architecture, some with Departments of Planning, where new ideas, taken not from the succession of original visionaries in this country—Morris, Geddes, Mackintosh, Ashbee, Lethaby among them—but from abroad, were beginning to take root. The most notable urban vision coming from this source was *Tomorrow Town*, designed just before the war by a brilliant group of fifth-year students of the Architectural Association School of Architecture. It integrated many of the new building forms into a coherent three-dimensional urban design. This vision, with a number from other Schools of Architecture, was used at a critical moment in wartime Coventry, to persuade the leading citizens of the need for new ways of thinking in the building and rebuilding of cities.

In Coventry itself, too, a modest vision model was used by us in Donald Gibson's new Architectural Department just before the outbreak of war. This will be described in a later chapter, since it had a real contribution to make to the ultimate rebuilding of the city centre.

A CITY CENTRE FOR TOMORROW. To close this brief list of urban visions, which of necessity omits so much, I would like to quote from a more recent exercise in theoretical design for the centre of a capital city, in this case Berlin. In 1958 an international competition was announced for the comprehensive replanning of the whole central area of Berlin in spite of the fact that it was still divided politically.

I was approached by Paul Boissevain, of Messrs Boissevain and Osmond, to join him in submitting an entry, and we invited Mr[1] Colin Buchanan, at present Special Advisor on Traffic Planning to the Ministry of Transport, to work with us, in order that he could apply some of the very exceptional experience he had accumulated on communications in relation to city planning. All three of us regarded the preparation of such a scheme more in the nature of an exercise in the theoretical principles of urban design than as a detailed practical solution to the complex problems of Berlin, and for this reason a few of our ideas may be useful to record. The relative prominence which I give to this study is not intended to suggest that, in quality of vision, it can rank with any of those already mentioned in this chapter. It is used here merely to illustrate in

[1] Now *Professor*.

greater detail the new conception of comprehensive development towards which we are moving today.

Principles. On general principles our report went as follows:

> We have approached the problem of replanning the Centre of Berlin in a spirit of humility at the magnitude of the task, and with the realization that it is a problem affecting the very roots of civilization. The replanning and rebuilding of Berlin after such an epic disaster represents one of those rare opportunities to use the latest scientific planning theories which are too often rendered impractical in normal cities. In doing so we have been very conscious that the application of these theories is only a means to an end, the end being an environment where civilization can flourish.
>
> Although our scheme is presented as a completed project we claim that it has organic unity both in space and time. In space each part is intended to be satisfying in itself but contributes to the design of the whole, and in time it is to have the organic quality of regeneration over a period. . . .
>
> . . . we have had in mind two salient facts. First, the conditions which must be met in planning such a complex organism as the centre of a city with an ultimate planned population of 4·5 million. Second, those of the highly specialized characteristics of a capital city and a world centre.
>
> Taking first the conditions for the centre of a metropolitan city; they may be summarized as follows:
>
> The centre must fulfil the functional requirements of all the various civic and economic activities of its citizens. It must be an efficient machine, providing healthy and adequate conditions for work and communication.
>
> It must provide adequately for social activities, for learning, culture and entertainment, for all those things which stimulate mind and emotions and for which men have always sought in cities.
>
> It must provide generously for its own citizens and the many others attracted to it as consumers, and as a great market it has a specialized function.
>
> Finally, it must provide for them all as spectators, so that it can form an adequate theatre for them both as actors and audience. The centre, then, is a totality of states or spaces for multifarious collective activity. In sum it is an arrangement of spaces within buildings, of spaces between and around buildings, of spaces intermingled with trees, verdure and water. And all these spaces must be interconnected with the environs of the city and with other cities in a manner which will be efficient, safe and gracious for today and for the foreseeable future.
>
> The highly specialized conditions for a capital city may be considered in two ways—in terms of the practical needs of government and in terms of an abstract idea; the capital embodying a noble expression of the psyche of the whole country.
>
> In addition, therefore, to giving the opportunities for spaciousness and beauty in urban design are the subtle problems of scale and dignity befitting a capital city.

The Basic Principles Adopted. We have endeavoured to keep our principles simple, even though the solution of such a complex problem as a capital city must inevitably be complex itself. Our basic principles are as follows: (1) *The Heart of the City.* We have accepted the fact of the historic heart of the City as the Unter den Linden with the seat of National Government at its western end, the great public buildings of national character grouped about its length and its culmination at the eastern end on Museum Island. Our first principle, therefore, is to retain this great Public Way and to develop it and its immediate environment as the innermost heart of the capital. All the major elements of the plan which constitute the special features of a great capital city are disposed about, or in close proximity to the Unter den Linden. (2) *The New City*—

Sector Planning. We have endeavoured to break down the mass of the central area around the heart with a series of nucleated and interconnected areas of a new type; each large enough to form a micro-city within the macro-city and each with its own autonomous nucleus. In a sense they will be an evolutionary form of the historic guild precinct of mediaeval days, and will form a great constellation around the heart of the city. (3) *Human Planning.* We regard it as a fundamental principle that the city should provide a civilized environment for human beings. Since the Industrial Revolution the misuse of a series of potential artefacts has threatened civilized values. To deal with this problem we have made the whole heart area a pedestrian precinct and for its surrounding nuclei have introduced a comprehensive upper-level pedestrian plane, separated completely from vehicles of all kinds.

The New City-Sector System. I had been intimately concerned with the first Coventry City Centre plan and its precintual proposals, and later with the joint London County Council/City Corporation Barbican Scheme, and all three of us studied the Boston Back Bay and Fort Worth projects. We came to the conclusion that the big city required not only a new kind of transport system, but also a new kind of urban unit, which we called the city-sector. We described it in this way:

> For all the economic activities we have designed a new kind of planning system. Instead of the chaotic muddle which has evolved in nearly all large cities we propose to develop the 'super-block' idea to such an extent as to create a whole series of what are almost micro-cities within the macro-city. These micro-cities or city-sectors are especially designed to enable the full benefits of speed, comfort and efficiency of the motor vehicle to be obtained, and still to preserve the advantages of the mediaeval city in terms of quiet, safety and urbanity.
>
> It is in fact an ancient and natural urban characteristic that the various economic activities of cities tend to group themselves together, and we visualize each main category, such as Insurance, the Newspaper and Printing Trade, etc., concentrating in one of the City-Sectors, but with a varied group of other economic components present as well. An important principle of their design is that they will be as self-contained as possible in regard to all those facilities which city workers should have in order to make their work enjoyable as well as useful.
>
> Each city sector will have an almost complete upper-level pedestrian podium covering the city-sector at about 20 feet above ground level. This podium will consist of squares, terraces, walkways, and a covered shopping centre. From this level the buildings will rise in a wide variety of forms and compositions, but whatever their form the principle means of access to them will be from the podium.
>
> Second, the ground level below will be almost completely given over to passenger vehicle access and public transport facilities. Access from the surrounding roads will be by a series of entrances on each side of the city-sector, and there will be a local vehicle circulating system which will serve the car parks.
>
> Third, for goods vehicles there will be a basement level road running right through the city-sector, with loading bays and lift connections to the buildings above.
>
> Fourth, there will be a central core running up through all the main levels of the city-sector. This will be municipally constructed and owned and will contain all the main services, i.e. water, electricity, district heating, escalators, etc., and may also contain moving walkways where desirable.
>
> Fifth, the city-sectors will be interconnected at podium level by walkways which will have the friendly character of the Rialto Bridge in Venice, or the quays of Paris, with bookstalls, kiosks, and other interesting features to attract the pedestrian.
>
> The space between the city-sectors will be of an average, but not regular, width of 300 feet. Through them the roads will run at ground level, except where they rise or

fall half a level at crossover intersections. The roads will have no pavements and no pedestrians will normally be permitted to cross them. Between them and the city-sectors there will be a strip of undulating landscaped ground which will rise gently to the upper level of the podiums.

A point to which we have given special consideration is the need for satisfactory public transport facilities for each of the city-sectors. For, in spite of the greatly improved facilities for private-car traffic, a high proportion of 'commuter' traffic coming from the suburbs will, no doubt, continue to be carried by public transport.

This applies, in particular, to the underground railways whose bulk carrying capacity cannot be replaced by road transport, and there already exists a very satisfactory coverage of the central area by existing and proposed new underground railway lines and suitable spaced stations.

It is therefore proposed to connect the centres of the blocks directly with the nearest underground station or stations by means of moving walkways and pedestrian subways, the latter to be so arranged that unnecessary gradients are avoided as far as possible.

Special attention has also been paid to the need for good bus access. The bus stops will take the form of lay-bys which ensure that stopping buses do not impede the general flow of traffic. The lay-bys will be enlarged towards the centre of the blocks so as to bring the buses nearer to the centre of gravity, without imposing an unduly long detour on through buses. Where bus terminal facilities are desired, these can be easily provided by enlarging the central bus stop on one of the long sides of the block by a system of terminal loop platforms at which departing buses for different destinations can be suitably segregated.

Road Communications. Our proposals amount to the freeing of most of the ground area of the city for vehicular traffic, and the resulting complete resolution of the pedestrian-vehicle conflict will be itself by a major contribution to the free circulation of motor traffic. Nevertheless it is still necessary to devise means whereby large numbers of vehicles can approach the various city-sectors from all parts of the city and beyond and circulate easily and swiftly amongst them. Some canalization of traffic is obviously needed. The servicing of the sectors by the insertion between and around them of conventional two-way roads is productive of insuperable difficulties. This system involves the constant problem of the 'left-hand turn' of one stream of vehicles against a stream approaching from the opposite direction. The system we have finally devised consists essentially of the servicing of the sectors from bounding one-way roads so arranged that they always abut the inner or slow lane of the road. It is thus possible, in a rectangular sector, to arrange ingress and egress at points on all four sides, and the system clearly lends itself to the easy separation of various types of traffic. The outer lanes of the road are left unobstructed for fast traffic and the various intersections are dealt with by means of grade separations of simple type.

It is impossible to devise a system for the distribution of vehicles amongst buildings which does not have some disadvantages—there may be a degree of traffic conflict involved, or detours for certain traffic flows, or intersections of enormous complexity or expense. We think that the system we have devised reduces the disadvantages to a minimum. The traffic is brought right in amongst the building blocks where clearly it needs to be; access to the blocks is always from the inner or slow side of the road; the outer side of the road is unobstructed for fast traffic; there is no 'cross traffic turns' or serious traffic conflicts of any kind; there are no traffic signals, roundabouts or sharp turns productive of pulsations or blockages of traffic; traffic flow should be swift and uniform. We have accepted grade-separated intersections, but the type we have introduced is reasonably simple. The disadvantage of the system is that for certain journeys circulation round blocks is involved. The detours are not excessive, however, in length and would be made on free-running roads (a new time-scale comes into operation where the longest detour at an average of 30 m.p.h. takes 2 minutes) and we think the system would rapidly become understandable to users. One feature in particular would soon be recognized—the one-way ring road closely bounding the whole central area and giving direct access to most of the city blocks.

A point to which we have given special consideration is the need for good bus access to the centre. We consider the system we have devised would meet this satisfactorily. By it suburban or longer distance buses would be able to penetrate right into the centre to bus stations arranged in the central core of the city-sectors from whence there would be stair or escalator access to the pedestrian level, and connections to the underground railway system.

TOMORROW'S VISIONS. Today we are still in the early groping stage of the new vision; the total design of the city depends on the evolution of the design forms of its many components and of their integration over a period of time, and many of the associated and organizational problems are still to be solved.

There are certain essential considerations in any visionary ideas for today's cities: first, they must be based on an understanding of the total needs of man, and not dominated by any one limited idea, no matter how dramatic. Ideas for today tend to emphasize the problem of 'getting there': no less important is to design for the 'having arrived' problem. Secondly, they must contain an awareness of tomorrow's problems, like the visions of Leonardo; but, above all they must be capable of being translated into reality.

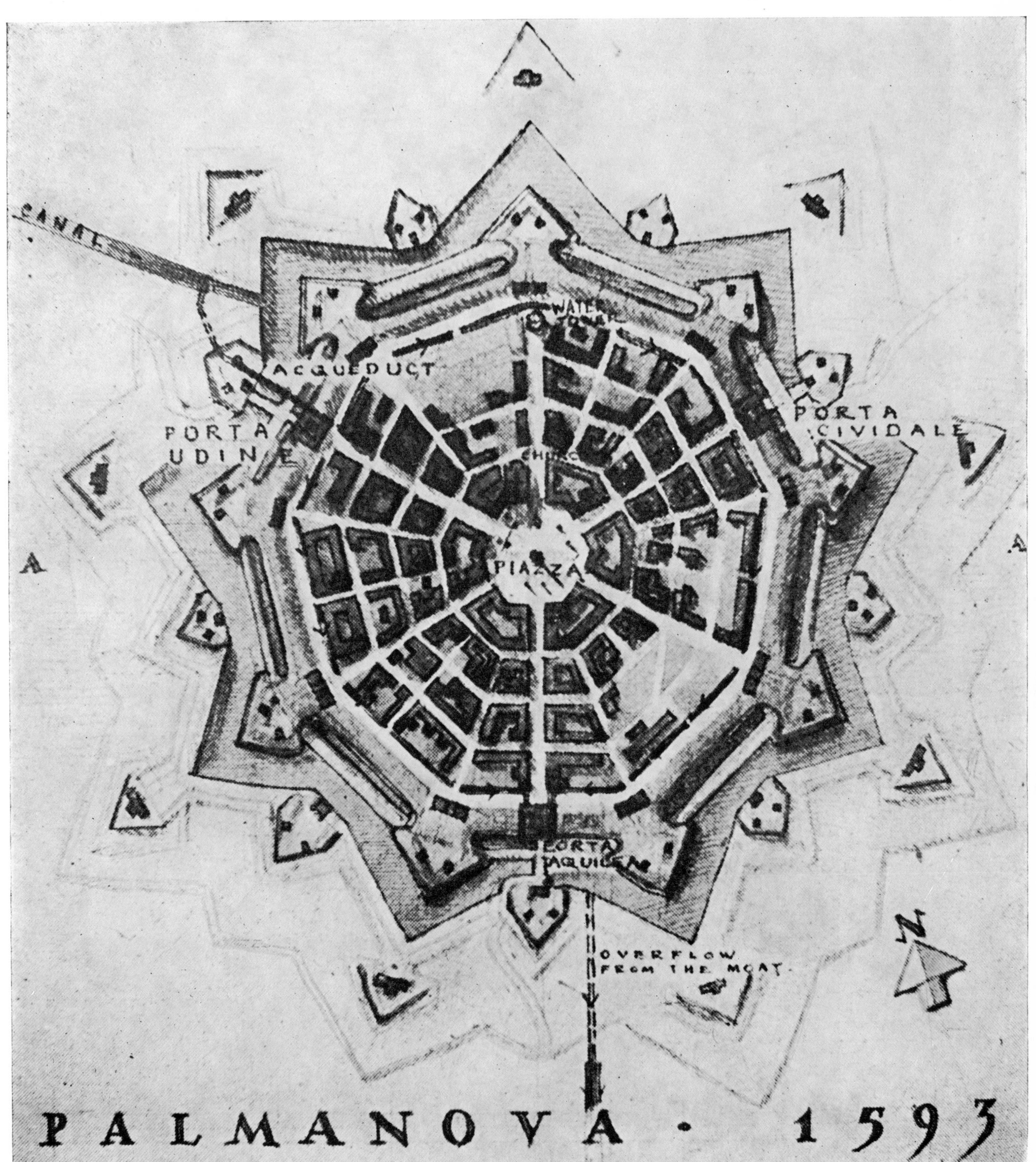

1

3 VISIONS AND DESIGNS

Formal Geometry

1. The Ideal City

In the design of the city of Palmanova in 1593 the theoretical principles of Renaissance planning were put into effect on an ideal site; but complete symmetry round a focal point, with streets radiating from it in all directions, almost automatically results in a series of distorted building forms. This is probably the greatest limitation of Renaissance planning, that it tends to force building forms into a rigid scenic mould, with little regard for their individual purpose. Yet the appeal of symmetry was so strong that it determined not merely the planning of most large cities, such as Rome, Paris, and Washington, from the sixteenth century onwards, but survived into the the twentieth century in New Delhi and in the wartime Academy plans for London.

2

3

2. The School of Athens, by Raphael (1483-1520)
Like most of the great Italian Renaissance artists, Raphael was also a sculptor and an architect. In this characteristic painting Raphael depicts a group of ideal people (philosophers) in an ideal setting. Many of the buildings and urban scenes imagined by the Renaissance painters were later transformed into reality.

3. St Mark Preaching in Alexandria
This is an astonishing townscape painting by Gentile and Giovanni Bellini, now in the Brera Gallery, Milan. The Bellinis, in endeavouring to illustrate a convincing setting for the patron Saint of Venice (whose bones had been brought by stealth from Alexandria to the capital of the Serene Republic) took the Square of St Mark as their model, and a modified Cathedral of St Mark as the dominant building. The rest is imagined, presumably based on a knowledge of North African cities; but how else could the Venetian painters have portrayed an event that had taken place over 1,400 years before?

4

5

4 & 5. The Renaissance theatre

One of the sources of inspiration for Renaissance urban planners was the theatre, where formal stage sets gave designers a wonderful opportunity to create imaginary townscapes. These in turn provided a potent source of ideas for town design. The illustrations show two typical Italian sets of the early seventeenth century which could easily be paralleled with actual building forms in Rome or Florence. Indeed it is likely that most of the great Renaissance urban set pieces were based on images taken from theatre sets or paintings.

6

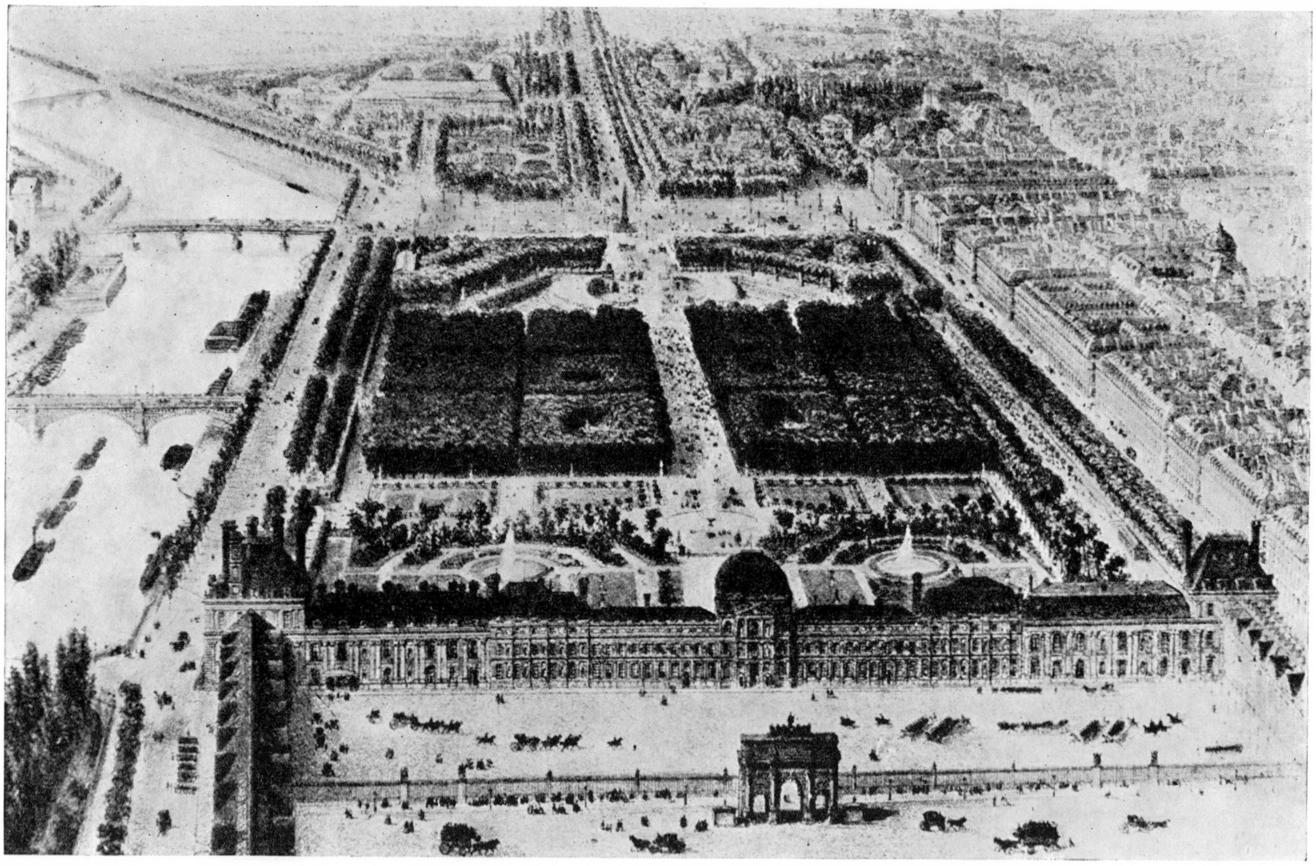

6. Paris: the Renaissance city

Renaissance Paris grew first from the sixteenth to the nineteenth centuries in isolated set-pieces, such as the Palais Royal, the Place Royale (later the Place des Vosges), the Place Vendome, Champ de Mars, les Invalides, and the great Louvre/Tuileries/Place de la Concorde/Champs-Elysées/Place de l'Etoile sequence. Napoleon III and Baron Haussmann finally connected them all together with great symmetrical avenues. With the ordered laying out of the bridges and quays of the river Seine and the generous formal tree-planting programme, the whole centre gave the appearance of a vast, planned, Renaissance city.

7

8

9

7. (*opposite*) Vienna: Otto Wagner's Scheme, 1910

Many of the early modern architects were unable to follow through the revolutionary new forms they had created for buildings to the broader integration with the design of the city as a whole. In this town planning scheme Wagner tamely reproduces a conventional beaux arts solution. It was left to le Corbusier to complete the synthesis.

8. New Delhi, 1926

Other capital cities followed the general Renaissance planning theories of Paris, but with varying success. Washington, first planned by L'Enfant at the end of the eighteenth century, was too vast to be comprehended except from a limited number of viewpoints, and never achieved the detailed design control that was so successful in Paris. The last great essay in the grand manner was New Delhi, planned for the former British/Indian imperial government by Sir Edwin Lutyens. He achieved a close integration of large-scale planning and detailed design. However, even in such an autocratic society, an important change from the original design was made. Lutyens planned the Viceroy's Palace as the closing form of a great three-sided place of government buildings. The wife of the Viceroy insisted that it should be moved well away from the Secretariat buildings, thus impairing the view up the main axis.

9. London: The Royal Academy Plan, 1943

The theoretical rules of Renaissance planning have held urban design in a vice grip from which only the modern movement in architecture has freed it. The British Royal Academy was still suggesting that London should be replanned like this during the last war. It is clear that these are imitation Renaissance Italian palaces (but twice as high, thus increasing the darkness within each courtyard) and are unsuitable for today's needs. The roads are half-way between monumental avenues and fast motorways: muddles would occur at the traffic junctions; while space for the pedestrian is negligible.

10

Three-dimensional form

10, 10a. Leonardo da Vinci

In contrast to the rigid formalism of his contemporaries, Leonardo da Vinci's approach to town planning is based not on the principles of abstract geometry but on the needs of society in an urban context. Such studies as those illustrated, coupled with his ideas for a theoretical new town, and, for example, a helicopter, are far in advance of his time. Although he used accepted Renaissance forms in detail, his approach is astonishingly far-sighted, with an extraordinary prescience of the need for multi-level communications.

10a

11

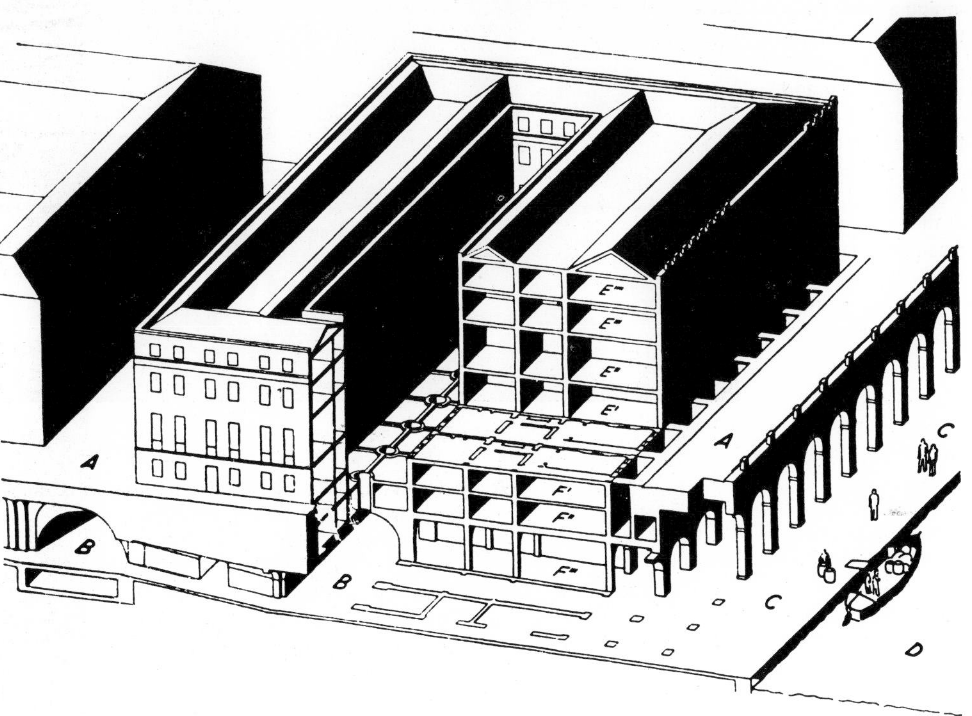

12

11. Chester: The Rows

In considering twentieth-century implementation of schemes to separate pedestrians from wheeled traffic, or of flyover junctions and the like, notice should be taken of the antiquity of such ideas, and credit should be given to the visionaries who put them into effect centuries ago. Probably the best-known example is the Rows at Chester, England, which consists of a two-level system of covered sidewalks (a more appropriate term than 'pavement' in this case) with shops at both levels. The half-timbered frame construction of the typical medieval town lent itself to this amazingly modern solution, although why in wet and windy climates we still tolerate unprotected shopping streets is astonishing to consider. The Chester Rows were the germ of the idea that led to the two level shopping precinct in Coventry.

12. London: the Adelphi, 1768-1774

This sectional drawing shows how the Adam brothers were alive to the problem of multi-level communications nearly 150 years before the motor vehicle. The Adelphi was a bold speculative venture by three architect/ developer brothers. The lower levels were designed as wharves and storage vaults, while on the main street-deck level were built terraces of spacious town houses.

13

13. Eighteenth-century Edinburgh

During the second half of the eighteenth and the first half of the nineteenth centuries Edinburgh was the scene of remarkable large-scale planning developments. The bold step having been taken of planning a great New Town across a deep valley from the old, it was necessary to join them at the same level. The contemporary drawing shows the North Bridge, with the eastern end of the New Town on the left and the Calton Hill in the background. The large building on the hillside was the gaol, since demolished to make way for St Andrew's House. North Bridge, which was also rebuilt at a later date, was at this time an integral part of the urban design of the city. Three other bridges with the same characteristics were built in Edinburgh at this time, all integrating communications with buildings.

14

14. The Fall of Babylon, by John Martin

A different kind of nineteenth-century vision is that of John Martin (1789-1854), the painter, whose large compositions, although usually of religious subjects, were inspired by scenes of contemporary Britain. He combined the architectural forms depicted by Piranesi and earlier artists of the Renaissance with the powerful atmospheric effect of the new mines, mills, and blast furnaces. Thus there is some analogy between Martin's lurid vision and that of such writers as Jack London, whose picture of Chicago in *The Iron Heel*, has the same feeling for the destructive power of the industrial city.

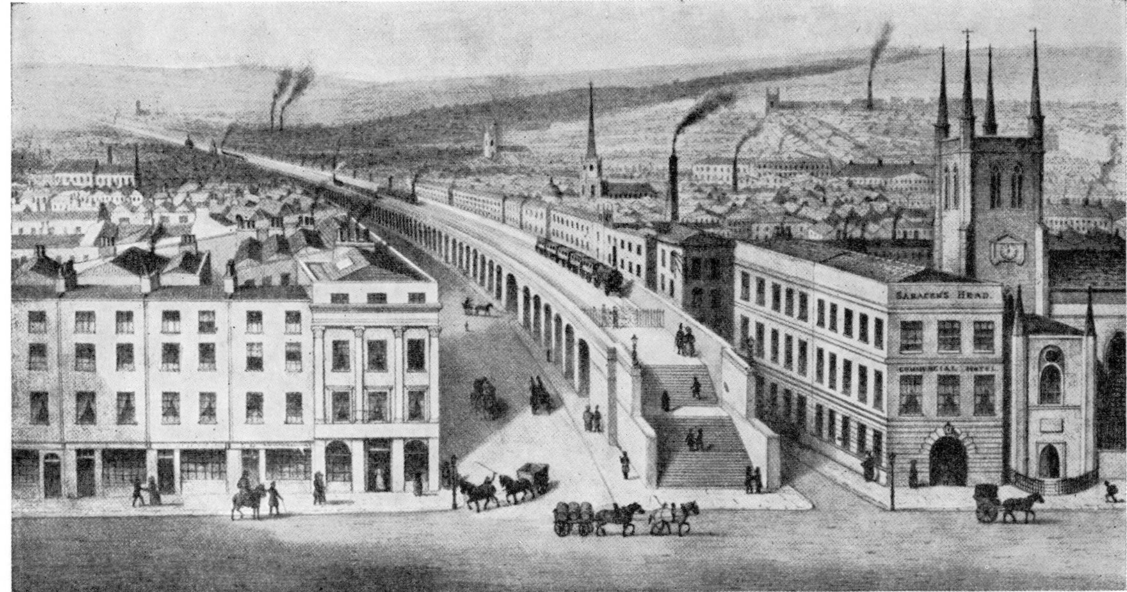

15

15. The Railway viaduct

The railway age stimulated development of new ideas. The imaginative drawing suggests how the new railways might be introduced into the urban scene. The multi-level problem is solved by a traditional viaduct, but the terminus needs more thought!

16

16. Multi-level traffic proposals

This nineteenth-century drawing is of multi-level proposals for Holborn in London. Here the new engineering techniques of steel bridge construction are used to solve the traffic problems which even then were worrying the municipal authorities. It can be observed that, while the motor vehicle was yet to be invented, the monorail was a practical proposition.

17

17. The Meigs Monorail

This early monorail project, invented by Captain J. V. Meigs of Lowell, Massachusetts, was actually built between 1873 and 1876. It was a far-sighted invention, and solved many of the problems posed by the monorail. The cylindrical form of the cars was of streamlined design to reduce wind resistance, while their entire interior surface was upholstered in case of accidents.

18

Social theories

18. Ville De Chaux

The 18th century conjunction of the *Enlightenment* and of the *Industrial Revolution* overthrew the old political systems and led to new urban visions in keeping with the new spirit of man. 19th century industrialism run riot imposed its own chaos, but the ideas of the revolution, in France and the United States, survived, to reappear in the work of the pioneers of the Garden City movement. Claude-Nicolas Ledoux (1736-1806) began life as an engraver, but later became an architect and built the Salt-works near Besançon. Later in life he wrote a book about himself and his work in which he described and illustrated the plan for an Ideal City (shown above), part of which was actually built for the Besançon Salt-works. In the centre is the Director's House, flanked by furnace rooms for drying the salt, and the whole group is set in a large elliptical place. Facing the latter are city blocks of houses and public buildings. Beyond are more public buildings in a romantic landscape. The theoretical ideas in the Ideal City were remarkable for their time; the plan was based on an ideal society, whose members would not only have well-planned dwellings and salubrious industrial buildings, but a wide range of public buildings for a large number of cultural and moral purposes.

18a. Reading, Pa. U.S.A.

The town of Reading, in Pennsylvania, was built after 1748 to a design by the son of William Penn. Like Savannah (1733) its regular logic goes beyond the simple chequerboard plan, to reveal something of the advanced urban vision of the Quaker and Non-Conformist communities of North America. In both cities a deliberate (if not wholly successful) attempt is made to separate traffic and pedestrian thoroughfares to the extent of stopping the latter short of the main street by dwelling houses at right angles to their axes.

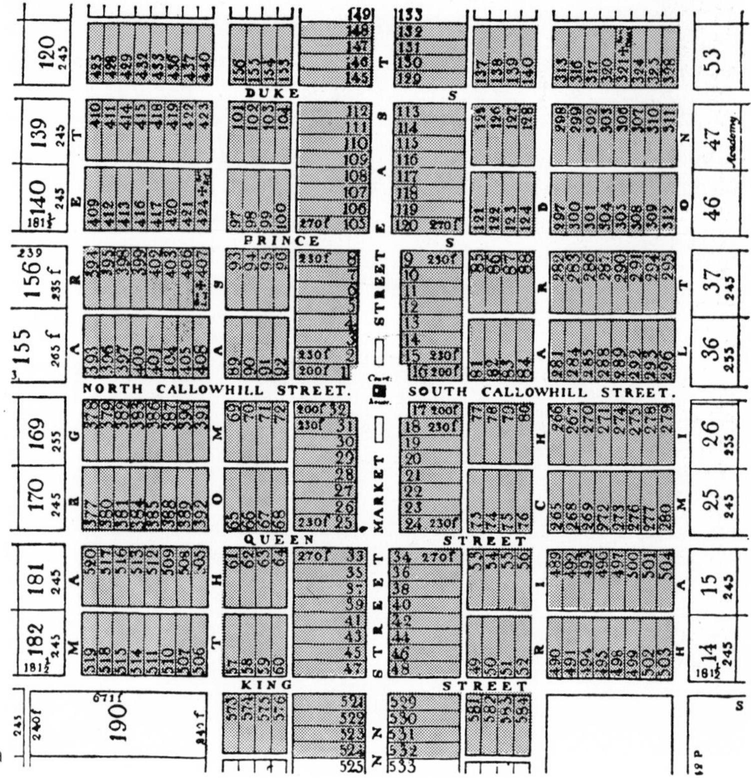

18a

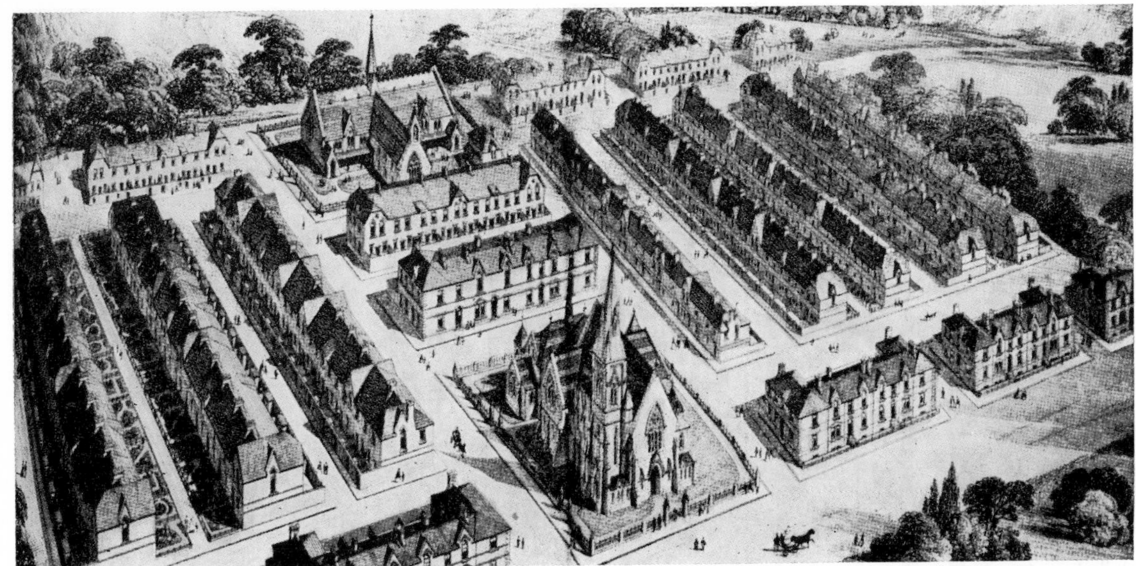

19

Nº 5.

— DIAGRAM —

ILLUSTRATING CORRECT PRINCIPLE OF A CITY'S GROWTH – OPEN COUNTRY EVER NEAR AT HAND, AND RAPID COMMUNICATION BETWEEN OFF-SHOOTS.

COUNTRY
HIGH ROAD
GARDEN CITY
CENTRAL CITY
INTER-MUNICIPAL RAILWAY
POPULATION 32,000
POPULATION 58,000
COUNTRY
COUNTRY
HIGH ROAD
INTER-MUNICIPAL RAILWAY
INTER-MUNICIPAL RAILWAY
COUNTRY
CONCORD
COUNTRY
HIGH ROAD
POPULATION 32,000
COUNTRY

20

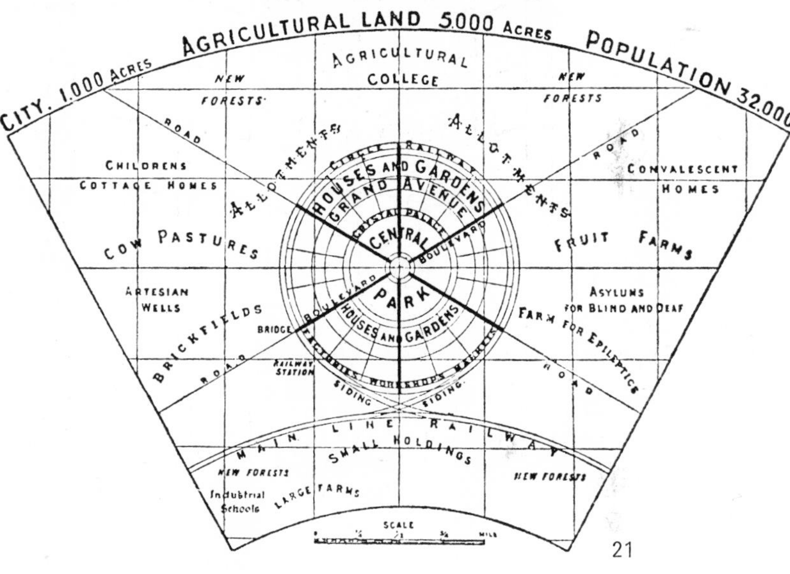

21

19. The nineteenth-century model town

West Hill Park, near Halifax, Yorks, was designed by John Crossley and built in 1862. It is typical of the practical visions of the more enlightened nineteenth-century industrialists. The movement for planned industrial towns really began with Ledoux in France and Robert Owen in Britain, and received an important impetus with Sir Titus Salt's Saltaire, near Bradford, Yorks. Halifax is not far away, and there are a number of these towns still in existence, where the industrialist purchased the land, usually adjacent to his mill or factory, and had planned and built for him rows of worker's dwellings, church and chapel, a school, and one or more shops. The movement continued with the Cadbury's Bournville near Birmingham, and Lever's Port Sunlight near Birkenhead.

20. The Garden City as a satellite

The Model Town movement received a theoretical contribution from William Morris in *News from Nowhere* (1890), in which he described his vision of an ideal city based on London. It was followed up by Ebenezer Howard, who developed an astonishingly thorough and complete theoretical study for an ideal Garden City. This diagram from his book *Tomorrow: A Peaceful Path to Real Reform* (1898) illustrates his theory of satellite garden cities around the central city, all separated by open country but connected by rail and road.

21. The Garden City in its setting

This diagram of Howard's shows his concentric garden city, complete with central park, houses and gardens, a shopping arcade, and industrial estate, in a setting of rural country-side. His idea was to take the maximum advantage of both town and country. The problems in the central city, however, remained unsolved.

2

Technological revolution

The development of the cast iron, later steel, framework, brought to early magnificence by Jenney and Sullivan (later Wright) in the Chicago of the 1880s and 1890s, gave architects and planners, a weapon of immense potential, for good or ill. Buildings could now be erected in the hearts of cities, to heights vastly greater than had been possible with stone and brick supporting walls.

22. Nuova Citta, by Sant' Elia

The young Italian futurist architect Antonio Sant' Elia, who was unfortunately killed at an early age during the First World War, was interested in the aesthetics of movement. In the unrealised vision for skyscraper apartment houses shown here this interest is manifested not only in the structural forms but also in the use of subways, elevators and multi-level lanes of communication.

23

23. The Ideal City, by Hugh Ferriss

During the inter-war period the idea of the skyscraper dominated much American thinking. The arch-prophet of this muddled vision was Hugh Ferriss, whose dreams look more like nightmares today.

24. New York: the Rockefeller Centre

The dreams of Hugh Ferriss were transformed into reality with the building of the Rockefeller Centre. This covered some twelve acres of office redevelopment in a hitherto undreamed of scale, which was only surpassed after the war by the United Nations Building. Unlike the latter, the Rockefeller Centre secures its pound and a half of real estate flesh from the site. Its minute open space, akin to the water in a well, was highly praised as real estate generosity, while a whole system of tunnels and passages provides the pedestrian with an underground shopping centre.

24

25 & 26. Russian revolutionary visions

These vigorous drawings of part of a new city were made by a Russian architect in the early 1920s, before the heavy hand of social realist theory imposed a stupid stylistic conformity based on an outdated beaux-arts Paris/Leningrad image.

25

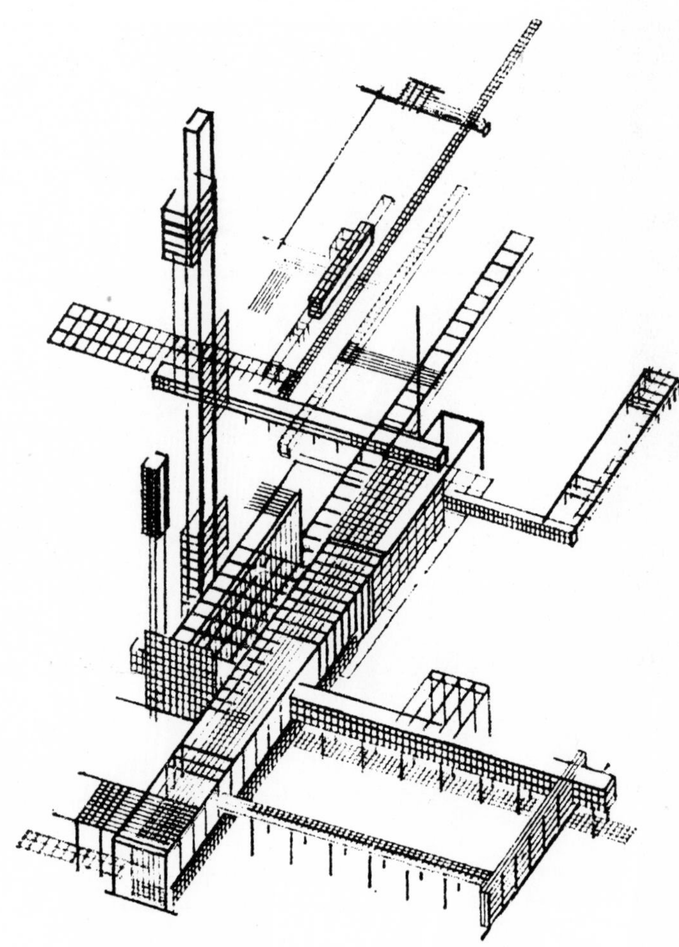

26

27

27. Plan for an Industrial City

Garnier's plan for an Industrial City (1901-4) of 35,000 people was the first really contemporary vision for a new city. He recognized the need for separating the industrial areas from other uses, and designed the whole urban area in great but coherent detail. The city centre is in the middle of the long rectangular residential area, the main railway line serving it from a lower level, while the industrial estate is at the top of the plan, with plenty of space for industrial communications and expansion.

[136]

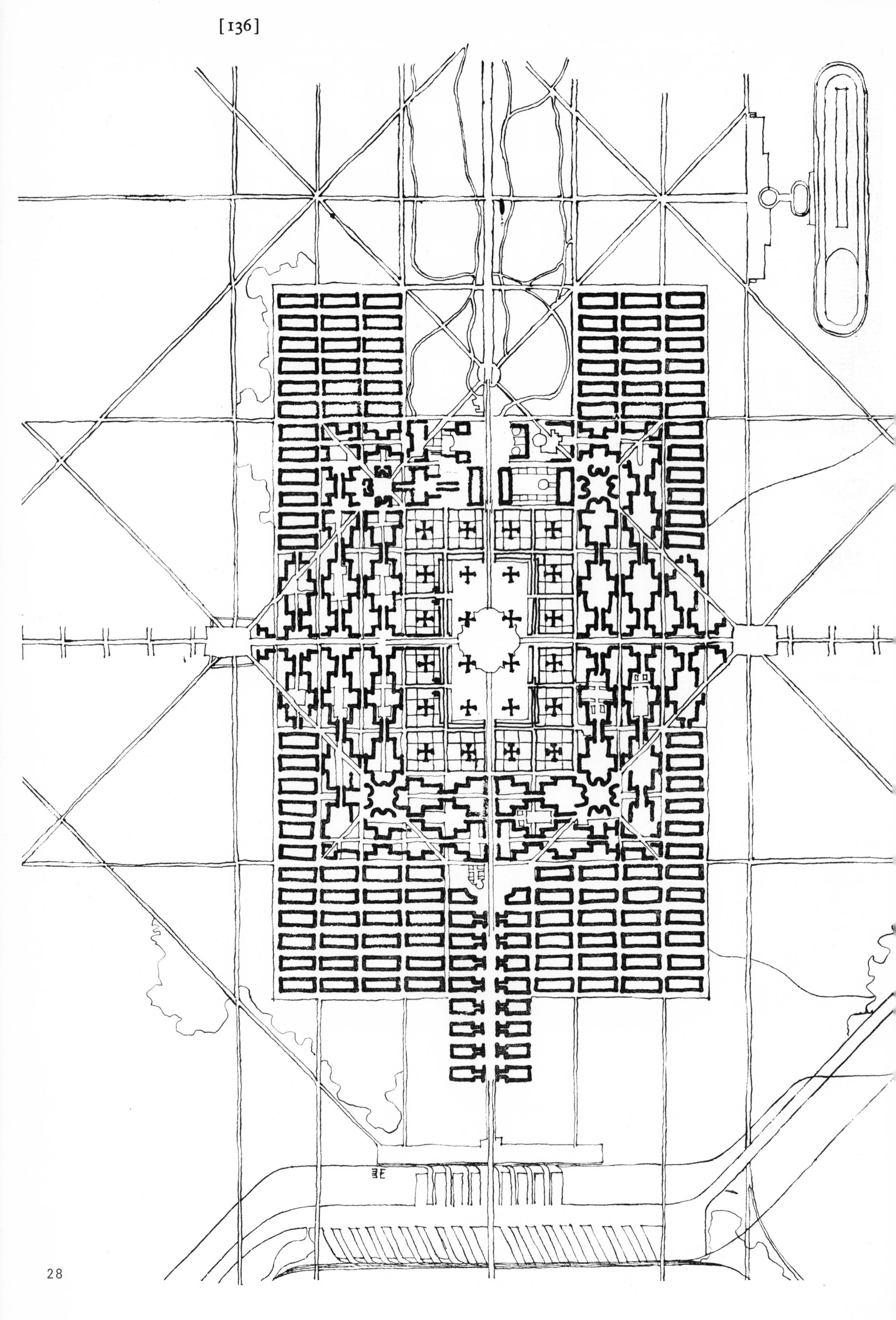

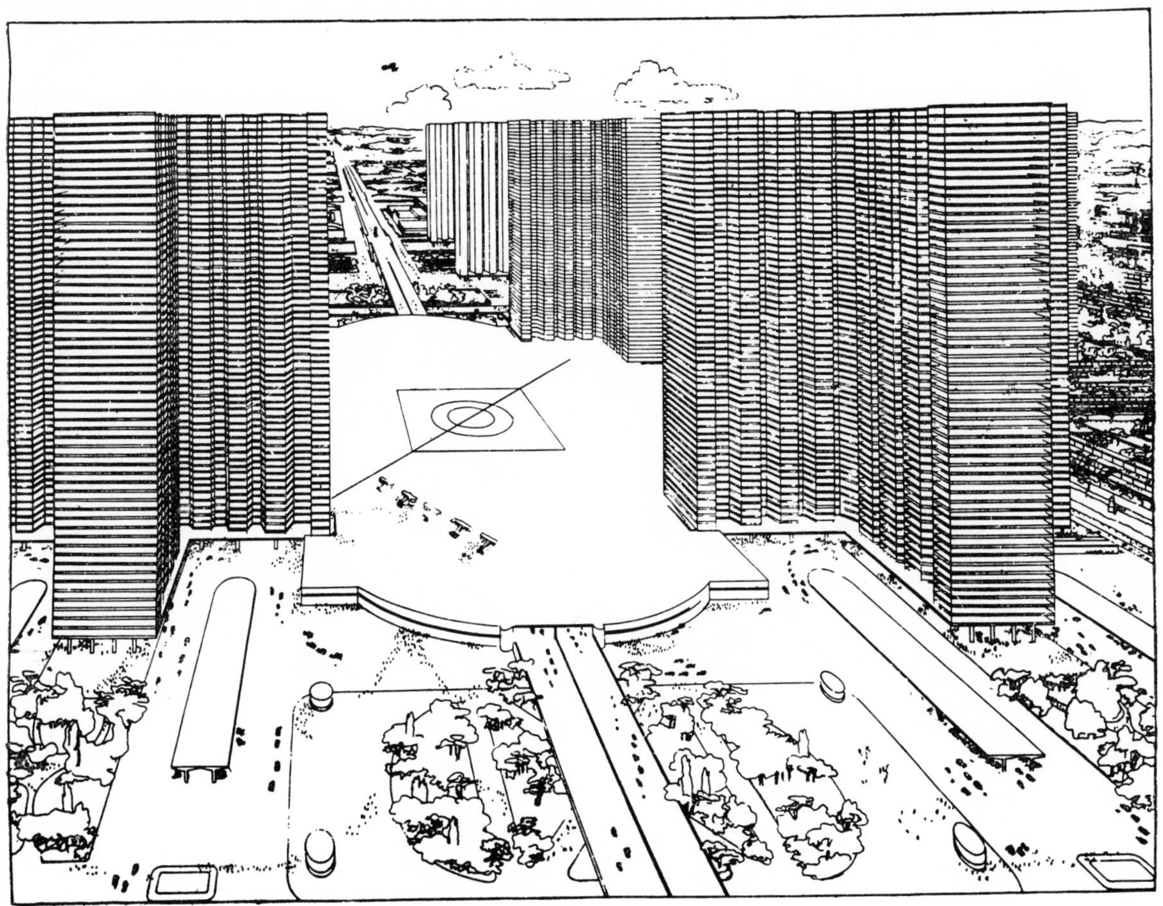

29

28 & 29. Plan for a Contemporary City

In this masterly plan for an ideal city of 3,000,000 inhabitants which he prepared in 1922, le Corbusier synthesized nearly all the planning ideas which had been evolving separately during the previous fifty years. In the centre there was to be a group of skyscrapers set well apart so as to take full advantage of building high. In the plan they may be seen as black cruciform shapes, and below the aero-taxi platform on which they stand is the main intersection for fast traffic. Below this are the main booking halls for the railways, which are tubes on the first level down, then local and suburban lines, and finally the main-line terminal. To the left of this business and central communication complex are the great public buildings, the museums, and the administrative offices. Further to the left is the city park. On the right are the warehouses, and then the main industrial area. All around the central business area are the garden cities or residential areas. The whole concept is a fantastically imaginative exercise in ideal city planning, relating all the then known technological advances and new architectural forms into a plan for a city; hitherto this kind of creative activity had only been done for individual building projects.

It was left to le Corbusier to conceive a totally new environment, developing the imaginative possibilities of the new technological advances in high buildings and multi-level communications. Like Leonardo, he freed himself from most of the worn-out theories, as this drawing of his vision of the city of the future shows. In doing so he gave direction of a fundamental nature to planning theory.

30

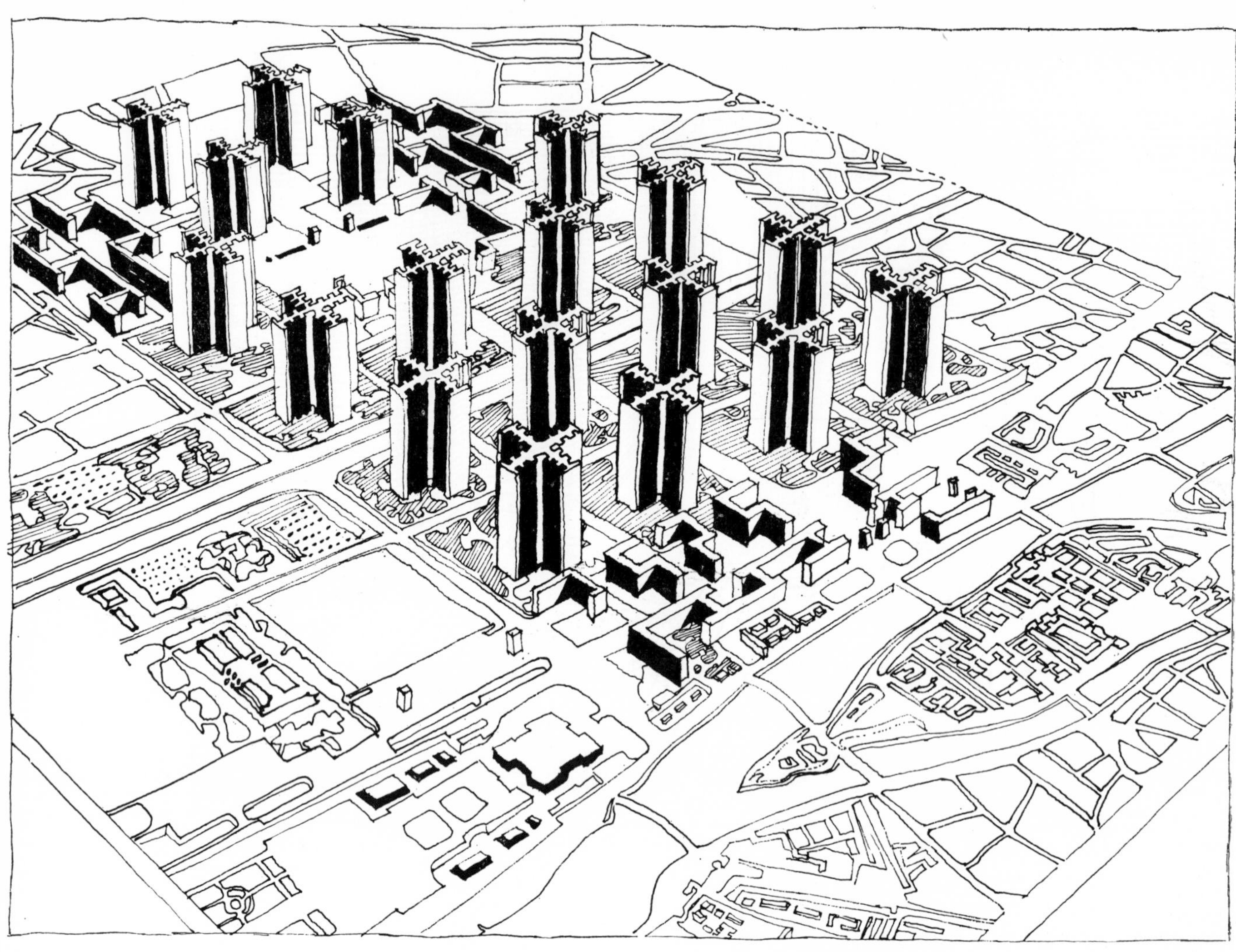

30. The Voisin Plan for Paris

In the Voisin Plan of 1925 le Corbusier and his colleagues applied the main physical features of the earlier plan to the centre of Paris. It was an interesting exercise, but showed dramatically what a great difference there was between a diagrammatic solution for a new city and successful urban renewal, in which a hundred problems of use, scale, and time are all intermingled.

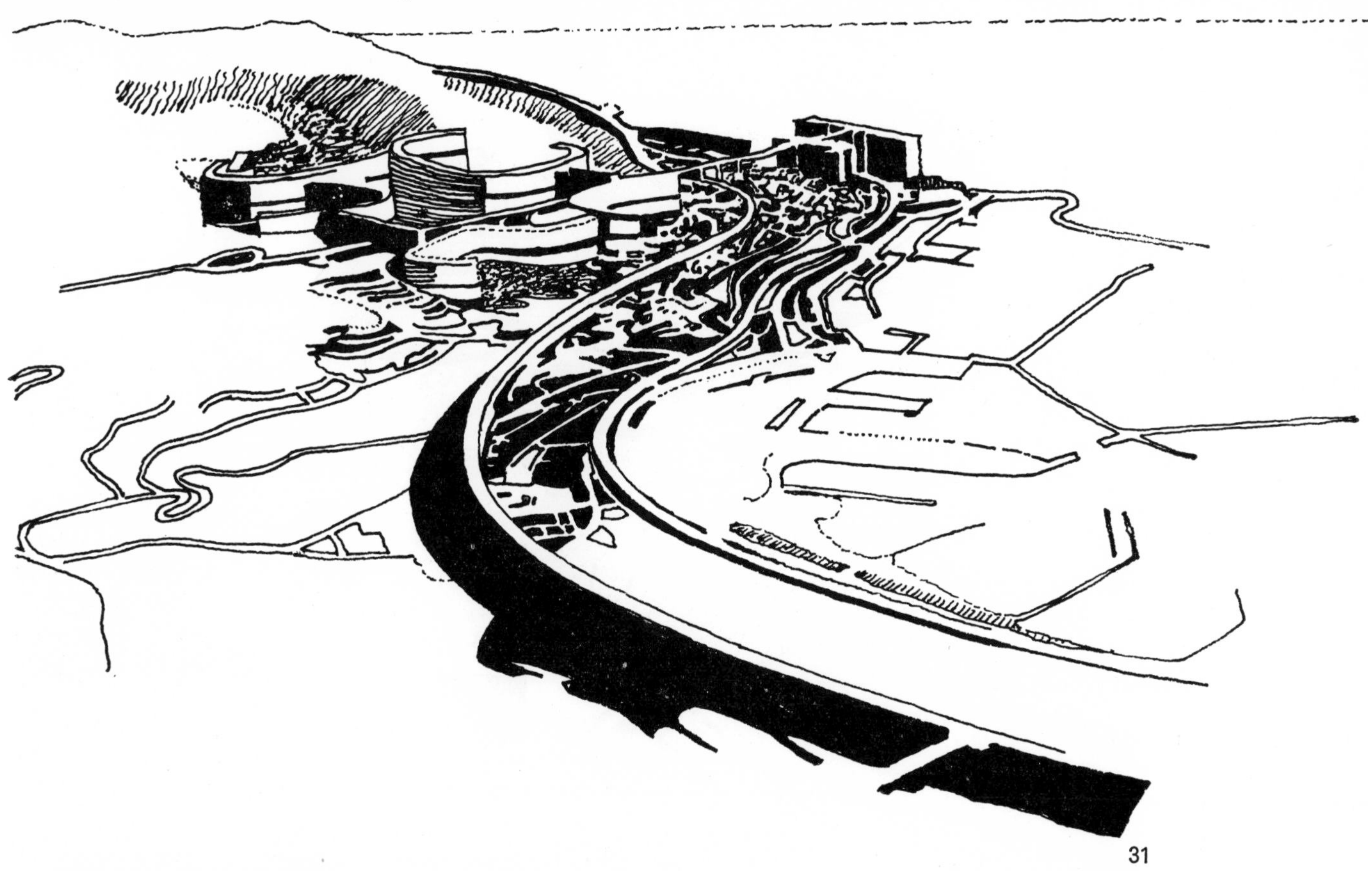

31

31. A plan for the city of Algiers

Here is a dramatic but expensive solution for a North African seaport (1930). The main commercial buildings are in high slabs down by the harbour, and are connected by a great viaduct with a vast curving group of interconnected blocks of flats. Running right along the sea coast is another enormous viaduct, the whole concept being Roman in scale but unrealizable in practice.

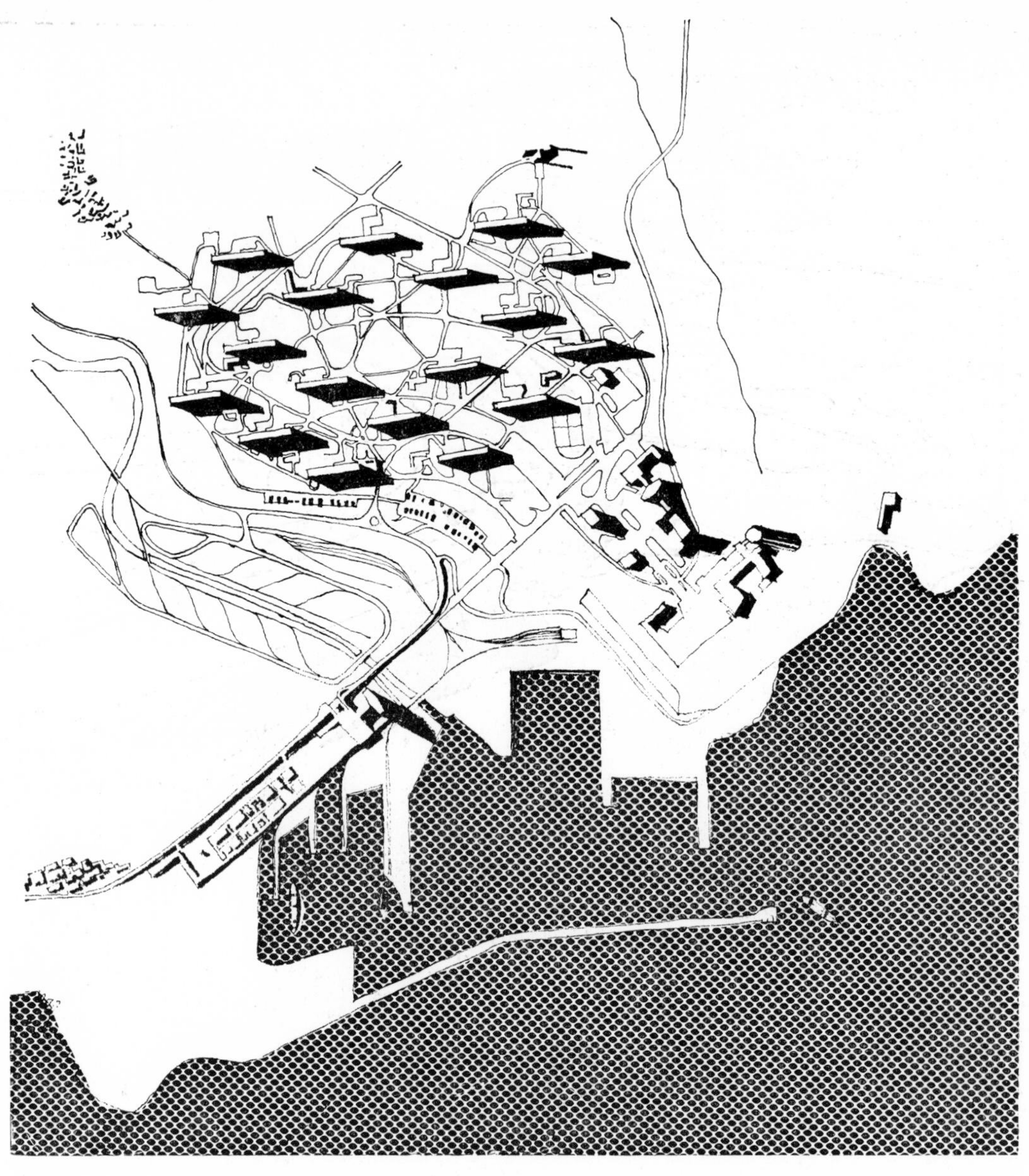

32

32. A Plan for the city of Nemours

This plan of 1934 was of more modest dimensions than that for Algiers. The main residential area was made up of eighteen large blocks of flats each contining 2,500 persons. These blocks foreshadowed the famous Unité d'Habitation block at Marseilles, which le Corbusier actually brought to reality after the war. Communications with the harbour are simple and direct, and the whole plan was a model of clarity.

33. A Plan for the town of St Die, 1945

The centre of the town is laid out in the bold, free, and imaginative manner which le Corbusier was evolving with each new planning project – compare it, for instance, with New Delhi, or with the near-contemporary Royal Academy plans for London, or indeed with most other French planning projects. All the buildings in the central area are themselves contemporary designs and they have all been carefully related to each other. Defining the centre of the town is the tall tower of the Administrative buildings, which faces a large central place. Nearby are grouped the various other public buildings, together with two 'unités', or large residential units. Across the river is the industrial area.

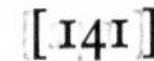
[141]

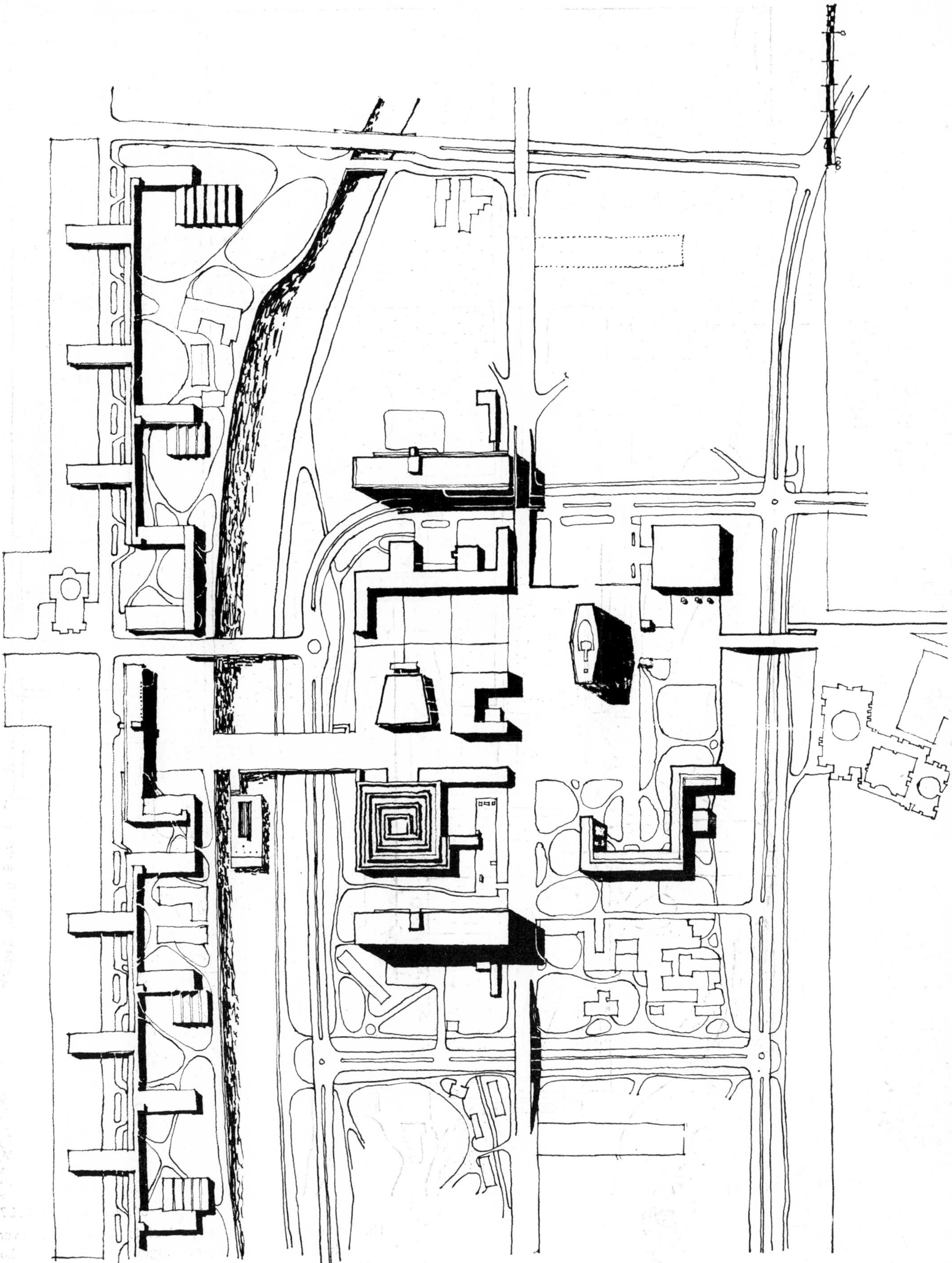

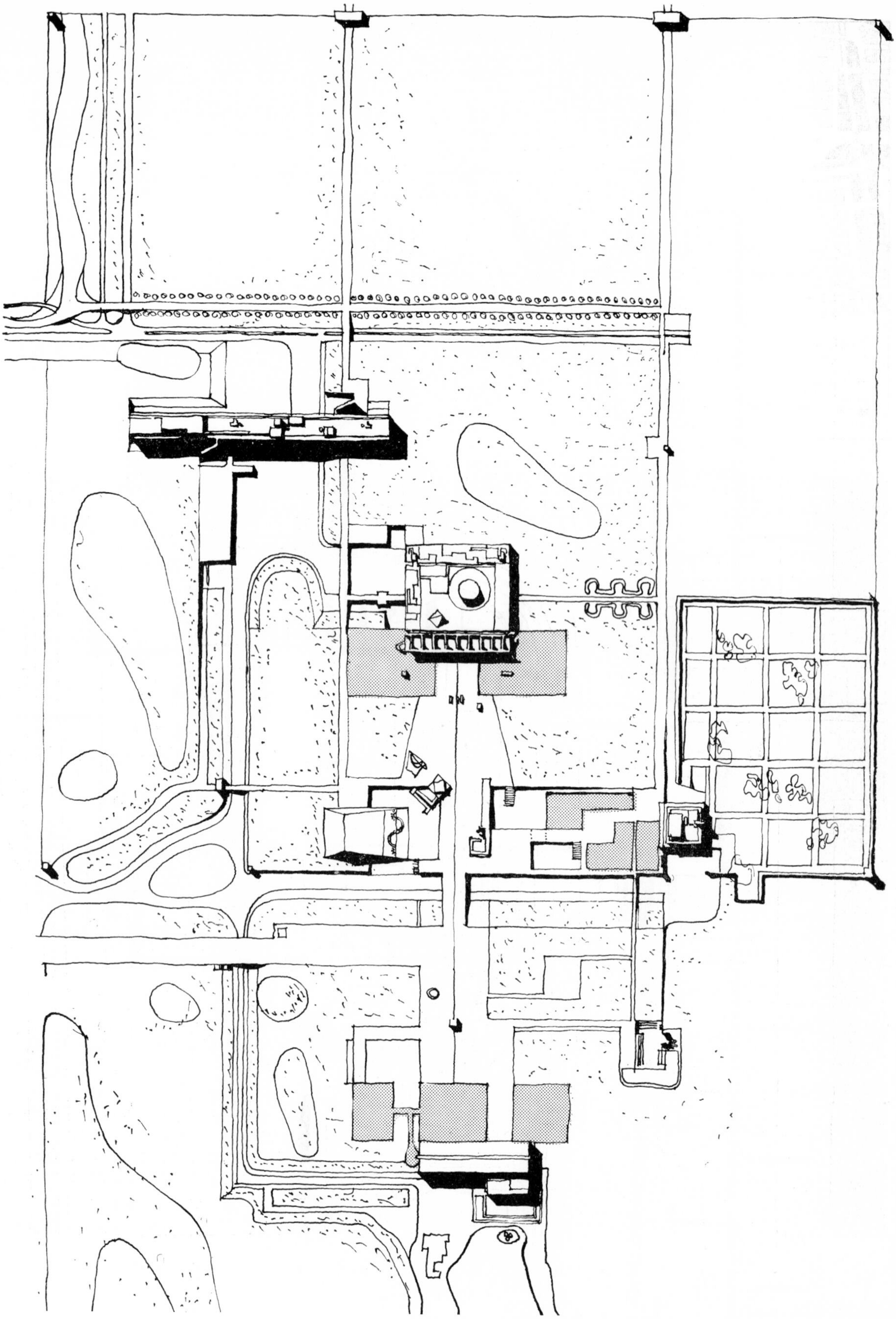

34

34. Chandigarh, 1957

This is the first plan for a city which le Corbusier has ever had the opportunity of bringing to reality; but, like Washington and Canberra, it will be many years before it reaches maturity. The drawing is of the government centre, with the Secretariat at the top, the Parliament building below it to the right, the Governor's Palace in the right centre, and the Court of Justice at the bottom

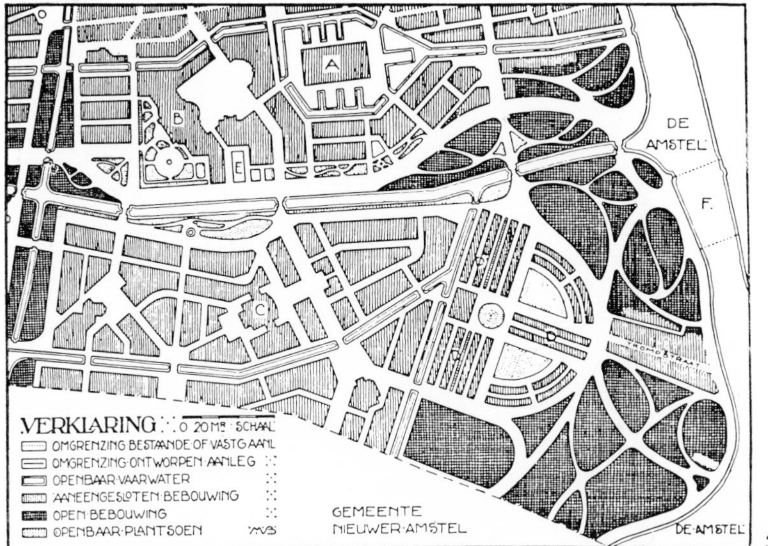

35

35. Amsterdam South: H. P. Berlage, 1902

A pioneer example of large-scale municipal enterprise at the turn of the century for lower-income groups. Berlage was an architect in private practice and prepared the scheme for the Department of Public Works. The main housing areas were grouped around a number of widely separated public buildings, and the urban pattern deliberately avoids the mechanical grid layout, substituting a romantic design derived in part from the *jardin anglais*. The scheme went through a number of modifications before it was built.

36

36. Amsterdam South, 1934

The section planned in the earlier scheme is on the right of the perspective, while the new Bosh Park is in the back-ground. A large part of the city was now the subject of an overall three-dimensional guide plan, by the Department of Public Works, and development work ever since has been under its overall control.

37

38

37. Moving sculpture by L. Moholy Nagy

This was one of the most visually exciting of a series of experiments by Moholy Nagy, who was endeavouring to discover new possibilities with the relationship of light, machines, and motion. This sculpture had 140 light bulbs so arranged that within a two-minute turning period various coloured and uncoloured spotlights were switched on, creating a light display on the inside walls of a cube. Here at last were artists exploring sensitivity in relation to machine forms.

38. *Things to Come*: the proposed film set

Moholy Nagy was invited by Alexander Korda to design a set for the film of H. G. Wells' book *Things to Come*. Nagy said that when the whole device was set in motion, with the cones revolving, and photographed with multiplying prisms, the effect was so rich that Korda dared not use it. The sequence of ideas from sculpture to film set and hence, possibly, to reality is fascinating.

39

39. *Things to Come*: the final film set

The film set that was actually used for Well's film was a good deal less imaginative than the earlier experiments, and is nearer in conception to those of the earlier futurist film *Metropolis*. A number of interesting ideas were, however, tried out, and prove that films, together with exhibitions, offer opportunities for experiment of a similar nature to the theatre sets and paintings of the Italian Renaissance.

40

41

42

40. The Greater New York Regional Plan

Among the many startling proposals in the Greater New York Plan of 1929, the bold and imaginative ideas for Manhattan were astonishing in their breadth of vision. A major thinning out of the urban jungle was proposed, and a series of brilliant sketches were prepared by the now famous British architect Maxwell Fry. This drawing shows Manhattan from the East River as it was at the time. Today, of course, it is even more overcrowded.

41. The Greater New York Regional Plan

Here is Maxwell Fry's imaginative sketch of Manhattan as it might look after a drastic thinning out process. Fry was greatly influenced by le Corbusier, but instead of proposing a totally new townscape of Ville Radieuse skyscrapers, he sensibly suggested that some of the existing skyscrapers be retained, but with enough space left around them to ensure a reasonable amount of light and air.

42. The Greater New York Regional Plan

Three of the finest planning documents ever produced have been the plans for Chicago by Burnham, New York by Adams, and London by Abercrombie. In each case a team of distinguished planners and designers took part, and developed imaginative ideas for the future. In this sketch for Manhattan, Maxwell Fry accepted the existing tower forms already evolved, but endeavoured to make urban design-sense out of their possibilities. The principle of having large pedestrian areas in the city centre is clearly demonstrated.

43 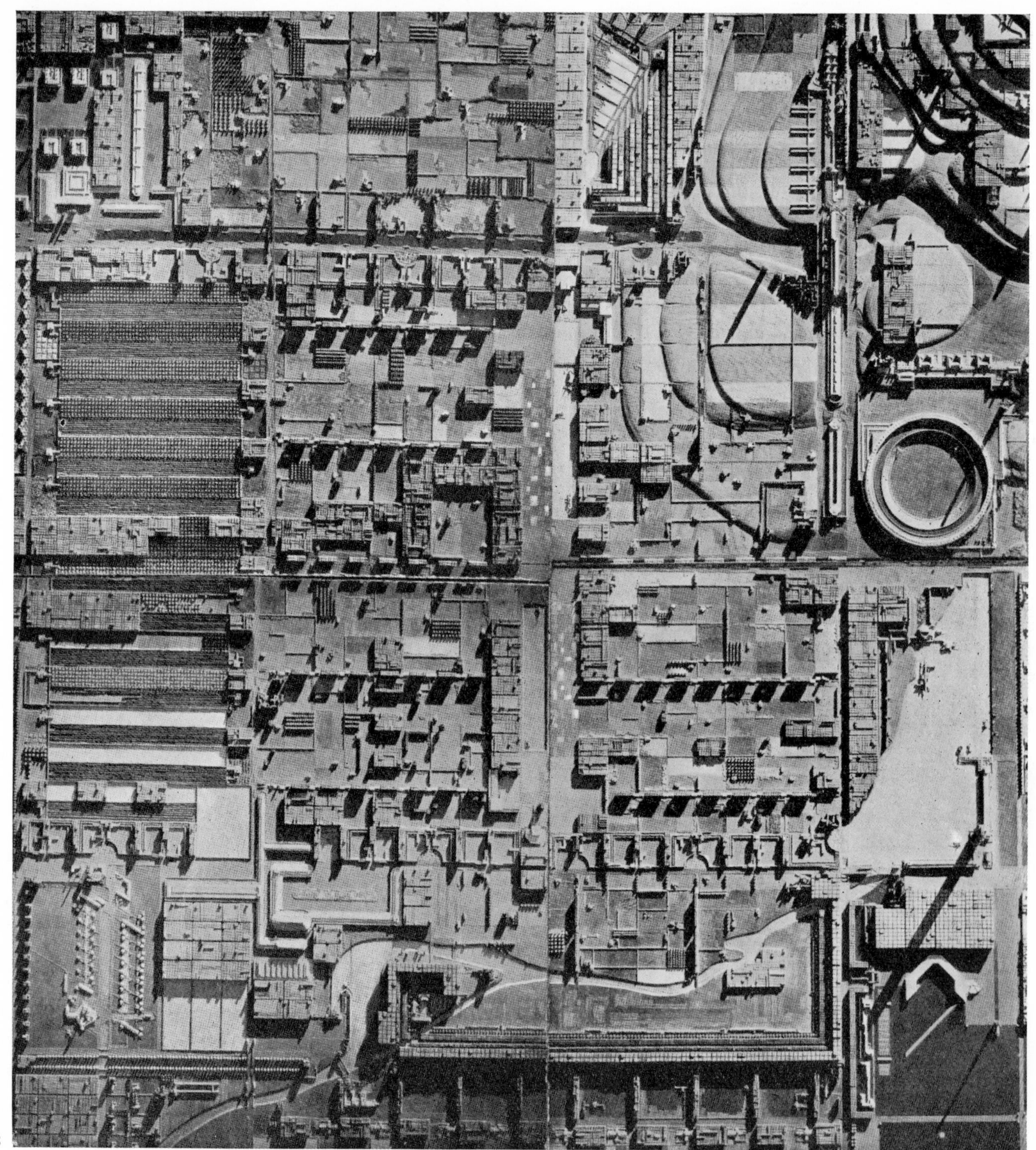

43. Broadacre City: Frank Lloyd Wright, 1935

Here America's famous pioneer architect turned his imaginative powers to the design of a whole community. Accepting his country's vast land potential, he proposed an extremely low-density solution. Running north/south down the centre of the model are schools surrounded by houses. On the left are vineyards, and above them a light industrial estate. Below them is a tourist camp, with another industrial estate. At lower centre are recreation facilities, with small farms at the bottom of the model. On the right the stadium shows up prominently, with various cultural facilities in its vicinity.

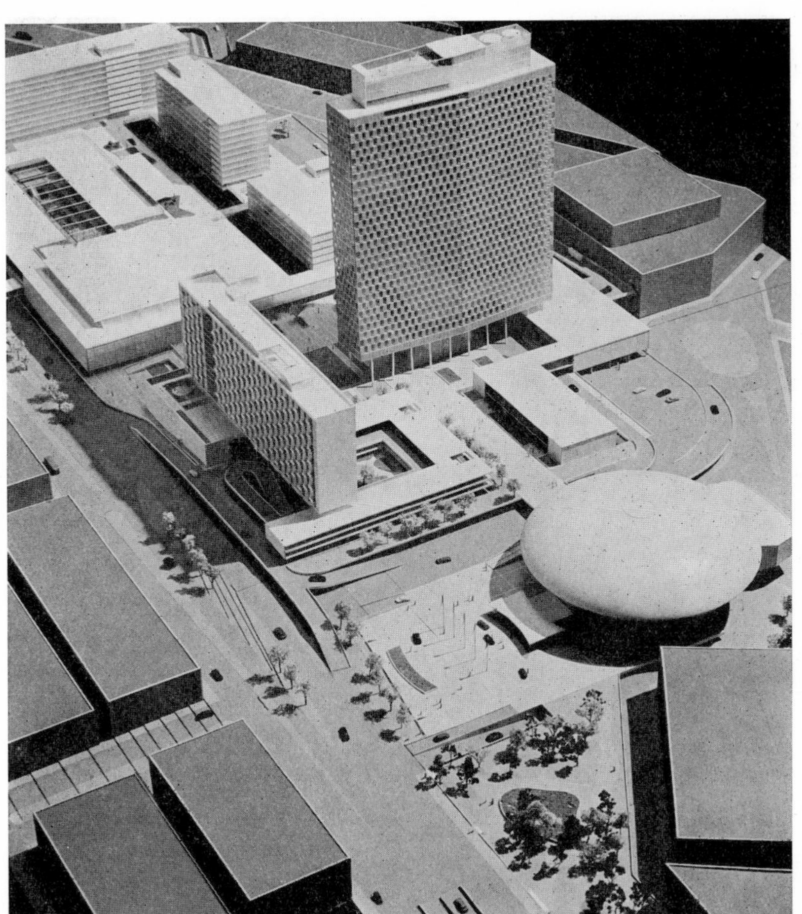

44

44. The Boston Center, 1953

This highly imaginative project, like that for Fort Worth, was unfortunately never realized. A real estate developer invited Professor Walter Gropius and his associates of Boston Center Architects to prepare a comprehensive plan for the redevelopment of thirty acres of redundant freight yards. The planners proposed three floors of car parking space for 5,000 cars below ground, thus releasing the whole surface area for pedestrains. A large shopping precinct was proposed at the upper level, together with offices, including the main office tower of forty storeys, an hotel, exhibition hall and a large Convention Hall for 7,500 people. In this photograph the Convention Hall is in the right foreground, adjacent to some existing buildings. It is joined by a pedestrian bridge to the main superblock. The shopping precinct is at upper left, and the complete separation of cars and pedestrians is evident. Although we had already been designing along similar lines at the L.C.C. in the South Bank and Barbican schemes, this project was a powerful stimulus to us, as it was to my colleagues and I in the preparation of our Berlin scheme. It is most unfortunate that Gropius' fine comprehensive plan, with its comparatively low site development, its careful disposition of the one high building so as to achieve light, air, and scale, and its traffic separation, was not taken as a guiding set of principles for American city redevelopment.

45

45. A plan for the centre of Fort Worth, Texas

In this imaginative and intensely realistic vision, Victor Gruen accepted the land realities of the existing city, but by conservative surgery radically improved the urban pattern. The whole city centre was treated as an island, surrounded by great rivers of motorway. Garage harbours were provided around the periphery, and for a number of access points service roads carried commercial vehicles to a lower level. Inferior and obsolete buildings were cleared away and the existing road pattern was transformed into a series of well designed pedestrian spaces. This was another project which could have had a powerful impact if it had been realized.

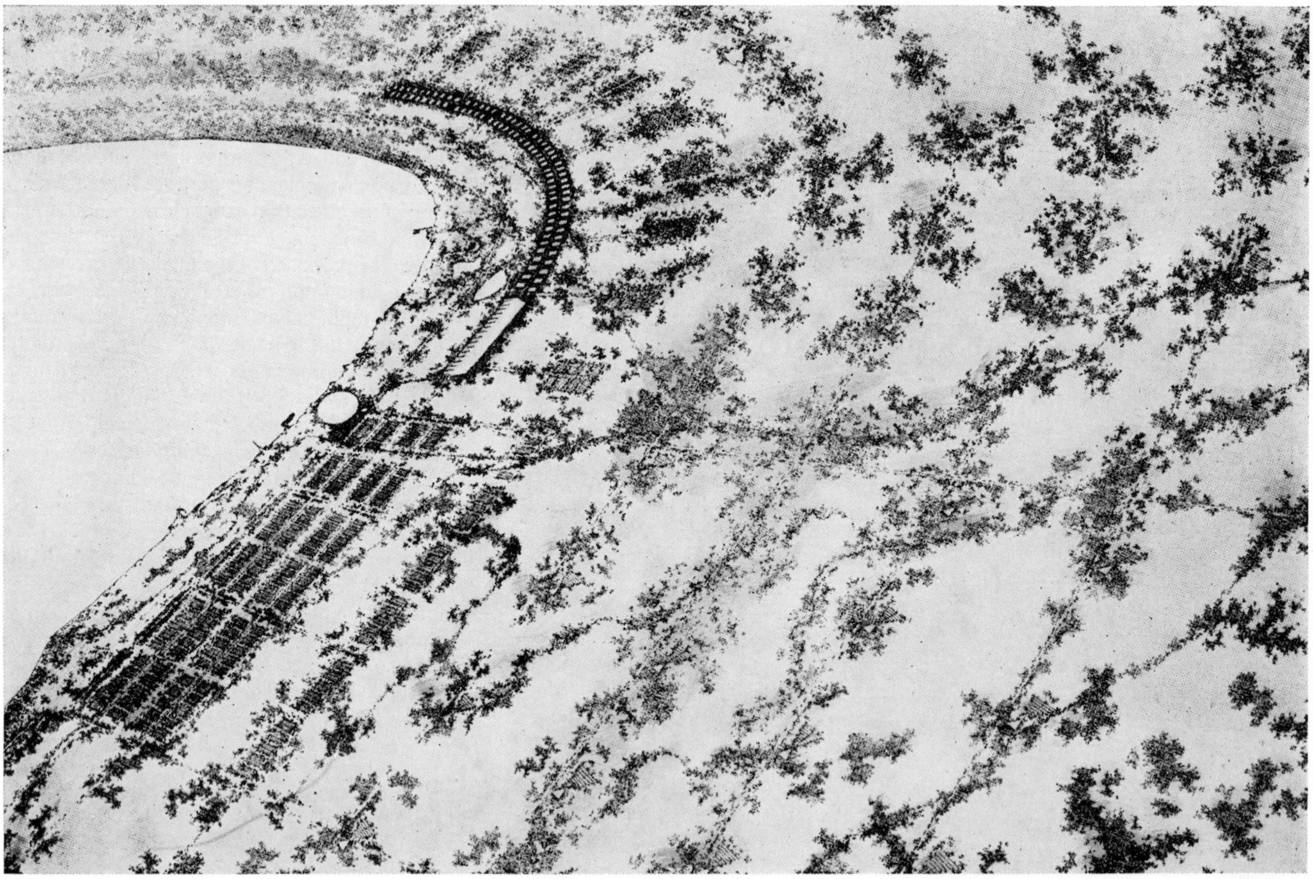

46

47

46. Plan for Chicago: by L. Hilberseimer

In some respects this vision is not dissimilar to Broadacre City. It is a totally new urban pattern, without much relevance to the vast and intractable urban problems of Chicago as they exist today. Many of Professor Hilberseimer's ideas are valuable, and would be well worth trying out in a new town.

47. Centre City, by Louis Kahn

In this imaginative study for Philadelphia, Kahn, like Hilberseimer in Chicago, pays little attention to the existing urban pattern. His concern is with ideas, and some of them would be more applicable to crystallography than architecture. It is important, however, to see them as diagrammatic symbols and not as realistic architectural solutions. The centre of the city is ringed with great cylinders, which are circular buildings with a core of garaging.

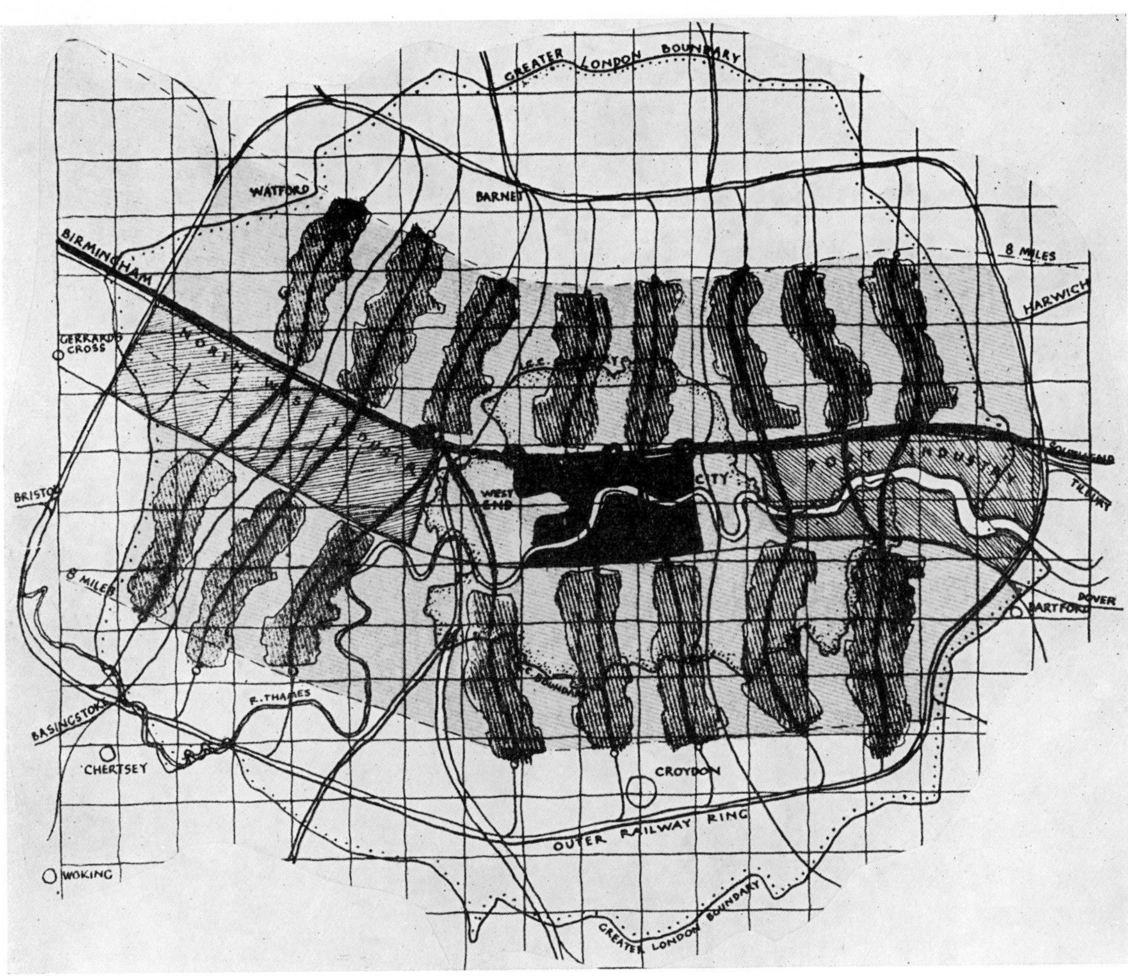

48

48. The M.A.R.S. plan for London, 1939

The new architectural ideas were late to arrive in Great Britain, but by the mid-1930s the Modern Architectural Research Group was functioning as a branch of the Congrés Internationaux d'Architecture Moderne (C.I.A.M.). In the late 1930s the group decided to prepare a plan for Greater London. It set out a number of new principles, based on those formulated at earlier C.I.A.M. Conferences. In outline, the plan proposed a wide band, running east-west, and consisting of all the main metropolitan commercial, cultural and entertainment functions in the centre, with industrial zones on either side. From this band linear blocks of residential development projected out, with wide open spaces between each. A comprehensive communications system was planned to serve this new urban pattern. Although the M.A.R.S. Plan had little to do with the real problems of London, it had great propaganda value, and among those who took part in its preparation was Arthur Ling (now Professor Ling) who later worked with Professor Abercrombie on the County of London Plan. Subsequently, as Senior Planning Officer in the London County Council, he was mainly responsible for the organisation of the L.C.C.'s Development Plan of 1951. The continuity of ideas was then maintained from sketch study through to statutory document.

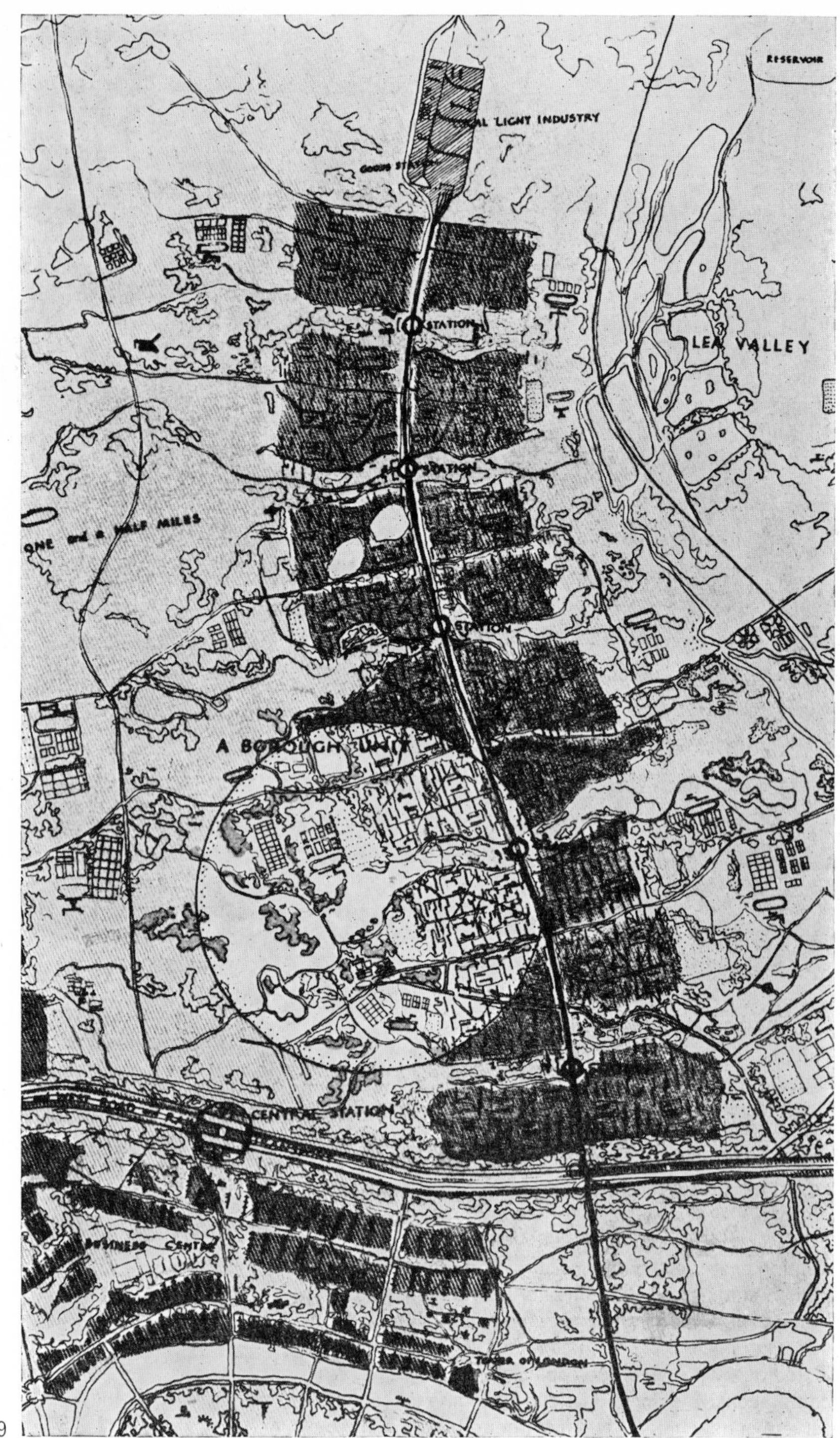

49

49. The M.A.R.S. plan for London, 1939
One of the great City Districts, planned as linear blocks of residential land, which were to run north-south, surrounded by spacious wedges of park land, approximately one and a half miles wide. If one studies the existing map of London one can see that this plan bore no relation to reality, but it was a powerful call to action. The population of a City District was suggested as 600,000 people.

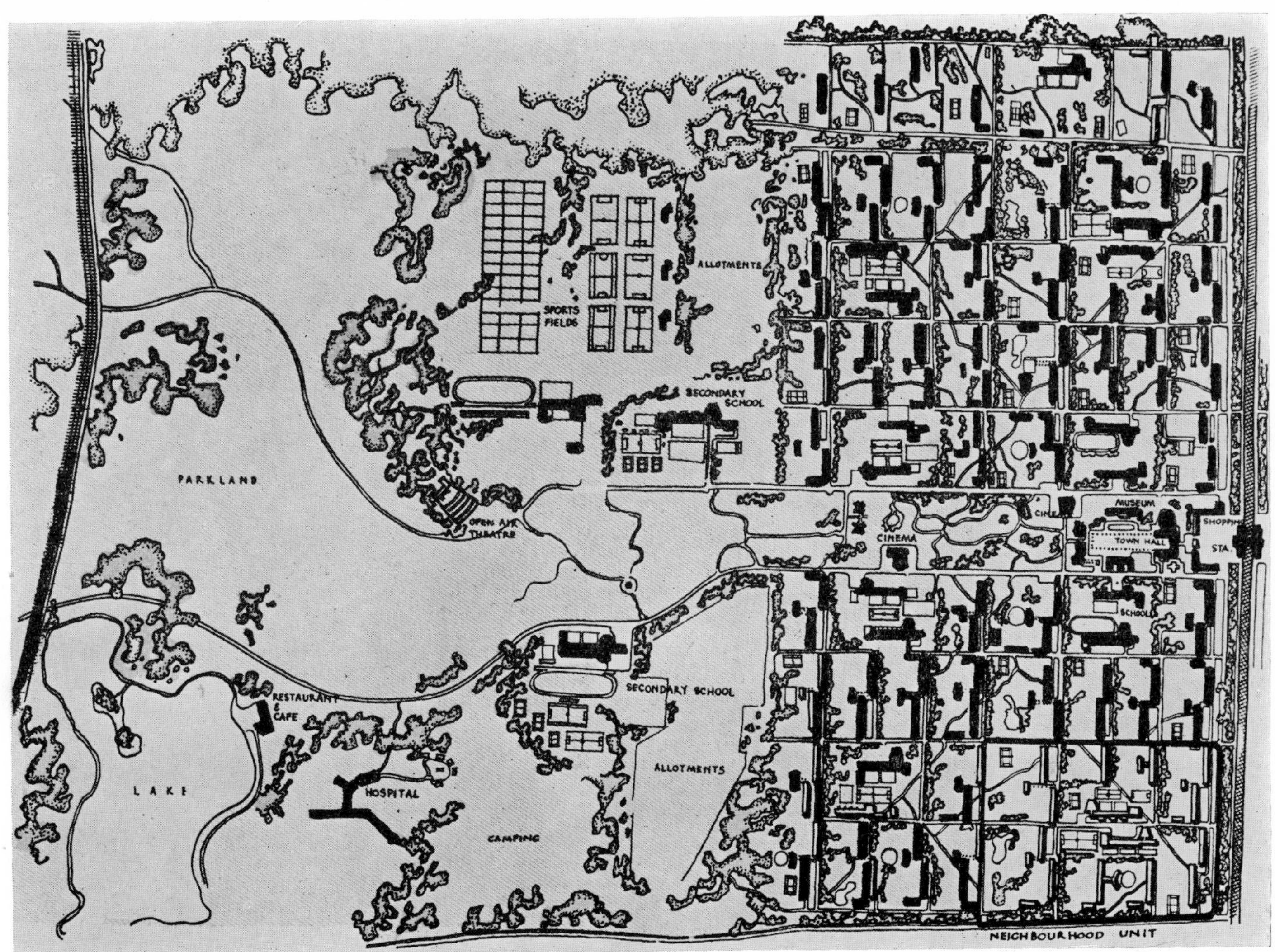

50

50. The M.A.R.S. plan for London, 1939

A proposed Borough Unit as part of one of the great residential blocks. This plan shows how the schools and other space-using public buildings were to be located in the green parkland, and, how each railway station could form the nucleus of a Town Centre, with Town Hall, Shopping Centre, and Museum. The population of the Borough Unit was suggested as 50,000 people.

51

51. The M.A.R.S. plan for London, 1939

A proposed Neighbourhood Unit within the larger Borough Unit. The suggested population is 1,000 people, accommodated entirely in apartment blocks, each equipped with a nursery school. There were also to be a Junior and Senior School, Clubs, and accommodation for aged persons. Although the whole plan was highly diagrammatic, it did follow through an idea consistently, right from the metropolitan scale down to the individual building.

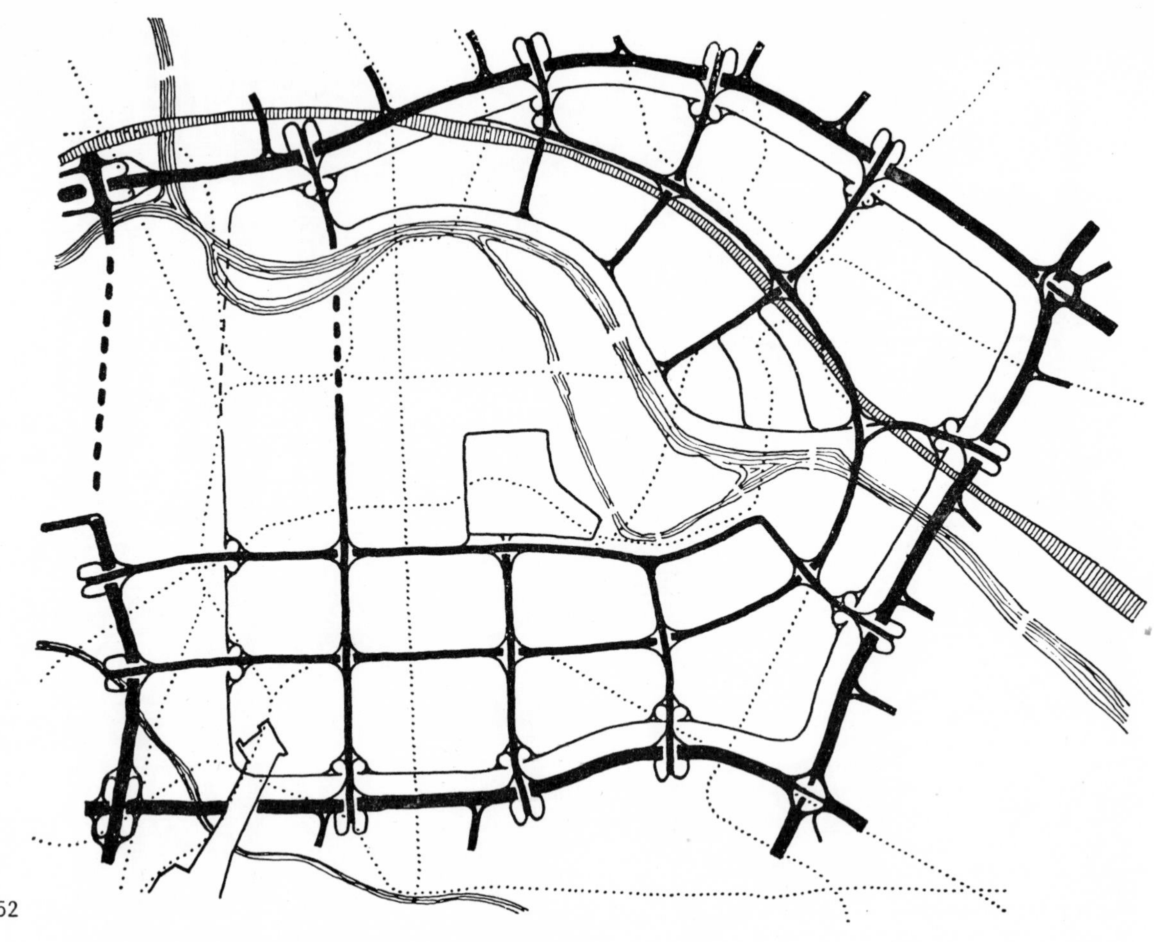

52

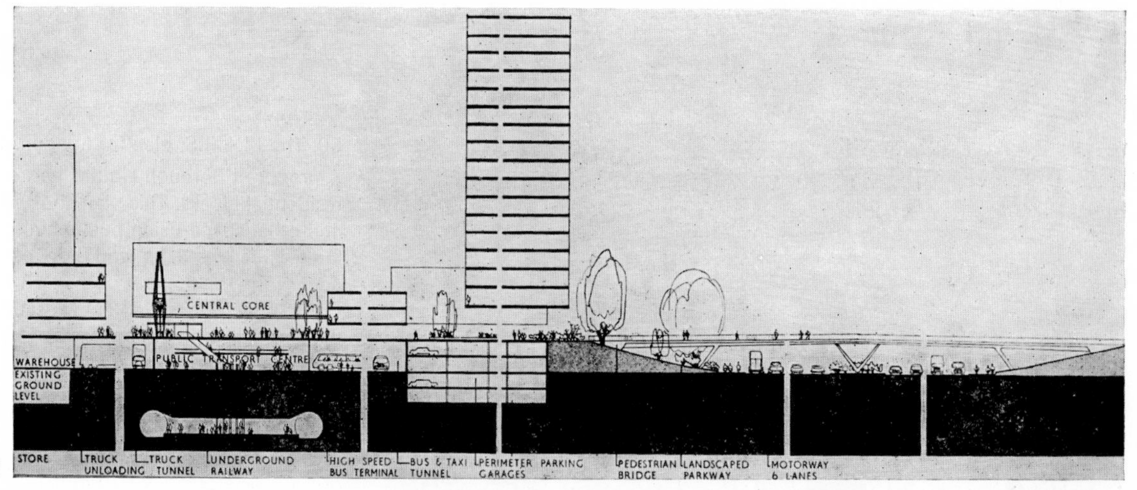

53

52. A plan for a two-level city, 1958

An international competition was held for the design of the bombed centre of Berlin, and Messrs Boissevain and Osmond, Colin Buchanan, and I entered a project which, while not pretending to be a detailed solution to the problems of such a complex city, did endeavour to suggest some possibilities for urban redevelopment. This plan of the main road pattern shows the central area divided into a number of city sectors. Each one would be totally raised to an upper level (the 'ground level' is a very artificial idea in most cities today), allowing the traffic to circulate freely below.

53. A plan for a two-level city, 1958

This sectional drawing shows everything below the main road level in black. It includes underground railway stations with lifts and escalators to carry commutors upwards. Above this are one or two levels of car parking or storage before the main pedestrian level is reached. Around the sides of the City Sectors a gentle grass and tree planted slope leads down to the main traffic roads, while bridges connect the City Sectors to each other. In this way the city is regained for the pedestrian, while the motor vehicle can circulate unhindered.

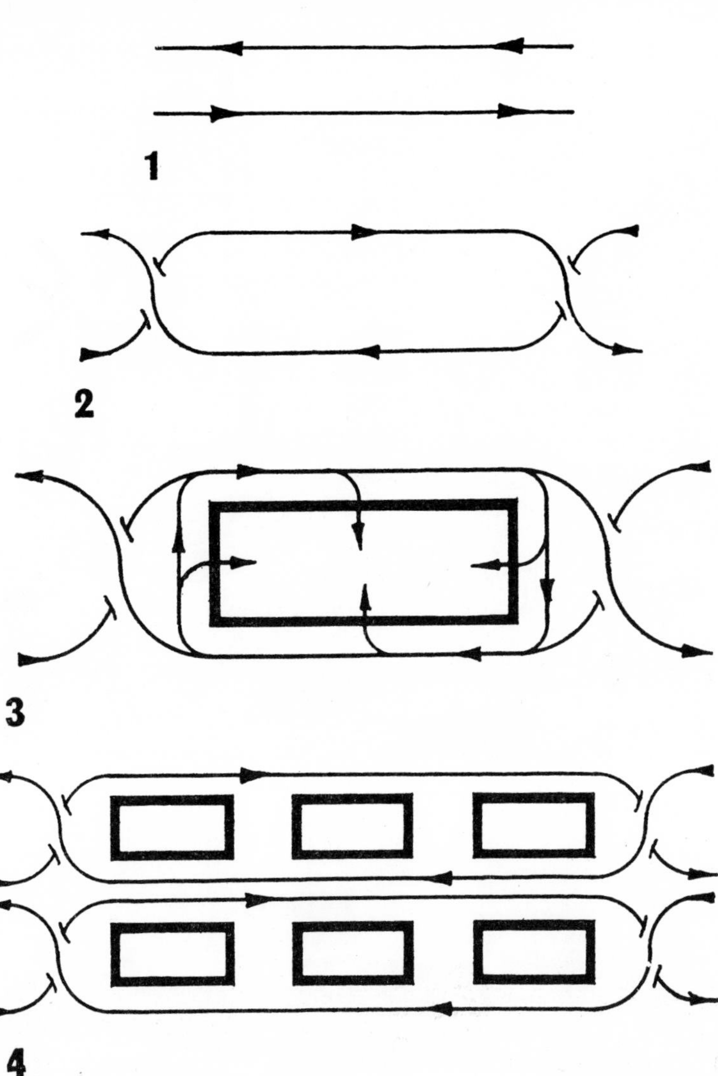

54

54. A plan for a two-level city, 1958

Diagrams of the traffic system: no. 1 is a normal double carriageway road (traffic on the right); no. 2 shows the two roads separated and flows reversed over a section; no. 3 shows a development block inserted between the reversed carriageways; while no. 4 shows the process continued over a number of blocks.

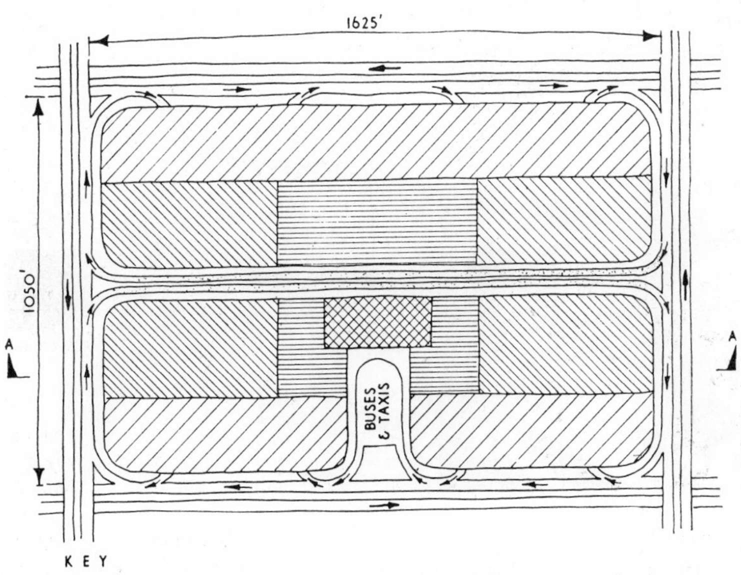

55

55. A plan for a two-level city, 1958

A City Sector in the new City Plan. The acreage is approximately 50 acres. At ground level the traffic circulates round the block in the reverse direction to that followed in a normal roundabout, entering the block from the slow lane. Truck access to the block is at each end and goes down to a lower level to loading and unloading platforms. Buses and taxis draw in and take passengers under cover to the Sector Centre. This is like a multi-level station, with access to Underground (or Subway) trains at the lower level, buses, taxis, and private cars at ground level, and with lifts and escalators going up to the main pedestrian level above. Almost the whole acreage of the sector could be given over to car parking, traffic, and storage, at three or more lower levels below the main pedestrian level.

56 

57 

56. New York: proposed upper-level walkways

The famous Greater New York Regional Plan of 1929 contains a large number of visionary ideas, and could have been a powerful stimulus for better city planning. In addition to Clarence Perry's neighbourhood theories there were a number of very interesting proposals for Manhattan. Perhaps the most immediately useful and practical idea was the suggestion that some of the major streets should be provided with upper-level pedestrian decks. Unfortunately the montage techniques used still leaves the existing ground level pavements full of pedestrians. Only now the Barbican scheme which we planned for London is actually bringing the upper level walkway idea into reality.

57. The moving walkway

What is interesting about many of these new theories is that precedents already exist, although in unexpected places. Clearly a moving walkway can only be justified economically where large numbers of people simultaneously wish to move in the same direction. In this photograph a 'speedwalk' installation is shown installed in the Goodyear Aircraft Plant at Akron, Ohio. It operates outside in all kinds of weather conditions without difficulty.

58

59

58. The moving walkway

The idea of making the ground move is almost a magic-carpet dream, but when actually put into practice in the dullest way possible – in a tunnel – loses all its glamorous possibilities. The photograph shows a 'speedwalk' installation for the Hudson and Manhattan Railroad in Jersey City; it is 227 feet long and runs up a ten per cent grade for the first 137 feet of its run. There is a similar moving walkway at the Bank Underground station in London, also in a tunnel. One could imagine exciting possibilities in new city centres with such moving walkways not only being used for mass pedestrian transit from one busy nodal point to another, but also affording fine urban vistas on their way.

59. The 'Speedwalk' moving walkway

This montage shows how the 'speedwalk' pedestrian walkway could look conveying pedestrians across a main street in Chicago's Loop (the central area formed by a bend in the Chicago River). It brings out the tremendous possibilities of this kind of technological discovery for both existing and new city centres.

60

61

60. The 'Carveyor' railcar

Here is another idea for local movement in city centres. It shows, first, how pedestrians can be placed above the traffic stream in an existing street (although it would have been more logical to omit the pavement at street level); second, how access to shops could be organised at the upper level of existing buildings; and, third, how a miniature railway service could speed up pedestrian movement.

61. The hovercraft

Communications by air are now repeating the story: the railcar replacing the stage coach and the motor vehicle overhauling the railway. It is, however, reasonable to assume that a reorganized rail system (dual or monorail) has an important role for mass transport in the big city, and that some form of surface motor vehicle will continue to be used. The hovercraft will therefore become an additional facility (and space user).

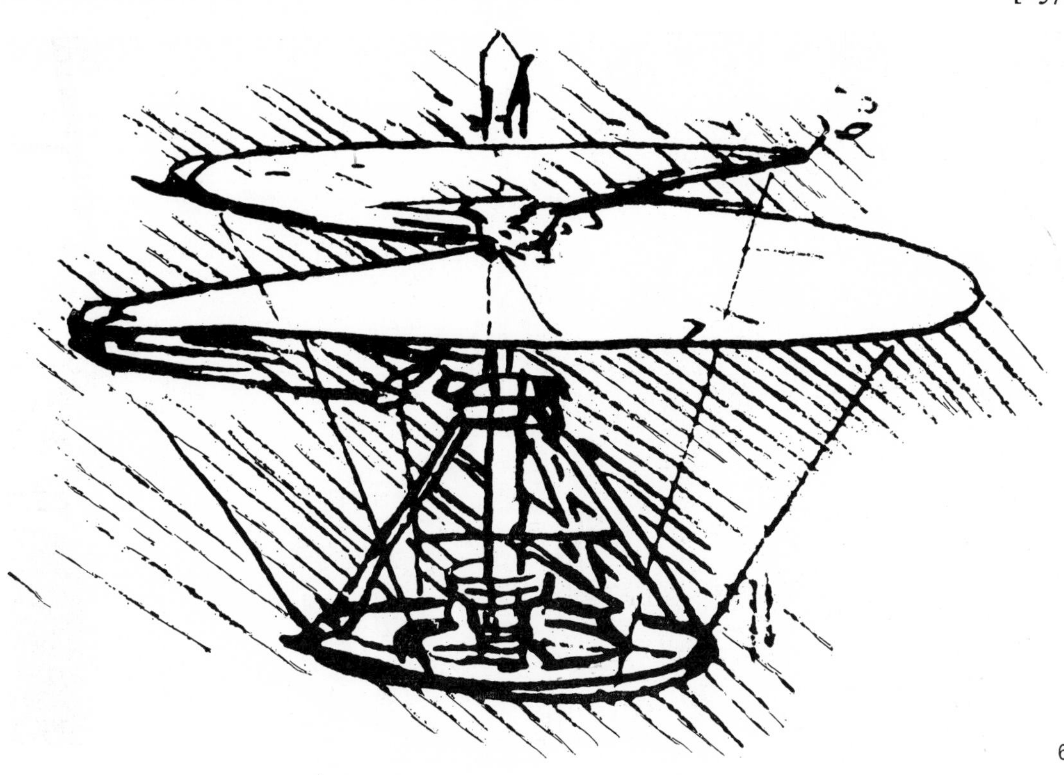

62

63

64

62. Leonardo da Vinci: the helicopter

Leonardo was a true universal genius in that he allowed his highly imaginative mind to play on almost every problem of the human environment, from regional studies down to a minutely observed analysis of the spinal column. In his studies of aircraft his fantastically powerful imagination is well displayed: 450 years later the helicopter uses the same principle of vertical take-off.

63. The 'Hoppicopter'

The Hoppicopter, which gives individual mobility a new vertical dimension, is one of the most exciting and at the same time potentially dangerous inventions for personal mobility yet produced. Terrifying possibilities emerge of thousands of office workers arriving at their skyscrapers at the appropriate floor, or of a thousand children dropping in to school like a swarm of bees. Clearly the Hoppicopter is bound to come, and planning for it should begin now.

64. The 'Skyway' monorail, Dallas

Many proposals have been made during the last hundred years for the construction of monorail public transport systems, but so far none has been developed, in spite of certain obvious advantages. Like any other upper-level rail or road system, there are serious environmental problems to be solved once the system is introduced into the existing urban pattern, such as noise, vibration, etc. It does, however, offer the minimum amount of obstruction at ground level.

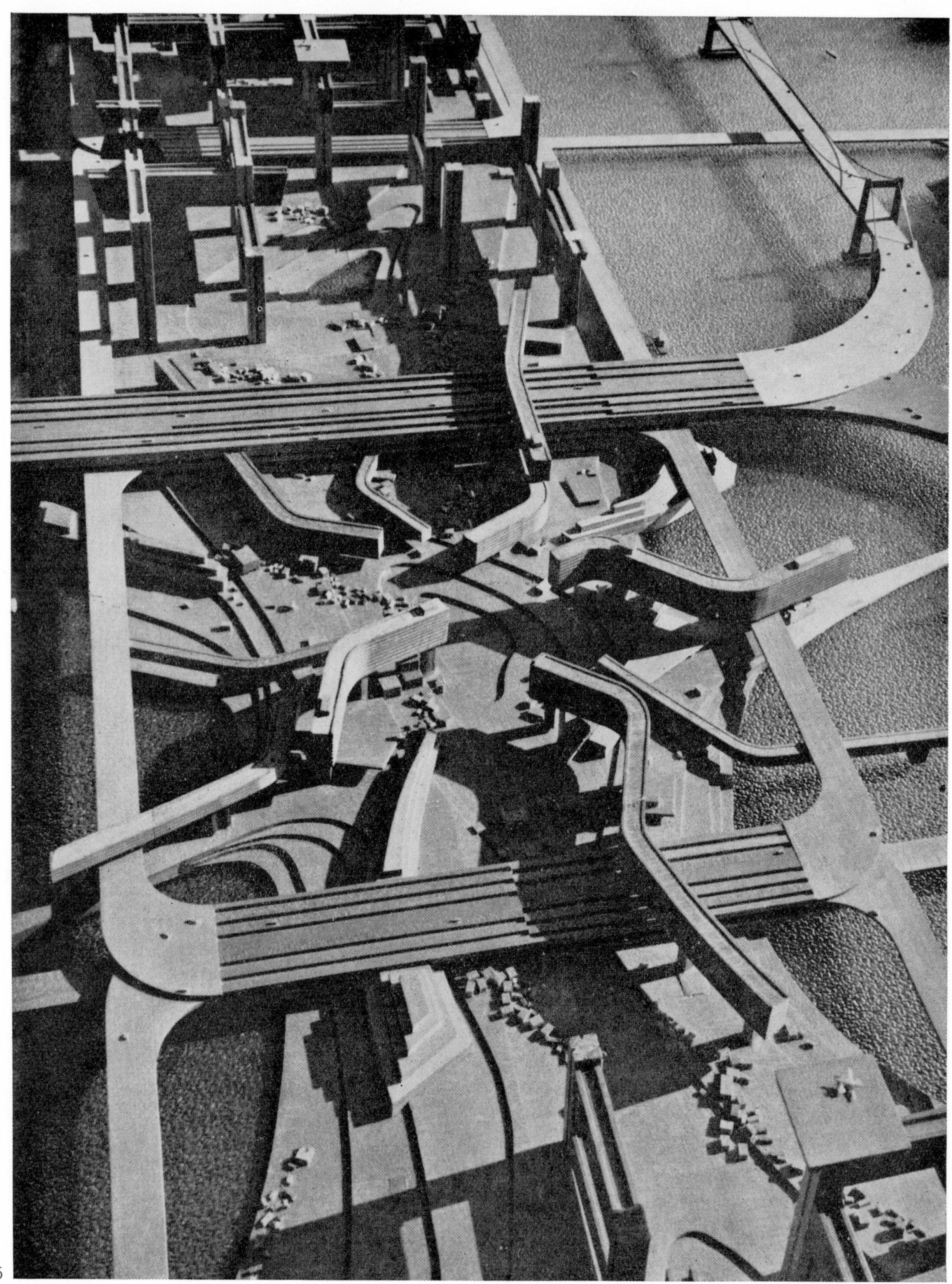

65

65. A plan for Tokyo: by Kenzo Tangye

Here, a well-known Japanese architect endeavours to present a solution to the problems of the world's largest city. The result is a slightly different kind of nightmare from that of Kahn's Philadelphia. Despairing of the existing city Tangye proposed to build a vast motorized complex across the shallow waters of Tokyo Bay. Sinuous shapes wind their way across great motorways, and towers for vertical circulation stand independently of buildings they serve.

PART TWO

4

New Planning Legislation and Techniques

During the thirties the planning movement in Britain developed rapidly, but owing to the inability of any city to put major planning proposals into practice, the attention of reformers had been devoted to endeavouring to convince the public of the *need* for planning, and to pressing successive governments for legislation to enable it to be carried out.

It was the shock of war and bombing, however, that really brought about positive action. For the first time people could see large areas in the centres of cities, which had been solidly built-up for generations, suddenly cleared. In one stroke all the major physical impediments to replanning were swept away. But, between wholesale destruction on the one hand and comprehensive reconstruction to form a live twentieth-century physical environment on the other, the gap was wide, and in one way it was fortunate that between the bombing of London, Coventry, Portsmouth and the other cities and the end of the war there was a period of some five years to work out not only plans and techniques but also the necessary legal and financial procedures.

THE THREE REPORTS. Before the war, planning matters in Britain had been the responsibility of the Ministry of Health, but this Ministry had been concerned only with the effects of a limited number of planning restrictions, and was not suitable administratively to co-ordinate vast new problems and possibilities which now appeared.

Under the impact of the aerial bombing of many of the larger cities, the Government set up a new Ministry of Works and Planning, with the dynamic politician Lord Reith as its Minister. It was Reith who met official delegations from bombed cities such as London and Coventry, and advised them to plan *boldly*, and who gave heart to sorely pressed civic leaders in a testing time.

It was Reith, too, who constituted two out of three famous Commissions concerned with national problems of planning. The Commission on the Distribution of the Industrial Population had already submitted its Report in 1939 (known as the Barlow

Report, after its Chairman Sir Montague Barlow). This Report had contained a large number of important planning recommendations, mainly of a strategical nature, including the setting up of a Ministry for Planning, and it had also suggested that the problems of compensation and betterment be further examined. As a result the Expert Committee on Compensation and Betterment was set up under the chairmanship of Lord Uthwatt in 1941, and the 'Uthwatt' Report appeared in 1942. Although this Report dealt mainly with the problems of unbuilt-on land, it recommended an increase in Planning Authorities' powers of compulsory purchase and recompense, and that legislation for the control of redevelopment consequent on reconstruction be expedited.

The third Committee, under the chairmanship of Lord Scott, dealt with Land Utilization in Rural Areas, and is for the most part outside the scope of this book. It did, however, include recommendations that local planning should be compulsory and not permissive, that expense incurred by local authorities through planning at a national scale should not be allowed to fall wholly on the authorities concerned, and it followed both its predecessors in recommending that a Central Planning Authority with Regional Offices be set up.

THE NEW MINISTRY. In 1943 the Ministry of Town and Country Planning Act transferred the planning functions in England and Wales[1] of the Ministry of Works and Planning to a new Ministry of Town and Country Planning. Although the main duty of this Ministry was concerned with 'securing consistency and continuity in the framing and execution of a national policy with respect to the use and development of land throughout England and Wales', and thus fell far short of the comprehensive powers envisaged by the Barlow Report, it began work with energy and enthusiasm. In addition to the usual administrative hierarchy, new technical and research offices were formed both at headquarters in London and in the regional headquarters of the regions—which had originally been set up for Civil Defence purposes. The headquarters technical research organization, which was known as the Planning Technique Office, first under the leadership of Professor Holford and then of Professor Stephenson, developed an astonishingly bold programme of urban planning studies, although of the dozen or so handbooks envisaged, only one appeared. This was known as the *Handbook on the Redevelopment of Central Areas*, and consisted not only of clear and easily understood methods of carrying out surveys, analyses, and plans for central areas, but also embodied the fruits of intensive studies into daylighting, floor space control, and use-class categories. In the hands of imaginative and intelligent planners it can still be a document of basic importance. Members of the staff also carried out a number of important development projects, of which the most important were the Greater London Plan (although Sir Patrick Abercrombie was in fact in charge of the whole of this operation) and the master plan for the first post-war New Town of Stevenage.

THE TOWN AND COUNTRY PLANNING ACT, 1944. An even more important priority was the need for planning legislation to deal with war-damaged areas, and closely following the establishment of the new Ministry a new Bill was prepared, which passed

[1] In Scotland planning responsibilities remained with the Department of Health, but the separate Acts of Parliament for Scotland relating to Planning corresponded closely to those for England and Wales.

into law as the *Town and Country Planning Act* of 1944. This Act could more appropriately have been called the Reconstruction Areas Act, since it dealt largely with this urgent problem.

Its main objective was to enable local[1] Planning Authorities to obtain control of areas of extensive war damage. Procedurally, the Planning Authority concerned could in the first instance apply to the Minister of Town and Country Planning for a 'Declaratory Order' over an area which had been extensively damaged. Any land adjacent or contiguous to it could also be included in order to deal with the area as a whole, even if it included existing buildings which were unlikely to be disturbed. The order could also cover land for overspill purposes (i.e. to take non-conforming uses from the reconstruction area) and was to be accompanied by plans showing how the area would be laid out. The primary object at this stage was to settle the principle of purchase for all the land covered by the Order. The Minister would then hold a Public Enquiry at which objections would be heard, and subsequently approve the Order, with any amendments he considered necessary (in the case of the L.C.C.'s Stepney-Poplar Reconstruction Area he reduced the Declaratory Order Area from approximately 2,000 to 1,300 acres).

The second stage would be for the Planning Authority to submit a Compulsory Purchase Order, or a series of such Orders, to the Minister for approval, and in this case, too, there would be a Public Enquiry to hear objections. Incidentally, when the 1947 Town and Country Planning Act came into force and set up the procedure for the submission of Development Plans, these also included the obligation to hold Public Enquiries, so that in some cases there were no less than three Public Enquiries held over the same area.

These procedural complications amounted to a serious financial and time-consuming burden, particularly for planning staffs, whose creative role tended to recede before the necessity of preparing long and onerous briefs, and of appearing for weeks on end as expert witnesses.

Having made provision for the large-scale acquisition of land to be legally possible, the next problem was to enable the Planning Authority to meet the very heavy cost of actually buying the land. Under Section 5 of the Act, the Central Government (i.e. the Treasury, advised by the Ministry of Town and Country Planning) would make grants payable which would be equal to the loan charges on the capital spent during the first two years, and a part of the loan charges during the next eight years.

Working under the provisions of this Act, 62 Declaratory Orders were made throughout England and Wales, covering 4,708 acres. The largest was the L.C.C.'s Stepney-Poplar Area of 1,300 acres, while the City of London[2] declared 231 acres in the busi-

[1] It should be emphasized that in Britain the responsibilities for Town Planning, Housing, Schools, and nearly all matters affecting the local environment, rest with the County Boroughs, as the larger municipalities are called. County Councils are also Planning Authorities.

[2] The local governmental administration of London is sometimes confusing to those who are unfamiliar with it. The City Corporation of the 'City' of London, covering approximately the square mile of the Roman city, has existed as a municipal organization for centuries. In 1888 the London County Council was set up comprising the built up area at the time and in 1899 a second tier of Borough Councils was created. Before the 1947 T. & C.P. Act only the L.C.C. and the City Corporation possessed separate planning powers. There was a further organisational change, which took effect in 1965. The Greater London Council, covering the enormously expanded built-up area of Greater London, replaced the London County Council. Several of the Boroughs were amalgamated to create larger lower-tier units.

ness heart of the capital, and Coventry declared 274 acres as a central Reconstruction Area.

THE DISTRIBUTION OF INDUSTRY ACT, 1945. The next piece of relevant legislation was the *Distribution of Industry Act* of 1945, the main purpose of which was to stimulate industrial development in the Development Areas, but which also contained a provision making it obligatory for any developer to inform the Board of Trade of any proposed industrial development of over 10,000 square feet. The objects of the provision were to assist the Board of Trade and to enable Planning Authorities in areas such as London (where it was the agreed planning policy) to prevent new industrial undertakings to be established, so that the consequent decongestion would enable redevelopment to take place more effectively. This matter of industrial relocation in London provided some interesting and useful lessons during the post-war period, particularly in, and adjacent to, the Reconstruction Areas (later known as Comprehensive Development Areas, or C.D.A.s for short). At first industrialists were unwilling to move, and owing to inelasticity in the compensation[1] provisions of the War Damage Act and to the high cost of acquisition of industrial land, great difficulties were experienced. Gradually, as it was realized that industrial sites outside London gave greater scope for expansion and flexibility, a change of attitude took place, with the result that several large industrial concerns, which until recently stood in the midst of comprehensively planned residential neighbourhoods, are now moving out altogether. A second example of this strategical decongestion policy followed in 1946, with the passing of the New Town Act, which, in so far as it affected London, was used to decongest the urban population by providing eight New Towns for this purpose.

THE TOWN AND COUNTRY PLANNING ACT, 1947. The following year came the comprehensive piece of planning legislation known as the *Town and Country Planning Act*, 1947. This Act set up an entirely new planning system throughout the country, and one can refer briefly to the more immediately relevant provisions. The submission by all local Planning Authorities (henceforth the Counties and the County Boroughs, as the larger cities are called) of Development Plans within three years of the passing of the Act was made mandatory, and in the Regulations and Circulars which followed it was made clear that these documents would provide an essential planning framework in time and two-dimensional space for all cities throughout the country. In so far as reconstruction and redevelopment were concerned, Reconstruction Areas gave way to Comprehensive Development Areas. In the latter the powers to define land were not limited to blitz and blight, but could include any land which the Planning Authority considered to be in need of replanning as a whole, the condition being that the purpose was to be specified, and that it could only be designated for compulsory purchase if it was required within a period of ten years.

The Regulations, which followed the Act in 1948, set out the detailed requirements of the Minister, both in respect of the Development Plan of the whole city and for the special requirement of Comprehensive Development Areas. Plans for the latter were to be the large scale of 1/2500, and in addition to Land Use, Floor Space and Residen-

[1] A money payment was only made where premises were completely demolished. Otherwise a 'Cost of Works' was awarded, whereby the Government undertook to reinstate the building back to its pre-war condition.

tial Density Surveys, there had to be a Proposals Map (i.e. Zoning Map), a Programme Map, Use Zone Table, and a Written Statement. The Scottish Department of Health went further and also required a Test Map, indicating three-dimensional proposals. This last requirement was an extraordinary omission by the Ministry of Town and Country Planning, although in the cases of both the London County Council and Coventry such proposals were in fact prepared and were accompanied by large-scale models.

The requirements for the Proposals Map were set out in considerable detail in Circular No. 59 of 1948. In addition to showing all the main uses, such as Business, Residential, Industrial, etc., they had to indicate floor space for Business Zones and the density of Residential Zones. They had also to show three categories of roads, Public and Private Open Spaces, and other proposals of importance such as Car Parks, land for Railway purposes, etc. The Programme Plan had to show the stages of development over twenty years in five-year periods.

All these requirements, with minor modifications, have since proved their usefulness and value in the test of implementation, and any other country wishing to embark on new planning legislation would be well advised to study the procedures and requirements embodied in the 1947 Act with its attendant Regulations and Circulars. At the present time (1965) they are under extensive review by the British Government in order to take advantage of experience gained since the Act was passed (see *The Future of Development Plans*, H.M.S.O., 1965).

1

4 NEW PLANNING LEGISLATION

1. London, 1941
Offices in the City ablaze during an air raid

BUILDING USE GROUPS Index Letter — TYPE	ZONE 1 Residential	ZONE 2 Business (Shops).	ZONE 3 Business (Offices).	ZONE 4 Business (Wholesale Warehouses)	ZONE 5 Educational Recreational and Public Buildings.	ZONE 6 Light Industrial	ZONE 7 Industrial	ZONE 8 Special Industrial
A Dwelling Houses	P	X	X	X	X	X	X	X
B Residential (other than dwelling houses)	P			X		X	X	X
C Schools and Residential Colleges		X	X	X	P	X	X	X
D Shops		P						
E Offices	X		P					
F Wholesale Warehouses	X			P	X			
G Storage Warehouses	X	X	X		X		P	
H Public Buildings and Places of Assembly					P			
I Special Places of Assembly	X			X				
J Light Industrial Buildings	X				X	P		
K Industrial Buildings	X	X	X		X		P	
L Special Industrial Buildings	X	X	X	X	X	X		P
M Other Buildings								

2

2. The Zoning Chart
This was one of the diagrams included in the *Handbook on the Redevelopment of Central Areas*, published by the British Ministry of Town and Country Planning in 1947. It shows a flexible technique in the application of use zones for central areas (enclosed by heavy line). In the Chart the letter P means permissible while X means not permissible. Spaces left blank indicate that the decision may depend on the circumstances of the case. For instance, in an Industrial Zone (Zone 7 in the chart), Industrial and Storage Warehouses would be permissible, Dwelling Houses would not be permissible, while shops and offices would depend on the particular situation. On the left hand side of the chart is the Index letter. Each letter stands for a Use Group, and elsewhere every kind of building use was put into one of thirteen main Use Categories.

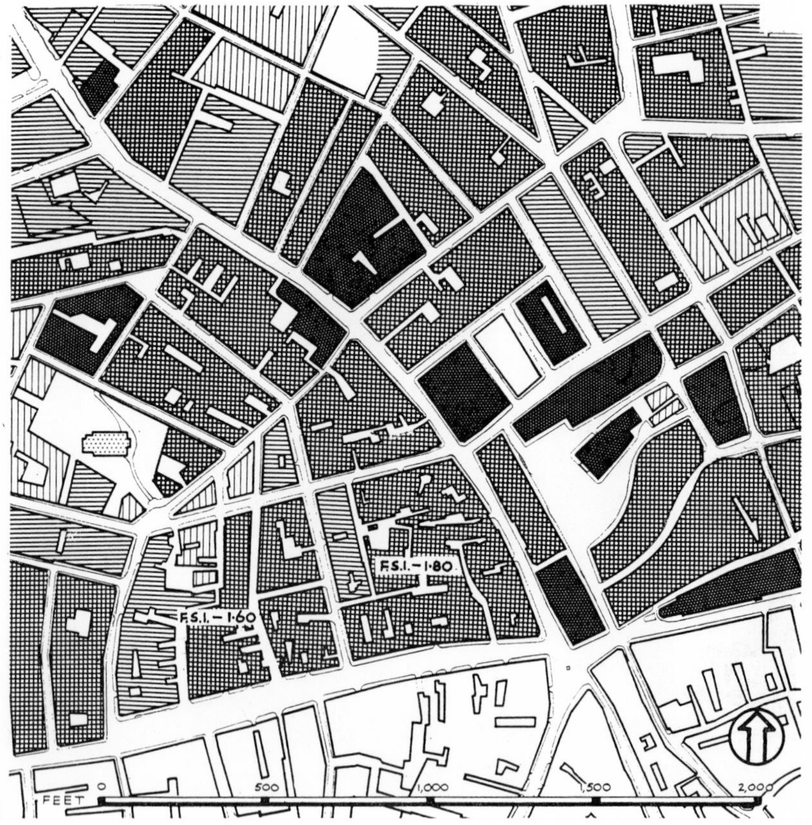

3

3. Floor space survey
This survey introduced a new technique to official planning: the control of the bulk of buildings on the site. In this survey, from the *Handbook*, each site is hatched to indicate the amount of floor space in relation to the site area. The dark hatching is over 2·0, the cross hatching is between 1·6 and 2·0, horizontal shading 1·2 to 1·6, vertical ·8 to 1·2, and dots up to ·8. In order to make the study more realistic, the Planning Technique Office of the Ministry, which was largely responsible for the *Handbook*, based it on an existing British city. Today this is regarded as an essential urban survey, but would be accompanied by an economic study as well.

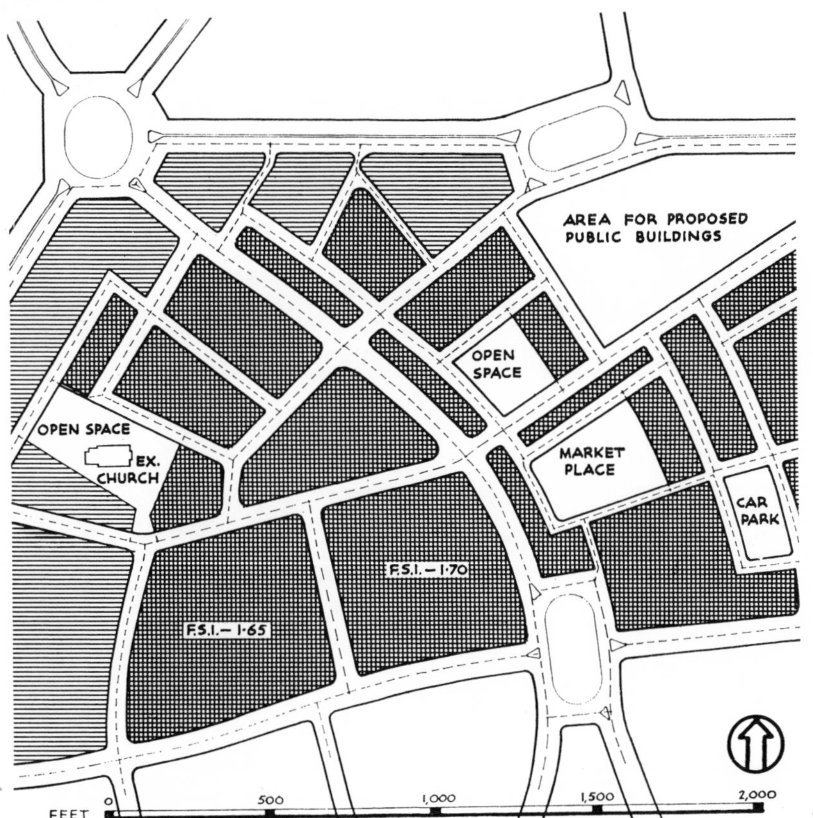

4

4. Floor space proposals plan

This is an example from the Handbook of one of the planning proposals which were to be submitted for the Central Area. Although the floor space indices (or bulk of building) proposed are reasonable (horizontal shading, 1·2 to 1·6; cross-hatching, 1·6 to 2·0), the road pattern is already out of date (particularly the roundabouts) and development would tend to be proposed in larger blocks.

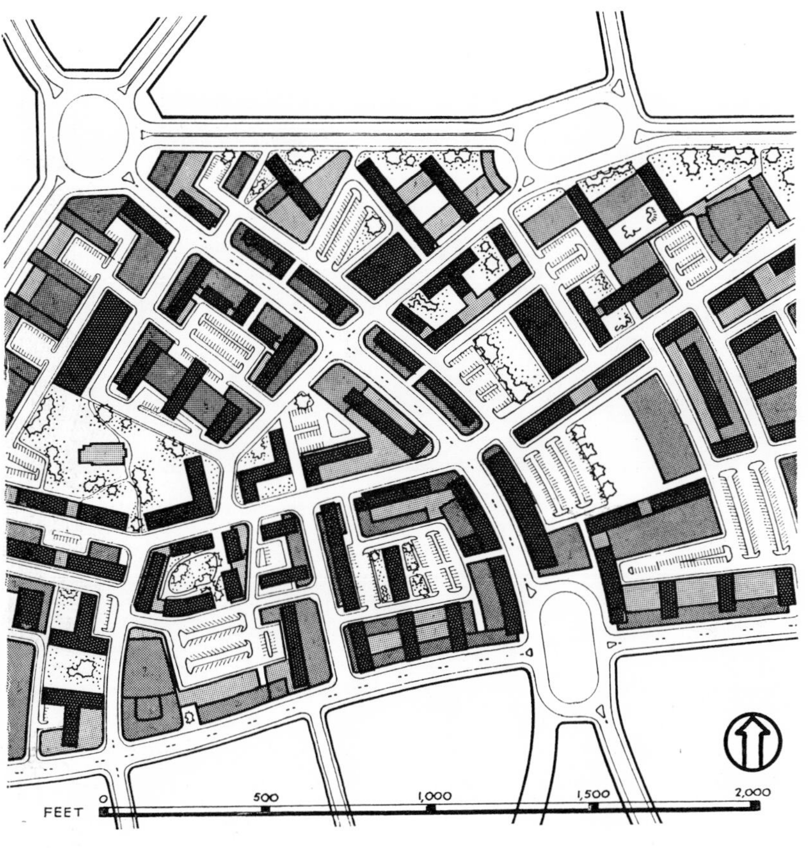

5

5. Three-dimensional proposals

This plan shows how part of the central area of a city could be redeveloped within the permitted floor space and daylighting requirements. Today we would criticize the small and isolated units of development, the shopping frontages facing on to traffic roads, the failure to separate pedestrian and vehicles, and the open areas of car parking. However, if the ideas had been generally adopted after the war, many of our cities and towns would have been greatly improved as urban environments.

6

development as existing in 1939

7

first stage of redevelopment

8

second stage of redevelopment

9

third stage of redevelopment

10

fourth stage of redevelopment

11

redevelopment complete

6, 7, 8, 9, 10, 11. Street block redevelopment in stages
This flexible planning model shows how part of a central area could be redeveloped over a period stage by stage from an unplanned muddle into a reasonable and planned environment. This was a good example of the excellent thinking done in the Ministry's Planning Technique Office under the guidance of Sir William Holford and Professor Gordon Stephenson.

(a) Development as existing in 1939

No planning; congestion of small buildings; car parking impossible; daylighting inadequate; sound insulation poor; ventilation unsatisfactory; no open space

12

(b) Pre-war type piecemeal redevelopment

Very limited improvement in planning; access and circulation confused; car parking facilities poor; daylighting fair to poor; ventilation slightly improved; no open space.

13

(c) Redevelopment in large courtyard units

Planning improved; access and circulation improved; parking for 30-40 cars in court-yards; daylighting, sound insulation and ventilation fair; two small areas of open space.

14

(d) Redevelopment in large units with open planning

Comprehensive and flexible planning; access and circulation clear and efficient; parking for 60-70 cars; daylighting good in all rooms; ventilation and sound insulation good; open space on all sides.

15

12, 13, 14, 15. Methods of developing an office area
Here the *Handbook* contrasted various forms of redevelopment for the same site, all based on different urban theories. Today we would probably add another one which would contain some of the more recent principles proposed in this book; but for its time this was a very valuable planning exercise.

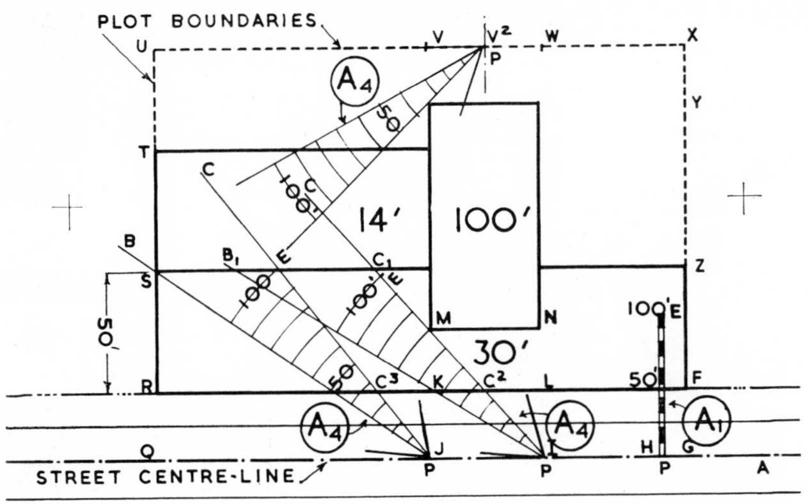

16

16. Daylighting control

This was a new method of ensuring that every building would receive an adequate amount of daylight to all its external surfaces, and hence internal accommodation. It was a brilliant simplification for general use of a complex scientific problem. Architects and planners could test the amount of daylight on any surface by means of protractors. It is fully explained in the *Handbook* and in the L.C.C.'s Development Plan of 1951. The background research studies took years of work in the Building Research Station and in the Ministry's Planning Technique Office.

2 : 1 **3½ : 1** **5 : 1**

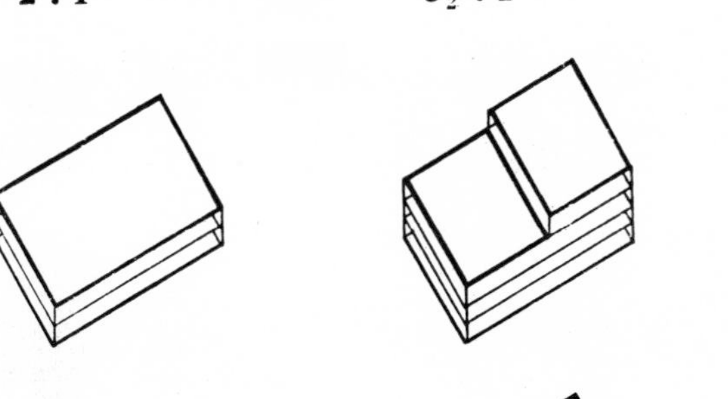

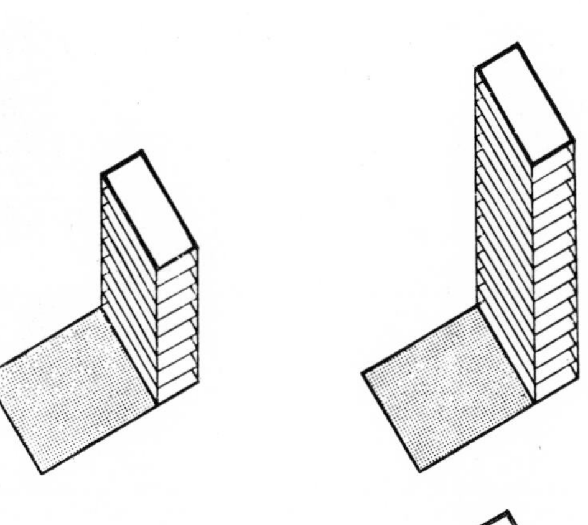

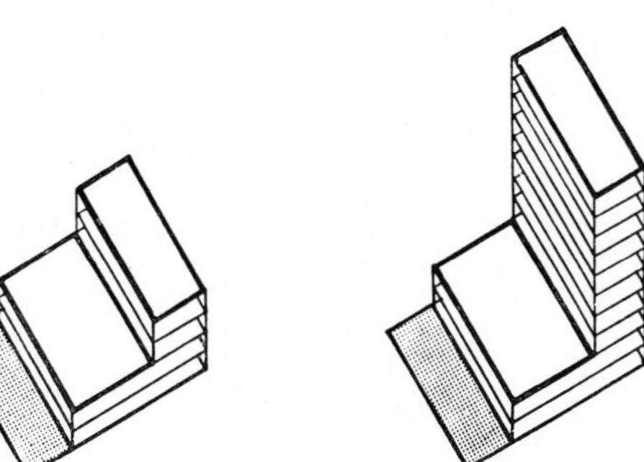

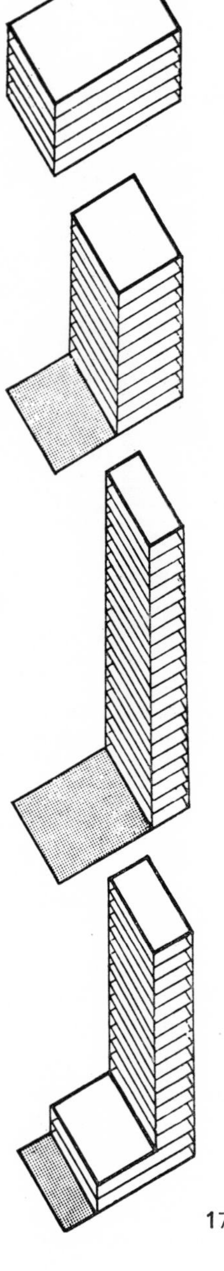

17

17. Plot ratio explained

This simple and clear diagram (from *A Plan to Combat Congestion in London*, London County Council, 1957) prepared by the Planning Division of the L.C.C. Architect's Department shows clearly what is meant by *plot ratio*: the relation between site area and building bulk. The diagram shows three alternative ways of building on a site at three different ratios.

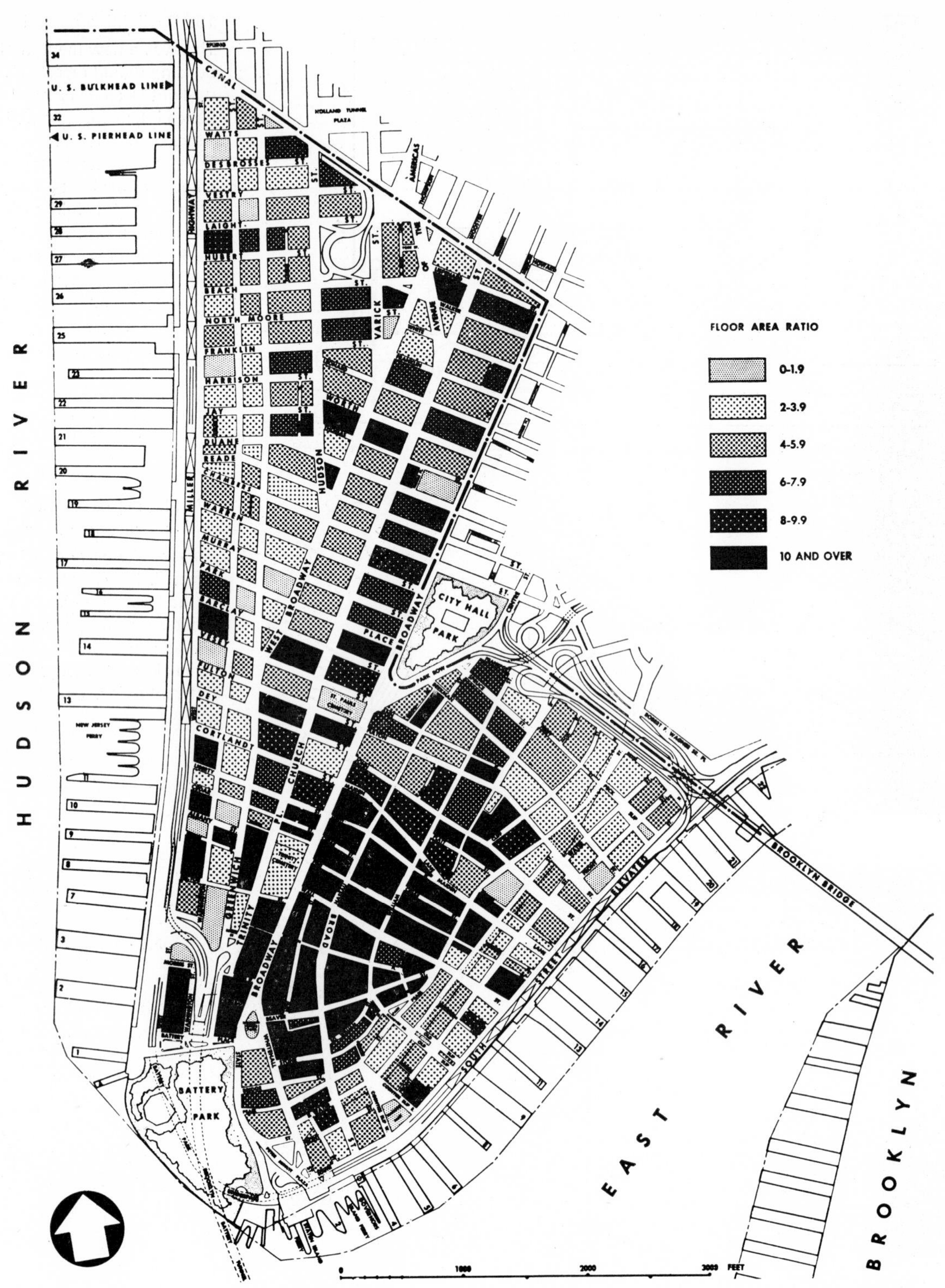

18

18. Manhattan: bulk of buildings

This bulk of buildings survey gives the plot ratios of each building block. Many are over 10:1, although there is a fringe of warehouse building near the docks which is much lower. Seen in conjunction with air and ground photographs it is clear that these high plot ratios are one of the factors which make effective urban redevelopment impossible. No matter how well the area is laid out the resulting congestion would make the achievement of a good urban environment impossible.

The photograph on page 66 shows what this urban pattern looks like from the air.

19

20

19. Copenhagen: land value model

The well-known model of Copenhagen which represents land values instead of building forms. Clearly when everyone wants to be in the middle of the city the laws of supply and demand bring congestion, even in such a comparatively well ordered city as Copenhagen.

20. Chicago: model of all-person trip destinations

The similarities between the physical silhouette of a city and other aspects are striking. Here is a model based on a scientific study of Chicago's traffic problems. The vast majority of person-trips are concerned with getting in and out of one small part of the city. It is a clear indication that either the bulk of building must be reduced, the central area made larger, or a number of sub-centres created; perhaps all three. To some extent the centre of San Francisco escaped this desperate congestion by having Oakland across the Bay as a down-town escape valve. In European cities the stricter building height controls have helped to keep the bulk of building in central areas below that of the larger North American cities.

21

22

21. Hamburg: residential density model, 1960

The model illustrates the pyramidal form of existing residential density. The old town in the centre contained a large number of high apartment blocks with densities of up to 200 persons per acre. Dr Hilbebrandt, the well known City Planning Director, and his staff proposed that the urban structure should be transformed over a period in order to enable a more uniform density pattern to be created, on the basis of equal amenity in all parts of the city.

22. Hamburg: density of work places model, 1960

Another model made in Dr Hilbebrandt's City Planning Department which shows a somewhat similar pyramidal form of building bulk to that of Residential Density. This model illustrates the proposed floor space for working areas. 240 workers per acre are catered for in the group of parallel buildings in the central area, and 480 per acre in the high density tower. New places of work are also proposed in the northern part of the city in order to create a more even distribution throughout the urban area.

5

Comprehensive Development in London

Since the days of Wren, Hooke and Evelyn, plans of many kinds have been prepared for London, but until the Second World War little enough came of any of them, because the basic economic, social and legal conditions required for their realization did not exist.

One pre-war plan, however, deserves a mention. This was the *MARS*[1] Group's *Plan* for London, which was prepared just before and at the outset of the war by an exceptionally able team of young and enthusiastic architects.

The proposals were based on an estimated population of 10 million. A band approximately two miles wide was drawn from East to West across the centre of London, and in this was contained most of the industrial, commercial and central area activity. On either side of this band a series of residential fingers projected outwards, each to contain about 600,000 people, and separated from each other by a green park of similar width. Each City District was subdivided into Borough and Neighbourhood Units, and a detailed three-dimensional layout was prepared of a typical District, Borough and Neighbourhood.

It was a bold, schematic plan, quite unrelated to the existing conditions of London, but nevertheless a fine study of great value as a demonstration of planning ideas.

In practical terms, London before the war had seemed to be a hopeless problem for comprehensive redevelopment. The only large recent central improvement—*Kingsway*—had taken over thirty years to complete, and residential rebuilding within the County was largely limited to slum clearance and the erection of tenement blocks. Although the London County Council, in building County Hall, had followed the Victorian lead of St. Thomas's Hospital in improving the *South Bank*, only students had dared to make three-dimensional studies for the whole river-side area.

[1] The Modern Architectural Research Group, which was the British section of C.I.A.M. (Congrès Internationaux des Architectes Modernes).

The Blitz, with its sudden clearing away of large built-up areas, made an enormous impact not only upon the authorities but also on the people as a whole. Its effects presented an opportunity that was too big and obvious to avoid, and the commissioning in 1941 of the *County of London Plan* was a direct result.

In the *County of London Plan* of 1943, the areas which had suffered the worst war damage were isolated as Reconstruction Areas and, for some of these, three-dimensional schemes were prepared, notably for the residential area of *Stepney* and for the central area of the *South Bank.*

The scheme for Stepney developed the idea of full social services on a community and neighbourhood basis. Dwellings were shown in the form of mixed development of flats and houses at a density of 136 persons to the acre; but not only was the three-dimensional form somewhat regimented in character, it inevitably lacked an adequate basis of survey. The planning was, however, comprehensive and bold, and presented a fine background from which further studies could take place.

The South Bank plan, too, was bold in conception, although somewhat disappointing in its three-dimensional detail. A broad green riverside garden was shown, with public buildings behind it, including, by the way, a theatre on the site where the Royal Festival Hall now stands. This scheme, too, formed a valuable background for comprehensive planning.

The most significant facts about these schemes were that they were part of an overall plan; that they were designed in time as well as space; and that they illustrated possible three-dimensional forms for large areas as a guide to development.

In 1944 the *Town and Country Planning Act* set out the procedure for Reconstruction Areas, whereby a Planning Authority could define a Designated Area, so as to deal comprehensively with blitzed and blighted areas.

It was under this Act that, in 1947, the L.C.C. created the *Stepney-Poplar* Reconstruction Area, and, in 1949, the *Bermondsey* Reconstruction Area; while the City Corporation, following the advice of their Consultants, in 1948, defined the major blitzed areas in the *City*. (The City Corporation was the Planning Authority for the City of London until the 1947 Act came into operation.) These procedural actions enabled a much greater control to be maintained over the blitzed areas, and enabled land to be acquired for broad planning purposes rather than for specific reasons (i.e. housing, education, etc.). The Town and Country Planning Act of 1947 not only made the submission of a Development Plan obligatory, but also enabled Planning Authorities to define areas of *Comprehensive* Development (a similar but more flexible idea than Reconstruction Areas). The Administrative County of London Development Plan of 1951 followed up the County of London Plan with a far more detailed study, and presented a broad but definite framework for the development of London over the next twenty years. The Development Plan Analysis stated that some 100 areas stood in need of comprehensive treatment; but in fact, owing to the financial liability likely to be incurred, only the eight most urgent areas were selected to be dealt with as Comprehensive Development Areas under the procedure of the Town and Country Planning Act of 1947. The Programme Map of the Development Plan did, however, throw up a clear picture of the areas most in need of redevelopment over the Country as a whole.

The eight areas selected included not only the *City* areas, *Stepney-Poplar* and *Bermondsey* (which had already been designated under the Town and Country Planning

Act of 1944), but also the *South Bank* and the *Elephant and Castle*, both areas of special character and interest in terms of urban reconstruction.

The first thing to bear in mind is the scale and complexity of the work of the Comprehensive Redevelopment of blitzed and blighted areas.

The Stepney-Poplar area alone, which has Lansbury and St Anne's as two of its neighbourhoods, has an area of nearly 2,000 acres with a planned population of some 100,000. A description of the main proposals was, of course, given in the section of the Development Plan Analysis on Comprehensive Development Areas, but as the work of implementation has developed, new techniques and procedures have been evolved which may eventually amount to an original contribution in the rebuilding of cities.

At the beginning of 1949 the Architect to the London County Council (then Robert Matthew)[1] set up a new Reconstruction Areas Group under my charge, within his Department's Planning Division, which was directed by Arthur Ling, to deal with this exceptional problem. The new Group's most pressing task was in connection with Neighbourhood 9 (or Lansbury) in the Stepney-Poplar Reconstruction Area, as it had been decided to develop the first stage of this neighbourhood for the Festival of Britain Exhibition of Live Architecture.

The Area was intended to be a kind of planning laboratory wherein the experience gained could be used not only in the rest of the Reconstruction Area, but throughout the County of London.

STEPNEY-POPLAR. This Area is an extremely complex one which possesses all the serious major defects to which attention was drawn in the County of London Plan. These include excessive density, over-crowding, and obsolescence of existing housing; lack of open space; intermixture of users, particularly with housing; and traffic congestion. In addition to these defects, the area was subject to extremely heavy war damage. The Council approved an average residential density of 136 persons per acre, which by 1971, when the major part of the redevelopment should have taken place, would, it was estimated, result in a total population of approximately 100,000. This compared with a 1951 population of 107,000, and a population in 1939 of 217,000. The overspill in this area would therefore amount to no more than 7,000. The drop in population since 1939 was accounted for almost entirely by war-time conditions, when people moved out of the area to other parts and never returned.

The area was replanned as a series of eleven neighbourhood units each containing its own community, educational, and shopping facilities. The shops were grouped into compact units forming either main or local shopping centres. These centres were designed in the form of precincts, off main traffic roads but adjacent to them. Their location was based on established concentrations of shops, for example, Chrisp Street and Watney Street, although most shops had been distributed along the main roads, or isolated within residential areas.

The area was seriously deficient in open space; there was only 0·52 acre per 1,000 persons compared with an ultimate provision of 3·6 acres per 1,000 persons and an interim objective of 2·15 acres per 1,000 persons. Most of the existing open space consisted of disused burial grounds and small squares, King Edward VII Memorial Park being the only area of open space of any considerable size.

[1] Professor Sir Robert Matthew, Head of the Department of Architecture in the University of Edinburgh.

The open-space proposals envisaged a distribution of small and large areas to cater respectively for the local needs of the neighbourhoods and for people living over a wider area. The most important of these larger areas was the broad belt of open space proposed to link the southern parts of Stepney with Victoria Park to the north. Included in this proposal was King George's Fields, of which 18 acres have already been laid out. The new open space system was to be linked together by green walks.

The problem of the existing intermixture of users is necessarily a difficult and expensive one to solve and the Comprehensive Development Area map indicated detailed zoning proposals for the area. The industrial zones were mainly located along the banks of the canals or near the docks, where many industries were already established. Certain areas of land, however, were set aside to accommodate nonconforming industrial users which would be disturbed by redevelopment and which were considered to be tied to London. Similar proposals were made for dealing with commercial and office users.

The proposals for reducing traffic congestion in the area indicated a considerable reduction in the number of intersections, particularly with regard to the number of minor roads abutting on to main roads. The major intersections included schemes at Gardiner's Corner (Aldgate), and the Rotherhithe Tunnel and Blackwall Tunnel approaches. Widening of most of the main routes was proposed, but this programme was of necessity long term.

The existing road network was quite irrational and wasteful of land; the new development was consequently planned on much larger and economical units of land than was previously the case. In all new development proper parking and unloading facilities were insisted upon unless it was quite impracticable to do so.

Progress. The first Compulsory Purchase Order was made in 1949 in respect of the Lansbury Area under the Town and Country Planning Act of 1944. Subsequent Orders have been made under the Town and Country Planning Act, 1947, and the Housing Act, 1936. By 1956 compulsory Purchase Orders had been confirmed over 165 acres in Stepney and 125 acres in Poplar, making a total of 290 acres (gross, i.e. including 20 feet of surrounding roads). Post-war development completed or in hand in the same year was as follows: L.C.C. 148 acres, Borough Councils 51 acres, other developers 9 acres; total 208 acres (These figures include housing, schools, public buildings, shops and open space. They refer to *net* site areas.)

Planning of the area in detail has been proceeding continuously and a considerable amount of building work has been completed or is under construction at the moment. The first large area of land to be redeveloped comprehensively and on a neighbourhood basis was the first stage of the Lansbury neighbourhood. Although the layout for this area was prepared by the Architect's Department, the design of most of the buildings was undertaken by private architects appointed by the Council.

An overall three-dimensional plan of the whole neighbourhood was prepared, and was planned so that the maximum number of social facilities, such as nursery, primary and secondary schools, two churches, pedestrian shopping centre, public open space, etc., could be included in the first stage. The opportunity was also taken in Lansbury to provide the maximum number of different forms of dwelling (i.e. six- and three-storey flats,[1] four-storey maisonettes, three- and two-storey terrace houses, houses

[1] At this time the Housing Committee refused to allow any flats for the L.C.C. to exceed six storeys in height.

with flats over them, etc.) with a full provision of children's play-spaces for different ages. The three-dimensional relationship between the various buildings and their materials was also carefully considered, and every attempt was made to achieve an improved standard in the design and siting of street furniture and other design details.

The exhibition area of Lansbury was extremely valuable, not only in being able to show a 'live' prototype of neighbourhood development, but also as a useful experiment for social studies of various kinds by our own sociologist as well as by those outside (for example, Dr Ruth Glass and Mr Westergaard).

Since then all new development in the various neighbourhoods always proceeded on the basis of overall three-dimensional plans. In the case of Lansbury, for instance, this overall design was amended several times to ensure that it represented a contemporary potential architectural solution for the various types of building, as well as taking into account any zoning modifications. The important fact was that every development should take place in relation to a larger design. It should be remembered that the Stepney-Poplar Comprehensive Development Area alone was equivalent to one large town (100,000 population approximately) or two smaller ones; also that work could not always go on in a too well-defined survey-analysis-plan order, since development was proceeding all the time. However, with the statutory requirements already mentioned demanding surveys and plans to both 6-inch and 25-inch scale, with the neighbourhood studies at 1,250 and the housing layouts at 32nd scales (leading on finally to working drawings), it was possible to carry out interrelated analysis reviews on both small and large scales.

This co-ordination at different scales was paralleled by a co-ordination of all development in the area. In one neighbourhood, for instance, not only might the L.C.C. be carrying out housing, schools, shops and open-space schemes, but the Borough Council might also be undertaking housing and perhaps a Branch Library, in addition to providing street lighting, etc. The Police might also have a housing site, and there might be a number of private developers building churches, community halls, commercial and industrial buildings, etc., while the various statutory authorities might have a post office, electricity sub-stations, and other types of buildings.

The evolution of housing layouts in the Comprehensive Development Areas naturally reflected the various experiments in flat and house design of recent years, and the close team work between planning and housing staffs ensured continuity from small-scale zoning plans right up to working drawings. The emerging forms of development which are now becoming the chief design elements are tall towers of flats set well apart and, wherever possible, integrated in an open-space system, with the main accommodation provided in four-storey maisonettes, which lend themselves well to a modern interpretation of the traditional British square. Groups of larger dwellings in the form of two-storey houses have also been provided in the larger schemes.

The preparation of the Comprehensive Development Area zoning and programming plans to 25-inch scale as part of the Development Plan undoubtedly proved of great value. Although they are, of course, subject to amendment, and are not completely inflexible, their scale alone enabled a very clear and precise set of proposals to be drawn up, and a large number of difficulties were revealed and dealt with which would not have been the case if the scale had been smaller.

An interesting variation in the neighbourhood pattern has been the emergence of

St Anne's as a twelfth neighbourhood. Originally it was part of Neighbourhood 4, but as studies were developed it became apparent that it should have an entity of its own. Somewhat similar in size was Neighbourhood 1, which had as a feature the Jewish shopping street of Hessell Street, eventually to be rebuilt as a pedestrian shopping centre.

The Group's sociologist (Miss Willis)[1] made studies of various kinds throughout the Comprehensive Development Areas, and her work influenced the planning in various ways. In addition to careful social studies of each neighbourhood, she undertook studies of particular subjects, such as shops and shopping habits, which caused ideas on the location of shops to be varied considerably.

In addition to the problems within the neighbourhoods there were the other major uses, such as communications, open spaces, industry and commerce. Railways remained more or less static (as have the statutory services), and road projects until recently were curtailed by Government limitation. A good deal of land has, however, been bought for safeguarding, as it has also been purchased for the accommodation of nonconforming industries.

SOUTH BANK. The area known as the South Bank lay along the Thames between Vauxhall and Southwark bridges. Much of it consists of low-lying land. Two railway viaducts cut across the northern part of the area and lead to Charing Cross and Blackfriars railway stations. There was an intermixture of commercial, industrial and residential users, and much of the property was obsolescent. The pre-war tendency of development to migrate to the south side of the river resulted in the erection of such buildings as W. H. Smith & Sons' offices, Waterloo Bridge House, Dorset House, etc., which, together with County Hall, formed a nucleus of improved development.

The South Bank was proposed as the southward extension of the central area of London. The intentions of the proposals were to improve traffic conditions; to allocate areas for central and local government purposes and for cultural, office, commercial and industrial uses; and to provide public open space combined with an extension of the river wall, with public buildings as the background.

The area can be roughly divided into five sectors: Albert Embankment, St Thomas's Hospital precinct, Permanent Development Scheme including County Hall, the area between Waterloo and Blackfriars bridges, and Bankside (between Blackfriars and Southwark bridges).

Albert Embankment is a narrow strip of land between the river and the railway viaduct. The main objective was to create along this important reach, a new river frontage consisting of co-ordinated office buildings with a high tower at the far end. This involved a series of prolonged negotiations with individual developers and re-resulted in the construction of a number of ten-storey office buildings of somewhat uneven architectural quality.

[1] Miss Margaret Willis was, regrettably, one of the very few Sociologists to be employed as a member of a planning team engaged on comprehensive redevelopment. She carried out a large number of studies while she was a member of the Reconstruction Areas Group, of which the following are a selection:

Play Areas (1951), Sandpits (1951), Laundries (1951), Amenity Open Spaces (1951), Living in High Flats (1951), Maisonettes (1952), Three-Storey Houses (1952), Living in a Layout (1952), Housing Needs of Single Persons (1953), Social Aspects of Space around Flats (1953), and Studies on Lansbury (1953).

St Thomas's Hospital Precinct. Negotiations took place with the Governors of St Thomas's Hospital—*via* their architect and their surveyor—in order to achieve a comprehensive development of this area. Part of this was a new block of flats east of Lambeth Palace Road erected by the Hospital for tenants disturbed by the scheme. Special importance was attached to the co-ordinated treatment of the Westminster Bridge approach and the immediate surroundings of the proposed roundabout.

Development Area. The total length of the South Bank Comprehensive Development Area runs from Vauxhall Bridge right down to Southwark Bridge, but, thanks to the Festival of Britain, 1951, the sector between County Hall and Waterloo Bridge is the part the public knows as South Bank, and is, of course, the sector in which comprehensive central-area planning was concentrated. In developing the three-dimensional overall plans for the South Bank scheme a number of main principles were followed. First, that the broad strip of open space along the river bank should be enlarged in depth at certain places so as not to create a continuous wall of building. Second, that the buildings immediately behind the open space should be of a lively character; and here the Royal Festival Hall was an excellent beginning. Third, that the buildings should, as far as possible, be grouped round squares or places. Fourth, that only one high building should be allowed in the immediate vicinity, the rest conforming generally to the existing basic height level (approximately 100 feet). Fifth, that communication should be at different levels, and that adequate car parking should be provided.

Although an interim layout was designed and carried out after the Festival of Britain was over, detailed plans for the permanent layout were only begun in earnest after the Government decided to forego its interest in having office buildings on the site.

The main users were provisionally as follows:

Private Office Buildings. It was decided that private office buildings should be restricted to the area behind Belvedere Road, and in fact the Shell Company took both the large sites above and below the Charing Cross railway viaduct.

National Theatre. The National Theatre was originally proposed on the site between the Festival Hall and Waterloo Bridge, but by agreement its location was moved to one adjacent to County Hall, thus leaving space for a Cultural Centre on its former site.

Hotel. It was thought that a hotel could well be situated across the railway viaduct from the Festival Hall.

Science Centre. The Government announced its intention of creating a Science Centre down-river from Waterloo Bridge, but later withdrew. The L.C.C. recently proposed that it should be redeveloped with a hotel and conference centre.

B.E.A. Terminal. British European Airways thought they would like to have an Air Terminal somewhere near where they were temporarily housed, in the Festival of Britain's Station Gate Building (although they changed their minds later on and decided to move to Kensington).

L.C.C. The L.C.C. was scheduled to complete its north block of offices along Chicheley Street, and all the land between York Road and Waterloo Station was proposed for offices.

From these basic decisions as to the chief uses, the three-dimensional designing developed.

Two main Places were developed on the 'upstream' site: one formed by the new County Hall offices, the Shell offices, offices on the further side of York Road, and the National Theatre, with the Air Terminal at a lower level in the middle; the other opening off the river bank, flanked by the proposed hotel and the National Theatre, and closed by the Shell offices. On this latter site it was proposed that the high building should be sited, which would give it a fine view right across the river. 'Downstream' were to be two smaller places of a less prominent character.

The communications were designed in three levels: there was to be main access at ground level, with an upper pedestrian walk-way (already begun in the Festival Hall terrace) and a basement car-parking level. Thus, in addition to parking space within each building (a normal L.C.C. planning requirement), most of the ground beneath the sites was to be excavated for parking.

An interesting aspect of the creation of the overall scheme was the way in which the design evolved. In certain parts of the area the building form already existed, i.e. the Royal Festival Hall, County Hall, Waterloo Station, and the new river wall. On the other sites the building programme was known and the architect chosen, i.e. the National Theatre. In others again this stage had not been reached, and it was therefore necessary for the planners to work out possible building programmes and potential designs. To ensure that these represented the best current development, at least a dozen alternatives were considered, for instance, for the design of the hotel before the proposal on the model was agreed.

On this part of the South Bank, the London County Council had the great advantage of owning all the land, thus giving landlord control in addition to planning control. In other sectors of the area co-ordination of a kind was obtained by negotiation, notably for instance, in the case of the prominent office area facing the river along the Albert Embankment, where a number of large office buildings have been built.

Problems of Implementation. The proposals described above were made public in 1953. As with the other Reconstruction projects, all kinds of problems emerged in endeavouring to turn the plans into reality. First, British European Airways decided to build their Air Terminal elsewhere, and the South Bank lost the possibility of becoming a nodal point for communications. After many tests, too, it was decided that the site was unsuitable for the landing of helicopters, on grounds of noise[1].

The first large building to be erected after the scheme was published was the London County Council's extension to the North Block of its own Headquarters; this was an odd looking affair which endeavoured to echo the highly individual form of the original main building, naturally without success. Then came the *cause célèbre* of the Shell Building. As has been explained, the great oil firm of Shell leased both upstream and downstream office sites. In the comprehensive design we suggested one tall, light and graceful tower with the rest of the development in long eleven-storey blocks in order to meet the very high plot ratio, which had been decided some years before. The form of these office buildings was not very satisfactory, although we tried dozens of alternatives for the two sites, but we did at least envisage that the whole complex would be built in a light airy and graceful manner. I had recently visited Rio de Janeiro and had been much impressed with the Ministry of Education building there, with its graceful,

[1] The L.C.C. carried out an extensive research study into the problems of the intensity of traffic noise.

glass walled tower standing on tall slender columns. It was this kind of architecture that we had in mind at the time—something that would express frankly the new structural techniques of today.

As it finally appeared on the site, the Shell building complex was a deep disappointment to us all. The bulk of the building blocks had been considerably increased, the considerable amount of open ground floor below the buildings had been filled in, while the architectural design went backwards instead of forwards for its inspiration. There is no doubt, however, that a high standard of internal working conditions has been achieved, and this includes a large indoor swimming pool and other amenities.

In so far as the riverside buildings are concerned, the National Theatre remained on paper for several years owing to lack of money, but recently the Government agreed to give financial support to the venture. Across the broad Place the site reserved for an hotel failed to find a developer and is now reserved for an Opera House. Below the railway viaduct, in the Royal Festival Hall sector, exciting developments are taking place. In 1961 the Council announced that the Hall itself would be considerably extended and that the Cultural Centre, which had been proposed adjacent to it, would be carried out. The latter is to include a small Concert Hall for 1,100 people and a large Exhibition Gallery. At the ground floor level, car parking for 170 cars is to be provided under the Gallery, and the total cost of this fine example of civic patronage will be approximately £3,704,000. The extensions to the Festival Hall are now complete.

A further development on the down-river side of Waterloo Bridge was also proposed in the form of a competition among private developers for an entertainment complex, to include a large hotel, restaurants, a convention centre and an art school.

At the same time as these new building projects are in progress it is also proposed to carry out the great riverside park as a broad pedestrian esplanade. Across Westminster Bridge Road from the County Hall, St Thomas's Hospital has a big redevelopment project in progress. The existing road to the east of the Hospital has been swung back to give more space for hospital rebuilding, and in addition to the large residential block already mentioned the Hospital Board has promoted a large office group immediately to its north.

Thus in a few years' time, and certainly within the twenty-year planning period, almost the whole stretch of the South Bank from the far side of Waterloo Bridge upstream as far as Vauxhall Bridge will have been redeveloped. Looking back, it is now clear that the Government allowed the London County Council too little money for road proposals, with the result that there will be a series of obsolete roundabouts; that the Plot Ratio was not reduced soon enough, and thus permitted an over-development of office buildings; and that there is too little architecture of high quality appear- in the Comprehensive Area. One of the best buildings, apart from the Royal Festival Hall, is in fact the National Film Theatre, which is rather like a soft shelled crab, being entirely contained within the abutments of Waterloo Bridge; but there is still time and the opportunity for a fine recovery to be made, of which the latest proposals for the National Theatre/Opera House complex give promise.

ELEPHANT AND CASTLE. The *Elephant and Castle* is the name given to the district around an important road junction south of the Thames, where the roads from Lambeth, Westminister, Waterloo and Blackfriars bridges converge, before joining the Kent Road. It is called after a famous coaching inn that stood at the junction.

The land around the Elephant and Castle was in a good location for development as a valuable business centre, and about 31 acres were defined as an area of comprehensive development. The main object was to take advantage of the extensive bomb damage to create a new centre for this part of London by a development surrounded on the east, west and south by buildings of similar height, and on the north by an imposing tall building worthy of this position. In addition, there was the problem of assimilating the existing important buildings which were to be retained. These were the 'Trocadero' and 'Elephant and Castle' cinemas and the Metropolitan Tabernacle. The cinemas, which were on the periphery of the design, were brought into the new scheme. The Tabernacle was in a prominent position opposite the main shopping concourse, and was brought into relationship with the proposed buildings on either side by incorporating it as a feature in a continuous frontage.

Consideration was given to complete pedestrian segregation at a lower level, passing below the roads, and excavating the roundabout (the Ministry of Transport had insisted on a one-level roundabout traffic solution on grounds of cost), but this again was turned down on the grounds of the high cost of excavation. In the end we had to be satisfied with the provision of new subways connecting the individual sites adjoining the roundabouts. It was also suggested that a direct link between the two shopping centres might be provided by means of a pedestrian way crossing the large roundabout at subway level.

Banks, public houses and one branch post office had to be provided and were to be distributed through the development. Developers were in certain cases to be asked to accommodate one or more of these uses on their sites and in most cases to incorporate them into the buildings. Developers were to be required to provide adequate parking space, in accordance with the Council's standards.

On the new public-buildings site on the west of Newington Butts the Southwark Metropolitan Borough Council were considering the erection of a building to contain a swimming pool, with subsidiary sports facilities, and a restaurant overlooking the extended open space to the south.

Only part of the land was in the ownership of the Council. To secure the comprehensive development of the area compulsory purchase orders have been submitted from time to time to the Minister of Housing and Local Government for confirmation.

Problems of Implementation. The Elephant and Castle C.D.A. got off to a slow start. Even the obsolete road layout was not completed until nearly six years after the design project was published. In the early 1950s no private developer was willing to risk money in the hinterland of South London when there were so many profitable sites to exploit in the West End. The L.C.C. became worried and decided to pump-prime the operation. The London College of Printing, which had been originally sited at the south end of the area, was moved up to the west side of the main roundabout, and an excellent design was prepared by the Schools Division of the Architect's Department. On the now vacant site the L.C.C. decided to build a high-density housing scheme, consisting of one high tower and lower flanking buildings (all appartment dwellings). When interest in the area had thus been revived by public enterprise, the L.C.C. then held limited competitions for the other available sites. The first was for the commercial area on the north-east, which included the Trocadero Cinema as an apparently fixed element. The competition was won by a boldly designed scheme submitted by the well known architect Mr Erno Goldfinger. Most unexpectedly, the Cinema has now been demolished, and this is obviously of great benefit to the overcrowded group to the north of it (the 5 : 1 Plot Ratio was regrettably retained). A third limited competition was held for the central shopping centre site, where it had been agreed that the Elephant and Castle cinema would now disappear (the only one of the pre-war buildings in the Area to be kept is the Tabernacle, which has recently been reconditioned—it was, incidentally, once the venue of the great revivalist preacher Spurgeon). This last and most important proposal was won by the outstanding young architectural firm of Messrs Boissevain and Osmond (readers may remember it was as Associates of this firm that Messrs Buchanan and I worked on the Berlin Competition, described in Chapter 3). Although again too much development has been crowded on to the site (over 200,000 square feet of shop space and 87,900 square feet of offices) this too should be an extremely interesting building. The shopping centre is planned on three levels, with a great glass-roofed arcade rising through two floors as its main feature. The arcade is cruciform in plan (similar in this respect to the Galleria in Milan) and its roof is designed to slide back in fine weather. Above the shopping area an office block is sited which is 170 feet high. There will be car parking for 154 cars in two basement levels.

Thus the late sixties should see most of the Elephant and Castle area redeveloped with a number of first-rate buildings. Looking back on the story of this area, one sees it before the war as a classic example of nineteenth—and early twentieth—century urban muddle, with main traffic arteries being choked at a nodal point by perimeter commercial development along all road frontages. In the County of London Plan it was treated to an academic exercise in 'grand manner' planning, with a vast public building surrounded by a hexagonal roundabout, the roads being lined with perimeter development. When we were considering its future during the preparation of the 1951 Development Plan, Arthur Ling and I suggested that it might be turned into a bold multi-level inter-section of a parkway type. This proposal met with favour neither from the traffic experts on financial grounds nor from the property experts on grounds of the potential loss of property values. Once, in fact, the Ministry of Transport had insisted on a one-level roundabout solution and the property experts had pressed for perimeter redevelopment of the adjacent sites, the whole terms of reference were inimical to a contemporary solution. There were also difficulties presented by substantial existing buildings, coupled with the unwillingness of the L.P.T.B.[1] to pay for the combining of their two separate underground stations and surface ticket offices into one. The 1953 scheme therefore could only be based on creating some degree of order in development, with one high building acting as a focal point: even the modest proposals for a lower level pedestrian connecting walkway were turned down (one must remember the financial stringency of the early 1950s), although the usual unattractive pedestrian tunnels were permitted.

A series of decisions made by the L.C.C. (taken after I had handed over responsibility for the area to Mr Gordon Logie, who took charge of the C.D.A.s south of the Thames in the reorganization of the Planning Division in 1956) changed the whole character of the scheme, and in fact made it an attractive proposition for development. First came the decision to site the London School of Printing as a prestige building in

[1] The London Passenger Transport Board.

a prominent site with a tower some 170 feet high, and to redevelop the site thus left vacant with a prominent housing block over 200 feet in height. Then came the series of limited competitions for the commercial sites, each producing bold and interesting buildings. At this stage there is no doubt that the L.C.C. should have gone for an upper-level deck right across all the arterial roads, but cost was still a paralysing factor. As it now stands, the scheme, instead of having one tall tower with a surrounding group of buildings of modest and ordered height, has a cluster of tall blocks of varying height, looking down on what will undoubtedly be a hopelessly congested traffic intersection. It is too reminiscent of Fifth Avenue in New York, where some of the world's finest and most expensive office buildings are so crowded along a corridor street that they fail to add up to a satisfactory total urban design solution.

BUNHILL FIELDS. The area is 41·53 acres. It suffered extensive war damage (73 per cent.), and immediately adjoins the City of London's Barbican Area. Before the war, the greater part of the area was divided among the following users: industrial, 16·41 acres; commercial, 13·37 acres; and residential, 6·34 acres. This accounted for 36·21 acres, and the remaining land was occupied by shops, schools, public buildings, and various other users.

The provision of residential accommodation was substantially increased to 14·53 acres, divided into three sites by Golden Lane and Whitecross Street. The western portion (Goswell Road to Golden Lane) has been developed by the Corporation of the City of London; the first stage of their Golden Lane Housing Scheme is completed and the second stage is now approaching completion. Work on the central portion (the greater part of the land between Golden Lane and Whitecross Street) is also completed in so far as existing tenement blocks permit; the scheme in this case is sponsored by the Peabody Fund. The eastern portion (Whitecross Street to Burnhill Row) is not cleared to the same extent as the others. Approximately half is owned by the Peabody Donation Fund and a number of their pre-war flats will remain. Those destroyed by enemy action have now been replaced by a single block which is erected and occupied, and forms the first stage of the Fund's ultimate redevelopment proposals which are unlikely to be carried out for some years.

The greater part of the 4·75 acres proposed for offices was in the vicinity of Chiswell Street and buildings were erected on the northern frontage, and in Bunhill Row. On the south side of Chiswell Street, another building is complete and schemes for the redevelopment of two large, cleared street blocks are under consideration. They have been designed to form an extension to the Joint London County Council and City detailed proposals for the Barbican Area to the south. The other office zones front on City Road and part of Goswell Road are in various stages of redevelopment.

The proposals envisaged the retention of the existing commercial development fronting on Old Street and rebuilding on cleared sites. Most of the shops in Whitecross Street escaped war damage and they will be retained as the main shopping area. Rebuilding has been taking place only as opportunities occur. In addition provision was made for one new school and the ultimate rebuilding and extension of two others.

Although acquisition of land is bound to be the most satisfactory method of solving the problems implicit in comprehensive development areas, experience in the Bunhill Fields Area showed that a degree of comprehensive development can be reached with the co-operation of owners, when it is forthcoming. Even so, much depends on the quality of the architects they employ, and their willingness to collaborate in urban design.

BARBICAN. The City Corporation and the L.C.C. were since 1947 jointly responsible for planning in the City of London. In April 1947 the planning consultants for the City, Dr C. H. Holden and Professor W. G. Holford,[1] presented their Final Report on Reconstruction in the City of London. In this they recommended the Court of Common Council to proceed with the application for a Declaratory Order under section 1 (1) of the Town and Country Planning Act, 1944, in respect of certain specific areas which had suffered extensive war damage together with minor contiguous areas to round off or complete the irregular boundaries.

The Minister made, on December 13th, 1948, the City of London Declaratory Order, 1948, in respect of 231 acres of the 272 acres applied for. In the Development Plan an area of approximately 244 acres was defined within the City of London as an Area of Comprehensive Development. After considerable pressure from the L.C.C., the City Corporation and the L.C.C. jointly prepared certain comprehensive three-dimensional schemes as a guide to development. The largest was that for the heavily bombed *Barbican* area, which was situated north of the Guildhall between Aldersgate and Moorgate, and covered an area of some 40 acres. It was recognized that much of the area would inevitably be rebuilt by private developers, and one of the chief problems was to subdivide the area into usable units of property, each of which could provide a reasonable return on investment. At the same time, however, it was considered fundamental that proposals for the site should conform to, and create, an overall design which would be both bold and practical, giving the best conditions for work coupled with maximum efficiency. The plan was to be flexible in both time and space in that various detailed modifications could be made on individual sites as the Scheme developed, and it was comprehensive in that it would include all the blitzed land in the Barbican area.

The area was divided into 19·5 acres for offices, 3·4 acres for commerce, 11·25 acres for residential use with approximately 6 acres of open space. A wide range of ancillary uses was suggested, depending partly on the wishes and needs of the various developers. The office buildings were proposed mainly in the form of tall towers on the west, south and east of the area, all surrounded by plenty of light and air. Each of the towers was to rise from a generous site (unlike those of American cities), most of which was to be covered by a platform or slab which would consist of one high or two low storeys above ground and two storeys below ground. These platforms would contain entrance halls, shopping terraces and arcades, showrooms, cafés, restaurants, public houses and other facilities. Generous space would also be provided for garden and roof terraces, and great scope was thus given for imaginative architecture. It was also suggested that there should be pedestrian ways on and between all sites at an upper level.

The siting of the office towers was arranged so that the highest ones were furthest away from St Paul's, and also adjacent to the underground stations of Aldersgate and Moorgate (which have a considerable additional passenger-carrying capacity); while the lower ones were on both sides of Route 11, thereby opening up this important new thoroughfare and giving a fine feeling of space and openness.

The residential area (which in the beginning could be expanded or contracted in

[1] Now Professor Lord Holford.

accordance with decisions then not yet taken as to its ultimate size) was shown centred on St Giles' Church, mainly with six-storey maisonettes in traditional squares. This would not only give a precinctual atmosphere, but take advantage of the proposed open space around the church and along the bastions of the Roman Wall. Residential use, largely in the form of tall towers, was also suggested to the north between the Metropolitan Railway and the Barbican.

A public open space was already proposed in the Development Plan for the area adjacent to the Roman Wall bastions south of St Giles', and a large new open space could have been created over the Metropolitan Railway had it been roofed over. Also, the proposed tower form of development would enable a number of new private open spaces and roof terraces to be created, which should all give a greenness to the scheme comparable to the Temple or the Inns of Court.

The Corporation planned (and has since built) a garage under Route 11 for 268 vehicles and it was proposed that two-level garaging and car parking should be provided in all the larger sites. It was envisaged that the majority of the large developers would include shopping arcades and rows as part of the first-floor accommodation. An adequate number of cafés, restaurants and public houses was also proposed as part of this development at the upper level.

A considerable number of former building owners and intending developers had made enquiries as to the future of the area, and a considerable amount of negotiation took place to ensure that all development should take place in accordance with the comprehensive scheme.

Problems of Implementation. One of the great difficulties in regard to the three-dimensional scheme for the Barbican was the reluctance of the City Corporation to accept such a scheme at all. It was in fact only after the submission of an extremely interesting but abortive project prepared for a private group by Messrs Kadleigh, Horsburgh and Whitfield and the ensuing Public Enquiry, that it became obvious that there would have to be an official project. Even then full acceptance at the political level took some time to achieve, although the need for some overall scheme had become critical, when, with the Government's lifting of the ban on office buildings, developers began to submit proposals haphazardly throughout the area.

The first scheme, initiated by us in the London County Council and completed jointly with the City Corporation, was an essential working basis. Certain building proposals had already gone too far to revoke and these were accepted as part of the brief. Greatly daring, we had as a matter of planning policy[1] suggested that a residential neighbourhood be included even though the City Corporation, as potential land owner, would stand to lose a great deal of money on loss of land value. To its credit the Corporation invited the private firm of architects (Messrs Chamberlin, Powell and Bon) who had already been responsible for the Golden Lane Housing Scheme in Bunhill Fields, to prepare a scheme for the residential area. At once they saw that the area could be enlarged to great advantage and suggested including the proposed commercial development to the west. Although negotiations for the use of this site had

[1] In a recent visit to the United States, I observed that a similar planning policy of introducing high-density middle-income residential development in the renewal of near downtown blighted areas was being adopted in such cities as Philadelphia (Society Hill), Washington (Capitol Hill), Detroit (Gratiot) and San Fransisco (Golden Gate).

already taken place, the Corporation eventually accepted the change of use, and thus gave the opportunity of preparing a much better project for the residential neighbourhood. The scheme finally approved after many discussions with both London County Council and City Corporation planners, was integrated into the overall comprehensive design, particularly in regard to the upper level walkway system. Unfortunately the building of this important residential area was badly delayed owing to one or two controversial aspects of its design: one factor was that it involved moving a stretch of the Metropolitan railway (which the original studies were careful to leave alone), and another was the proposal to provide a large number of flats with internal kitchens, to which the London County Council Members took strong objection. The construction of part of the scheme, however, is now proceeding.

The original overall design, however, did a good deal more than provide a convenient and flexible framework for a residential neighbourhood. Probably its most important contribution was to illustrate the new principle of pedestrian segregation as applied to a commercial area. Right from the beginning we designed the area with a low plot ratio (3½ : 1 instead of the 5 : 1 proposed in the Holford/Holden Plan and retained in the 1951 Development Plan), and thereby enabled the main office accommodation to be provided in tall towers spaced well apart for light, air, and for the possibility of obtaining fine views from them. We also (and this was an idea frankly borrowed from the form of the Lever Building in New York) proposed that each tower should sit on a low base or podium, and that all the decks thus created should be interconnected, so as to provide a continuous upper-level walkway throughout the scheme. When an acceptable division of the land had been worked out the City Corporation had no difficulty in negotiating leases—leases which specified that each developer should provide an upper-level deck (with shops, public houses, etc., in accordance with the plan, and that they would accept a considerable degree of design control throughout. The main group of office towers was arranged on either side of the New Route 11, and the first to be erected was Moor House, a design which happily met the requirements in a sensible way. Since then four other towers with their decks have been built, and when the bridges are provided a major theoretical idea in the scheme will have achieved reality. You can actually walk round the area today and see a planning dream carried out in much the same way as it had originally been visualized.

ST PAUL'S PRECINCT. During the war the precincts of St Paul's were the subject of a latter-day essay in the classical manner by Royal Academy planners, and the outline proposals which emerged from the Holford/Holden Plan of 1947 were limited and dull in character. During the early fifties prolonged discussions took place between the planners of the City Corporation and the London County Council (although Arthur Ling as Senior Planning Officer was grappling with planning strategy over the whole of London, he nevertheless found time to take a leading and distinguished role in many of these complicated meetings with the City). The very difficult urban design problem presented by St Paul's obviously carried a powerful national and even international degree of public interest.

Eventually it was decided by the City Corporation in agreement with the L.C.C. to invite Sir William Holford to prepare a scheme for the Precinct. During its preparation he was to be guided by a lay committee consisting of the Minister of Housing and Local Government (then Mr Duncan Sandys), and both the Chairmen of the L.C.C.

and City Corporation Planning Committees. A number of well-known elder statesmen of the architectural and planning professions were invited by the Minister to give their views, and at one stage Sir William was under strong pressure to give St Paul's a 'St Peter's' type of forecourt. We were able to assist him in a minor way at this juncture by preparing a series of overlays showing how various types of cathedral forecourt would look in the context of St Paul's, and it was clear that while St Peter's was the wrong source of inspiration, the Duomo in Florence had remarkable similarities in scale and space relationship. Sir William's final design was an original and distinguished contribution, in spite of all the difficulties with which he had to contend. The Cathedral had always been closely (too closely) surrounded by commercial buildings, and while providing a large amount of new commercial accommodation he found it necessary to reduce the Plot Ratio (from 5 : 1 to 4·2 : 1), although not sufficiently, in my opinion. He did however solve the forecourt problem excellently, by proposing a solution which was harmonious in scale, formal in character, and yet asymmetrical in design. Perhaps the only feature open to serious criticism was a very tall office building as part of a great office complex on the north side of the Cathedral, and this was later reduced in height at the request of the Minister.

In providing an extensive upper deck in this office complex with two levels of car parking beneath it he also took the opportunity of giving it a dignified approach from the forecourt with a great flight of steps. The deck itself will ultimately join up with that now coming into existence in the Barbican area, which is some way to the north. Most of the buildings which will compose the Precinct design are now under construction, so that within a comparatively short period this scheme too will have achieved reality. Another adjacent development of comprehensive urban designing by the City Corporation and L.C.C. planners was attempted in the area between the St Paul's Precinct and the river, but this will involve extensive demolition of a large number of substantial commercial buildings, and its implementation is still in the future.

TOWER OF LONDON. The precincts of the historic Tower of London are almost as important to many thousands of the public as are those of St Paul's or Westminster Abbey (of this I was made acutely aware whenever I lectured on London in the United States of America). Owing to its proximity to the docks, however, the area had before the war reached a sad state of blight and urban squalor. Gallant efforts by public spirited citizens, led by the famous Rev. 'Tubby' Clayton of first World War Toc H fame, had made a beginning, notably in securing the removal of a large disfiguring warehouse between the Tower and the church of All Hallows, of which the Rev. Clayton was the incumbent. The bombing cleared away most of the adjacent warehouse buildings, but as with other areas, it was sporadic, and much unseemly urban muddle still remained. The urban design for this area was again the product of collaboration between the City Corporation and the L.C.C. planners of my Group (at this time the North-East London Group). Our general principles were basically to give this great and powerful historic monument a spacious and attractive setting, while still providing as much building accommodation as possible. One small open space existed on the north-west of the Tower in Trinity Square and we endeavoured to extend this eastwards along the north aspect and southwards down to the river to provide a great pedestrian terrace. The extensive car and coach parking was to be provided in a three-floor car park beyond the terrace, while above it would be an office building limited to 5 storeys (including a largely open ground floor) with a higher tower of 16 storeys set at the extreme westward end of the site and as far away from the Tower itself as possible. Behind the open space to the north we proposed a group of commercial buildings, with a multi-storey car park for 750 cars set well back, and as a pump-priming operation, a National school for the L.C.C. itself.

In this scheme we were constantly bedevilled by the road proposals. We would have liked to take the main east-west road, which had long been planned along the north side of the Tower (and which already existed, although in inadequate fashion) into a tunnel so that we could have had an uninterrupted pedestrian terrace around both west and northern sides, but again the cost of such an operation ruled it out.

The procedural problems involved in this comprehensive scheme should also be mentioned. In addition to the L.C.C. and City Corporation planners, Planning Committees, and associated Departments (e.g. Engineering Departments for Roads, Parks Department for open spaces, Valuer's Departments for property, etc.), there was the Stepney Borough Council, in which lay half of the area, the Keeper of the Tower and the Ministry of Works, the Port of London Authority, and the L.P.T.B. for the underground railway (who were proposing to move a station in the area). In addition to all these official bodies there was the Rev. Tubby Clayton himself, a formidable figure of great influence. Truly, planning in the modern city is very much a diplomatic activity, apart from the highly complex technical design problems involved.

PROBLEMS OF COMPREHENSIVE DEVELOPMENT. It is perhaps a truism to say that, just as the various rooms of a building have to be planned together, so do the buildings in a city. There is, in fact, a major design problem involved, and one in which time is as important as space.

The development of modern architectural design has demanded the maximum freedom for the evolution of new forms in various types of building, and in many cases each modern building has been a possible prototype of a new vernacular. It is still vitally important for an evolving architecture that as much tolerance in form is present in any building project as possible, but it is equally important that every building in an urban environment is considered as an integral part of a larger design. In any case, most new buildings in cities are built as infillings of vacant sites surrounded by existing buildings, which often create rigid conditions in terms of rights of property, daylight, and height limitations.

Town design, therefore, affects building design in a number of ways. It begins, as with building design, with several scientifically measurable controlling factors. There are the current planning controls of plot ratio, which limit the bulk of building, and day-lighting, which seek to ensure that no building will obstruct the daylight from another. There are car-parking standards, and also those necessitated by fire precautions. But then come the subtle, difficult problem of positive design. It is very important that tall buildings should be sited in certain places in a city and not in others, and that certain definite spatial urban forms be achieved. But the central area of a large city is very varied—more, or less, formality is demanded in the different parts; dignity and even solemnity may be required in one place, contrasted with informality and even surprise in another. There should be room for all kinds of visual effects, but not, of course, at the expense of the building designs themselves.

One could sum up by saying that the old Haussmann idea of rigid street façade control has given way to a more difficult, more flexible and more subtle process of design co-ordination of a great variety of spatial forms.

Private Developers. One of the key things in urban design is that the total design effect of a city should add up to much more than a simple sum of its individual buildings. Whether an area is cleared, partly built, or in need of redevelopment, the building or rebuilding will take place over a period, and each building can make a greater or lesser contribution. The experience in the London County Council's Comprehensive Development Areas has shown that the majority of individual developers and their architects are well aware of this, and hence come at an early stage to discuss the planning implications before proceeding too far with building design.

In some cases the decision of the first developer to build is the moment for the planners to treat the whole surrounding area as a priority design problem, and the first buildings in a comprehensive area naturally have a considerable influence on the later ones. One good planning application, too, can often help greatly to stimulate development where it is most required.

Aesthetic Control. Aesthetic, including 'elevational', control was probably one of the most vexed of post-war planning problems, as it was only too easy for planners to take up an arbitrary and even unjustified attitude to architectural design. This does not mean, however, that the problem does not exist today, as a visit to almost any nineteenth- or twentieth-century city bears witness.

The important thing is that experienced and imaginative designers should be thinking and working on the larger problem of town design. If the broad ideas of these designers are in harmony with those of the best contemporary architects, then any aesthetic problems which arise can be resolved in a spirit of team work between architects and planners, since the best architects always see their buildings as part of a larger design and not as isolated monuments to themselves.

Multi-level Zoning and Communications. Any scheme of urban design today is inevitably the product of the minds of many experts, the major task of the planners being one of co-ordination and integration, and no plan can be judged finally until at least the larger part of it has achieved three dimensions. It is, in fact, possible for a plan to be fairly successful in two dimensions and a failure in three. Zoning is a case in point: it is an invaluable guide, but the Use Zone chart itself is a reminder that flexibility in interpretation is essential.

In the Barbican, for instance, it was proposed that office towers should rise over low slabs whose upper floors would consist of shops, canteens and similar uses, while the lower underground floors would be car-parks and storage rooms.

Communications, too, as has already been indicated, were proposed at different levels. London has, of course, one of the oldest examples of this in evidence in its overhead railway system, and in proposing two levels of vehicular circulation, and yet another for pedestrians, the Comprehensive Development Area proposals were only extending an idea with a long precedent.

Design Details in the Urban Scene. One of the most distressing facts of the present-day urban scheme has been the unco-ordinated medley of often badly designed articles of what is known as 'street furniture'. Around almost any important road junction one may see street lamps, bus signs, direction signs, telephone boxes, pillar boxes, police kiosks, litter baskets, and so on, scattered about in an incoherent way.

Determined efforts were made in the Reconstruction Areas to ensure that both the design of these various articles should be of a high standard and that their siting should be co-ordinated. Lansbury was a good example: in the Live Architecture area, a prolonged search was made for a well-designed lamp-post of standard make, and although the one selected has faults, it was the best available at the time. The difficulty of designing a special one is, of course, that manufacturers require a very large order before they will undertake to make them at a reasonable price. Then, their siting was carefully considered, in collaboration with the Borough Councils, whose responsibility they were (the Borough Councils concerned with the C.D.A.s were nearly always extremely co-operative). At the same time the siting of other standard articles was worked out on a large model with the various authorities responsible—full collaboration was achieved, for instance, with the Post Office on telephone kiosks and pillar boxes, with the various architects in regard to boundary walls and railings, and with the others concerned. Later, for the South Bank, a special lamp-standard was designed by a young member of the Group, in collaboration with L.C.C. electrical engineers.

In regard to trees, which are so scarce in cities today, every effort was made to preserve those existing on sites or roads which were being closed, and, of course, new ones are being planted throughout the Areas. The failure of the L.C.C. to undertake large-scale planting of mature trees was very unfortunate.

Finance of Redevelopment. A complete book could be written by the financial and land acquisition experts on the particular problems presented by the C.D.A.s, and the closest collaboration between them and the planners is obviously essential. A few comments from the planning point of view only can be mentioned.

Although the Minister of Housing and Local Government in the first instance authorized high-percentage grants for C.D.A.s, (since modified to a lower scale), he restricted compulsory acquisition largely to those heavily damaged areas where the local authority was proposing to develop in the immediate future; in addition, the process of acquisition has proved to be long and involved, so that, combined with the various restrictions on capital expenditure, redevelopment, apart from housing, has in many cases been slower than might have been expected. It has, too, been rather sporadic visually, and even now only an aerial view of the East End of London shows how much is actually completed or under construction.

Under the planning Acts, too, the planners, valuers and other local authority officers are faced with long preparation for, and appearance at, Public Enquiries, which must always precede compulsory acquisition. Having purchased land, however, the local authority, where it is not itself the developer, is in a position to ensure that the best form of development takes place, by means of 'landlord', as well as normal, planning control. Where co-ordinated development of a number of sites is taking place this is obviously a great advantage, as the historical case of the great West End estates, and the more recent Hampstead Garden Suburb and the Garden Cities have shown.

It is not always realized what an enormous capital sum has been spent in the past on underground services. This problem is perhaps more acute in London than in other cities, for the scale is so much larger. A comparatively unimportant road may carry underneath it trunk electricity or telephone cables, large-diameter sewers and gas conduits, or even hydraulic or gas liquor mains, while there is also the underground railway system as an additional complicating factor.

This problem accentuates the difference between redeveloping the existing city and creating the new town, for in many cases any alteration in the layout of these existing services is a prohibitively expensive matter. The actual siting of buildings is thus conditioned in no small way by this unseen factor, for it is one which cannot be ignored.

Social Studies and Sociological Advice. An important contribution which influenced the planning of the Comprehensive Areas was made by our Group's sociologist, Miss Willis. For the first time a sociologist was employed continuously as part of a planning team. Her task was two-fold: to find out social facts about the Areas and to prepare reports on them, and to advise the planners in the day-to-day work. Her reports dealt with a wide variety of problems, and in addition, she carried out a number of studies on housing problems of various kinds as the various housing experiments developed.

Different Scales of Planning. For planning to be completely successful, it is necessary that there should be a relationship starting from the region, continuing through the city, community, neighbourhood, right on to the completed individual dwelling. The need for this can be appreciated most easily in the case of dwellings, since the determination of various densities will decide whether there is to be a decentralization problem, what proportion of the dwellings can be in houses or flats, and so on.

The basic Development Plan zoning map is to a scale of 6 inches to 1 mile, and determines the main land uses. The legal Comprehensive Development plans are 25 inches to 1 mile, and use zoning becomes much more precise. At the next scale, 1/1,250, the basic Ordinance scale for urban areas, the three-dimensional relationship between buildings can be clearly determined. Then comes $\frac{1}{32}$ inch to 1 foot, where architectural design really begins, and so on up to full size.

An important part of the process of planning has been the designing, checking and reviewing of schemes at different scales. In the case of the South Bank, for instance, it was necessary to work out preliminary possible designs for buildings at $\frac{1}{16}$ inch to 1 foot in order to prepare the smaller scale-model, and in the same way the small-scale zoning is revised after the larger scales have thrown up the need for variation.

Planning Procedure. It is important to remember that the London County Council had a large number of Departments, and the procedure involved in preparing a plan and putting it into execution is worth mentioning. Every single action had to be taken by means of reports to various Committees, and in a neighbourhood where there were houses, open spaces and schools, four or five Committees would probably be concerned, the Finance Committee along with the others. The Architect's Department, too, was not the only one concerned; there were also the Controller's (Finance), the Chief Engineer's, the Valuer's and other Departments. It was necessary for the staff to co-ordinate ideas before schemes were submitted to Committees. The London County Council Committees made the decision, but beyond them were the controls exercised by the Government Departments. Nothing could be done until the money was forthcoming from the Treasury, and the Treasury acted on the advice of the relevant Ministries. On planning generally, among other authorities which had to be consulted were the General Post Office, which was interested in the siting of Post

Offices, Telephone Exchanges and the laying of telecommunications and cables; the London Transport Board for underground railways, bus routes, etc.; and the Regional Boards controlling gas, electricity, water and railways. Then there were the Borough Councils doing fifty per cent of the housing, and with powers over street lighting, minor roads, etc. Finally there were various voluntary bodies. Altogether the time between first conceiving the idea and actually getting a brick on the ground was apt to be long, and one difficulty was to keep a continuation of thought over the necessary period. The War Damage Act, the Distribution of Industries Act, and other legislation had to be kept in mind. There were the many technical problems concerned with applying planning principles of such matters as density, floor space, types and distance of open spaces, shopping centres, and these had all to be considered at each scale and stage of the plan.

A very important matter was that of trying to explain to the people generally what planning was about and how it would make their lives happier. It was vitally important to get the people to interest themselves and learn how planning affected them socially and economically. It is too easy for architects to feel that architecture is the centre of the drama, but it is essential for the experts to realize that *people* are the centre and architecture the stage setting.

War damage and blight often consisted of small isolated plots so that no large-scale reconstruction could be carried out at once, and where a large area was to be cleared there were always blocks of property that had been left standing, and it took time to get rid of them. Plans must be comprehensive, but they must be flexible.

CONCLUSIONS. First: the London County Council's experience was generally that, under the economy existing in this country, the current planning procedure has much to recommend it, although it tends to be over-complicated and slow. Also, the ability to acquire large areas of land, and hence achieve landlord, in addition to planning, control, can be of great assistance to the replanning of an area.

Second: the planning of such areas should form an integral part of a broader general Development Plan.

Third: having carried out surveys and analyses, there yet remains the vital task of three-dimensional urban design. This should deal with the problems of time while remaining flexible in spatial form. Thus, although only great architects can achieve great architecture, this broad design approach can do a great deal to ensure a standard of order and fitness in cities, in contrast to the urban chaos to which we are only too accustomed.

Fourth: the work involved demands a high degree of group or team work over a considerable period, in addition to close collaboration and liaison with many different specialists; and it demands, too, a considerable amount of devotion and idealism towards the job.

The Planning Team. In such a large and complex task, and one spread over a number of years, it is impossible to mention all those concerned with the planning of the London County Council's Reconstruction or Comprehensive Development Areas. Within the County Council it has always been a team effort with the officers of other Departments, notably with those of the Clerk, the Controller, the Chief Engineer, the Valuer, the Superintendent of Parks, and the Solicitor.

Basically, too, in accordance with democratic procedure, the decisions had to be taken by the elected representatives of the people, acting through the various Committees, the most important being the Planning Committee. The L.C.C. has been fortunate in having a tradition of outstanding Council members extending back to Bernard Shaw.

In addition to the L.C.C. there was of course the City of London and the Boroughs concerned with the Comprehensive Development Areas. Long and continuous collaboration was maintained particularly with the Boroughs of Stepney and Poplar, since a large part of their territory consisted of the area being comprehensively developed. A special case was, of course, the ancient City of London. Schemes such as the Barbican and the Tower were treated as combined operations of the L.C.C. and the City Corporation and close and regular collaboration was maintained continuously with the City Planning Officer (then Mr A. Mealand) and his staff.

Within the L.C.C. Architect's Department (the largest in the world) is the Town Planning Division, and within that again was the Reconstruction Areas Group. It was set up in 1949, but in 1956 was reorganized into the North-East London Group, thereby relinquishing the Comprehensive Areas south of the Thames, but retaining the City and the two eastern Boroughs of Stepney and Poplar, and adding Finsbury, Shoreditch, Bethnal Green, Hackney, Islington, and Stoke Newington.

Because the Architect's Department included Housing, Schools, General Buildings (i.e. Fire Stations, Old People's Homes, etc.), and Building Regulations (Byelaws) in its very wide sphere of responsibilities, and was therefore a combined operations of planning and building organization, very close collaboration was possible between planners and architects at an early stage; this was particularly valuable in the case of neighbourhood planning.

It will be remembered that Mr J. H. Forshaw, as the London County Council's Architect, collaborated with Sir Patrick Abercrombie in the preparation of the County of London Plan. Mr (now Professor Sir Robert) Matthew was appointed to this position shortly after the end of the war, and there is no doubt that the London County Council and planning as well as architecture in London owes to this one man a great enduring debt. He was followed by Dr (now Professor Sir Leslie) Martin in 1953 and by Mr Hubert Bennett in 1955.

Thanks to Mr Matthew, the Planning Division (amounting to some 250 planners) was set up under the direction of Arthur Ling, one of the most brilliant planners of the day, and one who took a leading part in the pre-war *MARS* Plan. Mr Ling left in 1956 to take over the leadership of the City Architectural and Planning Department in Coventry, and his more recent achievements are described elsewhere. His place was taken by Mr L. W. Lane, also a planner of great ability. To work with these leaders (among whom must be included Mr F. G. West, the present Deputy Architect and Planning Officer) was, for the members of my Group and myself, a great experience. The Group itself, with approximately 50 planners, naturally changed in its personnel from time to time. In 1956, when it was re-organized, the three Senior Planners were Messrs W. G. Bor, G. C. Logie, and C. G. L. Shankland, supported by Messrs R. T. Bigwood, V. Coppock, W. Kay, R. King, P. Kreisis, Mrs Ann MacEwan, G. Owen and R. Stone. Others, such as Mr J. K. Buczynski, played a notable part in the urban designing, and after 1956 the Group was joined by Messrs E. Farrow, B. Schlaffenberg and J. M. Hirsh as senior planners. In mentioning these names I am acutely conscious of omitting others who have dedicated several years of their lives to an infinitely worthwhile task, and I must apologize to them all.

1

5 LONDON

1. St Clement Danes church, 1941

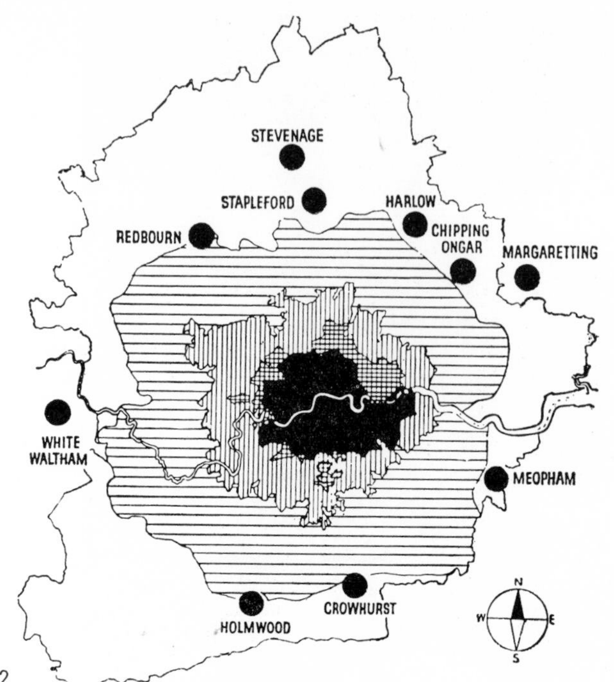

2

2. The Greater London Plan, 1944

The Greater London Plan, here shown diagrammatically, was the basic regional document, fundamental to urban renewal. The Plan followed the general ideas recommended for the whole country by the Barlow Report that there should be a major decentralization of industry and population from the congested areas of London. The diagram shows the L.C.C. area in the centre, with density proposals for the whole urban area of the metropolis. Around the latter a green belt would be consolidated, while beyond would be a reception area for some of the decentralized population in carefully planned New Towns. Eight of these are now largely completed.

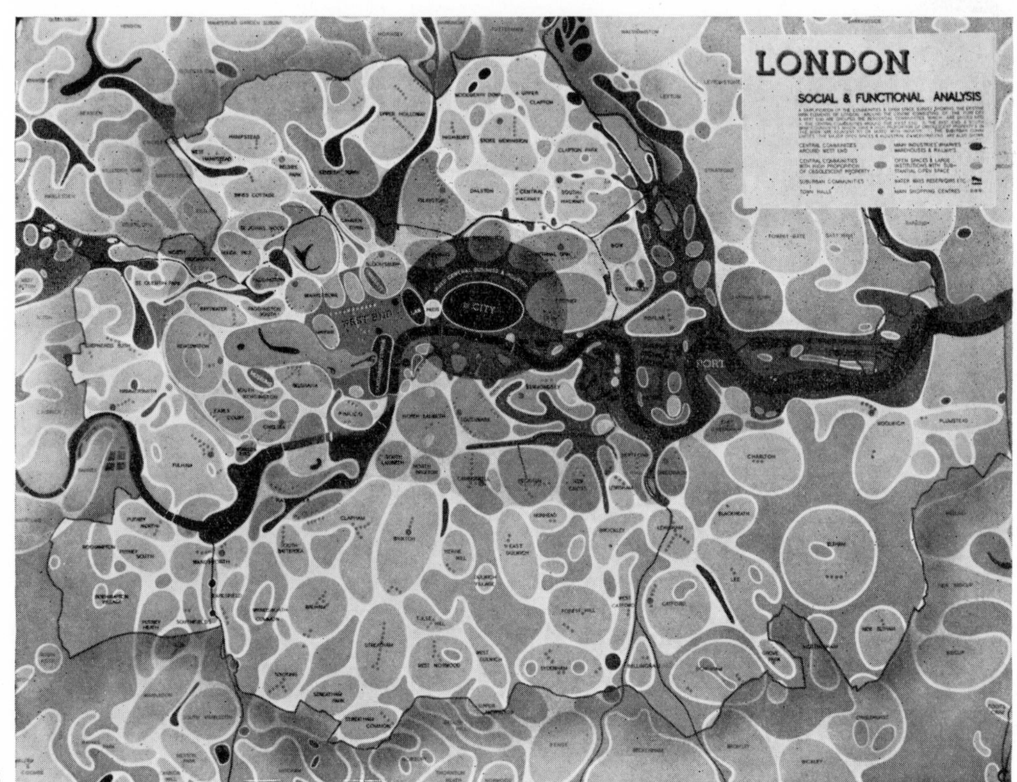

3

3. The County of London Plan, social and functional analysis

This diagram from the famous Report of the 1943 County of London Plan shows London's triple core of Westminster (government), the West End (shopping and entertainment), and the City (commerce). The egg shapes around this core indicate the re-creation of London's many submerged communities. The proposed communities of Stepney, Poplar, and Bow and Bromley (the heavily war damaged East End) may be seen immediately to the right of the City, above the Dock area.

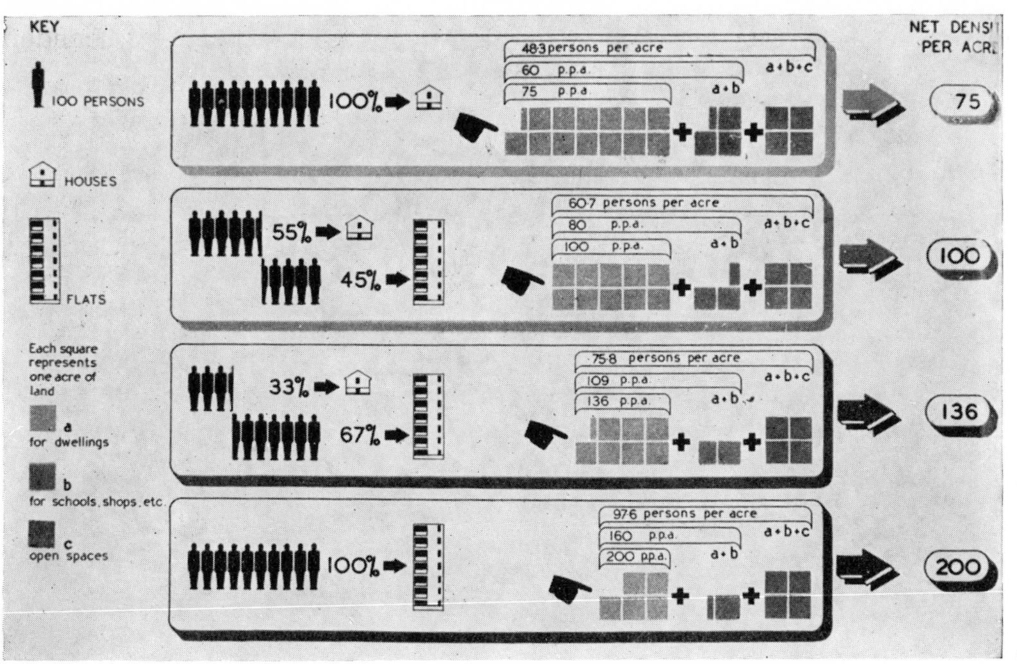

4

4. The County of London Plan: residential density study

In this famous Plan many new planning principles were evolved, notably those concerned with residential areas. This study, reproduced from an excellent Penguin booklet on the Plan by Messrs Carter and Goldfinger, shows the relationship between the main net residential density proposals, gross density, and dwelling types. At 75 persons per acre (net, or land for housing use only) all may live in houses; at 100 and 136 it is mixed; and at 200 it is all in flats. On the right the diagram shows the density for dwellings only, the reductions caused by schools and shops, and by open spaces.

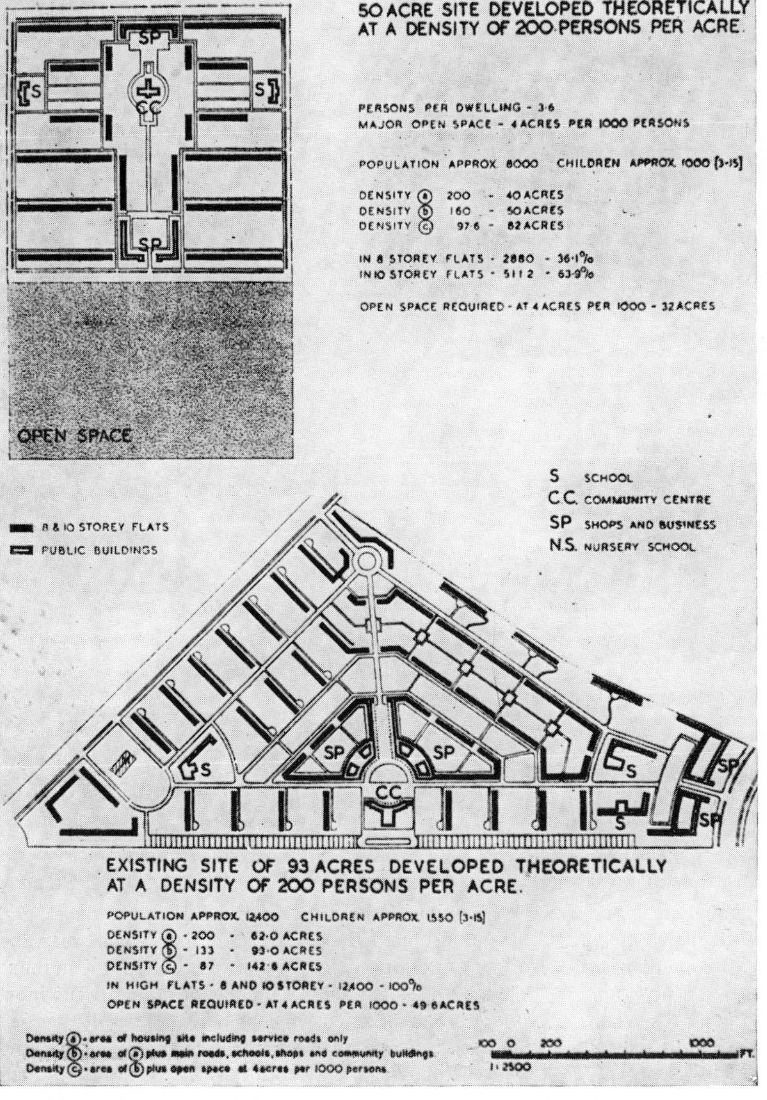

5

5. The County of London Plan: theoretical neighbourhood Study

Having worked out a series of guiding theories for residential development, the County of London Planners then proceeded to try them out on a number of theoretical sites. They assumed a given residential density with a due proportion of dwellings in houses and flats, and then included shops, a community centre, schools and open spaces, all based on agreed standards. These studies owe a debt to the earlier ones carried out by Clarence Perry and his colleagues when contributing to the New York Regional Plan of 1929.

6 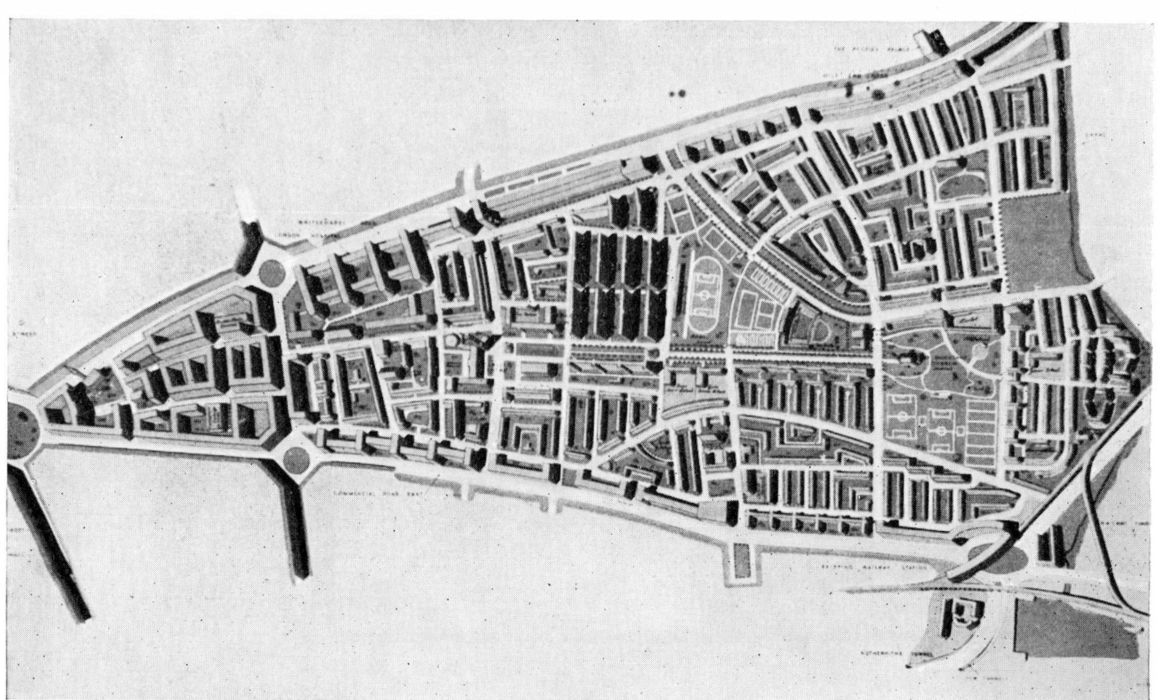

7 

6. The County of London Plan: proposals for Stepney
After the principles and standards for residential areas had been evolved, the most heavily bomb-damaged areas were chosen as Reconstruction Areas. Comprehensive three-dimensional layouts were then prepared. The Community of Stepney, here illustrated, was one of the worst slum areas of London before the war. The forms used for the various buildings compare interestingly with pre-war schemes in Germany and the Netherlands. There is a marked tendency to place most of the blocks north and south, so as to get the morning sun for the bedrooms and the afternoon sun for living-rooms. The main roads are lined with commercial buildings, and roundabouts are proposed for road junctions.

7. The County of London Plan: proposals for Stepney
Having worked out a set of planning standards, and having also carried out studies on theoretical areas, the County of London Planners then proceeded to use these ideas on selected bombed areas of London. The most important comprehensive scheme was that for Stepney in the East End, and a large model was made to show the public the general character of the new planning. In fact, of course, there was insufficient information available in 1943 to make these proposals effective in detail, although they were of very great help to us when we finally came to the reality of redevelopment in the 1950s.

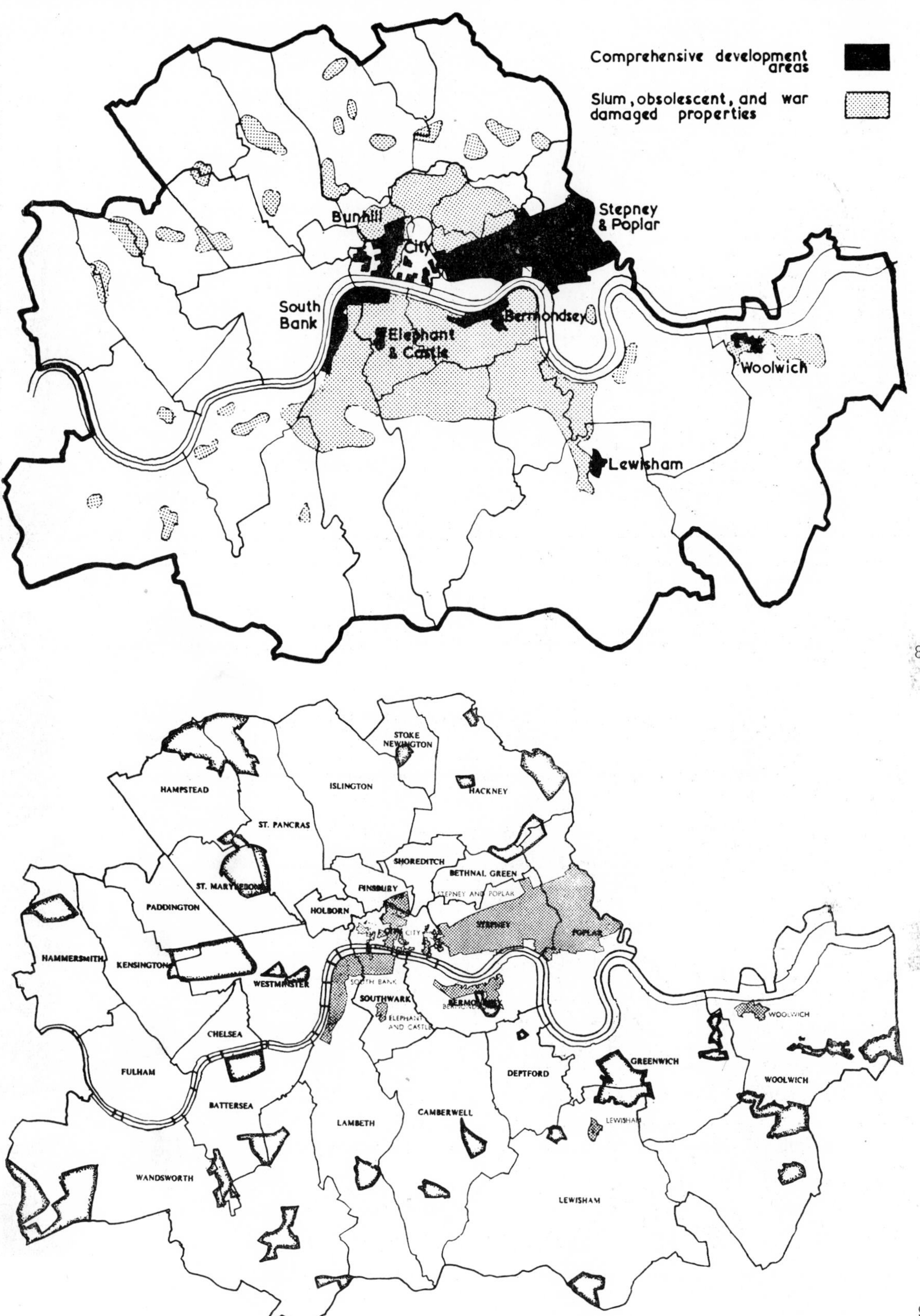

8. Urban conditions and the C.D.A.s

The diagram plan shows the eight Comprehensive Development Areas in relation to the other parts of London which suffered from urban blight. The C.D.A.s were as follows: The City of London (244 acres); Stepney/Poplar (2,000 acres, of which 1,312 acres are subject to Compulsory Purchase powers); Bermondsey (117 acres); The South Bank (288 acres); Elephant and Castle (31 acres); Bunhill Fields (41 acres); Lewisham Clock Tower (40 acres); Woolwich, St Mary's (63 acres).

9. Boroughs, parks, and the C.D.A.s

This diagram plan outlines the 123 square miles of the L.C.C. area with its 28 lower tier Metropolitan Boroughs and the City Corporation at the centre. The L.C.C. itself was created in 1878 and the Metropolitan Boroughs in 1899. The City Corporation, once the totality of Roman and later medieval London, has changed in character drastically, although it still keeps up many of its medieval trappings. The whole of London's government has now been reorganized. The diagram also shows the eight Comprehensive Development Areas (shaded) in relation to the major open spaces.

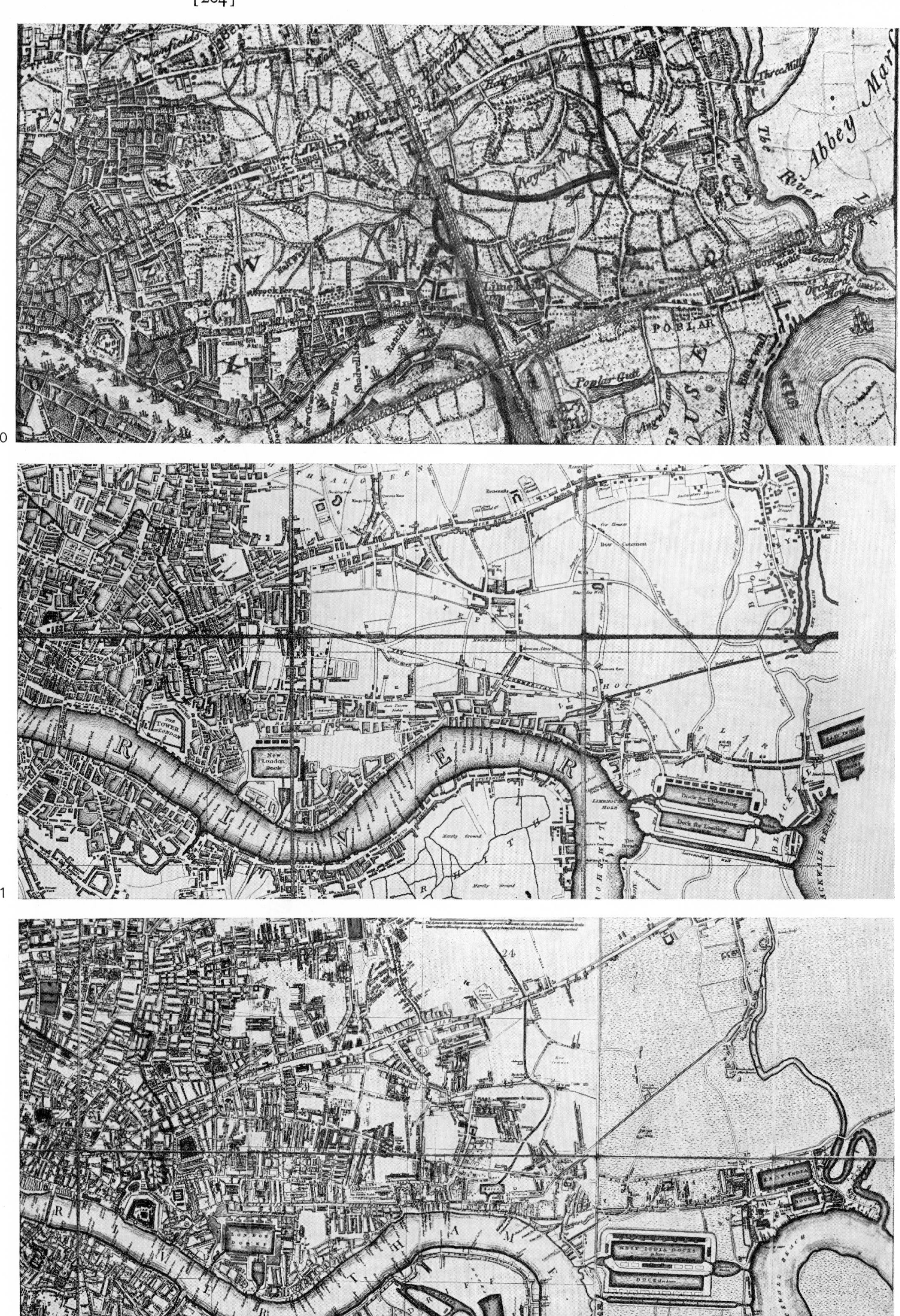
Spitalfields
Three Mill
Abbey Mars
The River
Limehouse
POPLAR
Poplar Gutt
Shadwell
Tower
BETHNAL GREEN
MILE END
Bow Common
STEPNEY
LIMEHOUSE
POPLAR
New London Dock
THE TOWER of LONDON
Dock for Unloading
Dock for Loading
Marshy Ground
BLACKWALL REACH
24
WEST INDIA DOCKS
THAMES

10

11

12

Stepney and Poplar

10. Stepney/Poplar, 1754

In this map, in which due allowance must be made for the current standard of map making, London is still a very small city by today's standards. The City itself has overflowed into the Liberties, outside its eastern walls, and a sizeable mercantile community already exists in West Stepney and Wapping. Otherwise there are green fields with villages, although some ribbon development is taking place along Whitechapel Street. By the eighteenth century several industries and other commercial enterprises were already established in Stepney, notably weaving at Spitalfields.

11. Stepney/Poplar, 1804

By 1804 a large dock-building programme had been completed, including the New Dock at Wapping and the two West Indian Docks across the neck of the Isle of Dogs. The first canal has already been cut, in 1770, from the Thames at Limehouse to the River Lee at Bromley, known as the Limehouse Cut; while a second canal parallels the West India Docks across the Isle of Dogs, which became an island for the first time. A major new road from the docks has also been built – the New Commercial Road, although it has not yet been joined up to the White Chapel High Street. Large parts of Stepney have now been built over, and the ribbon development has spread along White Chapel Road and Mile End Road to Stepney Village, with its Green and ancient parish church of St Dunstan, dating back to the thirteenth and fifteenth centuries. Another ribbon has spread from the Tower along Cable Street and the Ratcliffe Highway right along the river to the villages of Limehouse and Poplar. Poplar and Bow are still comparatively clear, with cow houses on Bow Common and farmers' cottages at Limehouse.

12. Stepney/Poplar, 1822

The full burst of the early nineteenth-century industrial explosion is now in full swing. The Regent's Canal has been built, connecting the River Thames by continuous waterway all the way to the Midlands. Stepney is now largely built over, and the earlier residential square development has now changed to long rows of the poorest type of artisans' dwellings. The docks have been lined with great warehouses, some of fine design and great durability. Rope walks and industries concerned with shipbuilding abound. Poplar and Bow still remain meadow lands although even here one sees the beginnings of the unplanned tomorrow in the scatter of 'Callico Houses' and 'Manufactories'. The new industrial areas are exciting and horrible, stimulating, and yet charnel houses, all at the same time. In the early part of the century Stepney had many thousands of looms which over the century disappeared and became clothing factories.

WEST HAM
ABBEY
MARSH
BOW
COMMON
LONDON DOCK
WEST INDIA
IMPORT
DOCKS
TIMBER DOCK
EAST INDIA
DOCK
BLACKWALL RAILWAY
BUGSBYS
MARSHES

13

TOWER HAMLETS CEMETERY
BROMLEY
NEW
TOWN
BROMLEY
BOW
COMMON
WEST HAM AB
CANNING
TOWN
RIVER LEE
BROMLEY MARSH
EAST INDIA DOCK
POPLAR
BLACKWALL RAILWAY
LONDON
DOCK
WEST INDIA DOCK
WEST INDIA DOCK
TIMBER DOCK
BUGSBYS
MARSHES
THE POOL

14

TOWER HAMLETS
CEMETERY
BROMLEY
BROMLEY
WEST HAM ABBEY
RIVER LEA
CANNING
TOWN
EAST INDIA DOCK
LONDON
DOCK
WEST INDIA DOCK
WEST INDIA DOCK
MARSHES

15

13. Stepney/Poplar, 1848

In this sombre year of political upheaval Stepney has probably reached its most wretched state for urban habitation. Cholera came the following year, and again in 1856 and 1866. The new railways have now arrived as a major element in urban expansion. In the already built-up areas they are constructed at prodigious expense on great viaducts – a costly but extremely valuable example of traffic segregation. All kinds of new industries are now being started, including a Commercial Gas Works at World's End (an appropriate name), and factories for Pearl Ash, Pot Ash, and Patent Cables. A large new cemetery has also been laid out at Tower Hamlets, and the living population of Stepney is now over 200,000.

14. Stepney/Poplar, 1860

Poplar is now rapidly filling up, almost entirely with long streets of cheap artisans' dwellings. The development is more regular in form, as the speculative builders were building in larger blocks of property, and the effects of the rising standards were beginning to be felt. In 1856 Sir Joseph Bazalgette, Chief Engineer to the Metropolitan Board of Works, prepared a main drainage scheme for London, and this was completed in 1875; as a result the health of the people and the state of the River Thames were both improved considerably. Two years before, Brunel's mighty steamship, the *Great Eastern*, had been launched after great difficulty at Milwall in the Isle of Dogs (just off the map below the Telegraph Cable Company).

15. Stepney/Poplar, 1879

Both Stepney and Poplar are now almost solidly built up – built up in the worst possible way, without open spaces or social facilities of any kinds, except churches and public houses. Endless rows of artisan dwellings are packed cheek by jowl for hundreds of continuous and evil-smelling acres. The population of Stepney is, unbelievable as it may sound, now approaching 290,000. Reformers were, of course, hard at work and already there were a number of benevolent institutions endeavouring to provide something better. Notable were the Metropolitan Association for the Improving of The Dwellings of the Poor and the American Peabody Trust, both of which built what are now giant barrack-like tenements, but which Dickens hailed as a great enterprise. From then on there was a long succession of desperate attempts to do something for the hopeless thousands in the East End, but only wholesale destruction by enemy action in the last war finally cleared the area for a fresh start.

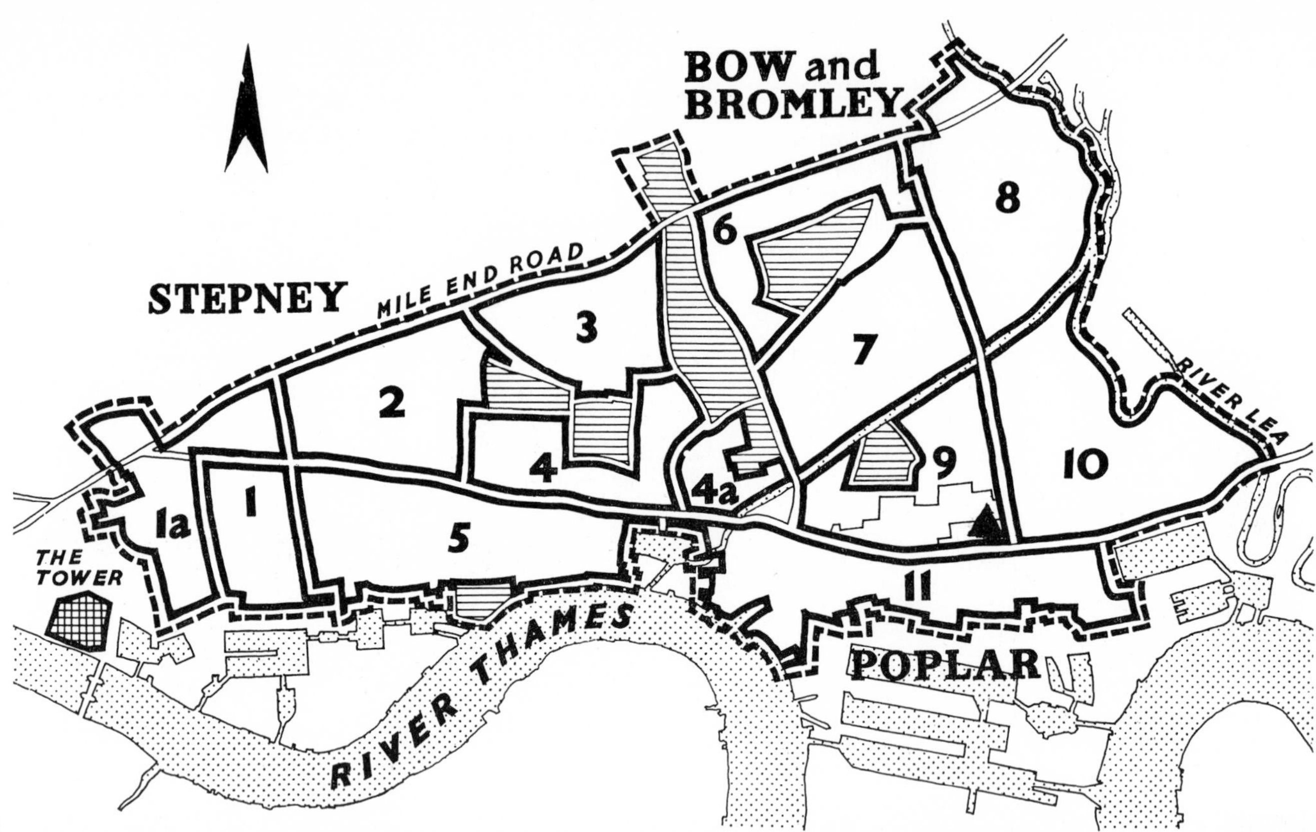

16

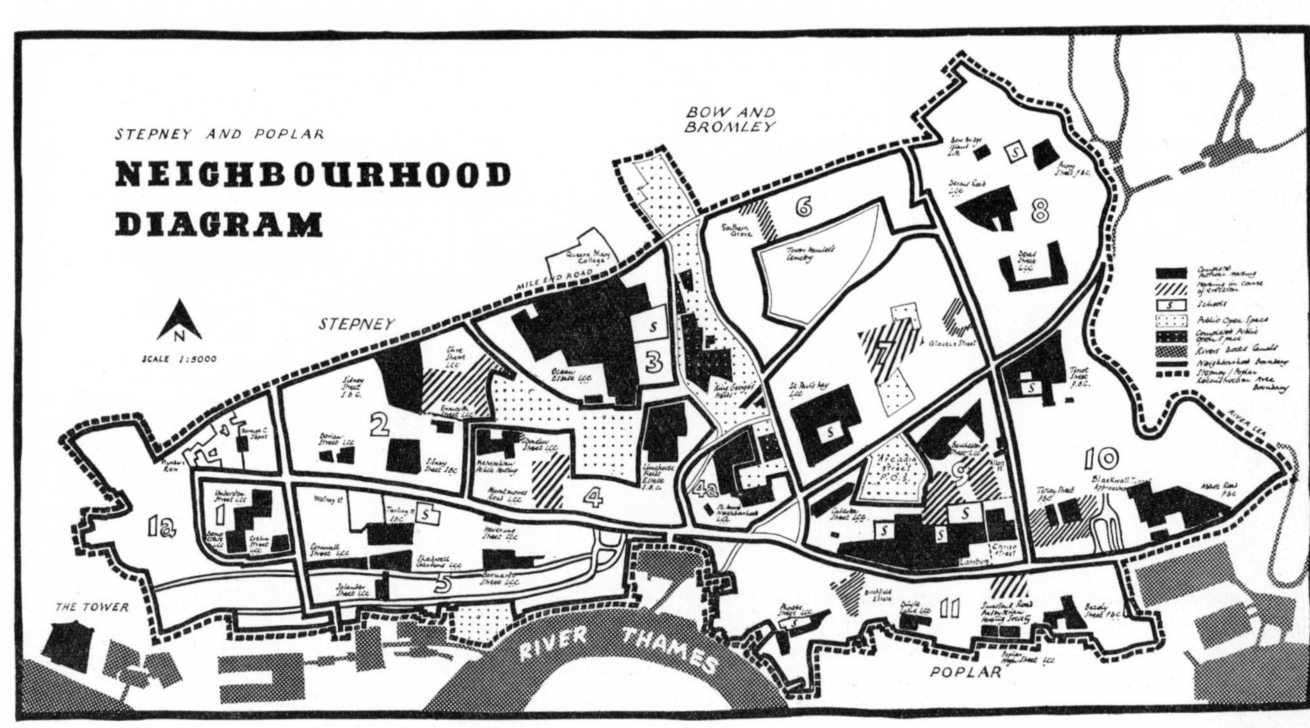

17

16. Communities and Neighbourhoods

During the late 1940's the original studies of the County of London Plan were taken up and a Community and Neighbourhood pattern was established. The Community of Stepney (which formed only a part of the Municipal Borough of Stepney) was divided into six Neighbourhoods. No. 2 was mostly residential but contained the London Hospital within it; no. 3 was partly planned and rebuilt by the L.C.C. Valuer's Department before the Reconstruction Areas Group was created; no. 4 was a long attenuated area, and at an early stage we separated from it the new Neighbourhood of St Anne's (named after the adjacent church of St Anne's, Limehouse).

17. Progress plan, 1956

The diagram shows the general state of progress in development up to 1956 throughout this new town in an old city. Completed housing schemes are shown in black, those in progress hatched. Completed schools are outlined and indicated with an S, open spaces with dots. The area within the dotted line is nearly 2,000 acres, with a planned population of approximately 100,000. Current planning standards for the area were: residential density 136 persons per acre, with car parking at one car space to four dwellings; commercial and industrial plot ratio $2\frac{1}{2}$ to 1, with car parking at one car space to 2,500 sq ft; public open space $3\frac{1}{2}$ acres per 1,000 people; secondary and primary schools at approximately $5\frac{1}{2}$ and $2\frac{1}{2}$ acres respectively.

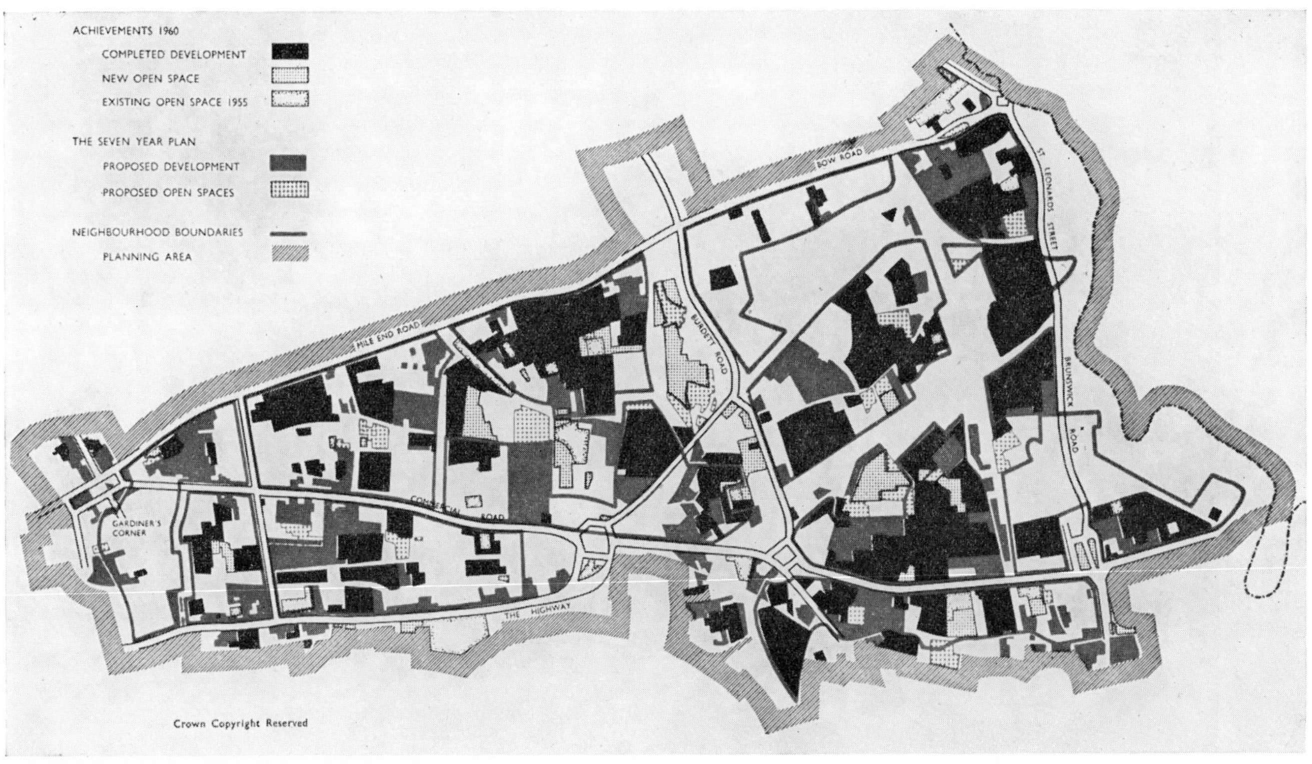

18

19

18. Progress and the next stage, 1960

This plan, taken from the London County Council's Five Yearly Review of its Development Plan, shows how much of the 2,000 acres of the Stepney/Poplar Comprehensive Development Area had been carried out since the plan was first made. It also shows the areas proposed for redevelopment in the next seven years, which include a further 100 acres of new housing, 40 acres of new parks, 30 acres of new schools, 2 new shopping centres and a new commercial/industrial area. As can be seen, the rebuilding of existing urban areas, even when subject to the heavy bomb damage of the last war, can only be undertaken in a patchwork pattern, as it depends on so many site factors.

19. Stepney: a pre-war air view

This air photograph, taken before war damage had wrought such changes and possibilities for improvement in the area, shows a typical nineteenth-century urban problem. Mixed development is here seen at its worst, with long rows of terrace houses and tenement blocks mixed up with large and small industries and commercial buildings of all kinds. There was practically no open space of any kind, and children and old people were in constant danger from motor vehicles. The area in the foreground became Neighbourhood no. 1, and except for the tenement blocks, has been almost completely redeveloped.

20

21

20. Stepney: a post-war air view

This photograph, looking north-west from a position over the River Thames (more or less where the famous *Great Eastern* was built at Milwall), shows Stepney after the war. One or two large post-war housing schemes have already started, but for the most part the area is characterized by a muddle of mixed industrial, commercial, and residential uses.

21. Stepney: Neighbourhoods nos. 2, 3, and 4

This model shows how planning policies such as the relocation of non-conforming industry, the new Open Space and School Space standards, a new road pattern, and mixed residential development at 136 persons per acre, are all making fundamental changes in the urban form of the East End. For the first time the East Enders will have adequate recreational space near their homes.

Wherever possible we tried to locate high residential towers (or point blocks) near to these green parks. In an area such as this there are two secondary schools, half a dozen primary schools and nursery schools, four minor shopping centres, and all kinds of ancillary social buildings for a complex community, all being redeveloped over a twenty-year planning period. The team leader in the Stepney Reconstruction Group was Walter Bor.

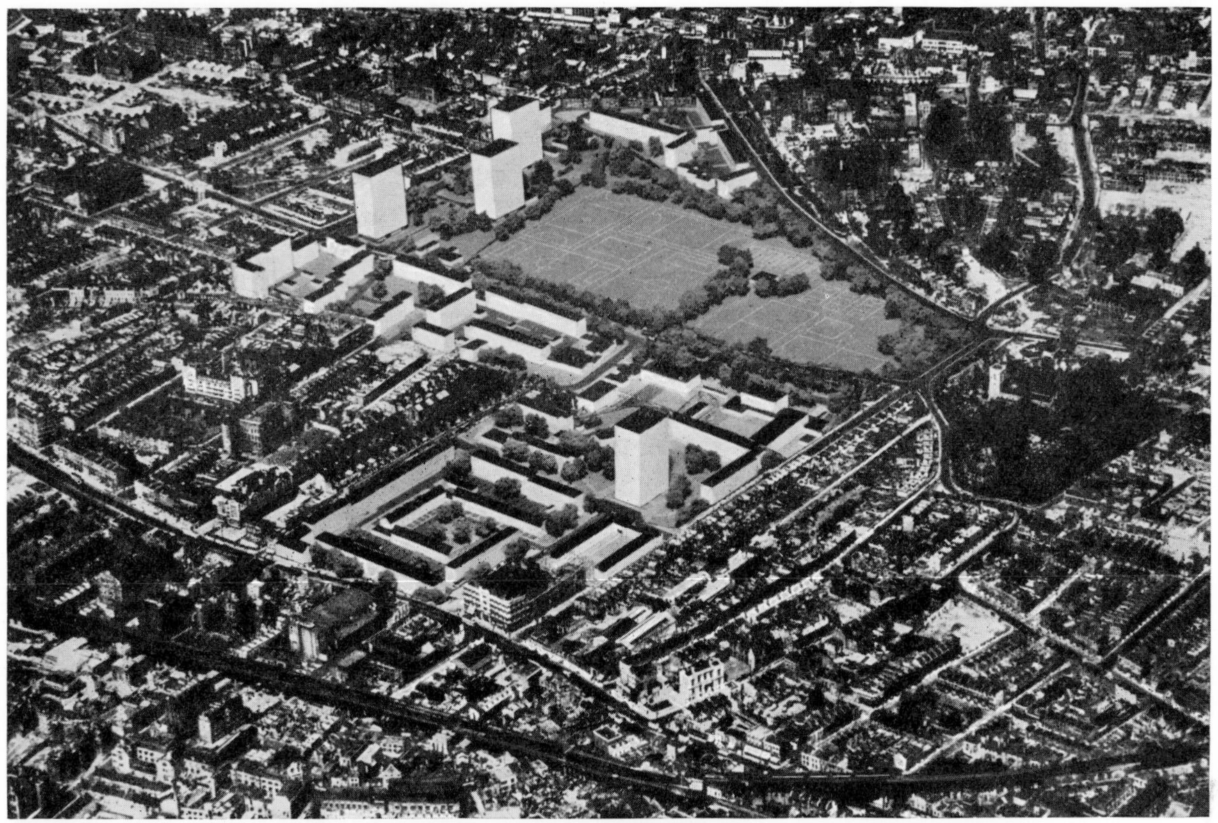

22

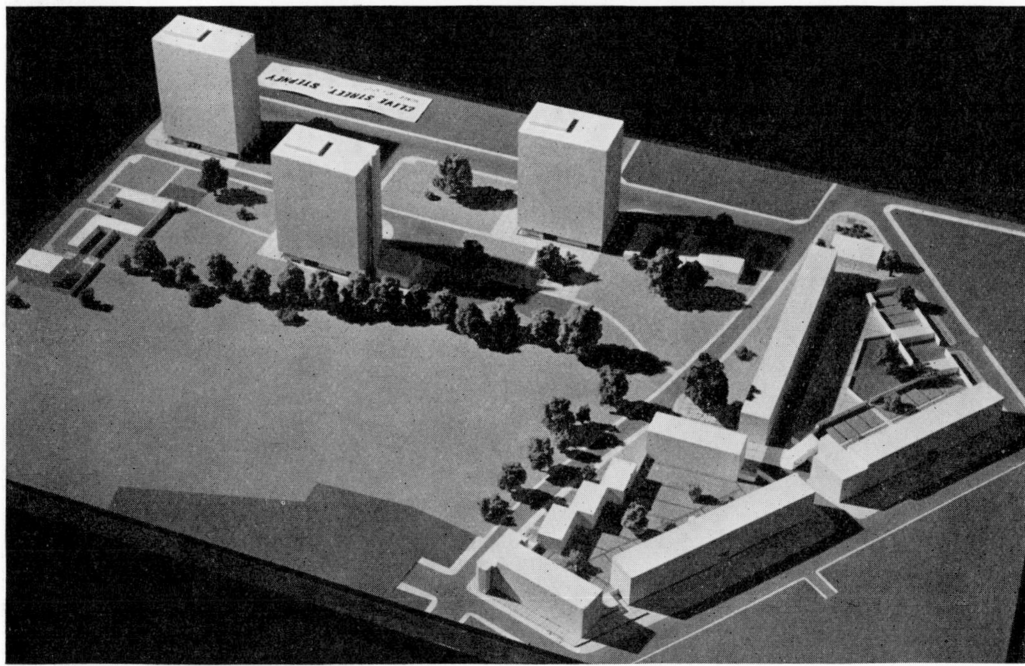

23

22. Stepney: new housing projects

In this photo-montage, four new housing projects have been superimposed on the air photograph, for comparison with the before and after views. The project at the top with three high towers is in Clive Street, now completed, together with five acres of Park land. Then comes a Metropolitan Police housing group completed in the early 1950s. Adjacent to it is an L.C.C. housing group by the Architect's Department Housing Division, also of the early 1950s; while next to this, with another high tower, is the Mountmorres Road scheme, now under construction. This scheme has a spacious two-storey square of houses with private gardens for large families.

23. Stepney: Stifford Estate

The design process started with the whole Comprehensive Development Area, and proceeded down from Community Plan, Neighbourhood layout, and on to the actual architectural design of the buildings. This housing project was worked out in close collaboration between the planners and the housing architects. The three seventeen-storey tower blocks are planned to get views over the new Park (five acres of which had been already laid out) while the area to the north (right in the photograph) has five four-storey blocks of maisonettes, a terrace of six houses, three shops, 138 tenants' stores, thirty-eight garages, a clubroom, an estate workshop, a fitted playground, and three toddlers' playspaces. Central heating was provided from a central boiler house, and the estimated cost of the whole scheme was £1,218,300.

24. Stepney: Stifford Estate

This large-scale model of one of the Clive Street seventeen-storey maisonette towers was included in a public exhibition of progress in the Stepney/Poplar area. These exhibitions were extremely helpful in giving the public an idea of what was being planned, as this was not always easy to understand by persons visiting or even living in the area.

24

25. Stepney: Stifford Estate

From being a small block in a planning model the towers finally achieve reality on the ground. The site still awaits the trees and landscaping which is so essential to any scheme, but in the East End almost everything had to be done afresh – in contrast to such schemes as Roehampton, where the area was already beautifully landscaped with mature trees.

25

26

26. Stepney: progress

This recent air photograph was taken from a similar viewpoint to that in the earlier air photograph of Neighbourhoods nos. 2, 3 and 4. In the centre of the photograph can be seen the three Stifford Estate towers, while a large area of land to their left is being cleared for a Stepney Borough Council housing scheme (since completed), and to their right clearance is in progress for open space and for the Mountmorres housing scheme. At lower centre is an early nineteenth-century residential square, which was severely affected a hundred years ago by the railway viaduct and to its right are the original buildings of Dr Barnardo's Homes. This side of the railway viaduct a residential area, which is part of Neighbourhood no. 5, has just been completed. The unusual pattern of long rows of buildings in the older urban pattern is in part due to ropewalks, of which a large number existed in the East End during the Napoleonic Wars.

27

28

27. Stepney: Stepney Green School

This secondary school, designed for Neighbourhood no. 3, and now under construction, is one of a number of well-designed school buildings at present being built in the Comprehensive Development Area, by the Schools Division of the L.C.C. Architect's Department. The sites of some of these schools, destined to form a prominent architectural element in neighbourhood layouts, were left vacant for a number of years, as the drop in population owing to war damage gave the East End a lower priority for school building than other hard-pressed areas of London.

28. Stepney: the Trinity Hospital Almshouses

The Trinity Hospital Almshouses, just across the Mile End Road from Neighbourhood no. 2, pick up a footpath planned to run right through the Neighbourhood. The Almshouses were originally erected in 1695 by The Corporation of Trinity House for masters and commanders of ships, or their widows. The whole group, including a small chapel, were badly damaged in the war, and the L.C.C. decided to put them back into their original condition and to integrate them with a large housing scheme immediately to the north. The rehabilitation was an expensive undertaking and was done with loving skill by the Historic Buildings Section of the L.C.C. Architect's Department – a work of which the L.C.C. (or any other Public Authority) might well feel proud.

29

30

Lansbury

29. After war damage

T. S. Eliot's poem *The Waste Land* might well have been composed in this area. A ruined school, a shattered tree, and rows of derelict houses are the only remnants of a thoroughly bad sub-standard environment. The sombre twilight conditions of before the war gave way to a sharp devastating tragedy for thousands as the wartime bombing destroyed their families, friends, homes, and their whole familiar world.

30. After the war

A typical post-war scene: cleared sites with a scrub of hardy vegetation. Above, a corner house has been entirely demolished leaving patched remnants. On the left a Roman Catholic primary school is still intact (and has since been incorporated into the new neighbourhood).

31

32

31. After the war

Here is a comparatively undamaged part of the area. The back gardens have gradually been filled with shacks and sheds and here and there an Anderson air-raid shelter. We were always surprised at the number of trees that had managed to survive, and our Parks Department did their best to preserve them.

32. After the war

The Upper North Street School managed to survive intact, and overlooked a small graveyard. As the building was in good condition it was decided to retain it in the new scheme and use it as a Community and Evening Studies Centre. The cemetery in the foreground was to become a Public Open Space.

33

33. The old Chrisp Street Market

This was one of the liveliest street markets of the East End. In fact, it was so popular that it completely blocked an important road. In the plan a new pedestrian market square was provided.

34

35

34. Site of the Second Stage

The large-scale devastation of north Lansbury was selected for the second stage of redevelopment, and was known as the Barchester Street Scheme. It was near – too near – to the line of industries on both sides of the Limehouse Cut Canal. Squatters in caravans made their appearance on vacant sites after the war and were a new problem on redevelopment.

35. An air view, 1939

This view is taken from a point over the Thames looking northwards and shows most of the Borough of Poplar in 1939. In the foreground are the West and East India Docks; behind is Poplar High Street, by this time an industrial travesty of a village street, and beyond is the broad East India Dock Road running right across the photograph. Running up northwards from the docks is the old North Western and Dock Junction Railway, mostly in open cut. At the right the River Lee winds a tortuous way up through its marshy valley to Hertfordshire, the lower reaches lined with Gas and Chemical Works and Power Stations. The future Lansbury Neighbourhood (named after the great political reformer George Lansbury) lies north of the East India Dock Road and west of the railway.

36

36. An air view, 1948

This air photograph gives a good impression of this part of the East End after war damage. In the foreground is the East India Dock Road, and running across the middle of the view is the Limehouse Cut Canal bounded on either side by industry. The black rectangle, lower right, is a war-time static water tank.

37

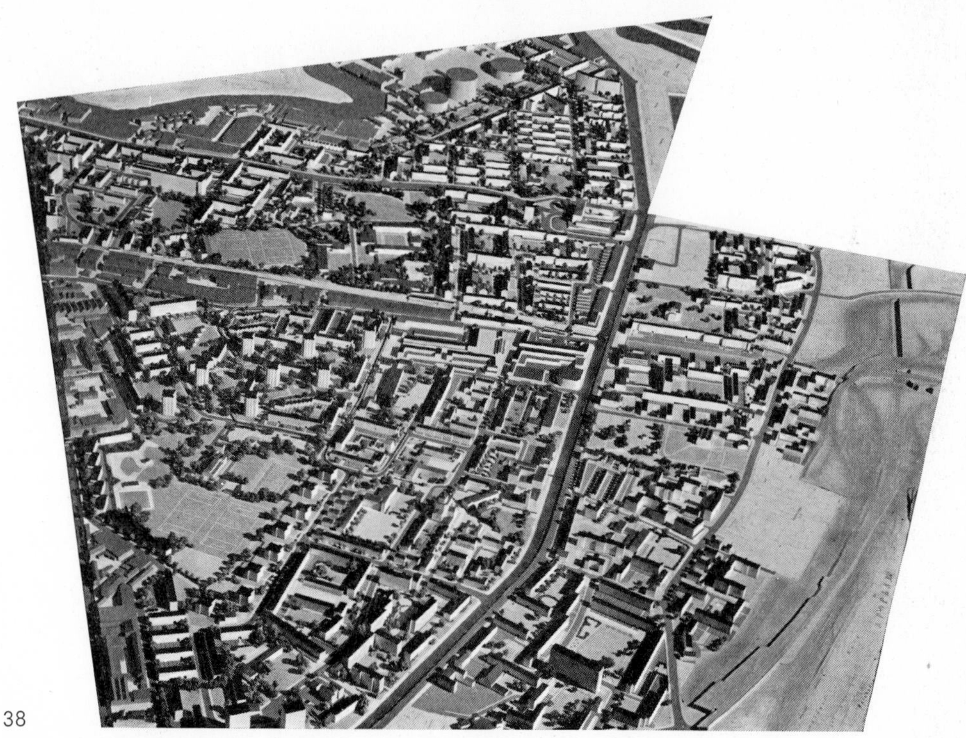

38

37. Planning exhibitions, 1958

Periodic exhibitons of planning progress are an important part of the planning task. Pointing at a model of the Stepney/Poplar Reconstruction Area is Mr Hubert Bennett, the Architect to the Council, who co-ordinated both the Planning and Architectural duties of the L.C.C. On the right is Mr L. W. Lane, then the Senior Planning Officer in the Architect's Department and in charge of the Planning Division, consisting of some 250 Planners. On the left is myself, then Group Planning Officer in charge of the North-East London Group, which included Stepney/Poplar as part of its planning duties.

38. Poplar Community Model

Here is a model of the whole Poplar Community, combining Neighbourhoods nos. 9, 10 and 11. The docks and railway sidings are on the right; the River Lee and its industries along the top, and the Limehouse Cut Canal with its industries along the left of the photograph. A light industrial zone lines the railway line running across the centre and separating Neighbourhood nos. 9 and 10 while the East India Dock Road separates them from no. 11. The team leader for Poplar until 1956 was Gordon Logie.

39

39. Poplar Community: the site

An air view of the site of the three neighbourhoods of the future Poplar Community. Running diagonally up left is the Limehouse Cut Canal, and bounding the top is the River Lee. The docks form the southern boundary along the right of the photograph.

40

40. Lansbury: The first stage
It was decided that as part of the 1951 Festival of Britain, a section of the Stepney/Poplar Reconstruction Area should be made into a Live Architecture Exhibition. The most appropriate area proved to be the south part of Neighbourhood no. 9 (later Lansbury). The white line on the photograph shows the land to be acquired for the purpose.

---

41. Lansbury: first model
This model is the one prepared for the whole Neighbourhood in order that the first stage could proceed within an overall planned framework. It was prepared under difficult conditions; for instance, the L.C.C. Housing Committee at the time would agree to no flats being over six storeys in height. Cinemas, too, were planned, but television removed their possibility of realization. There was one major Open Space in the north-centre of the Neighbourhood to supply the much-needed recreational space, and this was to be connected visually by green ways to smaller open spaces throughout the area.

42. Lansbury: third model
This is the third overall scheme for the Neighbourhood. Since this model was prepared, amendments have been made to the main shopping centre (bottom) and to other buildings, although always within the planned framework. This model reflects the general pattern which evolved in the East End for mixed development at 136 persons per acre: tower (point) blocks for the small families, four-storey maisonettes in traditional London squares for the medium sized ones, and terraces or squares of attached houses for the large ones.

41

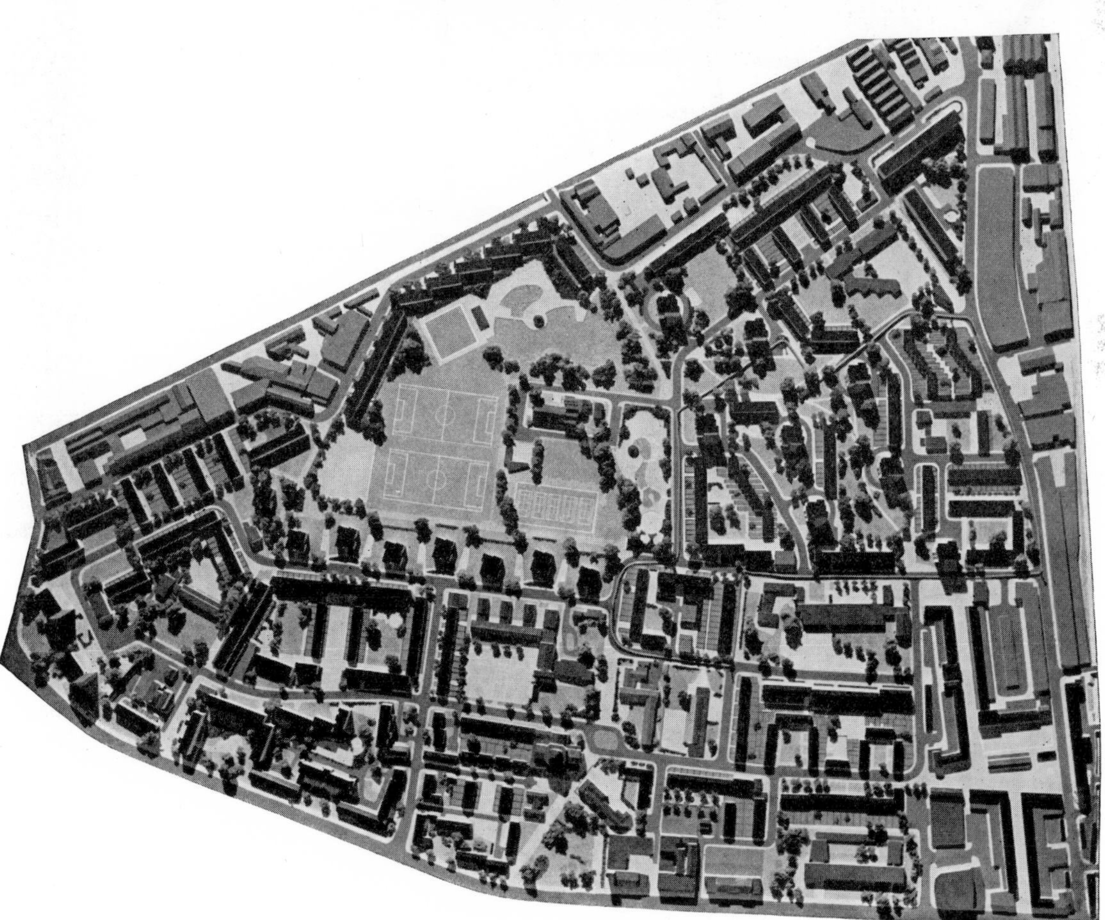

42

43 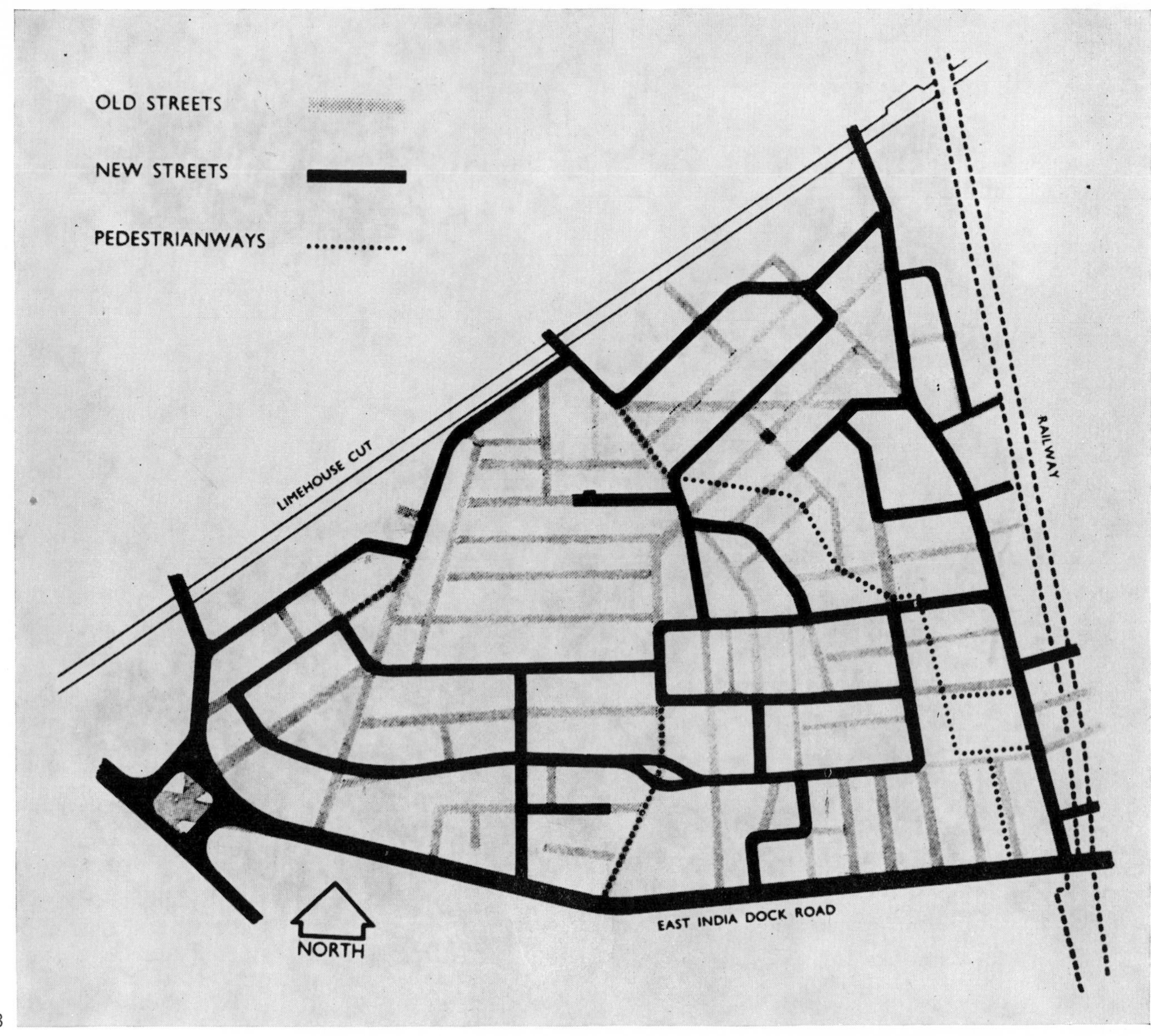

43. Lansbury: road pattern

This diagram of the new road pattern superimposed on the old one of the Neighbourhood shows the main traffic artery of the East India Dock Road running along the south, with an obsolete roundabout (which expressed the lack of Government finance available then for new road improvements). Running north along the east flank of the Neighbourhood is the connecting Community road of Chrisp Street (formerly blocked regularly by a street market). A similar connecting road runs along the north western boundary. Otherwise the pattern endeavours to serve each housing area without providing any traffic routes through the Neighbourhood.

44

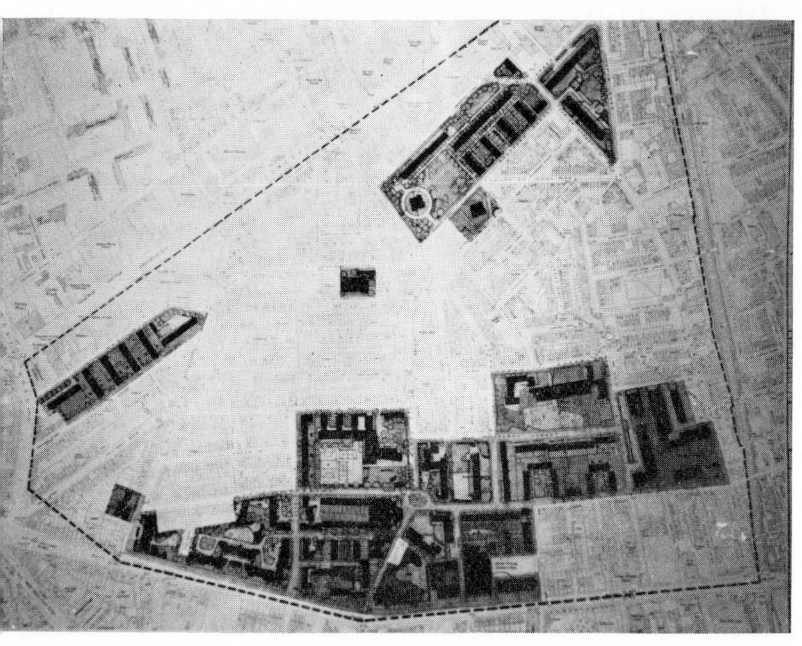
45

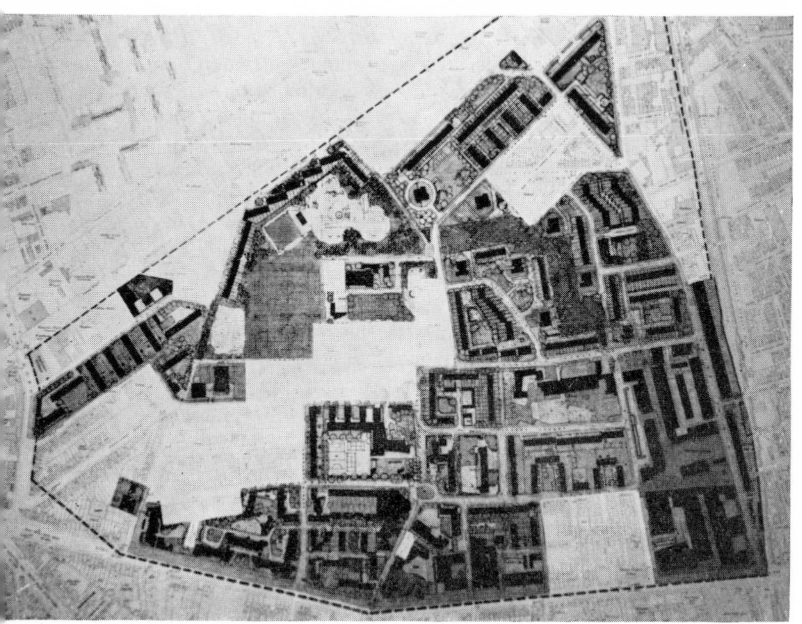
46

44, 45, 46. Lansbury: stages of development

After preparing the zoning and programming plans a three dimensional solution was worked out for each building group which had to create a satisfactory urban design in time as well as space. Stage One was for the Festival of Britain at the south part of the Neighbourhood. Stage Two consisted of two isolated sites, which in most cities would be dealt with in isolated fashion (the two point blocks, however, give a clue to the larger urban design); and in Stage Three the isolated sites are integrated, except for a school site, which had to wait owing to the substantial nature of the existing school.

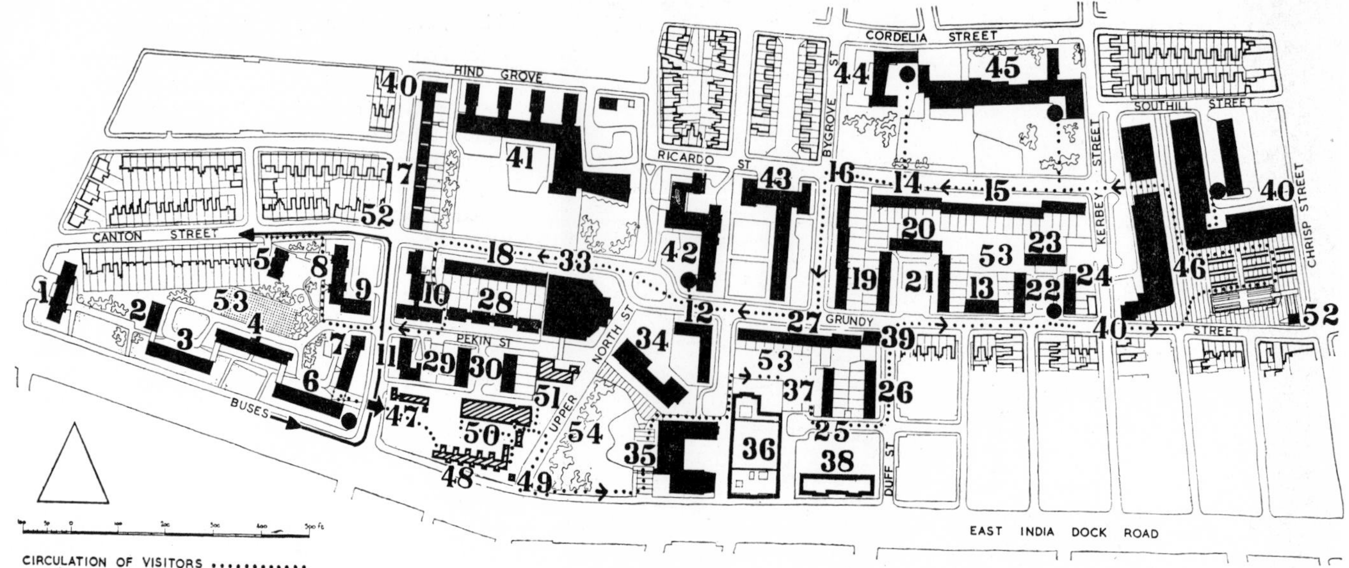

KEY

1 Six storey flats.
2 Six storey flats.
3 Three storey flats.
4 Six storey flats.
5 Six storey flats.
6 Three storey flats.
7 Three storey flats.
8 Six storey flats.
9 Three storey flats.
10 Three storey flats.
11 Three storey flats.
12 Two storey flats for old people.
13 Three storey flats (Existing).
14 Four storey maisonettes.
15 Four storey maisonettes.
16 Three storey (Two storey maisonettes with flats over).
17 Three storey (Two storey maisonettes with flats over).
18 Two storey terraced houses.
19-24 Three storey terraced houses with a few single room flats for old people.
25 Two storey terraced houses.
26 Two storey terraced houses.
27 Two storey terraced houses.
28 Two storey linked houses.
29 Two storey terraced houses.
30 Two storey terraced houses.
31 (Not shown). Future Health Centre on the site of 47-50.
32 (Not shown). Future R.C. Presbytery on the site of 51.
33 R.C. Church.
34 Upper North Street School (Existing) will be used for future Community Centre.
35 Trinity Church and Hall.
36 Seamans Mission and future extensions.
37 Trinity Church Manse.
38 Board of Trade Offices (Existing).
39 Public House (Existing).
40 New Public Houses.
41 R.C. Secondary School.
42 Old Peoples Home.
43 R.C. Primary School (Existing school and future extensions).
44 Ricardo Street Nursery School.
45 Ricardo Street Primary School.
46 Shopping Centre and Market Place.
47 Main Entrance and Administration Block.
48 Building Research Pavilion.
49 Vertical Feature.
50 Town Planning Pavilion.
51 Cafeteria.
52 Lavatories.
53 Childrens playgrounds.
54 Amenity Park.
● Show flats, show houses and show classrooms.

47

47. Lansbury: Stage One

Stage One was the live Architecture Exhibition for the 1951 Festival of Britain. In this first big attempt at post-war Neighbourhood planning and development every effort was made to show as great a variety of social facilities as possible. Homes were provided in two-storey terrace houses with gardens; three-storey houses, houses with a flat over or maisonettes with a flat below; four storey maisonettes; and three- and six-storey flats. There were also special flats for old people and an Old People's Home. A careful distribution of sandpits for under-five-year-old children, and playgrounds for the five to eleven group, was provided; while the older than eleven group would be catered for in the new larger Open Spaces and School Playgrounds (we tried to arrange for these to be opened after school hours). In addition to living accommodation there was a new Secondary, Primary, and Nursery School besides the existing Roman Catholic Primary School. The first stage of the new Community consisted of a Shopping Centre, Clock Tower, covered arcades, two Public Houses, and maisonettes over the shops. There were two new churches, one for Roman Catholics and one for Congregationalists (with Church Hall and Club Rooms) to replace buildings that had been destroyed. The existing Upper North Street School was converted into a Community and Evening Educational Centre, and finally the Seamen's Mission and Hostel was to be reconstructed. A comprehensive Health Centre was also proposed, but was vetoed by the Government at the last minute on grounds of economy; it was to have been sited on the area used for the Festival Town Planning Exhibition.

48

49

48. Lansbury: model of Stage One

This large-scale ($\frac{1}{32}$-inch) model, photographed from the east, was made to show how the new urban pattern would be seen in contrast to the existing buildings, most of which have now been replaced by new development. In the foreground is the first stage of the Lansbury Market, with its market stalls and flats over the shops. At middle right is the new Susan Lawrence Primary School with its Nursery School and 2½ acres of playground. On the left of this was the first block of four-storey maisonettes to be designed for the L.C.C., with two three-storey squares, and a children's play-ground in the centre. Beyond this group are the Roman Catholic Primary School (an existing building), an Old People's Home, and the Cardinal Griffin Secondary School.

49. Lansbury: model of Stage One

A photograph taken from the north-west, with the Secondary School in the foreground, and a terrace of three-storey houses (with flats over them) and corner Public House (one of four in Stage One) alongside. Beyond is the Roman Catholic Church, and to the right of it is the excellent group of houses and flats designed by Peter Shepheard. To the left of the Secondary School is the Old People's Home. A difficult part of the urban design was in the relationship of the open spaces enclosed by the buildings.

50 

50. Lansbury: model of Stage One

This shows the western end of the Neighbourhood and illustrates some of the difficulties of redevelopment. The site available had a long awkward shape with an existing Welfare Building in the middle of it. On its left perimeter was a long row of substantial three-storey terrace houses with gardens, part of a street that could only be redeveloped at a later period. Remember, too, that the Housing Committee's height limit was six storeys and that the detailed design was then the responsibility of the Valuer's Department (Housing as a technical task was transferred to the Architect's Department in 1951). Low three-storey blocks were sited near to, but well back from, the main East India Road (right on photograph) with the higher blocks further back still. In the centre of the scheme is a 5-11 years children's playground, while three sandpits are sited in other parts of the scheme.

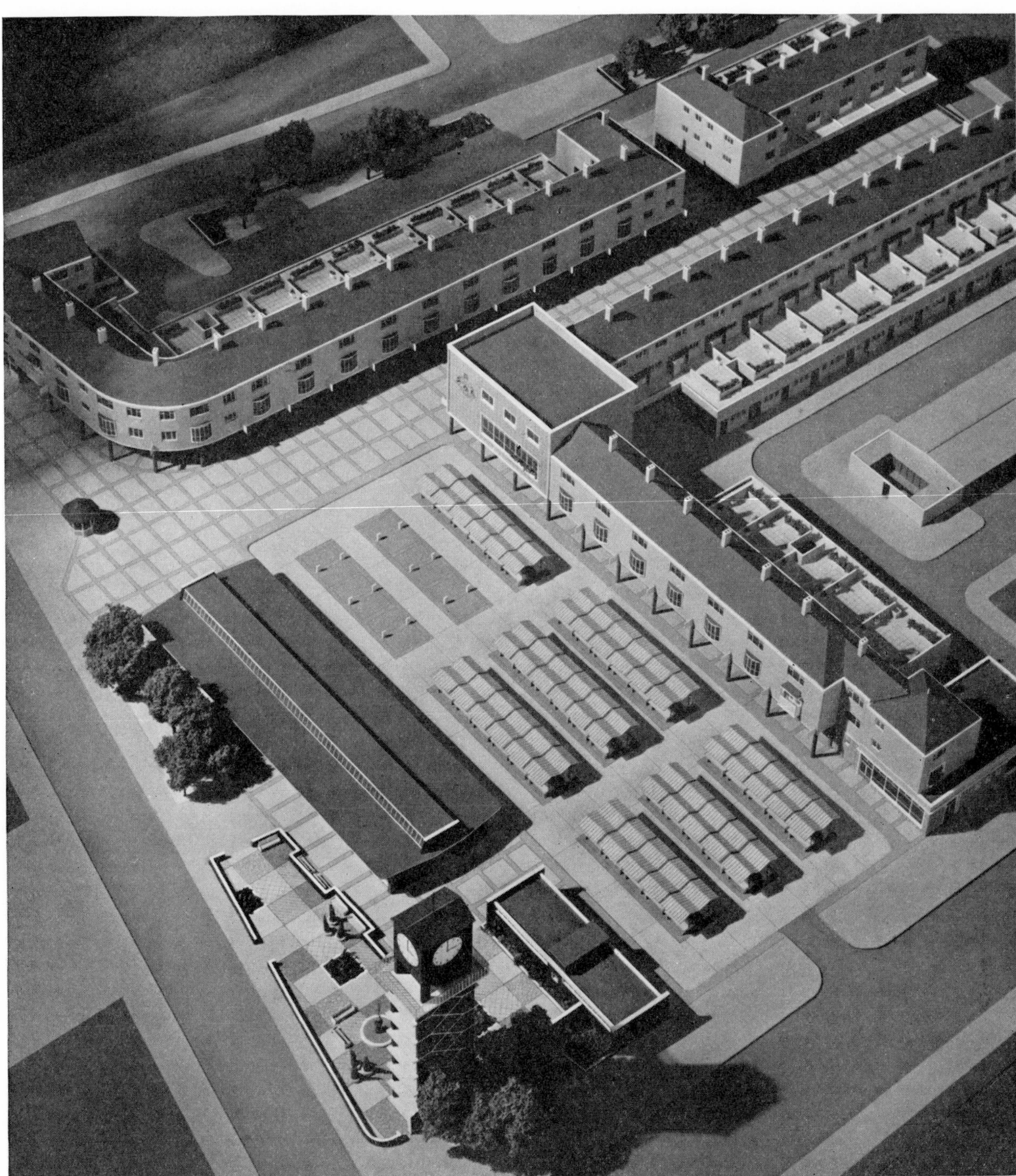

51

51. Lansbury: the Shopping Centre

The first stage of the Lansbury Shopping Centre was designed by Frederick Gibberd, and could well be the subject of a book itself. Arthur Ling had always wanted to have a market clock tower in the Centre, and Gibberd, with considerable diplomacy, was able to provide it (although it is not high enough, in my opinion). The covered market seen just above the clock tower was intended, at the request of the Ministry of Food, to hold the food stalls, but in the end these remained in the open air. The flat-roofed building at the centre was planned to be a restaurant, but the L.C.C. Valuers had earmarked another site outside the Centre, and so it had to be rented to a furniture store. The upper-level terrace gardens above the shops have proved to be excellent, and the arcade a real amenity.

52

52. Lansbury: progress on Stage One

An air view of Lansbury while the construction of Stage One was in progress. The East India Dock Road runs east to west in the foreground. At left centre is the Town Planning Exhibition erected for the Festival of Britain (since developed for housing), and behind it a mixed scheme of houses and flats in progress of erection. The Roman Catholic Church is still a vacant site, but behind, the Secondary School is well ahead. In the centre foreground the new small Public Open Space has its ornamental pond laid out, and to its right the Congregational Church is clothed in scaffolding. Behind it the foundations of the Old Peoples' flats make an inverted 'L' and beyond this the Old Peoples' Home is nearly completed. Further right various types of housing are in course of erection, while at centre right the Primary and Nursery School have been erected.

53

54

53. Lansbury: progress on Stage One

All kinds of unexpected things happen during the redevelopment of a large area: in the city of London, for instance, the foundations of a Roman temple of Mithras were discovered. In the East End it was less romantic, since the whole area had been largely open fields until the nineteenth century. But there were odd incidents, nevertheless, such as the navvy digging out the foundations for the new primary school and driving his pick within half an inch of a high-tension electricity cable that had been inaccurately charted; the unexpected discovery of a number of graves; an old tree that Peter Shepheard, the architect of the houses seen in the photograph, had made the building contractors preserve with endless patience only to find that the occupier of the house and garden wherein it stood had it uprooted within a few days of occupation. At the far right the teaching block and playground of the new secondary school are almost completed, while in the foreground the site is being cleared for the Roman Catholic church.

54. Lansbury: the Shopping Centre in use

Lansbury Shopping Centre with its new Market Place in use. The architect, Frederick Gibberd, offered to design new stalls for the traders, but they preferred to carry on with their untidy and shabby old stalls. Nevertheless the atmosphere on a market day is lively in the extreme, with all the quick bantering humour of the Cockney. In the foreground is the covered market, which was lined throughout with vitreous tiles for the fresh food stalls. The traders in fresh foods, however, preferred to sell their goods off their old stalls.

55

56

55. Lansbury: the new entrance road

Only one new road was built in the new development, but over one third of the existing roads were made redundant owing to the larger size of the building sites. Here the new road, named Saracen Street, is seen as one of the entrances to the Neighbourhood. The flats on either side are by different architects, but both by agreement used low-pitched slate roofs and London 'stock' type bricks. Every effort was made to preserve the few existing mature trees.

56. Lansbury: Nursery and Primary School

For the Primary School the architect, the late F. R. S. Yorke, used many of the building components pioneered by the world famous Hertfordshire Schools Programme, and it was erected very rapidly. In an area where a large building programme is in progress it is very important that as many of the buildings as possible should be completed at the same time so that the total new landscape can be achieved. Where sites are left in a derelict or unfinished condition the new dwellers get used to inferior surroundings and tend to adapt their behaviour accordingly. These two schools were fortunate in having first-class head teachers and staff, who made it their business to see that the children were aware of the new urban surroundings, and we gave a number of lectures to them on reconstruction. On the first day all the children arrived spotlessly clean and with new clothes, except one boy who had to do an early morning coal round. There was a good deal of pessimism among the non-architects about the large windows: they feared that in a 'tough' area like this all the windows would soon be smashed. In the event five windows were broken in three years, three by staff moving furniture. The Primary School houses 520 pupils and the Nursery School 80.

57

58

57. Lansbury: Trinity Congregational Church

On a site near by, the former church, built by a ship-builder in 1841, was totally demolished by bombing. The church authorities were provided with a new site in Lansbury and decided to build a church for 400, together with large and small halls and Clubrooms. For planning reasons it was decided to provide a small public open space in front of the church, and this was carefully land-scaped with a pool to reflect the building.

58. Lansbury: Peking Close

This small residential square is still one of the most attractive and human features in the area. Designed by Peter Shepheard, it provides an attractive hard-surfaced area which is sensible for walking or for children's play. The unprotected front gardens are carefully looked after and the newly planted trees are growing well. In the background the 'attached' houses for large families are equally successful.

59

60

59. Lansbury: the Old Peoples' Home

This quiet unobtrusive design was by a woman architect, Judith Ledeboer. It was well detailed and landscaped, and has been greatly liked by the old people. Originally we planned the Old Peoples' Home in the quietest part of the Neighbourhood, but the Welfare Committee found that the old people wanted to be near a lively active part of the area, so we sited it between two schools; sometimes this has been almost too noisy for them, but on the whole it has fitted in very successfully. It was designed for forty-nine old persons and a staff of five. Adjacent to it is a small block of flats for elderly people who can still look after themselves.

60. Lansbury: the Secondary School

The Cardinal Griffin Catholic Secondary School was designed for 450 boys and girls from 11 to 15 years old. The photograph shows the end of the main classroom block on the left with the gymnasium superimposed on the school hall in the centre and the dining-room with staffrooms over it on the left.

61

62

61. Lansbury: Stage One after ten years

Gradually the new development settles in to make a normal and natural environment, but an environment which provides very different standards of living from the older one. The trees, newly planted in 1951, have now matured considerably, and interesting play objects, such as the old caravan on the right, all help to humanize the scene. We spent a great deal of time in obtaining simple and unobtrusive railings (one day it will be possible to do without them altogether as they do in Holland today). To the north of the Primary School (known as the Susan Lawrence School) is a newly completed four-storey maisonette block, while behind it rises a new eleven storey 'point' or tower block of flats for small families.

62. Lansbury: Stage Three

A view looking north from Stage One. Off the photograph to the right is the Nursery School while on the left is a newly completed terrace of four-storey maisonettes, with gallery access at the third floor for the upper row of dwellings. What was once a through road has been turned into a cul-de-sac. In the background may be seen the new tower blocks between which a parkway leads to the new park.

63 

63. Lansbury: the Second and Third Stages

In the foreground is one of two tower blocks erected as part of Stage Two. By this time over 100 of these eleven-storey buildings had been erected by the L.C.C., and a high standard of low-income accommodation had had been achieved. Immediately to the right of the block is the row of small shops which we had built in Stage One to house temporarily the displaced traders while the new shopping centre was being built. Beyond is Stage Three under construction, with more tower blocks for small families. When the scheme is completed the tower blocks will be in the middle of a leafy parkway leading from the shopping centre to a major seventeen-acre open space.

64

64. Lansbury: progress

This view gives a good idea of progress in the Neighbourhood up to 1961, approximately ten years after redevelopment began. In the foreground is the Shopping Centre, with its Market and Clock Tower, but it still awaits the second stage which is now taking place between it and the main East India Dock Road (bottom left). The rest of Stage One runs diagonally leftwards up the photograph, and the Primary and Nursery Schools can be seen adjacent to the Shopping Centre. To their left is the super block of maisonettes with two three-storey squares, while beyond is another Primary School and the Old Peoples' Home. Above the latter is the Secondary School. At middle left is the over-large Roman Catholic Church (we originally planned for a much more modest building). At middle right is the large housing scheme called Alton Street (sometimes confused with the Alton Estate, now renamed Roehampton I), with its five tower blocks, four-storey maisonette terraces, two-storey square for elderly people, and two-storey echeloned terrace houses. In this scheme the garage accommodation was increased from the 10 per cent provided in Stage One to $33\frac{1}{3}$ per cent, while additional garages were added to Stage One in spaces which had been left for the purpose. At middle right is the Barchester Street Scheme which formed Stage Two. It consisted of two tower blocks, and a series of squares of four-storey maisonettes with (off the photograph) two six-storey maisonette blocks. At upper centre may be seen the First Stage of the seventeen-acre new Park. To its left is an isolated block of flats carried out as part of Stage Three, and behind it some lower blocks built as part of Stage Two. In the distance, above the railway line, is the St Anne's Neighbourhood with the clearly marked new Park of King George's Fields.

65 

St. Anne's

65. St Anne's Neighbourhood: as it was

An air photograph of East Stepney taken after the war. Large areas cleared by bombing can be seen, as can a large number of damaged buildings with their roofs repaired. In the foreground are docks, warehouses, and St Anne's Church (from which the new Neighbourhood derives its name – the Church was built between 1712 and 1730 to the designs of Hawksmoore). Above it the Commercial Road can be seen running across the photograph. Beyond the road is a triangular area bounded by the railway viaduct and the Burdett Road which is the site of the Neighbourhood. Running backwards into the distance and parallel with the latter road is the Regent's Canal, between which and Burdett Road Abercrombie proposed a great green parkway right up to Victoria Park.

66

66. St Anne's Neighbourhood: as it will be

A photo-montage showing the model of the proposed Neighbourhood and Parkway superimposed on the air photograph. The contrasting patterns of nineteenth- and twentieth-century urban development show clearly in this presentation. The broad green Parkway planned in the County of London Plan 1943 envisaged a continuous green strip from Victoria Park right down to the river. In implementing the Plan we found that the industries near the river were too expensive to move, so the Parkway now terminates at St Anne's, as in the photograph. Three-quarters of the Open Space shown in the photograph is completed, but not, alas, with its mature trees.

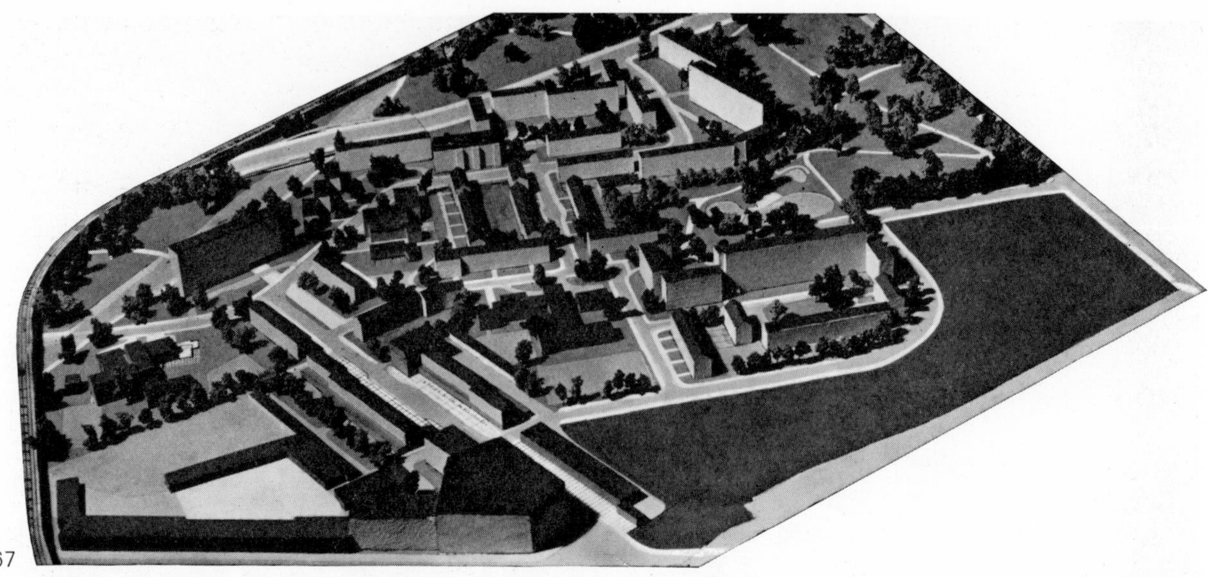
67

67. St Anne's: first model

An early scheme for the Neighbourhood. At this stage (1952) we were still restricted by the Housing Committee to six-storey blocks of flats (at the density of 136 persons per acre, approximately two-thirds of the population were to be housed in flats). The large pentagonally shaped building at the bottom of the photograph was an existing and very substantial Sailors' Club and Hostel. The road running diagonally to the left above it was Salmon Lane, an old Stepney shopping street which had to be retained as a local traffic way in the scheme.

68

68. St Anne's: model of the final scheme, 1955

This is typical of the mixed development as advocated in the County of London Plan. In the foreground is a L.C.C. Housing Depot and District Office, with the existing Sailors' Club and Hostel on the right. Immediately above is the Salmon Lane Shopping Centre, reduced after a careful social study from a pre-war total of 65 shops to 24 new ones. Both to the right and left of the Shopping Centre are Primary Schools, that on the right being for the Church of England for 320 children, while that on the left was for the Roman Catholic Church for 240 children. Adjacent to both schools are blocks of three-storey flats some of which were to frame a Place dominated by a fifteen-storey tower block. The tower block itself was to help to open up the Regent's Canal at this point (seen at far left). To the right of the tower block was to be a Mission Church and a Nursery School. Above this group may be seen a pre-war block of tenements, while to their right are three terraces of five-roomed houses for larger families with adequate private gardens. The programming for this scheme is up to date except for the Schools, and nearly everything except for them and the tower block has now been completed.

69

70

69. St Anne's: a detail of the final model

The square in the foreground has been lived in some time. Although the end of the great Parkway, which terminated in the open space with the paddling pool (far right), took some time to bring to reality, everything seen in the photograph (with the exception of the Primary School and Mission Church) is now completed. This large-scale model was very valuable during the negotiating stages of the scheme when meetings would be held around it, attended by those responsible for the street lighting fittings, tree planting, paving, litter bins, etc.

70. St Anne's: progress

A progress photograph showing the old slum and derelict housing being demolished while the new neighbourhood rises through rubble. Much of the original building in Stepney and Poplar, although substandard in function and condition was of good architectural quality. Efforts were made to continue certain aspects of the urban character by the use of London stock bricks, and low pitched roofs on the lower blocks.

71

71. St Anne's: the reality

The first residential Place to be created in the new Neighbourhood. Although the housing types here seen (eight- and three-storey flats) were later discontinued in preference to other types, the space remains pleasing and quiet. The tree in the foreground was planted at the time the buildings were completed, and artificial undulations were formed in the large grass area around the Gulliver (as the play-sculpture by Trevor Tennant is known locally). Small differences of level, changing textures and materials in paving, and hardy bushes, all help to make a medium-high density layout more interesting and attractive to live in.

72

72. St Anne's: a play-sculpture

A close-up of the Gulliver. This play-sculpture has proved to be very popular with all age-groups. It is set in a sand pit for safe play, and is in continuous use all summer. The sculptor, Trevor Tennant, came to see Mr Walter Bor (my Deputy Group Planning Officer at the time) and said that he wished to contribute as a sculptor to the new East End. Mr Bor suggested a play-sculpture, and the result has been an imaginative and popular success.

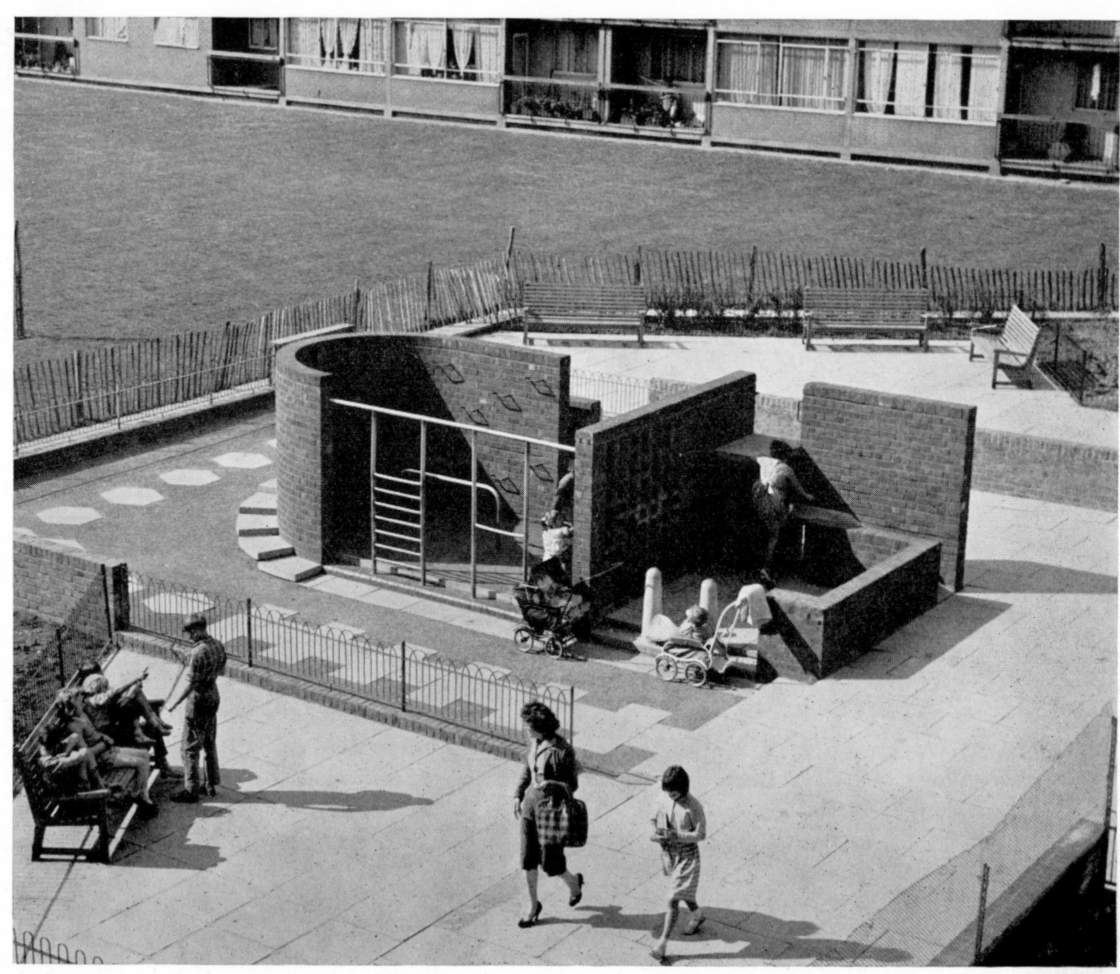

73

74

73. St Anne's: a play-space

This play-space is set in a square of the new Neighbourhood. The various types of open space provision and their distribution through the communities and neighbourhoods of Stepney and Poplar were the object of considerable social study. In this new square there is a sand pit for the infants, and the play space in the picture is fitted with a carefully designed piece of play equipment designed to exercise the 5 to 11 age-group. Seats are provided for parents, while the timber paling fence is a temporary barrier to give the newly planted grass a chance to grow (it did).

74. St Anne's: the Parkway

As there was a considerable amount of standing property, the great Parkway was programmed to be carried out in stages. The first major development was the 13 acres of St George's Fields, between Stepney and Poplar, and the photograph shows the new Open Space shortly after it was opened by the Duke of Edinburgh in 1952. This part was to be mainly devoted to much-needed playing fields. The line of factories in the background is along the Regent's Canal and at a later stage is scheduled to be removed to allow the Open Space to go right up to the Canal.

75

75. St Anne's: progress

An air photograph of the new Neighbourhood. The most prominent features from the air are still the docks, canals, and railway viaducts, while diminishing patches of the old development still remain, although by 1980 nearly all the bad old muddle will have gone.

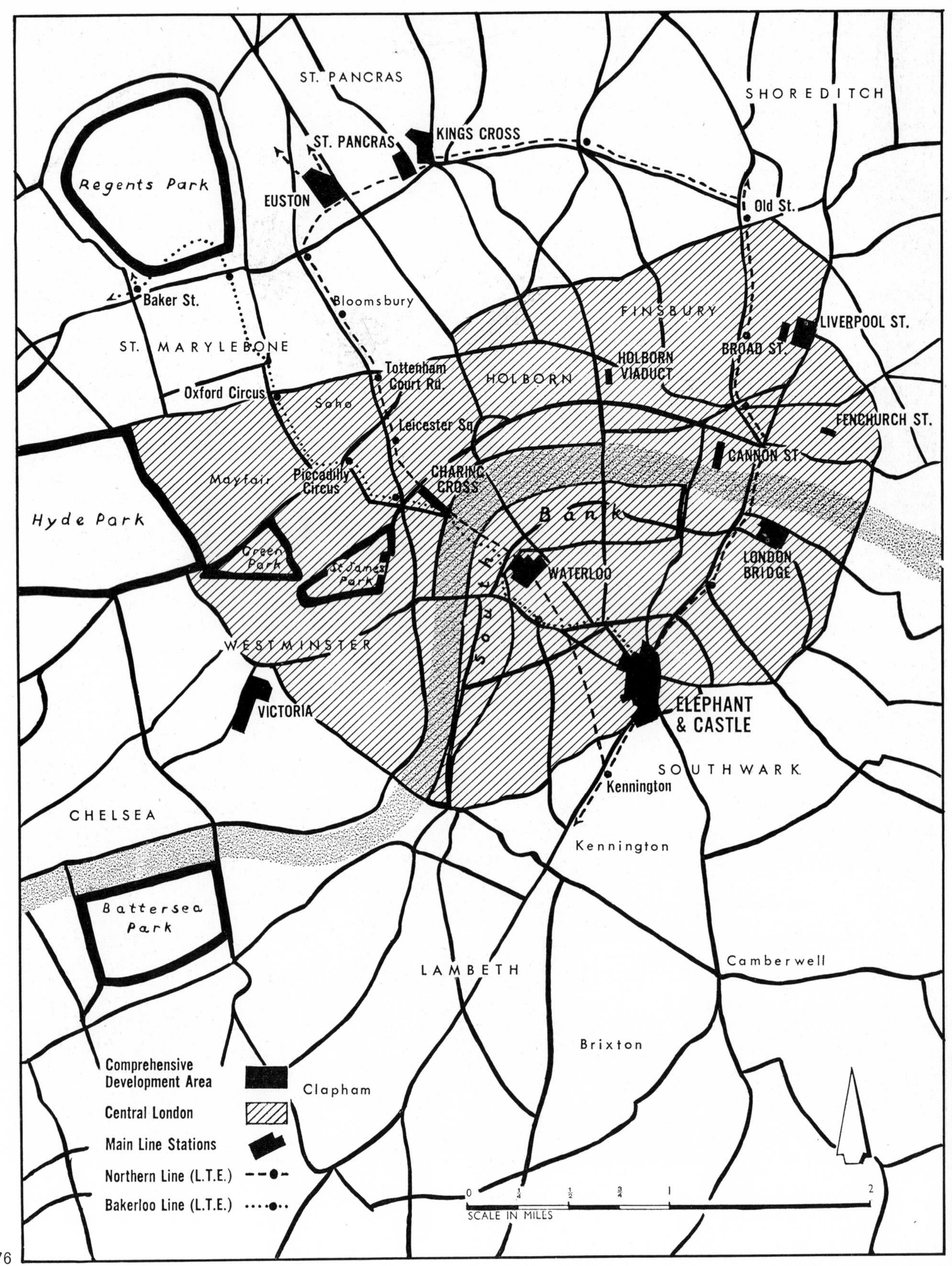

The South Bank

76. Central London

This plan shows the location of both South Bank and Elephant and Castle Areas of Comprehensive Development in relation to London's central area, together with the main roads, railway terminals, and underground lines.

77

77. South Bank

A general view looking over the Houses of Parliament with the great curve of the Thames, crossed by Westminster and Waterloo Bridges. Between the two road bridges is the Charing Cross railway bridge, destined to be replaced by a third road bridge at some future (unspecified) date. At the eastern end of Westminster Bridge can be seen the great monumental bulk of the L.C.C. County Hall, where so much of London's planning was done. Beyond it the too solid masses of the Shell office complex can be seen in course of erection.

78

78. South Bank, 1806

The South Bank has been through a number of phases of redevelopment: first as a cross-river entertainment centre, which included Shakespeare's Globe Theatre, then as a typical commercial and warehouse riverside muddle backed by slums and squalor. Even by the beginning of the nineteenth century, as this plan shows, it was a mass of wharves and warehouses. This part of the South Bank now contains the L.C.C.'s County Hall, adjacent to Westminster Bridge (and Wordsworth must have had his back to the contemporary muddle when he wrote his sonnet), with Waterloo Station in the hinterland. It is the site of the South Bank project which followed on from the Festival of Britain.

79 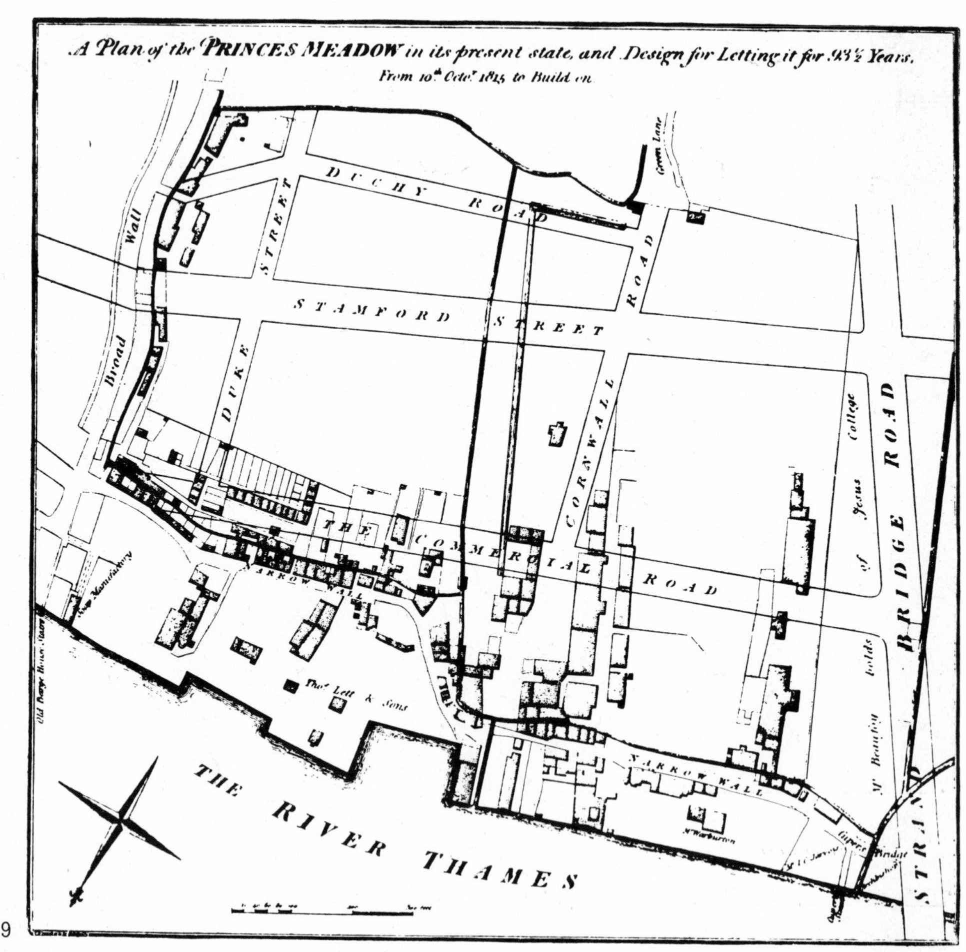

80 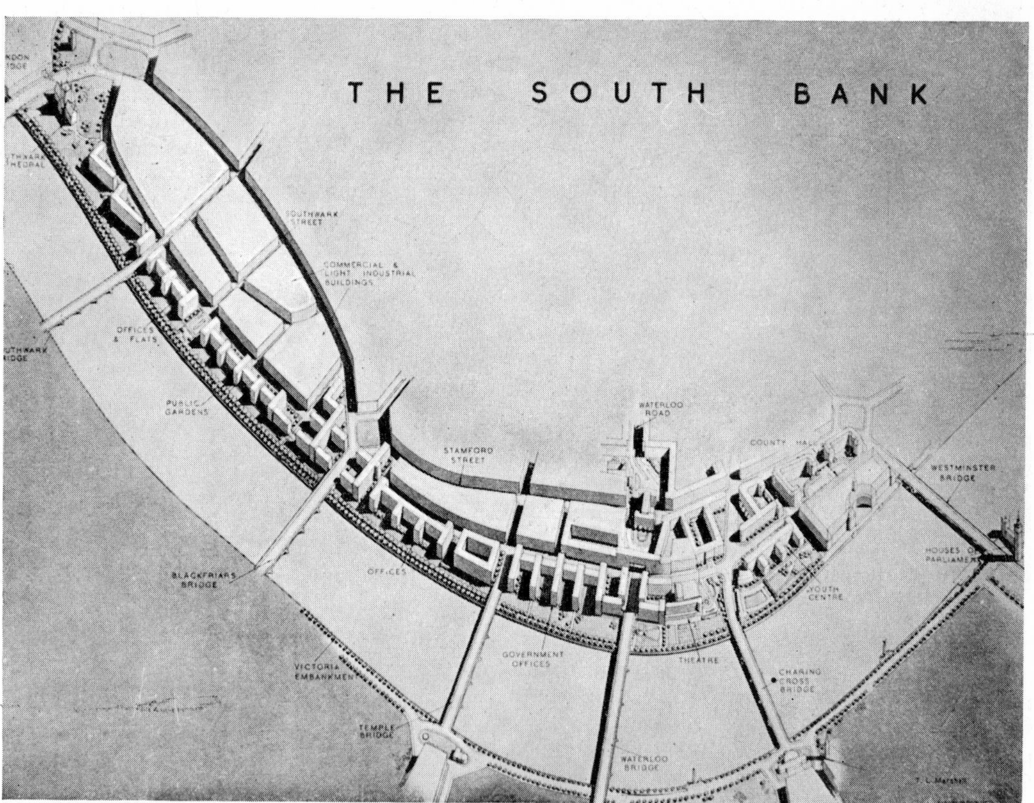

79. South Bank, 1815

By 1815 determined efforts were being made to achieve some degree of efficiency and order by driving a new road pattern through the area. The Strand Bridge Road in the drawing leads up to the then new Waterloo Bridge. This site is now proposed for a hotel and Convention Centre.

80. South Bank, 1943

An axonometric view prepared for the County of London Plan of 1943 by Mr T. L. Marshall, showing preliminary three dimensional proposals for the whole river frontage from Westminster Bridge down river to Southwark Bridge. Behind the broad riverside gardens there were to be cultural buildings, offices and flats.

81

81. South Bank: an early model

This little-known scheme for the South Bank was prepared by Dr Holden not long after the war, when the Government were still proposing to build an office complex on the area between County Hall and the Charing Cross (or Hungerford) Railway Bridge. The design conception is of a rather enlarged Paris-Haussmann category. The buildings are seen as very large palaces with internal courts, the roads as processional ways with totally unusable formal gardens in their midst, while the pedestrians have to be quick or dead. One must be fair and state that in my Reconstruction Group in the early 1950s we tried dozens of schemes keeping to the limitations of a Plot Ratio of 5:1 and the London Building Act provision restricting building heights, which amounted to '80 feet and two floors in the roof' – and we had little more success. Even now I would say unhesitatingly that a Plot Ratio of 5:1 is too high for London development, and that the standard of $3\frac{1}{2}$:1 that we evolved in the Barbican is much more suitable. More research into this problem is needed.

82

83

82. South Bank: The Festival of Britain, 1951

The site was chosen as the main area for the Festival of Britain (marking the centenary of the Great Exhibition of 1851, which saw the creation of the Crystal Palace). The whole area between County Hall and Waterloo Bridge was cleared completely, and a superb group of Exhibition buildings laid out by an outstanding team of designers, co-ordinated by Sir Hugh Casson. In the centre is the Royal Festival Hall, the only permanent building in the Exhibition area, and incidentally still one of the finest post-war buildings in Europe. It was designed by (then Mr) R. H. Matthew, Architect to the L.C.C., and his Deputy Dr J. L. Martin.

83. South Bank: the Royal Festival Hall

A view of the service entrance taken from under the arches of the Charing Cross railway viaduct. The upper-level deck provided along the main river front and on this side was connected to a footway across the river attached to the railway bridge. In the South Bank scheme of 1952 it was proposed to extend this deck throughout the area, and this is still one of the objectives of the plan. A major extension of the deck was approved in 1961 when the L.C.C. published its project for the extensions to the Festival Hall, together with an associated small Concert Hall and Exhibition Gallery. The photograph shows clearly the possibilities of the segregation of pedestrians and vehicular traffic.

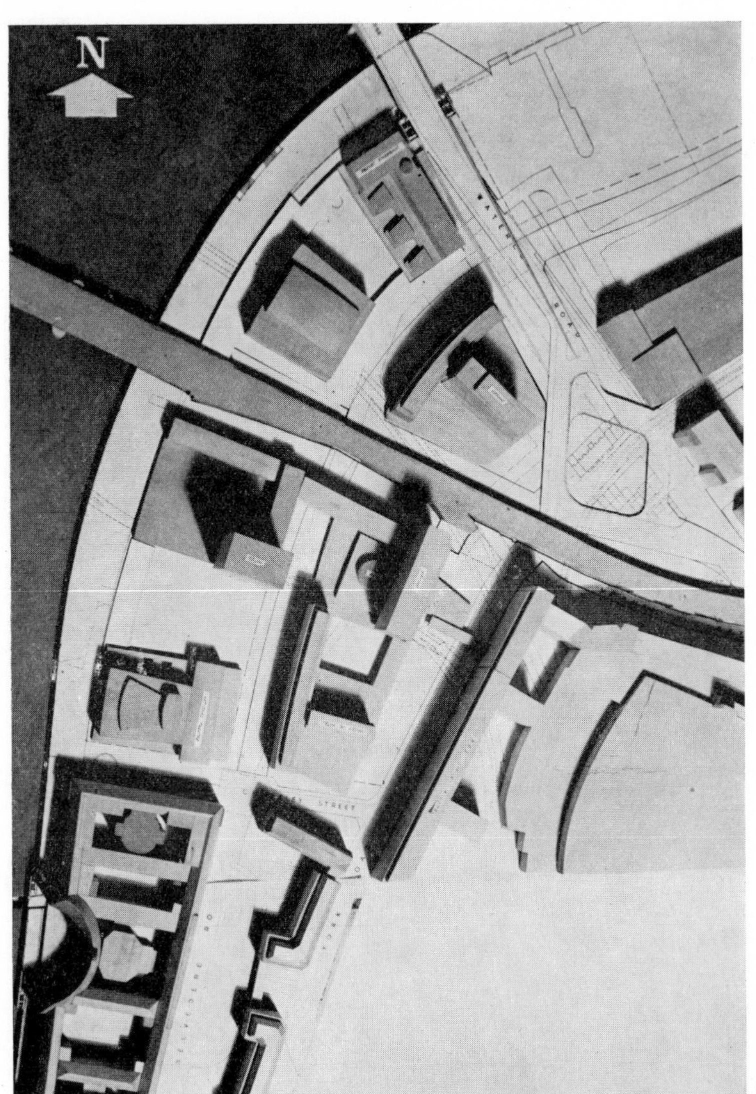

84

84. South Bank: design study for the 1953 scheme

Before arriving at the final solution, innumerable studies for alternative proposals were made, involving up to a dozen or more design possibilities for each building. Here is one of the many trial models: at this stage it was thought that the one high building agreed for the site as a whole might be the hotel on the riverside, but as no developers appeared for this site the high tower was transferred to the office complex behind, where the Shell Company wished to have a high building for prestige reasons.

85. South Bank: final studies for the 1953 scheme

This model shows the scheme nearing its final form. The circular building in the centre of the photograph was designed as the upper part of the British European Airways Air Terminal, but later they withdrew and went to a site in Kensington. The system of upper-level decks and connecting bridges can be clearly seen.

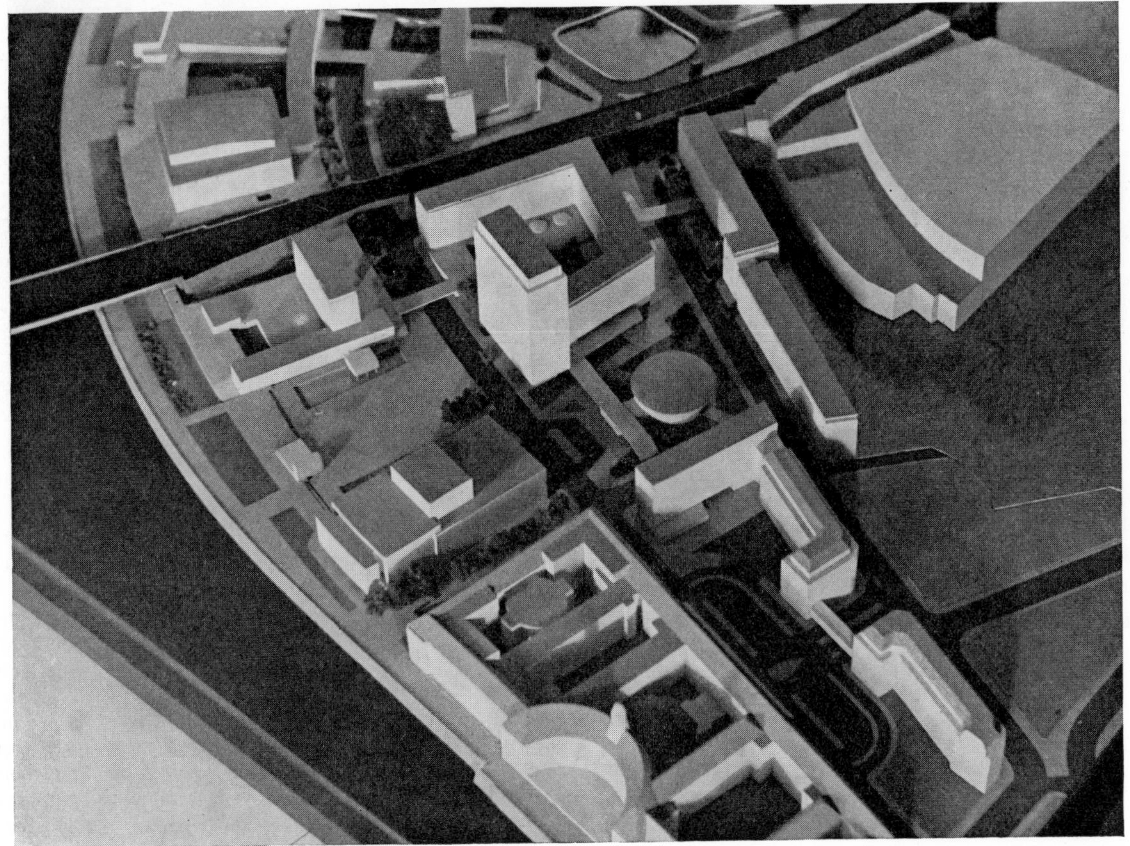

85

86. South Bank: the 1953 scheme

A vertical photograph of the final model at the time the scheme was published in 1952. A system of large enclosed squares was adopted. Above County Hall (bottom left) can be seen the National Theatre, which encloses the Theatre Square, together with the hotel opposite and the tall Shell office tower, which faces the uninterruptedly open west side to the river. The other adjacent squares are that facing the east front of the theatre and another enclosed by the office complex. North-east of the Royal Festival Hall is a smaller square enclosed on the far side by a proposed art and cultural centre, while a fifth square is enclosed by the office complex between the Festival Hall and the roundabout. The railway viaduct separating the two building groups was eventually to be replaced by a road. The team leader was Graeme Shankland.

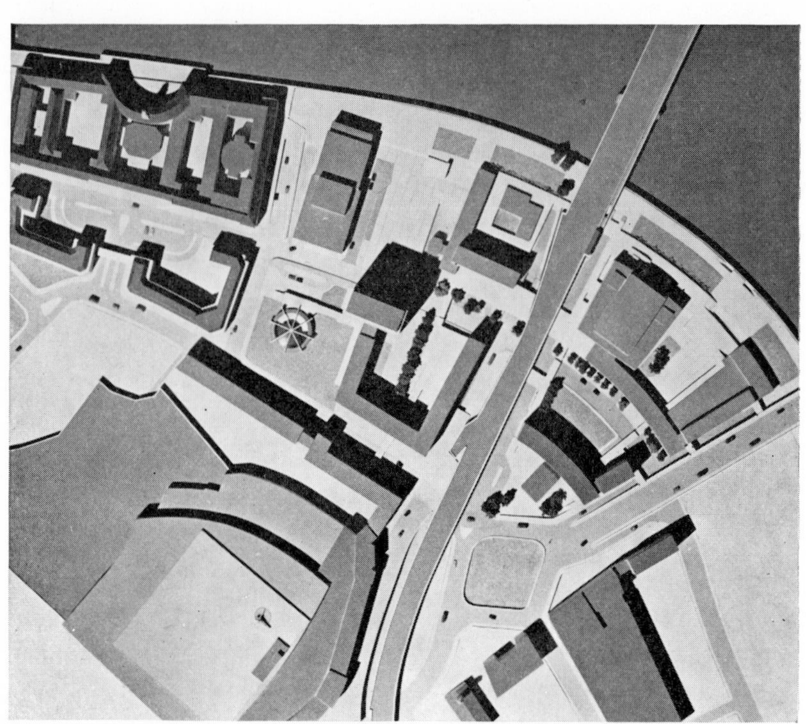

86

87

87. South Bank: the 1953 scheme

This montage was prepared in order to show how the urban spaces proposed in the scheme related to other familiar spaces in central London. The large square faced by the Shell tower compares in size with Trafalgar Square, while the others are similar to the Temple (top right) and Somerset House.

88

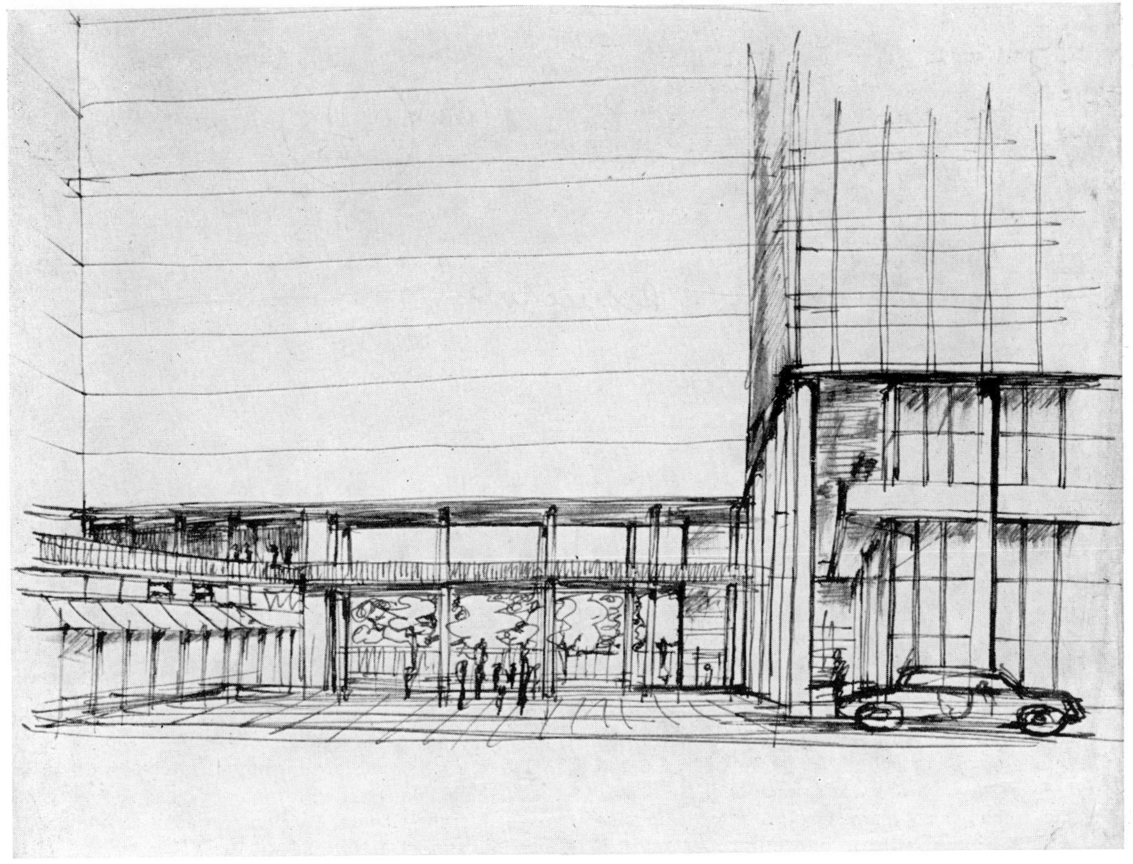

89

88. South Bank: a sketch of the 1953 scheme

This sketch was drawn by Dr (now Professor Sir) Leslie Martin after he had become Architect to the L.C.C. in succession to Mr (now Professor Sir) Robert Matthew in 1953. Messrs Matthew, Martin, and Ling (then Senior Planning Officer) all took a keen interest in the scheme.

89. South Bank: a sketch of the 1953 scheme

This sketch of mine was one of a large number done by various members of my group in order to indicate the character of the development we had in mind. This shows clearly that the idea was to have the office buildings resting on tall columns to which the upper-level walkways would be attached.

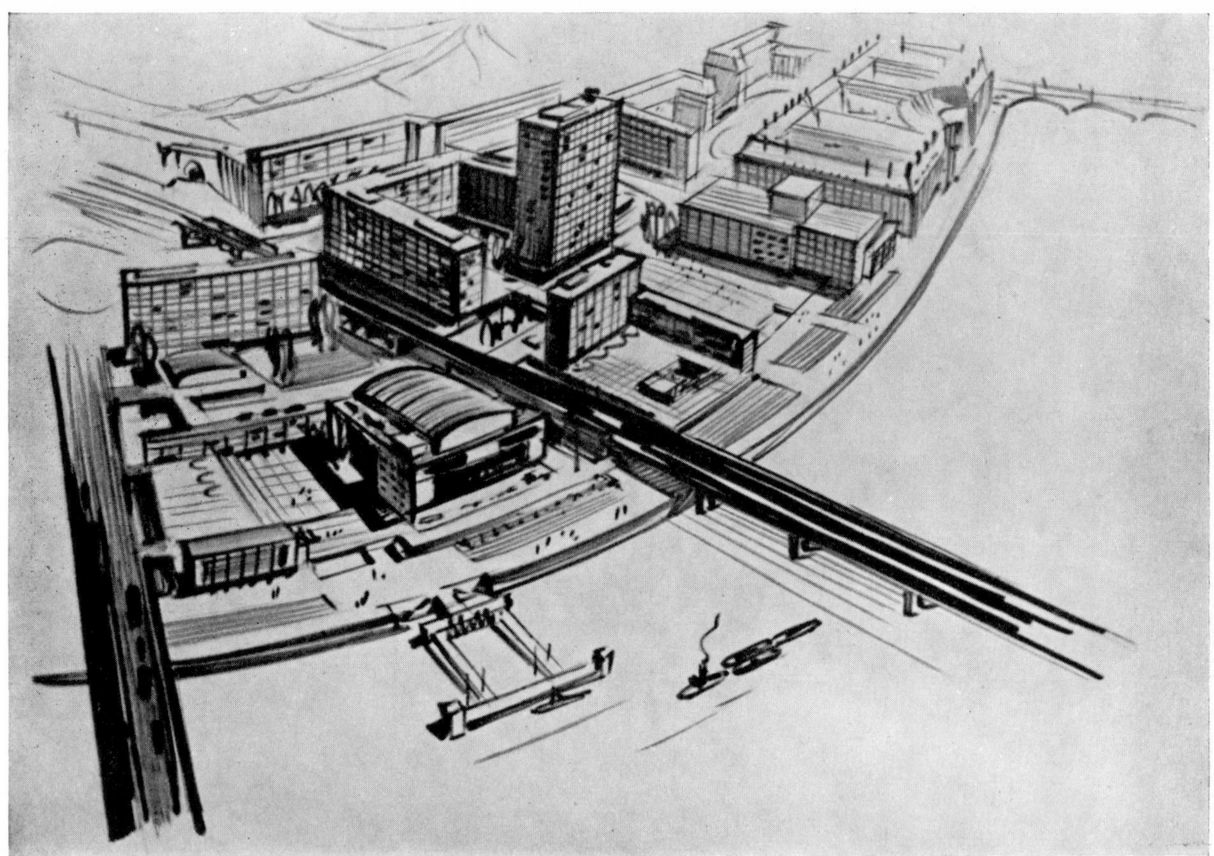

90

91

90. South Bank: a sketch of the 1953 scheme

This sketch, one of many drawn by the brilliant urban designer W. Kay, who was a member of our design team, shows the general arrangement of the buildings as proposed in 1952.

91. South Bank: National Film Theatre

One of the best designs in central London was that for the National Film Theatre, carried out by an Architectural Team in the General Division of the L.C.C. Architect's Department. Unfortunately, like a hermit crab which finds a convenient shell made by another crustacean, it is wholly enclosed within one of the abutments of the Waterloo Bridge.

92

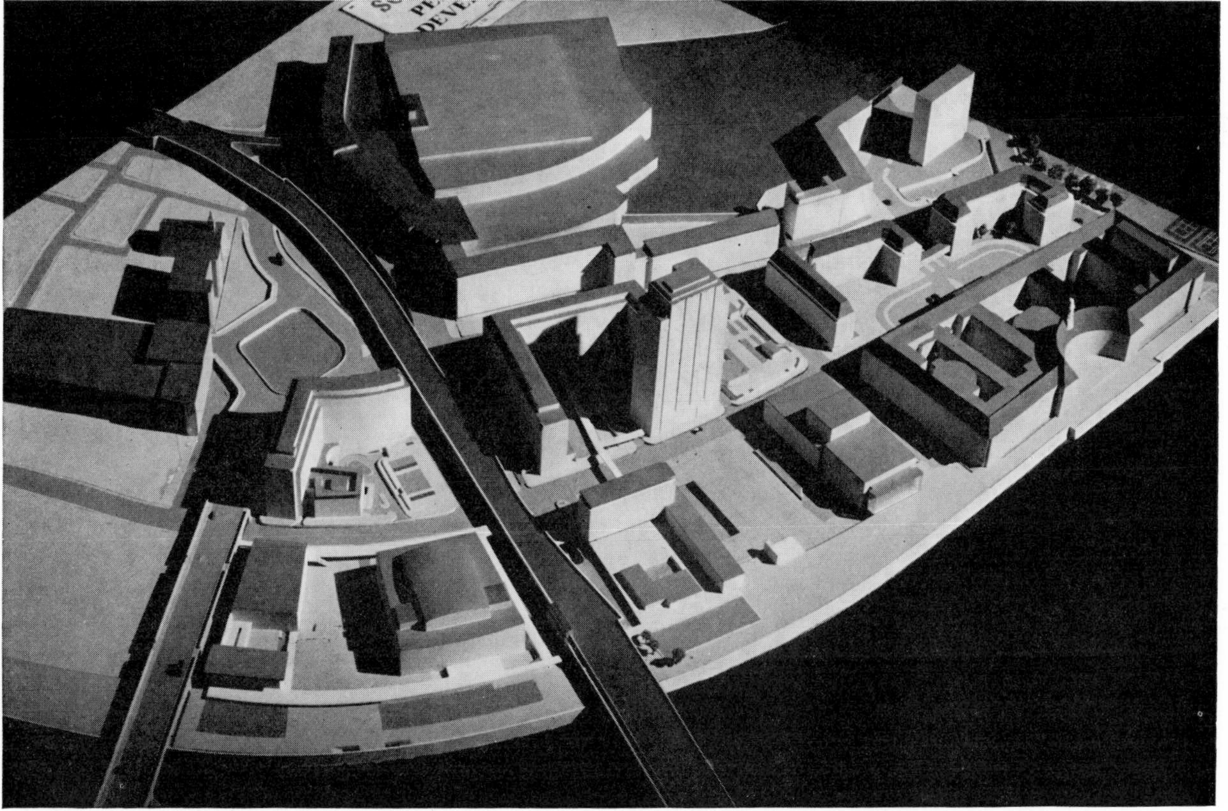

93

92. South Bank: the 1957 model

A photograph of a model of both sides of the River Thames. The bridges are, from left to right, Waterloo, Charing Cross railway, Westminster, Lambeth, and Vauxhall. It is interesting to compare this model of the South Bank Scheme with the proposals set out in the County of London Plan.

93. South Bank: central section of the 1957 model

By 1957 the Shell complex had begun to go ahead on the two sites set back from the river. This model shows how they were destined to change the urban scene – too large and too heavy blocks, giving a false impression of structural masonry.

94

95

94. South Bank: the Cultural Centre, 1961

By 1961 the London County Council was able to announce another major new development for the South Bank. The Royal Festival Hall itself was to be extended on both its river front and landward sites, while the long-awaited Cultural Centre adjacent to it was at last to become a reality. This was to consist of a Smaller Concert Hall, Recital Room and a large Exhibition Gallery, and the new building was to be joined to the Festival Hall pedestrian terrace by a major expansion of the upper level deck system. A car park for 170 vehicles would be provided under the Exhibition Gallery. The photograph shows a model of the proposed development.

95. South Bank: extensions to the Royal Festival Hall

When the Royal Festival Hall was built in time for the Festival of Britain in 1951, considerable additional accommodation had been allowed for in the future, notably a smaller Concert Hall. The Hall had, however, been built over an underground railway, and it was found that a smaller Hall set low down as part of the original building might have suffered acoustically. The decision was then made to move it to the adjacent site as part of the Cultural Centre. At the same time (1961) the extensions to the Festival Hall itself were announced. The photograph of the model shows the new riverside frontage with its upper-level terrace and lower riverside esplanade that is planned to extend right along the whole South Bank area. The extensions have since been completed.

96

96. South Bank

A recent vertical photograph showing current development. The vast Shell office complex, with its tower block, is nearing completion, as is the other Shell block across the railway bridge. Adjacent to this building is the first half of a new traffic roundabout (these roundabouts, although obsolete when planned, were rendered necessary by the Government's financial stringency after the war). The whole riverside area, apart from the Royal Festival Hall, still has the temporary landscape scheme carried out after the demolition of the Festival of Britain Exhibition buildings.

97 

The Elephant and Castle

97. The Elephant and Castle in 1826

The Elephant and Castle, which gave its name to the surrounding area, was an old coaching Inn erected in 1760 and rebuilt first in 1818, and again in 1898. A hundred and forty years ago it was already a considerable communications centre, but by 1940 it had become hopelessly congested.

98. Elephant and Castle: road diagram

The diagram shows how this part of South London had become a nodal point of communications. In addition to being a meeting-point of six major roads and an overhead rail station, it had two underground line stations, marked in the diagram with black dots.

98 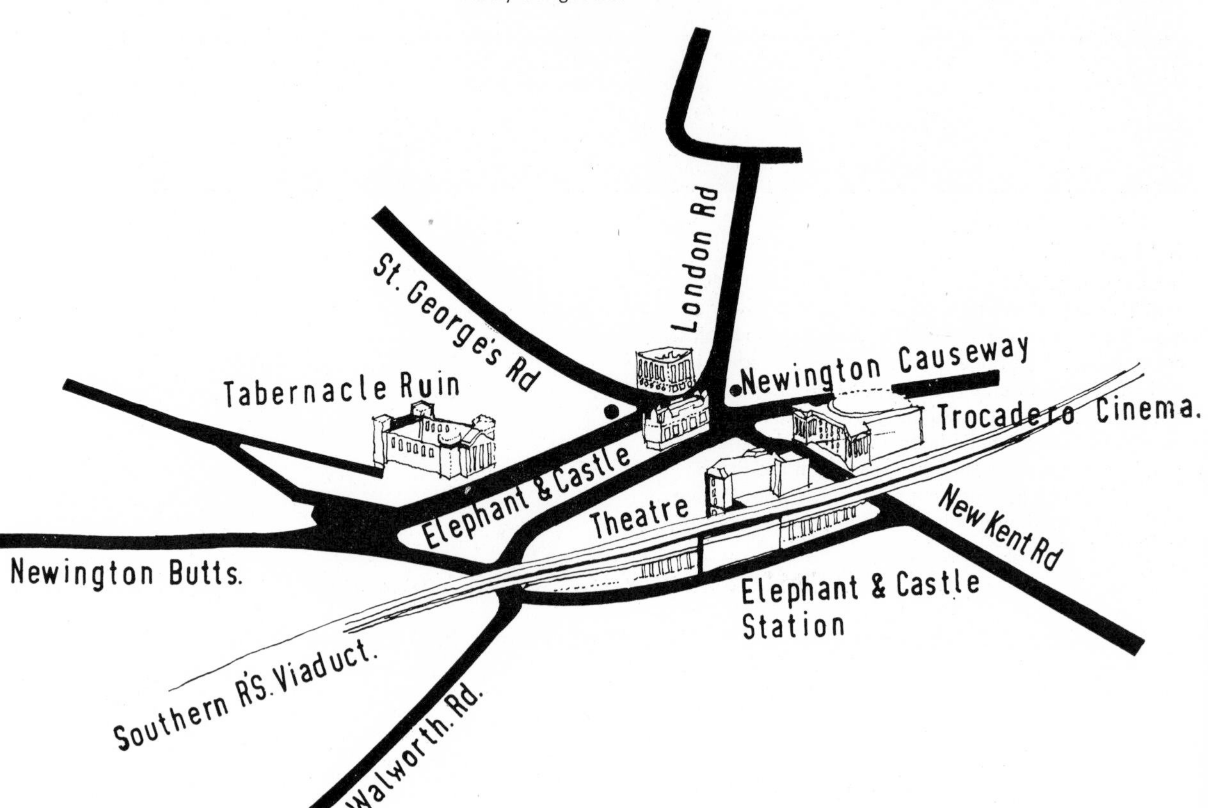

99

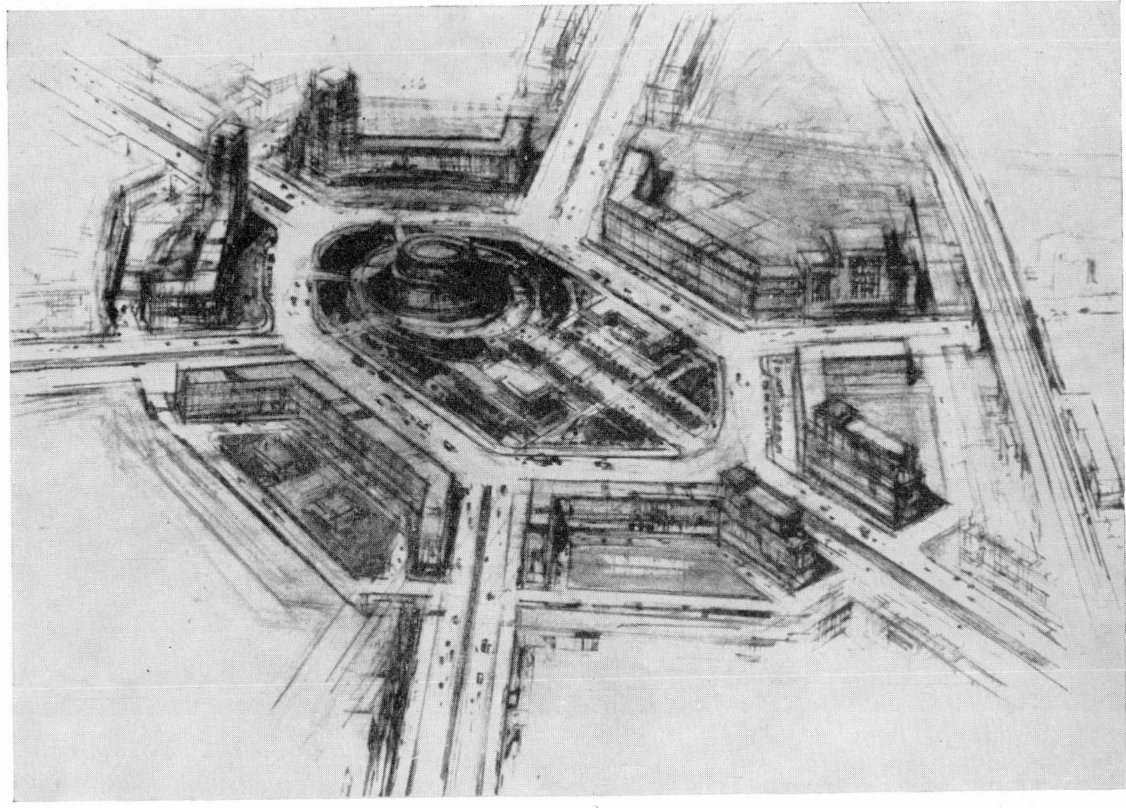

100

99. Elephant and Castle: after war damage

This photograph, taken in 1955, shows the area after bomb damage. The Elephant and Castle Inn itself, seen in the centre of the photograph, has since been demolished, as have the standing buildings both to its left and right.

100. Elephant and Castle: the 1943 proposals

In the County of London Plan of 1943 the Elephant and Castle area was the subject of an academic, backward-looking study in contrast to most of the creative ideas in the Plan. In the centre of a hexagonal roundabout is a large public building, while perimeter 'office and shop' type buildings front on to all sides of the intersection.

101

101. Elephant and Castle: a model of the 1954 scheme

The Ministry of Transport decided that the traffic intersection should be solved by a single level roundabout on financial grounds (the country was still in a state of financial difficulty in the early nineteen fifties). This, and the necessity to get the maximum value from the commercial sites in a commercially unattractive area, was the reason for a rather conventional perimeter-type development in the 1954 scheme. An attempt was made to mitigate these disadvantages by opening up the main shopping centre site with a broad terrace, on which were to be sited the underground surface stations and a cafe-restaurant. It was also hoped to connect the terrace by an underpass with the central reservation of the roundabout, which was to have been excavated and provided with a lower level shopping parade and car park (this was excluded from the scheme on the grounds of cost).

On the site in the foreground was to have been the London College of Printing, while across Newington Butts Road to the left Southwark Borough Council proposed to erect a large Swimming Pool. Beyond that may be seen the reconstructed Tabernacle Church, while at upper right is the Trocadero Cinema, then regarded as a permanent building, but recently demolished.

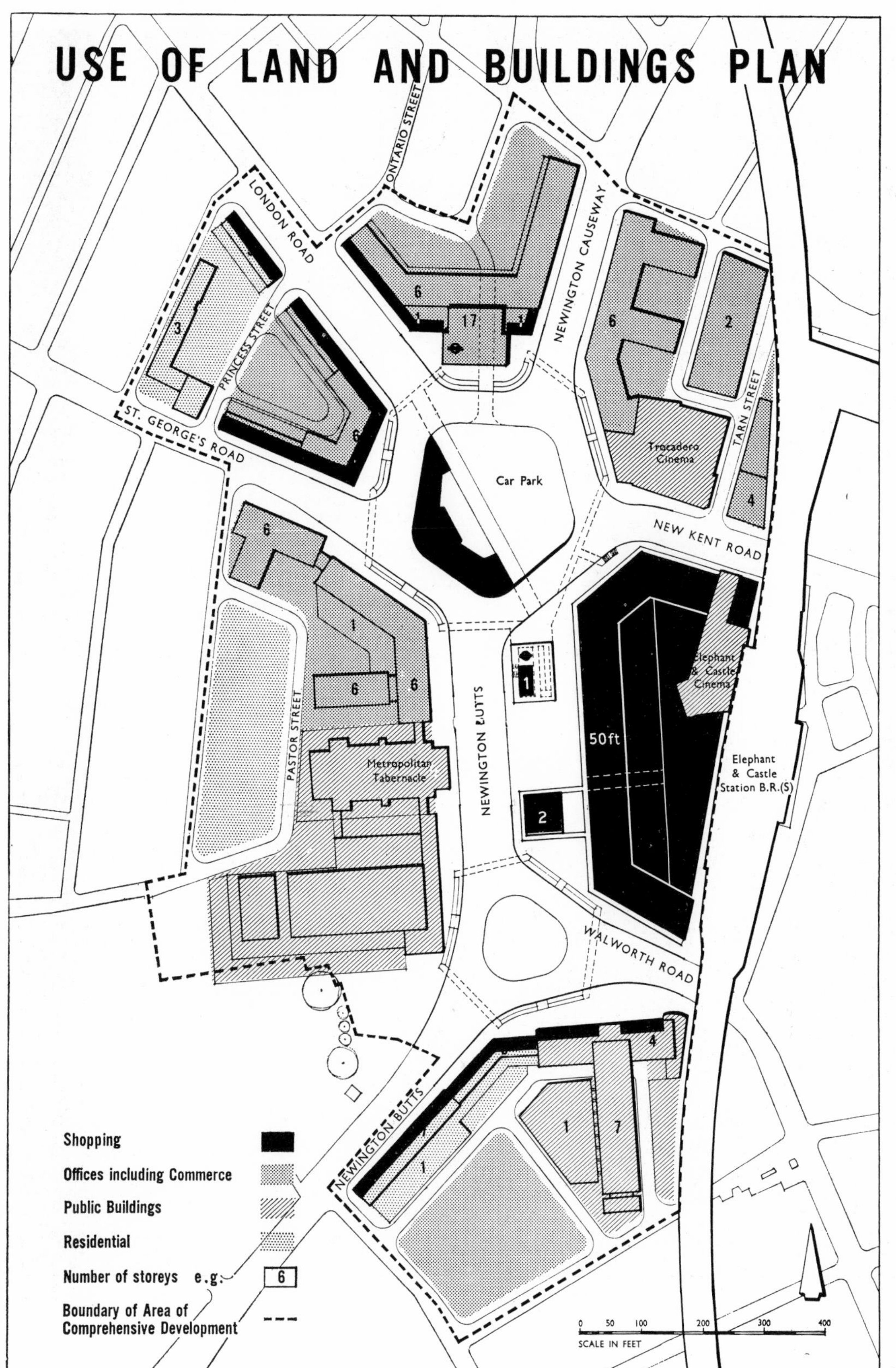

102. Elephant and Castle: plan of the 1954 scheme

This plan shows the position and heights of the various buildings proposed. There was to have been one high office building as a dominant feature of the whole area, with all the others of not more than seven storeys. The team leader was Graeme Shankland.

103

103. Elephant and Castle: the revised scheme, 1960

As few commercial developers had shown any interest in the area, the L.C.C. decided as a matter of planning policy to initiate development in the area itself. In addition to laying out the new road junction with its pedestrian underpasses, stairs, and ramps, the proposed College of Printing (a specialized Technical College) was moved up to the prominent site adjoining the large roundabout, and the imaginative design prepared for it by the Schools Division of the L.C.C. Architect's Department is seen, centre right. The original site on which it was to have been built was developed as a housing project by the Department's Housing Division, and may be seen at the top of the photograph. At lower left is a proposed high office building designed by Mr Erno Goldfinger, while to its left (off the photograph) another commercial building with a lower tower block by the same architect is completed. The Shopping Centre, designed by Messrs Boissevain and Osmond, is seen left-centre, with an office block above it, while the roundabout remains unexcavated but contains a memorial to Faraday. There are thus no less than five high buildings, all of which promise to be of high architectural quality individually, instead of the single one in the original scheme.

104

105

104. Elephant and Castle: commercial buildings

Commercial buildings designed by Mr Erno Goldfinger as part of the comprehensive redevelopment. The traffic roundabout is seen under construction in the right foreground. On the left are other sites being cleared for redevelopment, and on the right is the new Faraday Monument situated in the roundabout.

105. Elephant and Castle: the College of Printing

A model of the London College of Printing, now completed.

106

106. Elephant and Castle: the Shopping Centre

This building, by Messrs Boissevain and Osmond, was the winning scheme in a two stage competition organized by the L.C.C. for intending developers. There were thirty-six submissions in Stage One all accompanied by financial offers. The main shopping centre is in the form of a great cruciform arcade, rising through two floors. Above this is superimposed an office block rising to a height of 170 feet. Car parking for 154 cars is provided in two basement levels. The building is now complete.

The Barbican

107. The Barbican Area

This photograph, taken before reconstruction commenced, is a view looking across the area towards the Guildhall from the north-west. The church in the left foreground is that of St Giles', Cripplegate, built 1545-50, noted as being the church in which Cromwell was married. To the right of the St Giles' tower (the dark part at the top was added in 1683) is the north-west corner of the old city wall, with its prominent Roman Bastion. (Only the bottom four feet are supposed to be Roman work.)

107

108

108. The Barbican: the first scheme

This model, prepared by 1954, in my Reconstruction Group, shows the first scheme agreed between the L.C.C. and City Corporation Planners, and is montaged over an air photograph of the area. Along the bottom of the model, running from east to west, is Route 11, a road proposed in the Holford/Holden Plan for the City in 1947. Instead of the usual frontage type of development, we proposed a series of tall office towers along either side of the new road, each with a low slab, modelled on the Lever Building, which had been recently completed in New York, but with the low slabs all interconnected to form a continuous walkway at the upper level. Further north, on the east and west sides of the area, and near to the two underground stations of Aldersgate and Moorgate, we proposed two higher towers, which were intended to form part of a great circle of high towers around St Paul's Cathedral. Around the historic church of St Giles', left centre, we suggested that there might be a high-density residential neighbourhood. For locational purposes, the road running vertically up the left-hand side is Aldersgate, while that on the right is Moorgate. At lower right is Finsbury Circus, and at the top right is Finsbury Square (now provided with an underground car park).

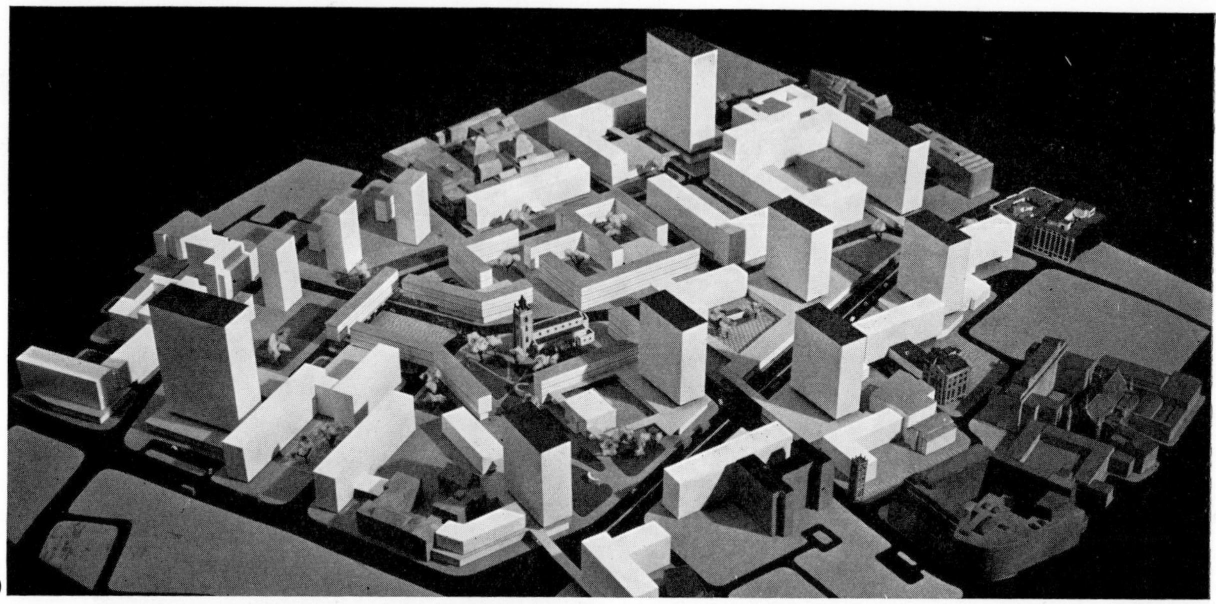

109

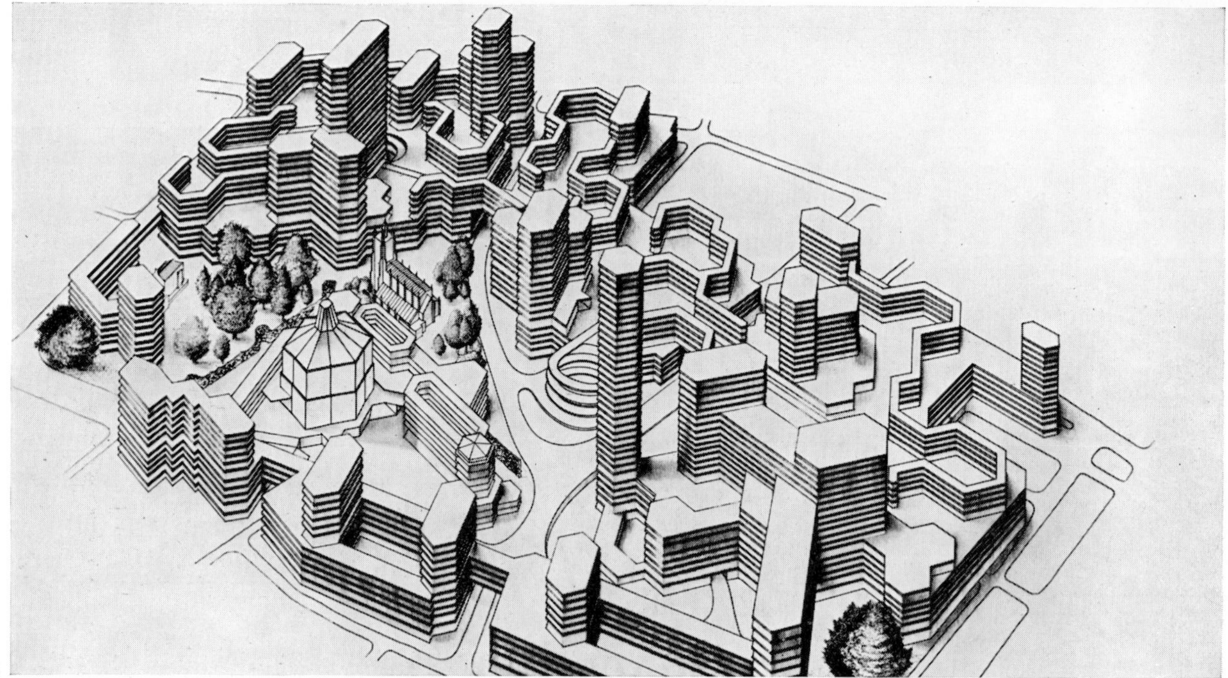

110

109. The Barbican: the first scheme extended

The extended model of 1954 shows two more tower blocks on the south side of Route 11, under which the City Engineer had planned (and later built) a continuous car park. Because of their proximity to St Paul's, we kept the height of these tower blocks down to a maximum of 200 feet, while the two higher ones further away were proposed at 300 feet. The team leader until 1955 was Gordon Logie.

110. New Barbican, 1954

During 1954 we were trying to persuade the City Corporation to accept our three-dimensional proposals for the Barbican Area. This scheme accepted the fact that the Corporation had already given some piecemeal approvals for development in the area on the basis of the old road pattern, and was designed to fit in with their wish to have the area redeveloped largely by private enterprise in units of acceptable size. Suddenly the area became a centre of acute controversy when a firm of very imaginative architects submitted a project as a planning application on behalf of a private group known as the New Barbican Committee. This was NEW BARBICAN, and it was proposed to redevelop the whole area of approximately 40 acres as one gigantic building complex. The majority of the area was to be excavated to a depth some 60 feet, and this excavated area was to be filled with four floors of warehouse accommodation and car parking for approximately 3000, vehicles. Above ground level it was proposed to build three floors of warehousing and industrial space with perimeter offices; on the roof deck of this would be a pattern of four-storey maisonettes, provided with shop, restaurants, pubs, etc. Above the residential area would rise five tall point blocks. There was also to be a centre of trade and commerce, with hotel, restaurant, etc. Although the scheme was not accepted, for various reasons, either by the City Corporation or the L.C.C. or by the Ministry on appeal, it did have the important effect of making it obvious to the public that there must be a comprehensive scheme for the Barbican Area. The architects were Messrs Kadleigh, Horsburgh, and Whitfield.

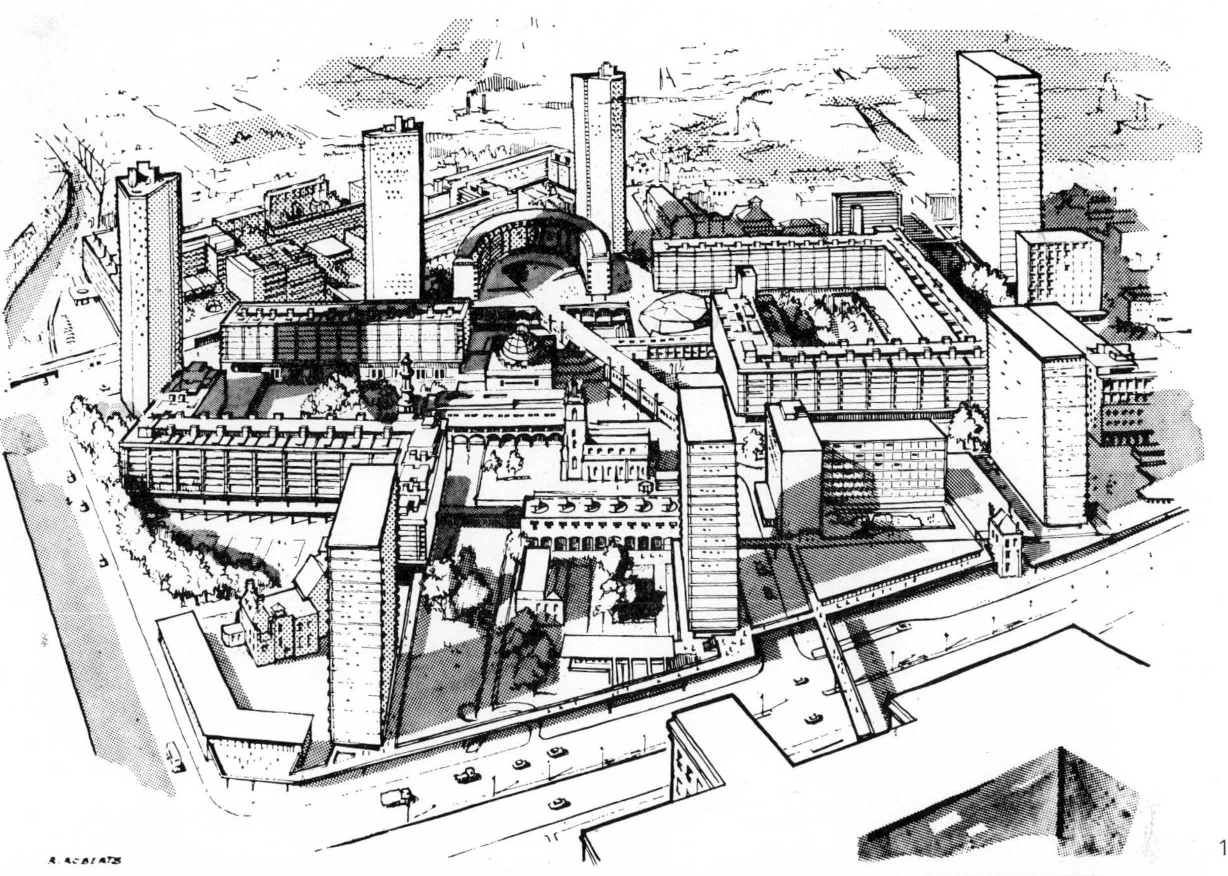

111

112

111. The Barbican

The drawing shows the residential neighbourhood designed by Messrs Chamberlain, Powell and Bon set within the larger context of the comprehensive design. In the foreground are three of the office towers, with a connected upper-level walkway system, all designed by different architects, and now built. Messrs Chamberlain, Powell and Bon made some revisions to the residential scheme as it developed. First, the omission of the Boys' Secondary School reduced the congestion in the great central space. Then they revised the western court in order to avoid daylighting infringements. Third, they altered the shape of the three tall residential towers along the north side of the scheme, from a rectangular to the less satisfactory triangular plan form.

112. The Barbican: residential neighbourhood

This close-up photograph looking west shows the group of office towers on the left and the taller one on the right. In the centre is the residential neighbourhood, with the eight-storey blocks of flats enclosing a great open space containing the luxurious social facilities, while in the background are the three thirty-seven-storey residential towers.

113

114

113. The Barbican: Roman House

Roman House was one of the designs for which approval had been given by the City of London before the comprehensive scheme was developed, and therefore had to be included as part of the design conditions. In the foreground the City Corporation carefully restored a section of the Medieval and Roman Wall, and laid out a small rest-garden around it.

114. The Barbican: the office group

This large-scale model of the main office area was made by the Department of the City Planning Officer (then Mr H. A. Mealand), in order to aid the detailed negotiations on the various sites, as the closest possible co-ordination was absolutely essential to ensure that the comprehensive upper-level deck system would work in detail.

115

115. The Barbican: Moor House

Moor House was the first of the high office towers planned on either side of Route II to be erected. The design followed the general idea of the original conception, and the upper-level deck can be clearly seen.

116 

117 

116. The Barbican: Route 11, 1961

Route II was first proposed in the Holford/Holden Plan of 1947 for the City of London as part of a bold network of communications. Like the County of London Plan road proposals, most of them were dropped or put off indefinitely, to the great detriment of London today. This part of Route 11 went ahead, as it traversed land cleared by bombing. The foreground of the photograph shows how difficult the problem is elsewhere. In the background the second office tower has reached full height, and work on the third and fourth is proceeding. The historic church of St Giles', Cripplegate, can be seen on the left.

117. The Barbican: an air view in 1962

In this view, looking north, four of the group of six office towers around Route II can be seen, and work on a fifth has begun. The upper-level decks are already equipped with shops, but as yet no bridges join them. In the centre background may be seen the Golden Lane and the Peabody Housing Schemes in the Bunhill Fields Area. In the centre foreground is the historic re-roofed Guildhall, with the large and ponderous new municipal office block behind it. The area reserved for the residential neighbourhood can be seen as a vacant site behind the towers.

118

118. The Barbican: an air view in 1962

This view, looking north-east, shows Route II and four of the associated office towers. Behind the towers can be seen the line of the Metropolitan Railway (the first underground railway in the world) which met with heated controversy when it was first proposed over 100 years ago. In the same way, the separation of pedestrians and vehicles was met with strong opposition, both in the case of the Coventry Shopping Precinct and the upper level deck of the Barbican. The photograph shows the decks at the base of each tower, with their shops and cafes, provided individually by each building owner. They have now been joined up by municipally provided pedestrian bridges, and form a good example of public and private collaboration.

119 

Bunhill Fields

119. Bunhill Fields

This model of the Bunhill Fields Comprehensive Development Area, which almost adjoins the Barbican Area (to the south – top right in the photograph) was a mixed up commercial, industrial, and residential area before the war. Bomb damage presented an opportunity, but the L.C.C.'s financial resources were heavily strained after the war and financial commitments were severely limited. For this reason the whole length of old Street in the foreground had to be left for piecemeal redevelopment, and the area between this C.D.A. and the Barbican Area also suffered for the same reason. The main objective was to secure a continuous residential area of high density (200 persons per acre) right through the area. The first section, seen at extreme right in the photograph, was almost entirely cleared by bombing, and the City Corporation (who owned the land, although it was actually in Finsbury) organized a competition for what was known as the Golden Lane site. It was won by a very able young firm of architects, Messrs Chamberlain, Powell and Bon, who, after a good deal of negotiation brought the scheme to a most interesting reality. Next to it (centre of photograph) was an area owned by the Peabody Trust, which already had two blocks of nineteenth-century tenements, thus rendering comprehensive development more difficult – the contrast between this scheme and that of Golden Lane is worth studying, since both are developed at the same density, and both are now completed. At far left on the model is the Bunhill Fields cemetery, resting-place of John Bunyan, and just beyond it (not shown in the model), in City Road, is the famous chapel of John Wesley, whose statue is in the forecourt. To the south of it is the Honourable Artillery Company's Field. Most of this part of the Area was zoned for commerce, and great difficulty was experienced in achieving any sort of co-ordinated development without having purchased any of the land. To the right of the Honourable Artillery Company's Ground (a *very* private Open Space) was a large vacant site which had been earmarked by the War Department. When this was relinquished it was taken over by the London County Council Education Committee for use as an extension to a Polytechnic College. To its right in the model is the very large and at present immovable brewery of Whitbread. The team leader was Gordon Logie.

120

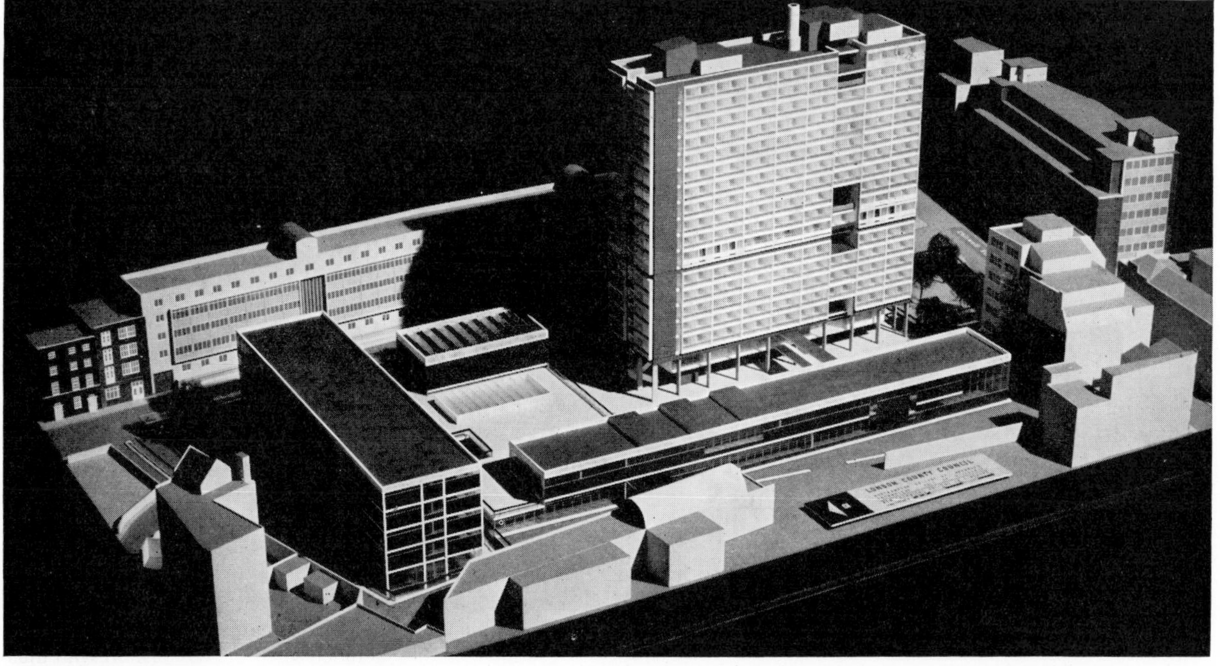

121

120. Bunhill Fields: the Golden Lane Scheme

As a result of a public competition the Golden Lane Housing Scheme was built for the City Corporation. In this scheme the Architects, Messrs Chamberlain, Powell and Bon showed what could be done with a modest budget at a density of 200 persons per acre. The photograph shows the high tower on the left facing a large area of hard paving with a surface pattern reminiscent of Lisbon or Rio. On the right is the Community Building and in the background are two blocks of six-storey maisonettes.

121. Bunhill Fields: extensions to the Northampton College of Advanced Technology

This large site, rendered vacant by war damage, was originally earmarked for the War Department. When relinquished it was taken over by the L.C.C.'s Education Committee for extensions to the Northampton College. An excellent design was prepared by the L.C.C. Architect's Department Schools Division. There is no doubt that the quality of the architecture is vital to the success of any comprehensive planning.

122

St. Paul's

122. Old St Paul's

This old study of Old St Paul's in its late medieval setting was drawn in Dean Colet's time. The City walls and gates are clearly visible, and the closely packed mass of building around the Cathedral is reminiscent of continental rather than British tradition.

123. St Paul's Precinct: before the war

This air photograph was taken in 1939, shortly before the area was devastated by bombing. By a miracle, and through the continuous vigilance of a volunteer group of architects, the Cathedral sustained comparatively minor damage. The Cathedral is here seen set in a mass of office and commercial buildings, most of them nineteenth-century replacements of earlier buildings, which had themselves replaced those destroyed in the earlier devastation of 1666. More recent buildings of larger bulk and greater height can be seen pushing through the congested muddle, and in fact increasing the congestion with their larger volume. Until the arrival of the electric lift St Paul's was safe in its dominating scale, but the new building at the bottom of the photograph was a portent of its possible overshadowing.

124. St Paul's Precinct: after the war

This air view, taken from an angle similar to the previous photograph, shows the extent of the war damage around the Cathedral. In spite of the devastation, enough pre-war building remained to cause great difficulties in the reorganization of the urban pattern.

123

124

125

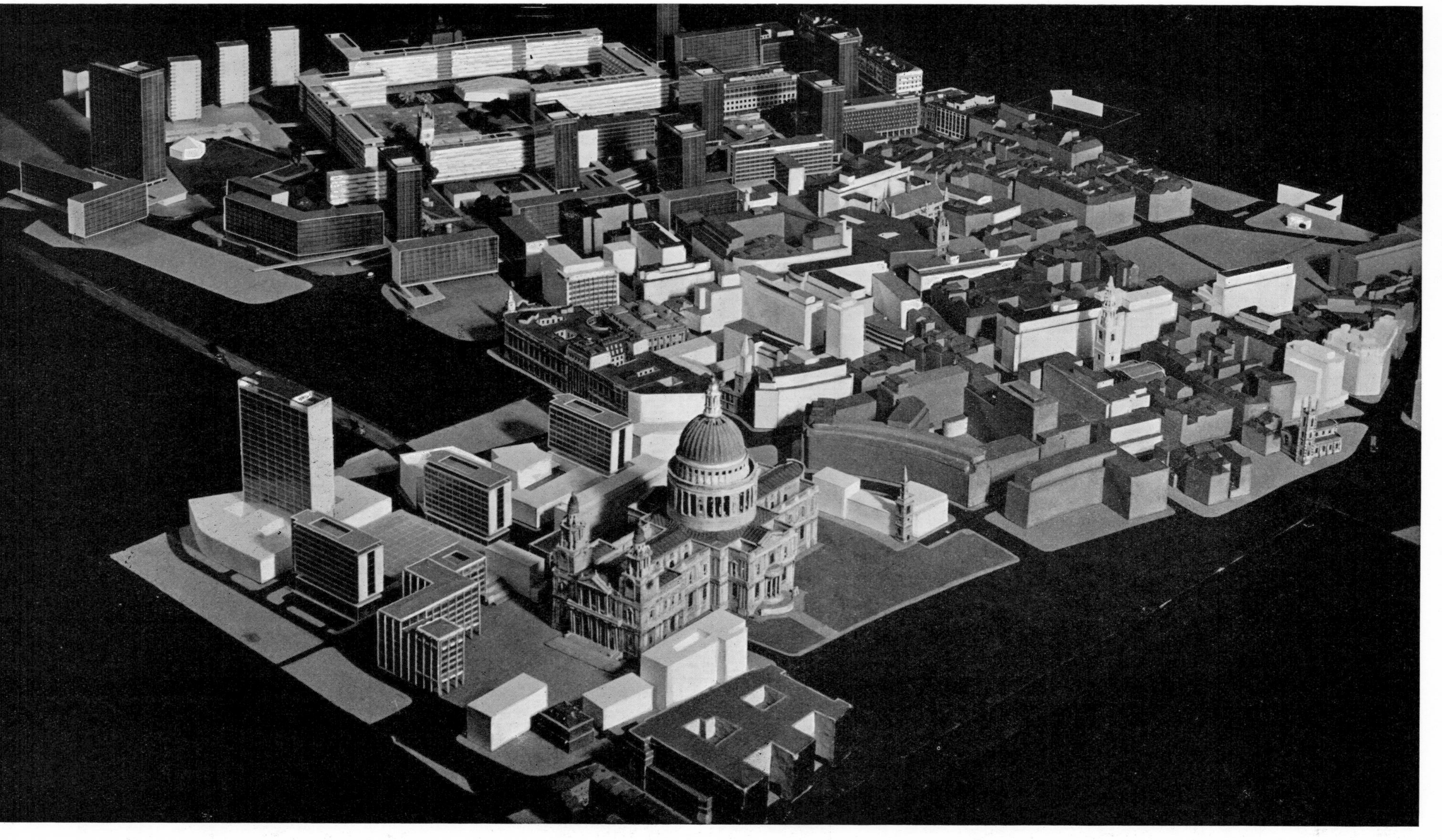

125. St Paul's Precinct: a composite view of the model

This photograph of a composite model built up by the City Corporation Planning Office is taken from an angle similar to the pre- and post-war air views. It shows the treatment proposed by Sir William Holford for the west, north, and east sides of the Precinct. Behind St Paul's may be seen a heavily damaged commercial area which was redeveloped at the recommended Plot Ratio of 5:1, and with all the buildings complying with the new Daylighting Code. It went ahead, however, without acquisition of the area and without an overall three dimensional scheme. After the Barbican (an intermediate proposal for which is seen in the background of the photograph) all large-scale redevelopment in the City, and elsewhere in London, was accompanied by a three-dimensional scheme for the whole area.

126

126. St Paul's Precinct: the model of the cathedral forecourt.

A view of the model from the south-west. In the foreground is the forecourt to the west front of the Cathedral. A broad flight of steps leads up to a large raised square on the north, under which are two levels of car parking. The high slab block of offices was judged to be too high (and rightly in my view) by the Minister of Housing and Local Government, who, when approving the scheme, asked for this block to be lowered. The office complex on the north is now almost completed.

127

127. St Paul's Precinct: from the West

A spirited drawing by Mr H. Mason, looking down on the Precinct from the west. At the bottom of the drawing Ludgate Hill comes up to a small and minor traffic Place, as the new main road going along the right hand side will eventually cut through the obsolete development at bottom right.

128. St Paul's Precinct: forecourt

Another clear drawing by Mr H. Mason of the west forecourt to St Paul's. The office building on the left was to be arcaded and to contain viewing balconies.

129. St Paul's Precinct

A cross-section from south to north passing through the main forecourt. This section shows the heights of the proposed buildings (except for the high tower) in relation to the Cathedral, and also the upper square with the two floors of car parking beneath it.

130

130. St Paul's Precinct
A recent air view taken from the north-west, with the Thames in the background. The area immediately to the south of the Cathedral has gone ahead, and here Sir William Holford adopted a suggestion we made that what had been a continuous wall of buildings should be opened up with a square so as to bring the old church of St Nicholas Coleabbey into the composition.

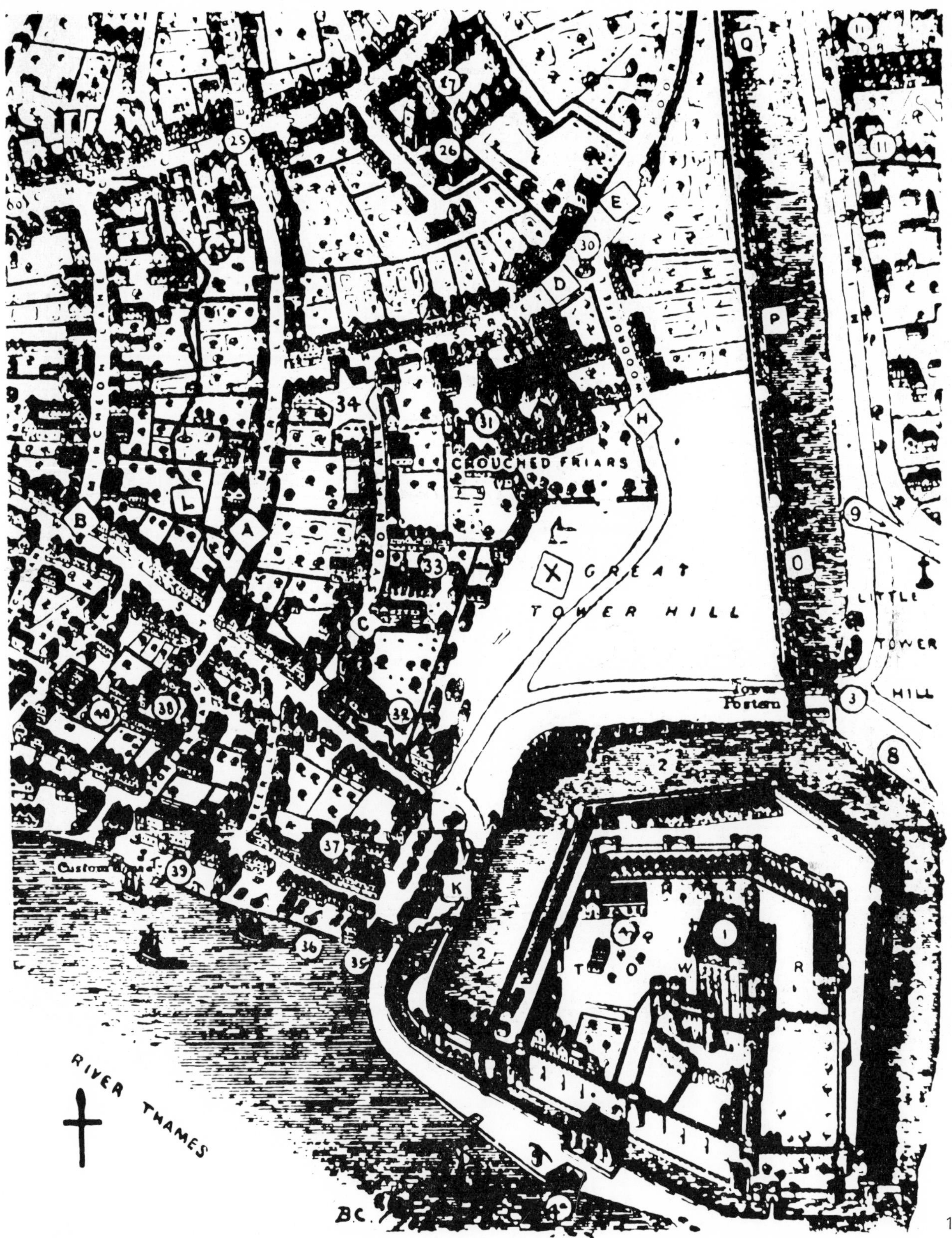

131

The Tower of London

131. The Tower, 1535

This map was drawn about 1535, when Henry VIII was on the throne, the poet William Dunbar probably still alive, and such figures as Cranmer, Tyndale, and Knox, were dominating the human stage. At this period the Tower was a great royal prison and fortress, and Great Tower Hill was formed by the necessity to keep a bowshot from its walls. On the hill stands the scaffold, which for many centuries was the scene of gruesome but popular executions.

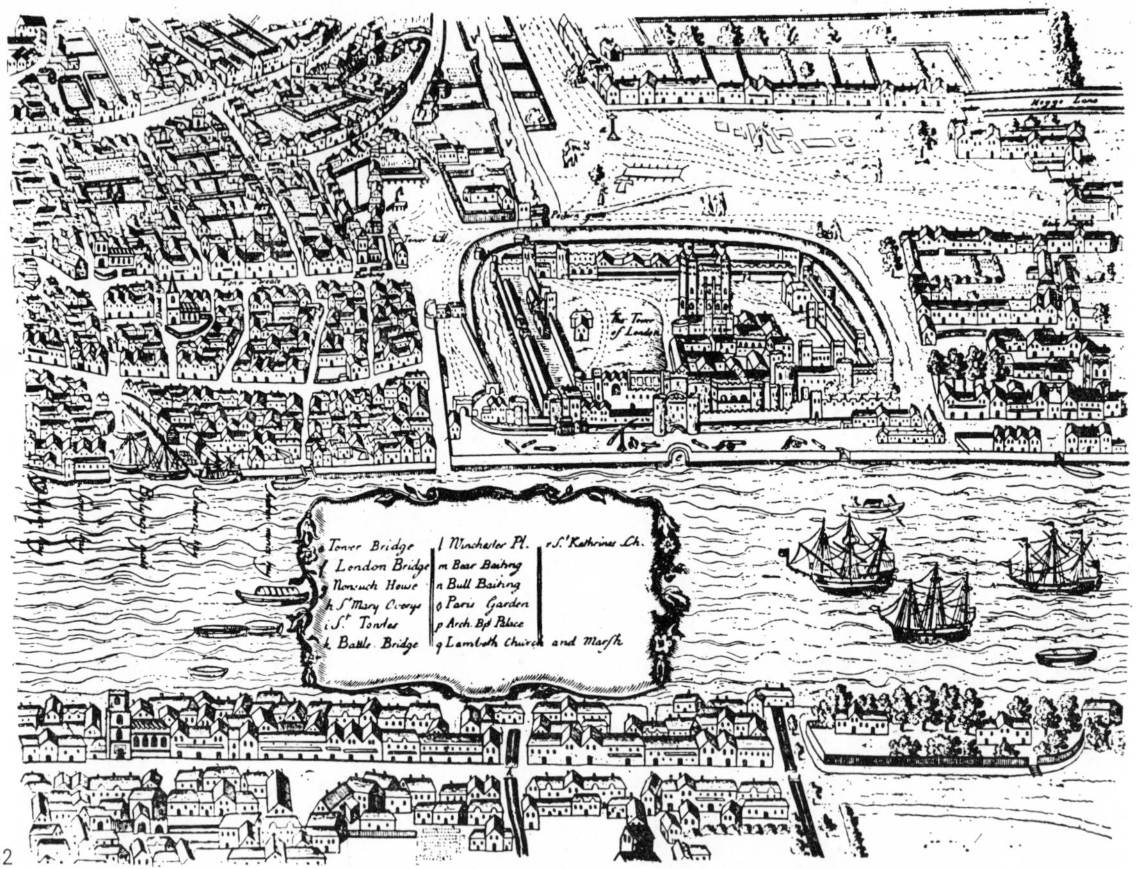

132

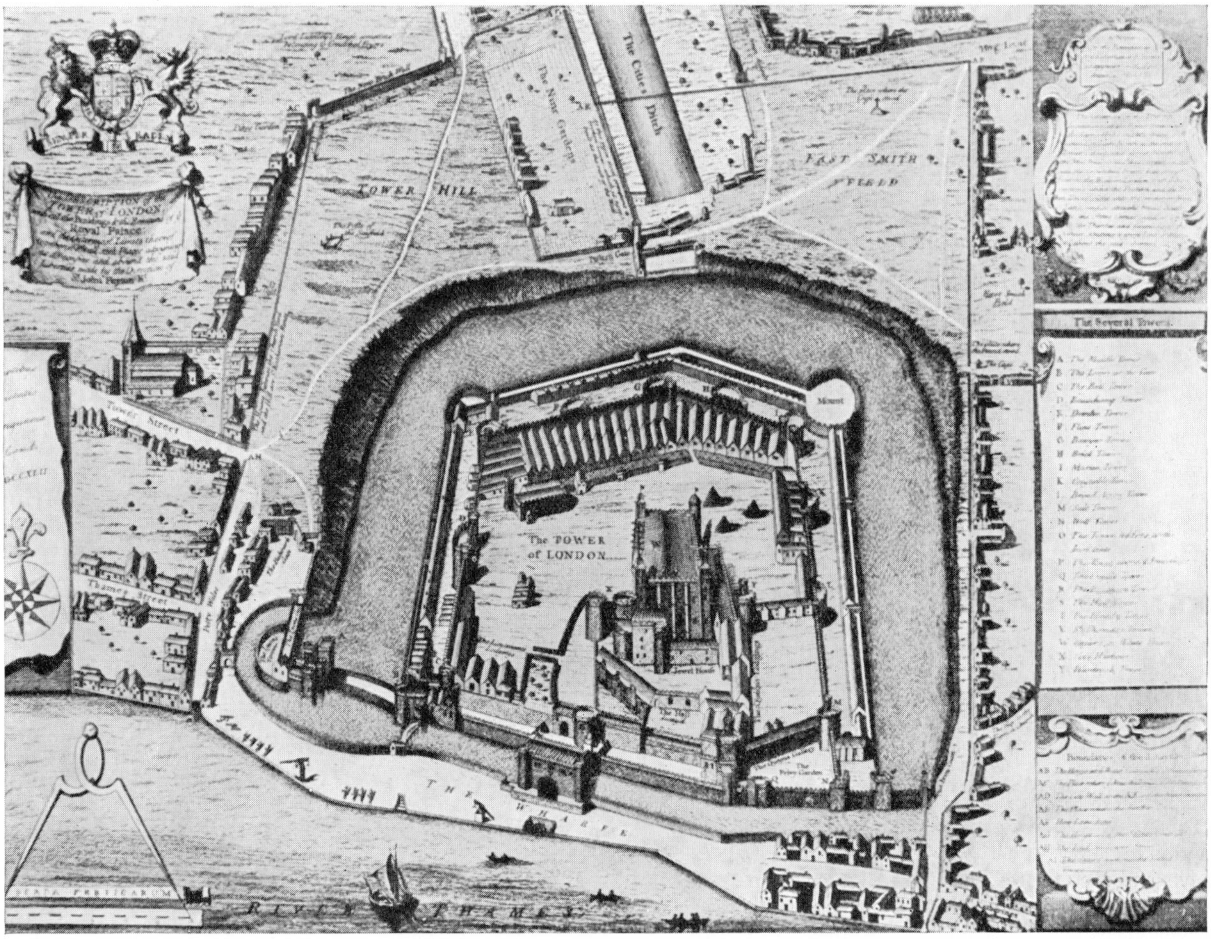

133

132. The Tower, 1570
In Ralph Agas' famous map the Tower itself is not depicted with too much accuracy, but the technique of showing buildings in perspective gives a strong effect of realism. The land beyond the city walls, known as the Liberties, is beginning to be developed.

133. The Tower, 1597
This beautifully drawn map, made to the order of Sir John Peyton in 1597, shows only the immediate environs of the Tower.

134

134. The Tower, 1641

Here is Tower Hill in use. The thousands of spectators have come to watch the execution of the Earl of Strafford and the north-west side of the Tower itself has been turned into a grandstand. Although the whole complex enclosed by the moat is called the Tower of London, the picture shows the Norman White Tower. The keep built by Bishop Gundulf for William I, still dominates the scene.

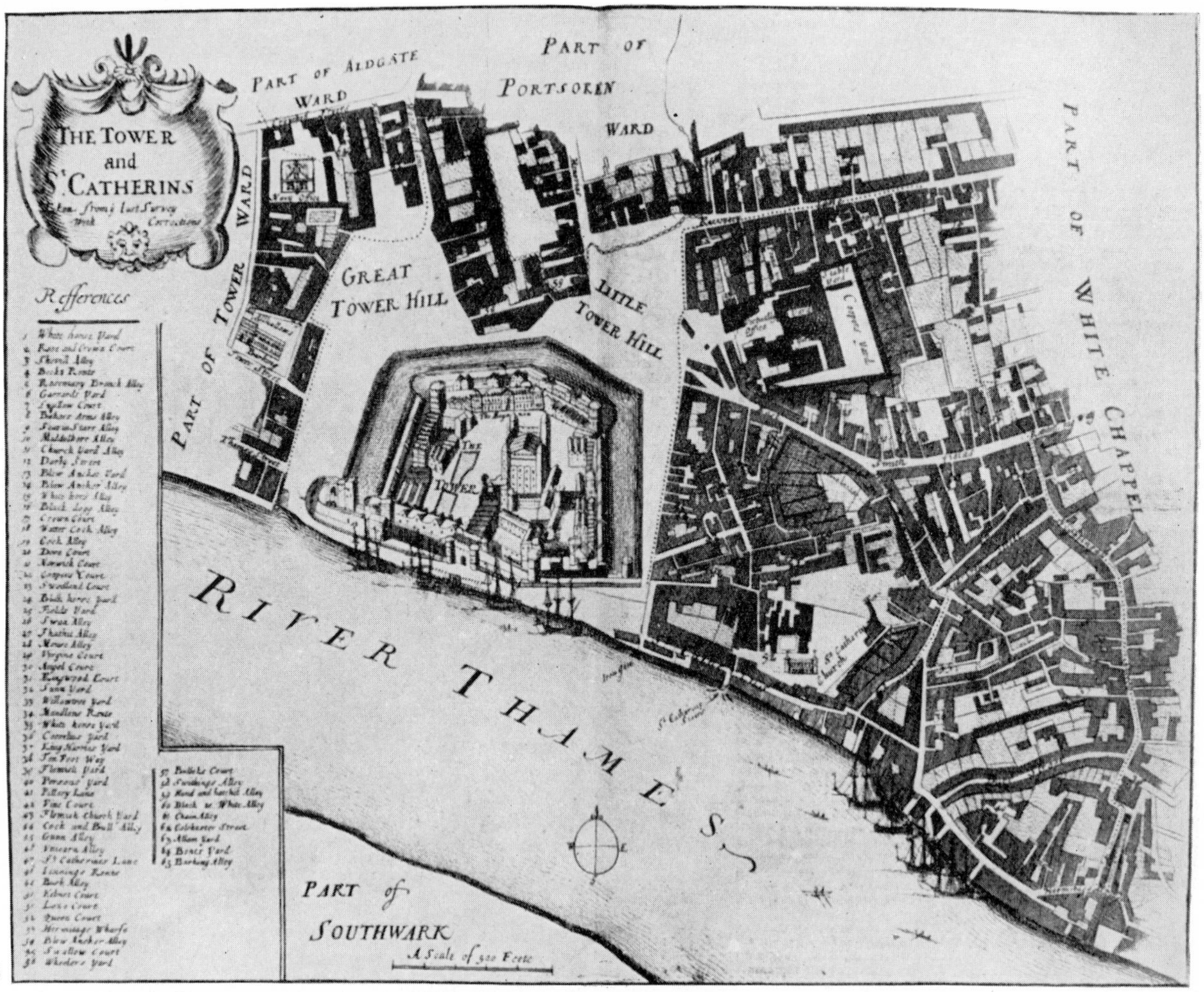

THE TOWER and St CATHERINS

References

PART OF ALDGATE WARD

PART OF PORTSOKEN WARD

PART OF WHITE CHAPPEL

PART OF TOWER WARD

GREAT TOWER HILL

LITTLE TOWER HILL

THE TOWER

RIVER THAMES

PART of SOUTHWARK

A Scale of 300 Feete

135

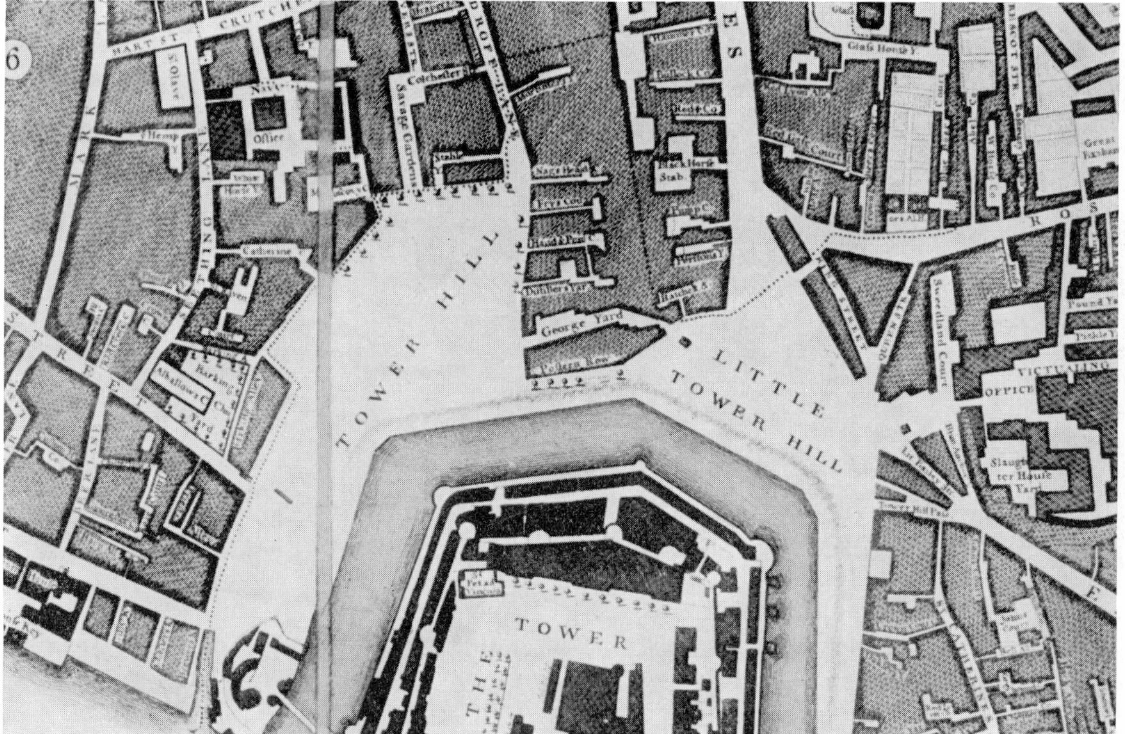

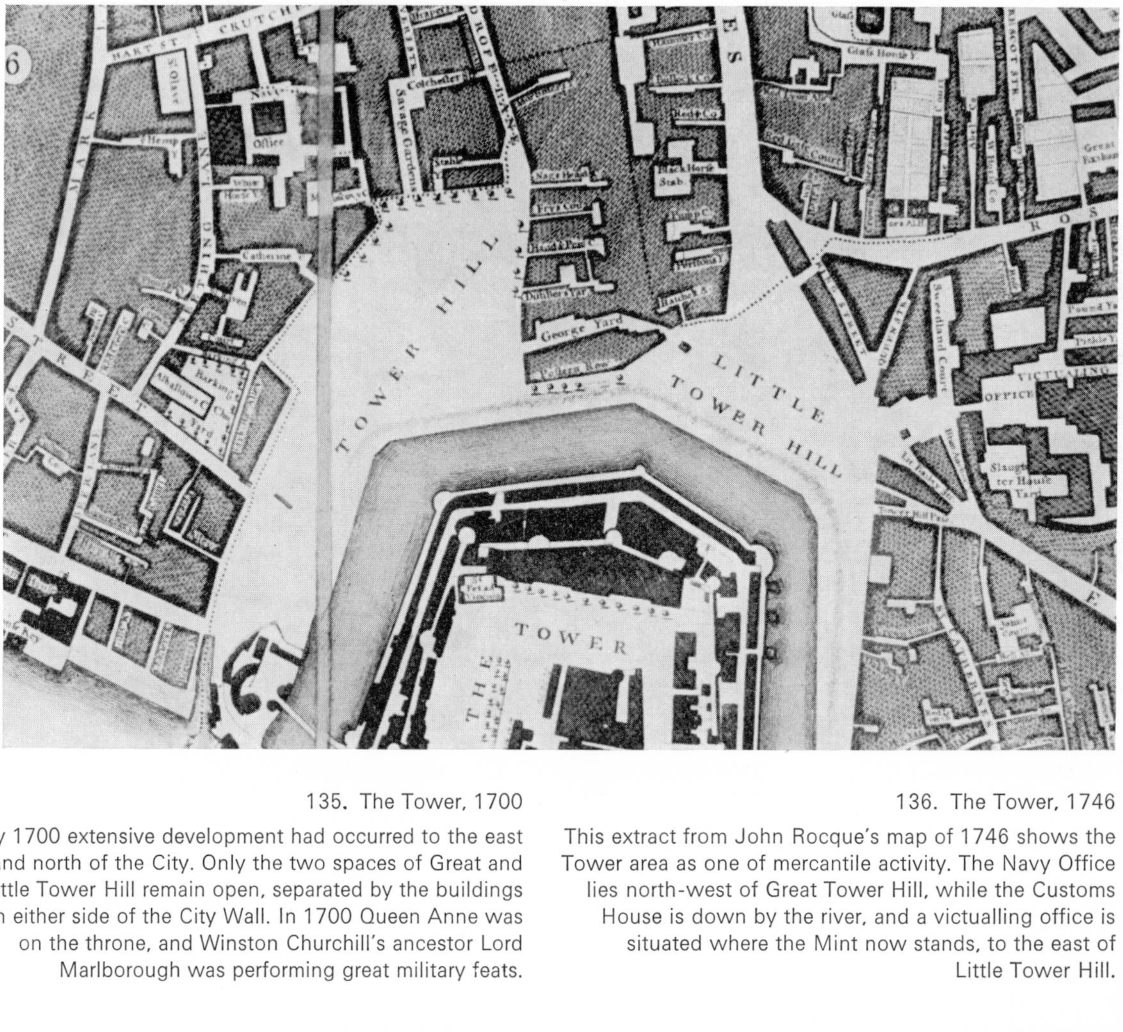

136

135. The Tower, 1700

By 1700 extensive development had occurred to the east and north of the City. Only the two spaces of Great and Little Tower Hill remain open, separated by the buildings on either side of the City Wall. In 1700 Queen Anne was on the throne, and Winston Churchill's ancestor Lord Marlborough was performing great military feats.

136. The Tower, 1746

This extract from John Rocque's map of 1746 shows the Tower area as one of mercantile activity. The Navy Office lies north-west of Great Tower Hill, while the Customs House is down by the river, and a victualling office is situated where the Mint now stands, to the east of Little Tower Hill.

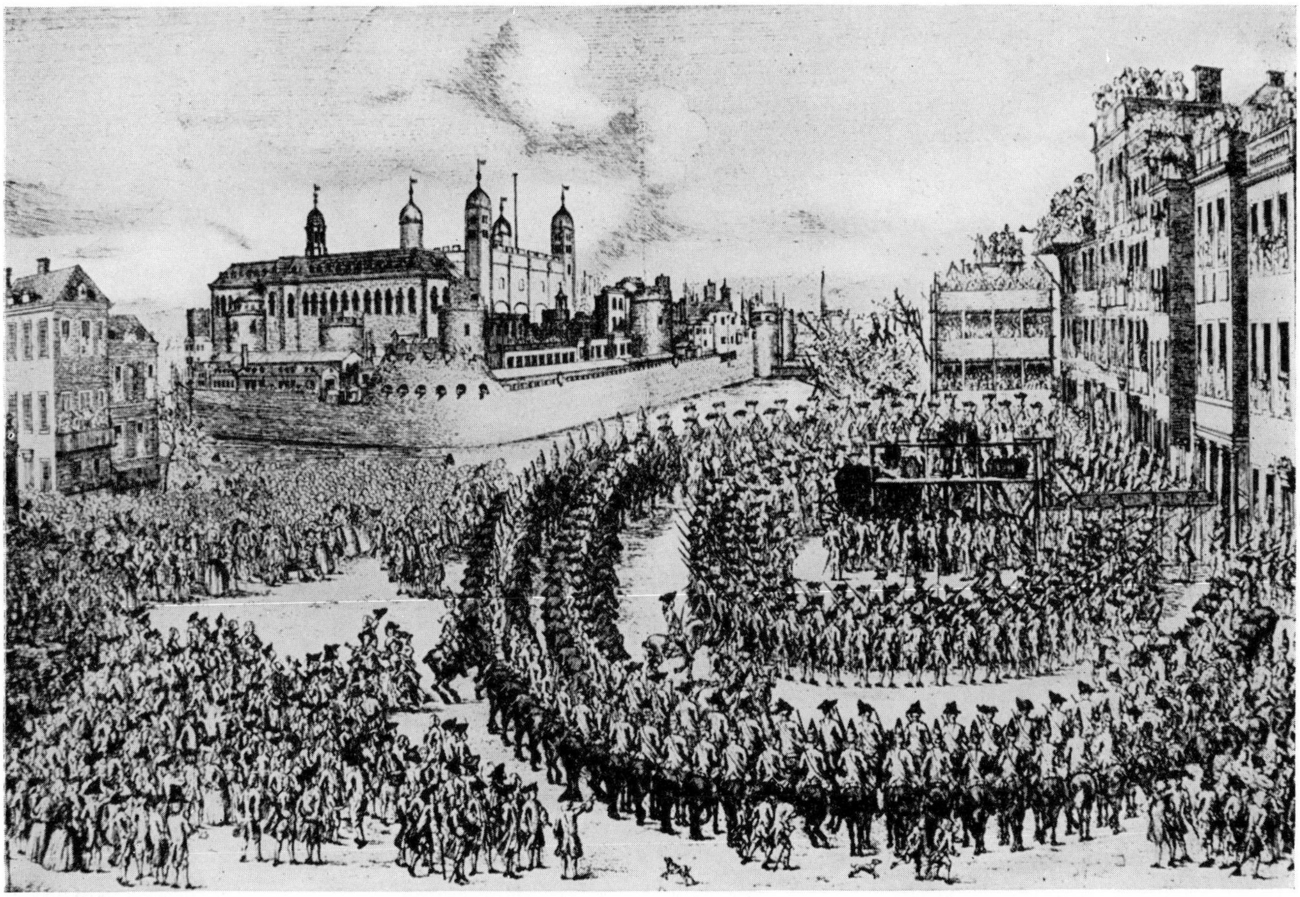

137

138

137. The Tower, 1747

Another great public scene is being enacted, this time the execution of Lord Lovat after the tragic '45', the last execution by the headsman's axe in Britain. The White Tower is now considerably screened by a large building, later rebuilt as the Waterloo Barracks, and which today impedes the view of the White Tower from the north.

138. The Tower, 1811

A panoramic view of the Tower from the north-west. The large expanse of open space, first left for military purposes, made an important space for all kinds of activities down the centuries. It continued to be a great meeting-place, and is still the scene of political meetings, the most famous being that arranged during the great Dock Strike of 1889, when Messrs John Burns and Tom Mann addressed the Dockers.

139 

139. The Tower, 1933

This air view shows the Tower Bridge in the foreground with the Tower itself beyond. The environs are now almost surrounded by great warehouses. The former Great Tower Hill has been given a romantically landscaped oval green, known as Trinity Square. Facing it is Trinity House, the headquarters of 'the Guild, Fraternity or Brotherhood of the Most Glorious and Undivided Trinity and of Saint Clement in the parish of Deptford Strond in the County of Kent', built in 1793 and responsible for the licensing of pilots, the marking of channels and sea marks and the lighthouses and lightships of the English coast.

The large monumental building seen behind Trinity Square is the headquarters of the Port of London Authority, built in 1908 on the site of the Pepys' neighbourhood and his old Navy Office. The road coming into the Tower environs at upper right is the Minories.

The Tower Bridge, underneath its romantic Gothic exterior provided by Sir Horace Jones, was an advanced engineering design of its time, incorporating bascule, cantilever, and suspension elements, the bascule section being operated by hydraulic power. It was designed by Sir John Wolfe Barry and built between 1886 and 1894. On the right of the photograph are the great St Katherine's Dock warehouses by Telford, 1825-8.

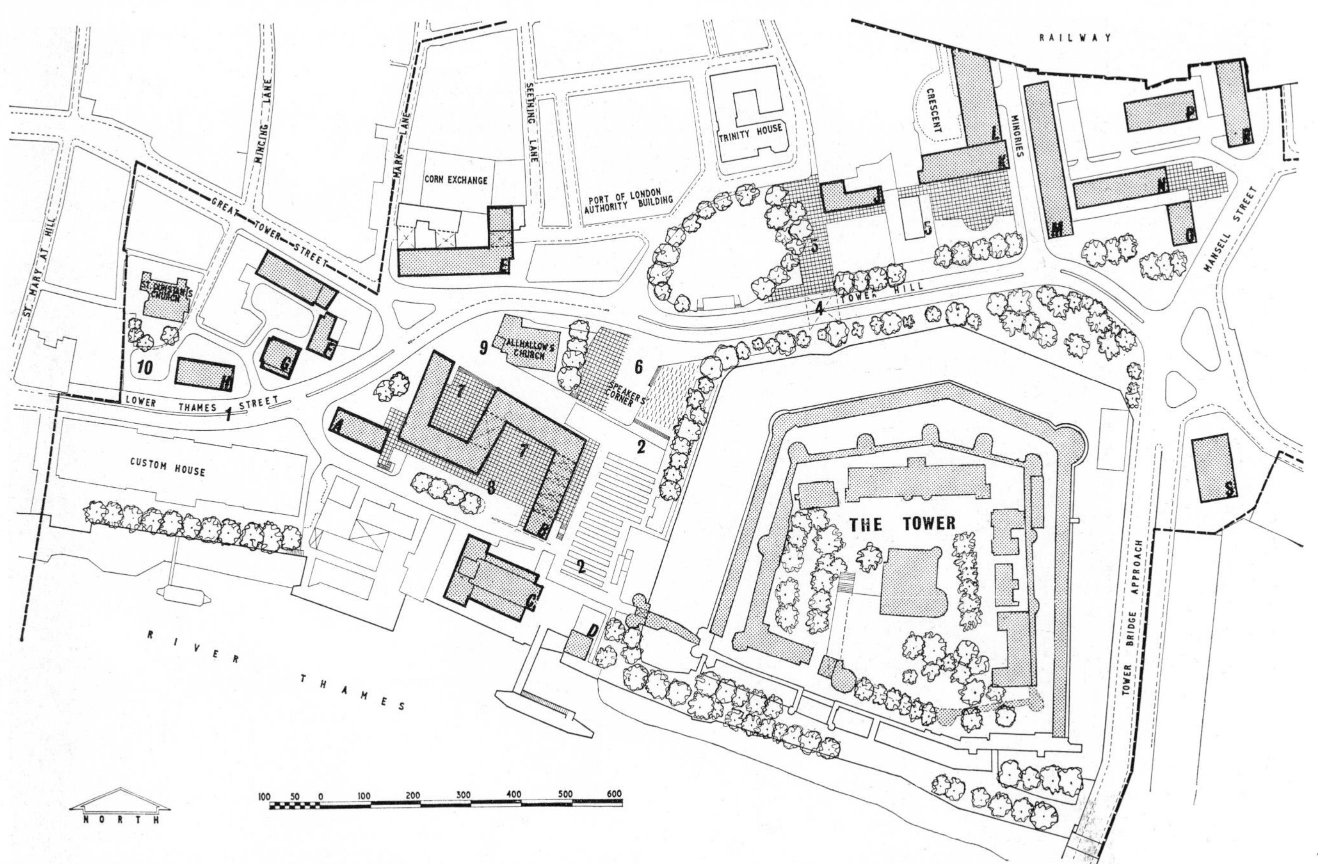

140

140. The Tower: the comprehensive scheme

The following is a key to the numbers and letters on the plan:

1. Lower Thames Street widened and diverted through to the Dock Area
2. Tower Hill Concourse, a large paved space for pedestrians
3. Trinity Square extended as open space and Cooper's Row diverted
4. A pedestrian underpass between the station and the pedestrian walk
5. New open space about the Roman Wall
6. Speakers' Place enlarged and modified
7. Shopping and Walking space
8. Accommodation for 400 cars and 30 coaches on three floors under this space
9. Open spaces to the south and west of All Hallows Church improve its setting
10. A new cul-de-sac in front of St Dunstan's Church embanked above the level of Lower Thames Street

A. Sixteen-storey office block
B. Five-storey office block with through views to the Tower. This building, which is opposite All Hallows Church, has been planned and sited with due deference to the Church; but an alternative development is being considered in relation to a particular objection
C. General Steam Navigation Company
D. Improved Riverside Restaurant and new jetty
E. A new eight-storey building at the south end of Seething Lane
F. Six-storey office block
G. Bakers' Hall
H. Eight-storey office and commercial building
J. Five-storey office building which may later house the Tower Hill Station
K. The five- and three-storey buildings, open on the ground floor, which enclose the Crescent
M. N. R. S. Commercial buildings
O. Proposed hostel
P. Multi-storey car park for 750 cars

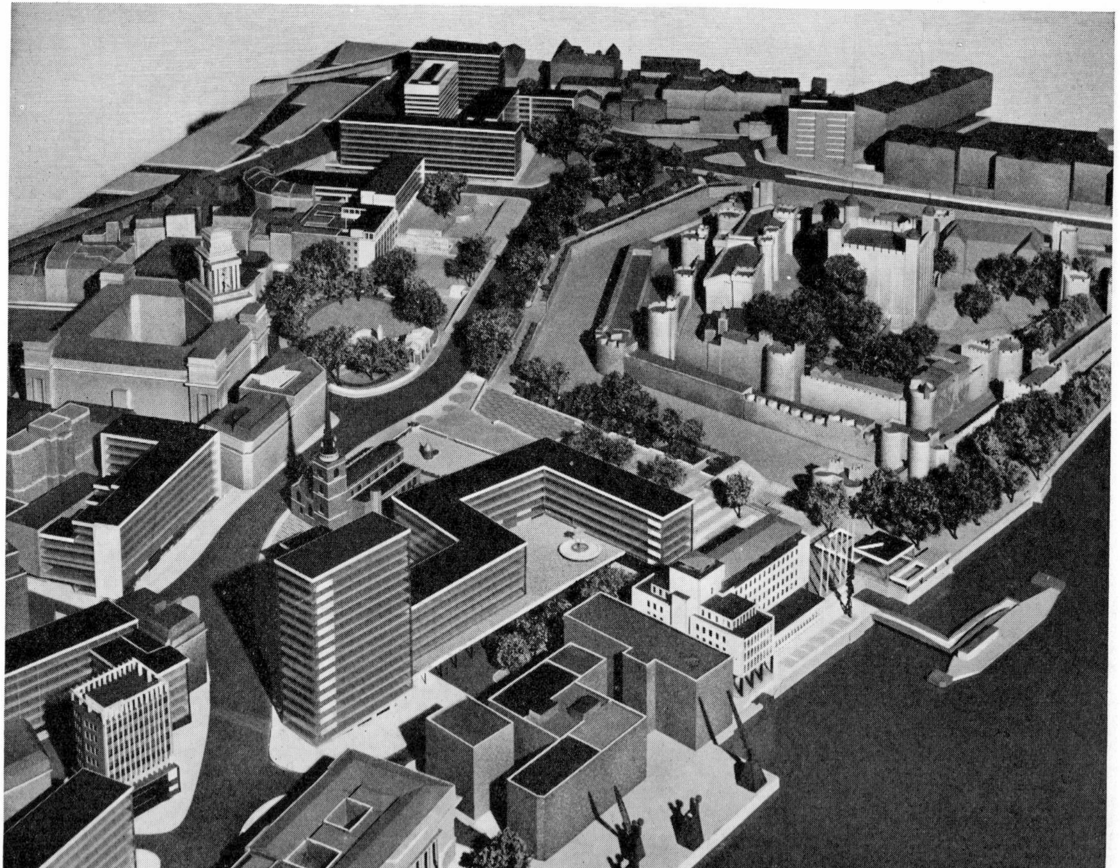

141

142

141. The Tower: the 1959 scheme

A view of the model from the south-west. Running diagonally across the model from lower left to top centre is Lower Thames Street, realigned to join up with Tower Hill. As planners we wished the whole of this street to be in tunnel to allow uninterrupted pedestrian access on the environs of the Tower. Financial difficulties prevented it. In the foreground is the proposed office complex, whose three levels of car parking may be seen.

142. The Tower: the comprehensive scheme

This close-up view of the model shows the great pedestrian Mall proposed along the west side of the Tower. On the left is a recently completed shipping office building, while above, centre, is the proposed office complex with its plot ratio kept low and its height near the tower kept down to five storeys (approximately 60 feet). The raised level in front of it is designed as a viewing terrace.

143

143. The Tower: the comprehensive scheme of 1959

A similar view to the pre-war air photograph from across the river. The montage shows upper left, All Hallows Church opened up to the Tower environs, where the traditional Great Tower Hill is made much greater and taken down in a spacious Mall right to the river, where new restaurant facilities are proposed. To the south of All Hallows Church, in what was once a jungle of commercial buildings, a new office complex is proposed. This has a low five-storey block facing the Tower which is continued to form two open squares – one facing the tower of All Hallows and the other facing the newly completed Peninsula and Oriental Steamship Company headquarters overlooking the river. In the background is a sixteen-storey office block, while three levels of car and coach parking are provided beneath the office buildings. Trinity Square, upper centre, now containing both First and Second War Memorials to Merchant Seamen, is continued along the north side of the tower, making one large continuous space of the ancient Great and Little Tower Hills. In this space is a surviving section of the Old Roman wall, now laid out for viewing in its own garden. Behind the new open space will rise low office and commercial buildings. In this scheme the Tower not only regains the scale it lost in the nineteenth century, but also a much greater surrounding open space, which it never had. The opening up of All Hallows Church to the Tower environs, for which the Reverend P. B. Clayton fought so hard, is also maintained.

144 

145 

144, 145. The Tower: perspective studies

In planning the Tower of London Precinct we aimed at achieving, not only a spacious and discreet framework to a great national monument, but also a lively and stimulating environment where tourists and holidaymakers could come on holidays and at week-ends to enjoy the river and the total atmosphere of this potentially exciting part of London. The team leader was Walter Bor.

6

Coventry

The history of Coventry reaches back as far as the seventh century. The name derives from the convent which was then founded by St Osburg. It was rebuilt in 1043—as a Benedictine monastery—by Earl Leofric of Mercia and his wife, the Countess Godiva. Although the famous legend with which her name is associated may or may not have a basis of historic fact, it is the kind of event which is a vital part of urban tradition, of similar character to Venice's symbolic marriage with the sea. The town was constituted as a Municipal Corporation by Edward III in 1345, and during the fifteenth century grew steadily in importance as a centre first for the buying and selling of wool, and then for the making of cloth, ranking at that time as the fourth wealthiest town in England. It was in fact a characteristic medieval centre, with a monastery, churches, merchants' houses, guilds which built the famous fifteenth-century St Mary's Hall, and almshouses that included an outstanding example of late half-timber architecture in Ford's Hospital, built in 1509. All these and many other buildings were grouped in a medieval road pattern on a small hill and were surrounded by a fairly solid town wall.

During the seventeenth century it became an important centre for the ribbon-making trade, and in the eighteenth and nineteenth this was superseded by watch- and clock-making. When the latter industry was killed by foreign competition, the citizens turned to making sewing machines and bicycles, which led to motor cars, engines and aircraft, and hence to the reason for its destruction in the last war.

Its population, which was estimated at 6,600 in 1520, was still only 16,034 in 1801, although by 1901 it had increased to 69,978. It then almost doubled itself by 1921, when it stood at 128,157, and again doubled itself to reach 254,900 by 1949. Typical of the changing scale of cities is the fact that, up to the second half of the nineteenth century, almost the whole of the old city was contained within what is now the central area.

The situation before the Second World War was of a rapidly expanding industrial city with a centre that was extremely inadequate for its ever-increasing tasks. Piecemeal redevelopment was taking place in what had been an attractive and ancient town, and was threatening to destroy much of its character in the process. However, a vigorous and progressive group of Councillors in the Labour-controlled City Council were alive to these problems, and were anxious to do their best for the city. To this end they took certain organizational steps, and the following account concerning them is taken from a small book of collected papers on Planning which I wrote in India during the last war, not long after the events had taken place:

'Like many English cities, Coventry was without a city Architectural Department until 1938, and the city Engineering Department had assumed the duties not only of Engineering but also of Municipal Architecture (with the exception of Housing), town planning, building inspection and the responsibility for building bye-laws. However, in 1938 the City Council decided to create a new City Architectural Department, and chose for their City Architect Mr D. E. E. Gibson,[1] a brilliant architect and planner, then in his early thirties. Many of the younger members of the architectural profession felt that it was a noteworthy step, and this may be judged by the fact that for some of the new appointments in the office there were over seven hundred applicants. Thus, when the new office opened at the beginning of 1939, it had a staff of keen, highly trained young men who were determined to show that a Municipal Authority could do work comparable to the best in private practice.

'The office began with a large programme of hospitals, schools and other municipal buildings, including several which were taken over from the City Engineer's Department, and, as the Housing Director retired shortly afterwards and his Department was absorbed in that of the City Architect, Corporation Housing also became one of its responsibilities.

'It was considered that architects, working as a City Department, have a great opportunity to influence the public taste in good design, not only through planning and building but also, by collaboration with the staffs of other corporation departments, by careful attention to the design of the countless objects of City equipment, i.e. gardens, lamp standards, litter baskets, bus shelters, signs, railings, etc. In order to stimulate keenness in design, spare-time competition *esquisses* were held in the office for the smaller design problems (when time permitted), and if possible the winner carried out his design.

'Most important of all was the basic layout or skeleton of the city. This was in the most deplorable condition, owing to the rapid and practically unplanned urban growth, especially in the preceding ten years, although there had been a Town Planning Section attached to the City Engineer's Department for the last seven years; and of the five separate planning schemes only one had got past what is significantly known as the Interim Stage, while the whole centre of the city was termed an Excluded Area for Planning purposes. However, the more progressive citizens had long felt the need of an adequate plan for this area, even if it was confined to the Civic Buildings which were so urgently required in a city which had almost quadrupled its population in twenty years. When the new architectural office was formed, public interest on this subject, stimulated by the local newspapers, was keen, and although the City Engineer's Planning Section had produced some plans, the only proposals worth considering had come from the City Guild, or local Civic Society, and were similar in conception to the Civic Centre schemes of such cities as Southampton or Swansea. Several acts

[1] Now Sir Donald Gibson.

served to make the problem more acute, such as (1) the erection by an Assurance Company of a large pseudo-Tudor office building on a site previously owned by the Corporation, between the Central Place (Broadgate) and the Cathedral, which everyone wished to see left open, and (2) the gift of a large sum by a wealthy local manufacturer for the immediate construction of an Art Gallery. The only site available to the Corporation for this purpose was one which would have continued the existing congestion, but in spite of energetic criticism by Mr Gibson work on this site was commenced.

'Realizing the urgency of the problem, Mr. Gibson set four members of his staff, Messrs J. T. Pinion, K. Lycett, P. F. Burgoyne and P. T. Powell, under my supervision, on the work of designing a correlated scheme for all the Civic Buildings considered necessary, and of preparing a large model for display purposes. This scheme took an area of forty acres around the Cathedral, and, using the latter as the centre piece, grouped a new Library, Museum, Civil Hall, Police and Law Courts and Municipal Offices, around a dignified and spacious Close. The group included a new Government Telephone Exchange and offices which were under consideration, and about the siting of which the Office of Works were found to be very helpful collaborators. All the buildings were kept comparatively low in order to emphasize the verticality of of the Cathedral and St Michael's Church, and were to be faced with brick and stone to harmonize with the local red sandstone of the latter buildings. The remainder of the area was laid out as a small central park with a lake. (It had been known since medieval days as Pool Meadow.) The old Fire Station and Bus Station were redesigned on the northern part of the site. The next step was to make the people of Coventry Planning and Design conscious, and a scheme was arranged with the Director of Education to enable qualified members of the staff to lecture to all the senior school-children in the city. Mr Gibson, too, led the way in giving talks to such bodies as the Rotarians, etc., and a large collection of coloured slides was built up by the staff for this purpose. Then the Coventry branch of the A.A.S.T.A.[1] (now A.B.T.[2]), which was almost entirely composed of members of the Department, decided to hold a Planning Exhibition, and with the financial assistance of the A.A.S.T.A., the City Guild, N.A.L.G.O.[3] (Coventry Branch) and the active co-operation of the Artists, Sculptors and Engineers, the "Coventry of Tomorrow" Exhibition took place. Large models were obtained from several Schools of Architecture, many photographs and the complete Small House Exhibition were loaned from the R.I.B.A., and famous Town Planners were invited to come down and lecture to the public. Thanks to energetic publicity which was greatly assisted by the three local newspapers, several thousands of people visited the Exhibition, as well as all the senior school-children of the city, and naturally the exhibit attracting most attention was the model of the proposed City Centre. After this the Department was wholly occupied by the many and varied demands of Civil Defence, and also the provision of housing for war-workers. Coventry was blitzed on the night of November the 14th, 1940. At the time, I was living only a few minutes' walk from Broadgate. In the morning I walked up over piles of smouldering rubble to Broadgate. It was an unforgettable and indescribable sight, almost as H.G. Wells had predicted in *Things to Come*—a shredded bus here, a car

[1] *Association of Architects, Surveyors and Technical Assistants.*
[2] *Association of Building Technicians.*
[3] *National Association of Local Government Officers.*

balanced crazily on the roof of a ruined building there, and the Cathedral, the Library and nearly everything one could see still burning and smouldering in great masses of devastation. Later that day the centre was cordoned off, and within a few weeks we were instructed to prepare a bold comprehensive plan. This was partly because Lord Reith, then Minister of Works and Buildings, had selected blitzed areas in three cities to assist in determining what new Planning legislation would be required for reconstruction. The centre of Coventry was one of these, and he asked the City Council to prepare a comprehensive scheme for this purpose. The Council then instructed the City Engineer to collaborate on the work, but owing to the fundamental divergence of opinion they submitted separate schemes to the Redevelopment Committee, who chose that of the City Architect. This scheme was then put before the Council, who decided to submit it to the Minister of Works and Buildings as their Comprehensive Scheme on February 28th, 1941. A new Redevelopment office was set up for Replanning purposes, consisting of three architects and three engineers, and they immediately commenced work on a Civic Survey. Although some kind of planning had been in existence for several years a negligible amount of the necessary survey information had been obtained. Within a few weeks, however, the three architects were called up. Although their places were taken over by women architects and men discharged from service owing to injuries received on active service, the work has been considerably hampered. Also, Lord Iliffe gave £1,000 for a model, 12 foot square, of the new scheme to be constructed and much research has been necessary to ensure that each individual building embodies the result of the latest technical research.'

This paper, written in 1942, ends on a worried note, but at least certain principles of urban design had been applied to a practical problem. A second statement, written some sixteen years later, is taken largely from a B.B.C. talk I gave in 1958.

The experimental model became the nucleus of a new plan, which now embraced the whole central area. It is worth remembering how little planning technique existed at the time the Coventry plan was first started. The Ministry of Town and Country Planning's Handbook on the Redevelopment of Central Areas, with its very full description of survey methods and floor space and day-lighting controls, came out only in 1947, and even Alker Tripp's book on Town Planning and Road Traffic, which dealt with traffic precincts, did not appear until 1942.

Looking back over twenty years one remembers it as a fascinating experience. At an early stage under Donald Gibson's leadership we decided to draw up a number of basic ideas; we would delineate the central area by a parkway ring, and within this ring there would be no through roads or industrial areas; we would group our main building types, such as shopping, entertainment and civic buildings, into several precincts. We rejected some of the ideas put forward in Le Corbusier's *City of Tomorrow*. We did not think, for instance, that very high buildings were necessary for the centre of a smallish city which was unlikely ever to have more than 400,000 people, and in any case we had the two undamaged church spires as vertical features in the centre. We would have liked to incorporate his dream of multi-level communications, but we were worried about expense, and felt that, anyway, our precinct form of development went a long way to bringing safety and convenience to the pedestrian. But we did try to bring green places back into the city centre by designing a new central park which was to act as a foil to the stone, glass and paving of the urban scene. We introduced one completely new building form in the shopping precinct, but otherwise fell back on the symbol forms for various types with which we were familiar, such as 'acoustic' wedge shapes for auditoria, a parabolic vault for the covered market and interconnecting blocks of flats for the high-density housing.

As far as possible we proposed to keep the main uses approximately in the positions they had always occupied, for in nearly every city there is a natural order of which things respond somehow to the way people live. At this point Lewis Mumford's ideas began to make their impact—his great book *The Culture of Cities* had recently arrived in England, and a colleague[1] had straight away sent it up from London. We thought it so important that we passed it on to our Councillors to read.

The key feature in our plan was the shopping centre. The traditional shopping street was Smithfield Street, which before its virtual destruction had twisted its narrow medieval way down from Broadgate at the top of the hill to St John's Church at the bottom, and after much discussion we decided to keep it more or less in the same position but to design a new kind of pedestrian shopping area rather than rebuilding the old shopping street. I had once worked in a multiple store, and had strong ideas about shopping being a pleasure and not a drudge. The big store did enable people to buy in comfort and safety, leave a child with an attendant, have a cup of tea or a meal, and in fact get all they wanted under one roof. This was the opportunity to put that experience to account. In addition, both Donald Gibson and I knew Chester well, with its historic two-level shopping rows. So we developed these two ideas in the form of a series of pedestrian squares down the hill, the idea being that one entered at the top or the bottom of the precinct at ground level, but owing to the slope the upper level would become a great gallery where one could shop or look at the scene of activity below.

On the north side of the shopping centre we planned a group of theatres and cinemas, roughly where they had been before, and in the space between provided a large two-floor car park; on the south we planned a large covered market with attendant banks and commercial buildings. Broadgate at the top we turned into a great square, flanked by a hotel and other important buildings, and opened its south side right up to the Cathedral spire. To the east and south of the Cathedral we slightly modified our pre-blitz scheme of a group of civic and cultural buildings and suggested a new higher education group beyond. Down the hill to the north of the Cathedral we proposed a small central park (it had once been Pool Meadow in pre-industrial times where the monks were said to have kept their Friday fish), and to the south the existing Hertford Street was to be realigned as a broad new approach round from the rebuilt station. For one or two of the other precincts we even included some high density residential groups, which included schools, shops, community centre, and multi-storey garages.

This then was the original scheme—conceived almost as a set of planning principles, and foreshadowing many of the requirements for city centres later embodied formally in the Ministry of Town and Country Planning's Handbook on the Redevelopment of Central Areas.

Between the cup and the lip, the conception and the realization, are inevitably many unknown factors. The fascinating thing about Coventry is that so many of the original ideas persist in the realization twenty years later. For this many people must share the

[1] Robert Gardner-Medwin, now Professor and Head of the School of Architecture in the University of Liverpool, who helped us in many ways.

credit. First of course, Donald Gibson, his successor Arthur Ling, and their design team; but without the steadfast holding to principles by the City Council and its Reconstruction Committee, and notably Alderman Hodgkinson, little would have been accomplished.

After the original scheme had been prepared and agreed as a basis for development, there was a lull. As I have described, I was given a joint team of architect and engineer planners working under Donald Gibson's direction, but within a matter of months most of us found ourselves in the Armed Services. Although by a strange coincidence I was given an Army posting back to within a few miles of Coventry, I could only help in a minor way. But Gibson persevered, and with Leslie Hulley, Joan Griffiths (now Mrs Burnett) and a number of other women architects, backed by a generous donation from Messrs Bassett-Lowke, the large-scale model was prepared. This in fact turned a planning sketch into an architectural design, and helped a great deal in public relations terms to enable the public to understand what the planners were proposing to do.

Nothing positive, however, could be done during the war except the tasks of clearing away the rubble, the demolition of derelict buildings and the erection of temporary shops for the bombed-out shopkeepers.

By 1945 it had been decided to align the ring road on a wider circumference, thus enlarging the central area considerably. It had also been decided, against the wiser judgment of Gibson, but in response to pressure from the business community, that a road should be cut right through the pedestrian shopping precinct. This road caused serious design consequences on the whole of this part of the scheme, but, in spite of Gibson's objections, was actually built as a traffic road. Much later it was closed at the instance of Arthur Ling and is now part of the pedestrian area.

One or two other aspects deserve special mention. First, as regards the realization of the shopping precinct. The Corporation decided to develop part of this themselves and the first block to be built facing Broadgate was designed by the City Architect and Planning Officer and built by the Corporation. The rest of the upper half of the precinct was also built by the Corporation and leased to shopkeepers, except the Leofric Hotel, designed by Messrs Hattrell and Partners, and the new Owen Owens Store, designed by Rolf Hellberg. Part of the transverse way buildings were built by individual developers under design control, but the Corporation continued to take a major part in construction, building the lower section, including the dance hall, the southern square and the market hall.

Car parking has of course been an ever-increasing problem. In the original scheme a three-deck car park was suggested on the north, a parking garage under the Market Hall and a multi-storey car park near the market-place. In the present scheme multi-storey car parks have been provided in the more restricted spaces to the north and south, and instead of a garage under the Market Hall parking has been provided over it with connections across to the roofs of low buildings.

A number of interesting minor structures have been included as the scheme has progressed. First, a memorial stone in the form of a Pheonix cut in bas relief by Trevor Tennant is set into the ground at the upper entrance of the precincts. Then a restaurant was built, spanning over Hertford Street at the point where it enters Broadgate. A charming circular café is sited in the middle of the lower precinct, and near it are large ceramic murals depicting various aspects of Coventry life, by Gordon Cullen. Interesting visual use is made of the lift of the dance hall by placing it externally in the pedestrian area.

Inevitably there are things which can be criticized. Apart from the near-disaster of the intruding road, a mistake in the levels enforces pedestrians to climb a flight of steps to the upper shopping-deck, whereas the original scheme had envisaged entry to this deck straight off Broadgate at the same level. This, combined with the vertical letting of shops, gave the upper deck a slow start. Here again, the upper deck should have had the more secluded type of shop such as hairdressers, jewellers, etc., but no doubt this can be rectified in due course.

Another mistake, flowing right from the original conception, was the creation of a traffic roundabout on Broadgate itself. This was always seen as the heart of the city and a large statue was suggested for this central place. Just before the war a citizen had commissioned the sculptor Reid Dick to design an equestrian statue commemorating the famous tradition of Lady Godiva's ride through the city. Immediately after the war Coventry was pressing the Government for permission to start rebuilding, and a present of Dutch bulbs from Holland gave them the chance to invite Royalty to open the new square, which was to be laid out with these plants. In order to display them, the central place was laid out as a roundabout, and a reluctant Ministry of Transport had to provide the financial grant. All this was duly carried out, and the Lady Godiva statue was erected as a centre piece to this slightly unfortunate conception.

On the east of Broadgate there was the problem of the destroyed cathedral, part of whose venerable walls and the noble spire still remained. After a number of abortive proposals it was decided to hold a competition, and this was won by Basil Spence, with an exciting project which placed the New Cathedral at right angles to the old one. Seven years later, in 1962, the new cathedral was opened and Coventry gained a remarkable building, immensely impressive and of a high quality of design and construction.

To the east of the Cathedral the educational precinct has been proceeding apace with a new Technical College, Art School, and Art Gallery. The last named was provided by a private citizen. Near by will come a new Museum, while across the road is the new City Architectural and Planning Department. This building is well worth visiting, as in addition to housing the new prototype town designer's office, it also has a large ground-floor exhibition room, where the citizen can see, in models and drawings, what the Council intends to create for them.

At long last the railway station, always one of Coventry's poorer public buildings, has been rebuilt to an excellent design by the Chief Architect of British Railways (North Midland Group), and with a new station hotel it should provide a worthy entrance to the central area. So, after twenty-five years a large part of the central area has been rebuilt—rebuilt from an original 'dream plan', which passed through many difficult stages, during which it suffered both misfortunes and improvements. No praise can be too high for the inspiring leadership given first by Donald Gibson and then by Arthur Ling over all these years.

The lessons of Coventry are clear. Cities are at heart a design problem and need teams of imaginative, devoted and practical designers, with outstanding leadership and with enlightened public patrons in order to create a civilized environment, but all this must be backed by legislation and adequate finance.

1

6 COVENTRY

1. Broadgate about 1900

The photograph was taken from Broadgate, looking down the main shopping street of Smithford Street, and with Hertford Street to the left. It gives an idea of the general character of the central area at the time. Most of the medieval houses had been rebuilt in the eighteenth and nineteenth centuries, but the scale was retained.

2. (*overleaf*) The pre-war centre

The centre of Coventry before the war had the medieval street pattern almost unchanged, with the exception of the eighteenth-century improvement of Hertford Street, seen running from the central town square of Broadgate down to Greyfriars Green, below the bottom of the photograph. The main pre-war shopping street was Smithford Street, which ran from Broadgate to Bablake on the left (or west) of the photograph. To the east of Broadgate is the Cathedral of St Michael (a parish church elevated to cathedral status only in 1912), with its superb fourteenth-century spire, which survived the bombing. Trinity Church, which was almost undamaged during the war, lies to the left (or north-west) of the Cathedral, while immediately to the right (or south) of the Spire is St Mary's Guild Hall, a fine fourteenth-century hall whose roof was destroyed in 1940 but has since been restored.

2

3

4

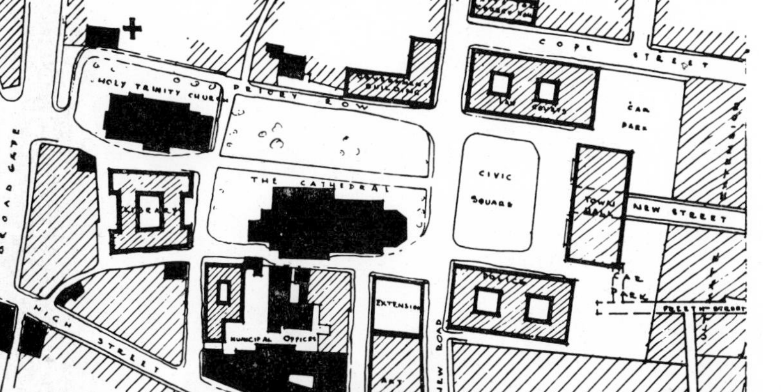

5

6

3. A view from the Cathedral spire

This photograph, which I took early in 1940, shows the general character of the old town before the bombing cleared nearly all of it away.

4. Broadgate, 1938

A view of the Central square of Coventry taken not long before the outbreak of the war. It is characteristic of old towns in the process of being redeveloped piecemeal, site by site. Along the east side of Broadgate (on the left in the photograph) is a terrace of Georgian and early Victorian houses, still comparatively untouched after a hundred years. On the west (or right-hand side) redevelopment has taken place at the same scale on the same sites, although the façades are different. At the south end (at the top of the photograph) a large new bank has seriously altered the scale of the centre. A number of sites were amalgamated and a much larger bulk and height of building has changed the character of Broadgate, although the roads remain as before. The war, incidentally spelt the death of the trams, and left the bus the sole means of local public transport.

5. The Civic Area: a pre-war suggestion

Even before the war Coventry had an active Civic Society strongly supported by the local architects. They made a number of studies for the improvement of the area immediately round the Cathedral, of which this is one. The most important proposal was to create a new Civic Square extending the Cathedral Close.

6. The 1939 model

This model was made in our spare time in the City Architectural Department, under the direction of the City Architect, Donald Gibson. At this time it was only an 'ideas' scheme to give the public an idea of what could be done to improve the city. The new civic buildings proposed by the Civic Society were taken as a basis for a redevelopment programme, but an attempt was made to exploit the contours of the hilltop site. In addition, a small central park was suggested down the hill to the north, to regain the ancient Pool Meadow. The whole area was designed as one large and mainly pedestrian precinct.

7. After the bombing

A model showing the extent of bomb damage in the centre of the city. The ruins of the Cathedral are on the right, and the model shows how the main shopping area of Broadgate and Smithford Street has been almost entirely demolished. In preparing the new plan we decided to locate the new shopping centre in the same area as before, but in the form of a pedestrian precinct instead a corridor street.

7

8

8. After the bombing

A view taken from the Cathedral spire looking down on Broadgate and Smithford Street after the devastation of the bombing. The majority of the buildings have been reduced to piles of rubble. A few damaged and burnt-out ruins remain, notably the chain store of Messrs Montague Burton, seen in the centre of the photograph, which was demolished after the war in order to clear the whole area.

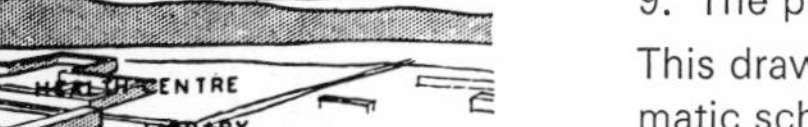

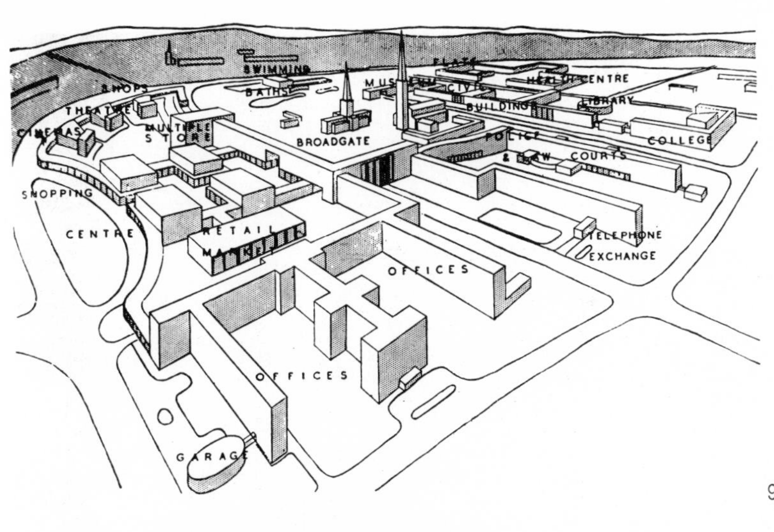

9

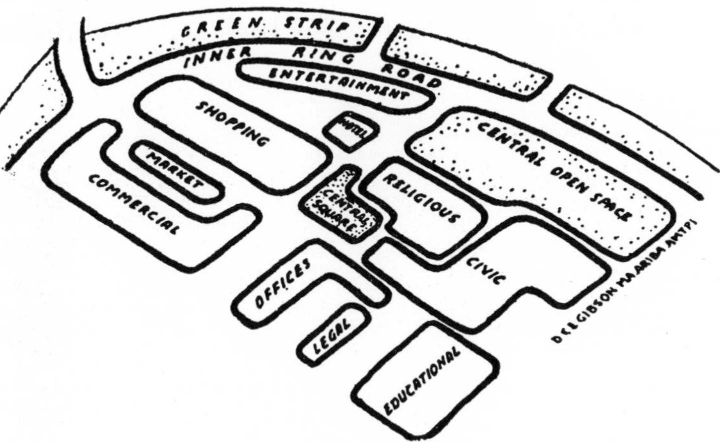

10

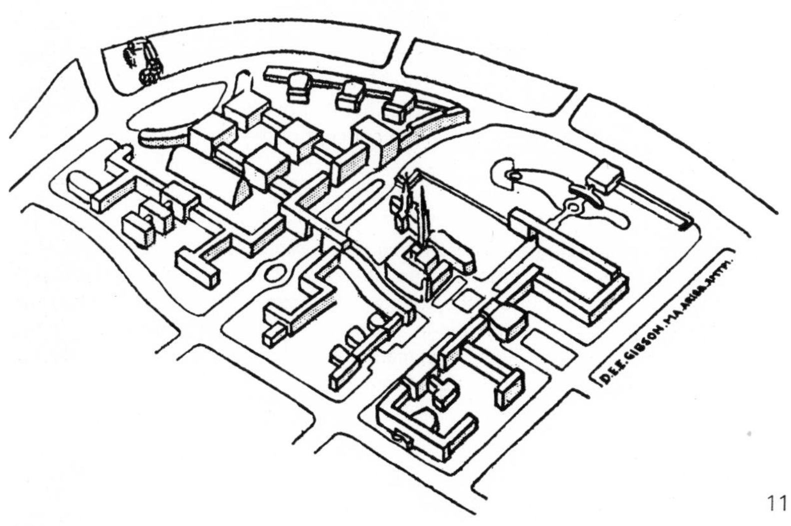

11

9. The plan of 1940

This drawing by Noel Musgrave is of the first diagrammatic scheme we prepared not long after the great 'blitz'. Both the City Architect and the City Engineer were invited to submit proposals to the City Council, who chose that submitted by the former. Thenceforth this scheme formed the basic guide plan for the central area. The precinct round the Cathedral remained somewhat similar to that shown in the 'pre-blitz' model (no. 6), and the new ideas were concentrated on the commercial area to the west. Here the old shopping street was replaced by a new shopping precinct, designed as a pedestrian area, with large and small stores all connected by covered ways. To the north of this was a group of theatres and cinemas with a three-storey garage in the middle, while to the south was a new Market Hall in a great place surrounded by commercial buildings. Below the market was to be a garage, while multi-storied garages, such as the one in the foreground, were distributed through the area.

10, 11. The first plan. 1941

These two diagrams illustrate the two-dimensional zoning (above) in which the main central uses, such as shopping, entertainment, commercial, etc., are grouped in compact precincts, while the three-dimensional study (below) shows how all the buildings on the sites could be designed to form an integrated group. A number of new planning ideas can be clearly seen, including the distribution of appropriate central area uses in functional groups, the introduction of pedestrian precincts, and a parkway along the inner ring road which was to contain all the main services in one large duct.

12

13

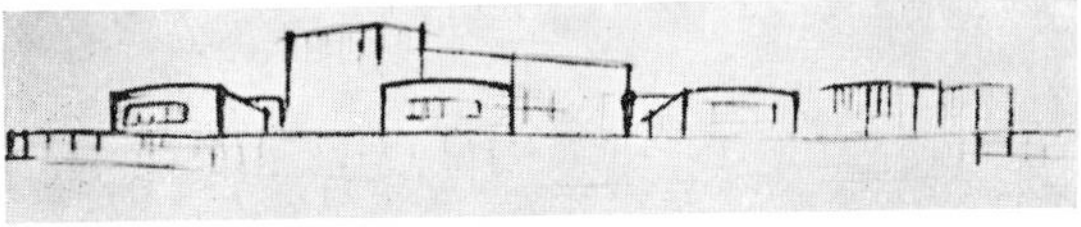

14

15

12. An early sketch of the shopping precinct

This is an early sketch of mine which shows the upper level walkways at the westward end of the proposed shopping precinct. For our initial ideas of the precinct we drew on the concept of the multiple store and of the ancient Rows at Chester.

13, 14, 15. New skylines, 1941

These rather rough sketches I drew on a wall in the office to illustrate some of the principles of the scheme to visitors. Later they were used by the Ministry of Information in a pamphlet on the replanning of Coventry. Planners sometimes need to beware of the unexpected uses to which casual sketch studies may be put.

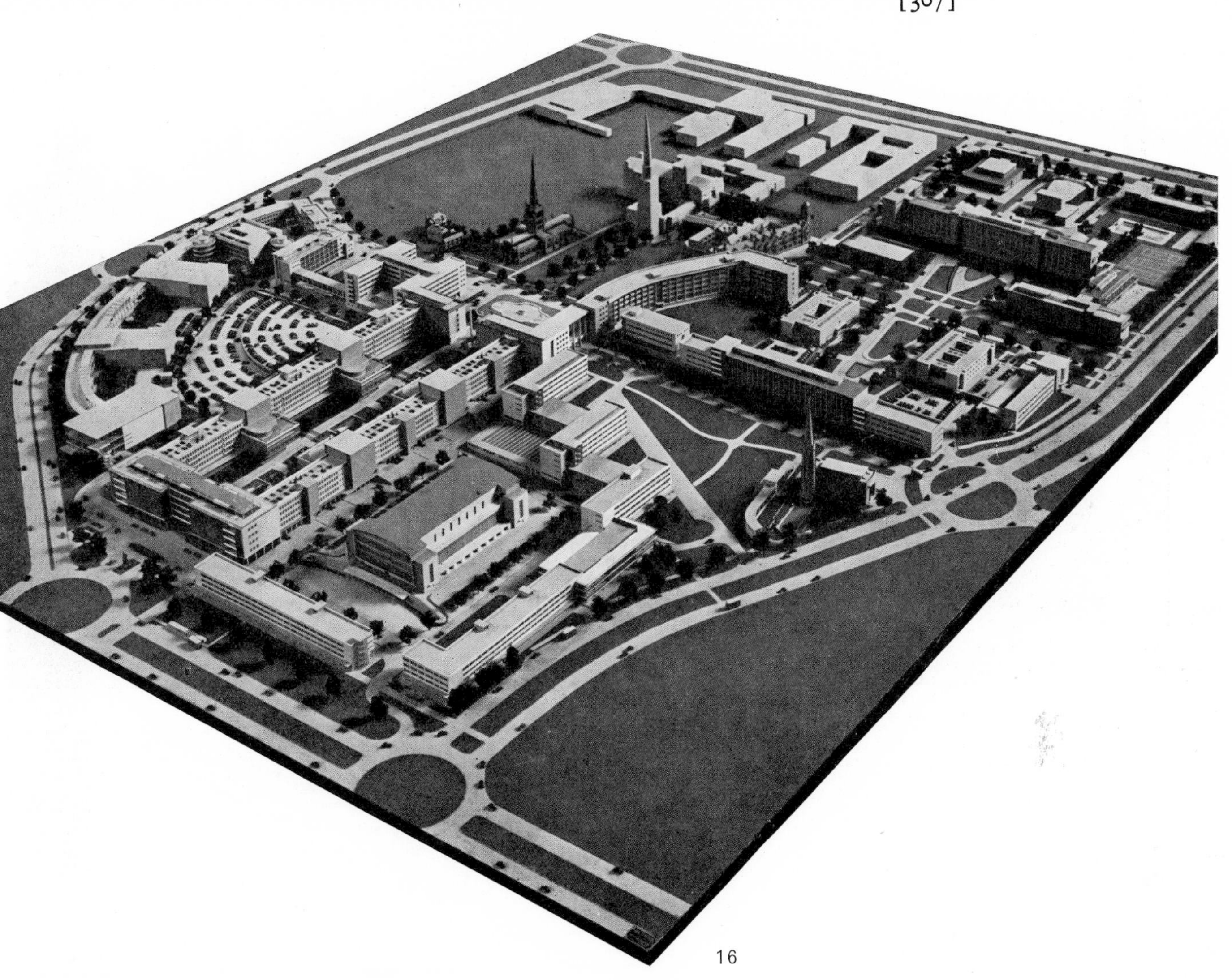

16

16. The third model, 1942

After the initial studies, work began on a more detailed scheme, and when Lord Iliffe gave £1,000 for a model it resulted in this carefully worked out three-dimensional study, which was extremely helpful in explaining the scheme to the public. At this stage the two original squares of the shopping precinct have become three, separated from each other by the low projecting blocks of large multiple stores. All the theatres and cinemas on the left (north) of the shopping precinct were to be connected to each other and to the former by a long upper-level gallery. At the west end of the shopping precinct was to be the Co-operative Society's big store, and at the eastern end (Broadgate) a new large hotel was proposed. Owing to the difficulty of removing existing buildings, Hertford Street had to be left in the same alignment, with the new buildings replacing the older ones over a period.

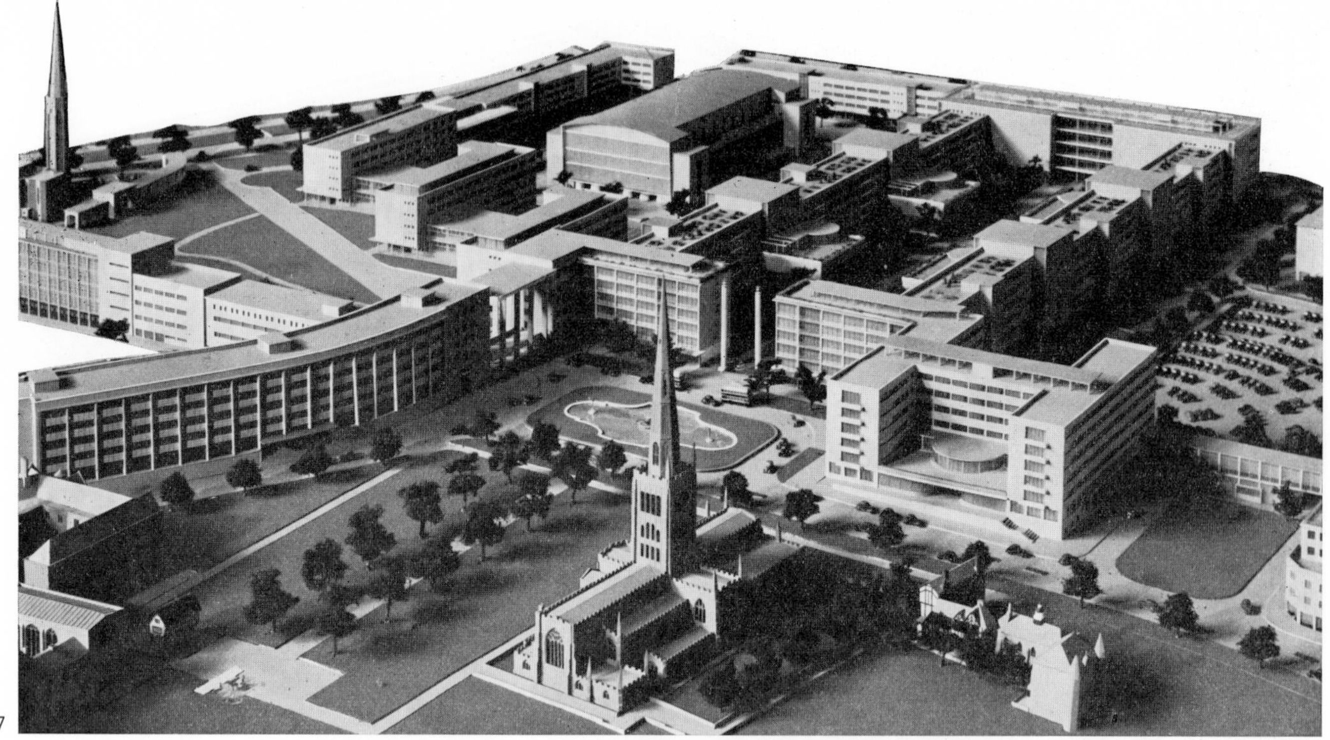
17

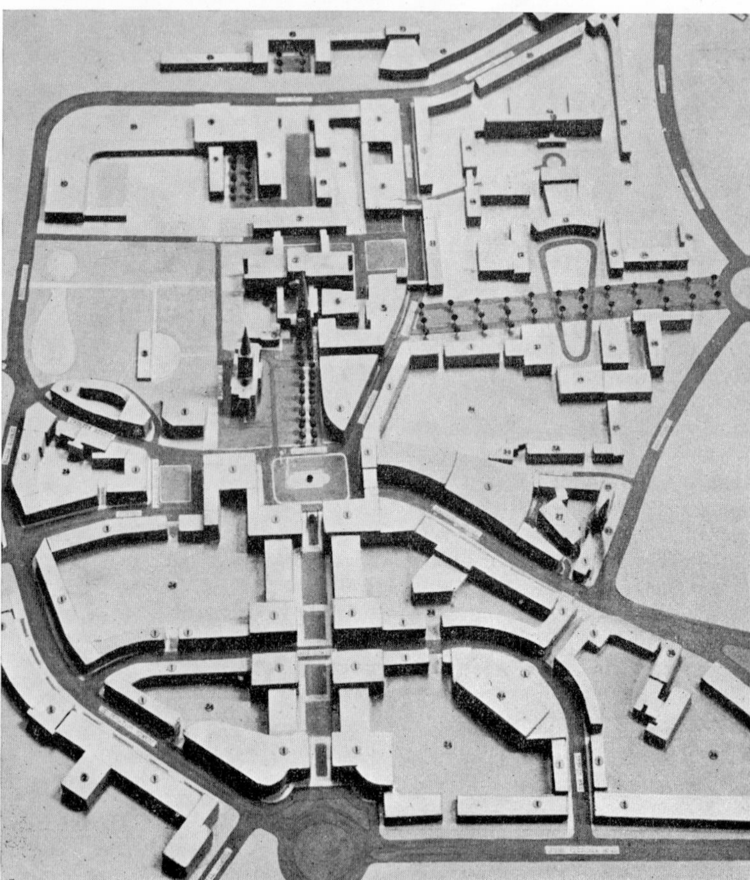
18

19

19. The 1958 model

This shows the city centre as planned in 1958. Many of the buildings were then completed, while others were in an advanced stage of detailed design. In the foreground is the civic and cultural precinct, then the Cathedral, with Broadgate in the centre of the photograph, and the shopping precinct at the top. Considerable modifications in detail have since been made to this model.

---

17. The third model: a detailed view

In this close-up view taken from the north-east, Trinity Church is in the foreground, with the re-designed Broadgate above it. Its design as a roundabout can now be seen to be a mistake, but it was an essential element in getting redevelopment started. After the war, when the Government economic restrictions prevented a start being made with the buildings, the City managed to persuade the Ministry of Transport that the present of a large quantity of bulbs from Holland, which were destined for the heart of the City, made it essential to construct the road round the roundabout. To the right of the roundabout the building then proposed was a large hotel; later this site was leased to Messrs Owen Owens, Coventry's big store, which had previously occupied part of the site.

18. The fourth model, 1945

A large number of negotiations had taken place since the early days after the bombing. Donald Gibson had continued to fight doughtily for the principles of his original plan, but although in certain respects the original proposals remained, at least one serious change for the worse had taken place. This model, photographed from the west, shows the shopping precinct in the foreground. Unfortunately it has been bisected by an intruding road which was deliberately inserted against Gibson's advice on the basis of the old theory of enabling shoppers to park their cars at the pavement and leave them while they did their shopping. This road not only disrupted the pedestrian precinct: it also made redevelopment in the original entertainment precinct to the north and the market precinct to the south extremely difficult. Fortunately Arthur Ling, the second City Architect and Planning Officer, was able to persuade the City Council to turn the road back into a pedestrian walkway. In the upper centre of the model the cathedral spire can be seen. At this stage Sir Giles Gilbert Scott had prepared a scheme for a new cathedral which assumed the complete demolition of the ruins of the old one. Later a competition was held, and won by Sir Basil Spence, in which he enabled the ruins to be retained, much to the benefit of the whole conception.

20

20. The 1962 Model

In the foreground is Broadgate, showing a possible re-use of two sides of the roundabout as pedestrian space. The City Council resolved in 1965 to close Hertford Street (to the left) and extend the pedestrian shopping area and to eliminate the north-south through traffic in the City Centre. This implies detailed reconsideration – not yet finalised – of the whole future of Broadgate. At the lower right is Trinity Church, and above it Messrs Owen Owens new store. Attached to it is the Leofric Hotel, which forms the top end of the shopping precinct, while above and to the right is the multi-storey car park completed in 1962. At the far end of the Precinct it was proposed firstly to site a long low slab. This was revised to the tall slab shown here – too tall in my opinion. It is now (1965) under construction as a slim point block, similar in scale to the tower terminating the cross axis (completed, with some modifications, in 1965), and more in scale with the rest of the development.

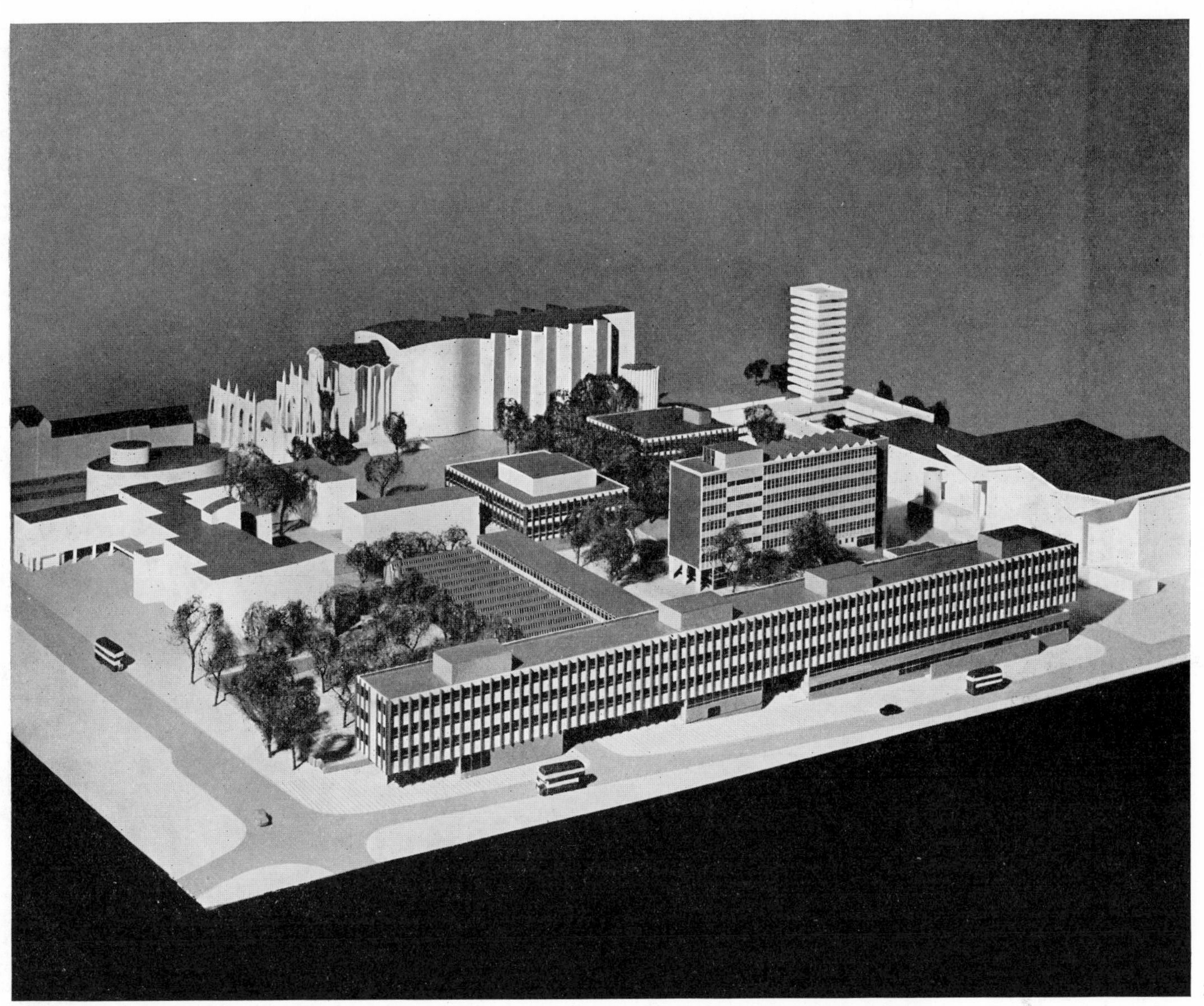

21

21. The civic and cultural precinct
This model shows the Lanchester College of Technology in the foreground, which was completed in 1964, except for the Halls of Residence. On the left is the completed Art Gallery and in the background is the Cathedral. On the right are the Central Baths, designed to Olympic standards and due to open in 1966.

22 

23 

22. Air view, 1945

In this view, taken from the south-east, the Council House, St Mary's Hall, Cathedral, and Trinity Church can be seen at lower right. To their left is Broadgate, with the devastated shopping area beyond.

23. Air view, 1949

The familiar group of Council House, Cathedral (in ruins), and Trinity Church, can be seen at lower right. Immediately to their left is the road layout of the new Broadgate, the first piece of redevelopment to be completed.

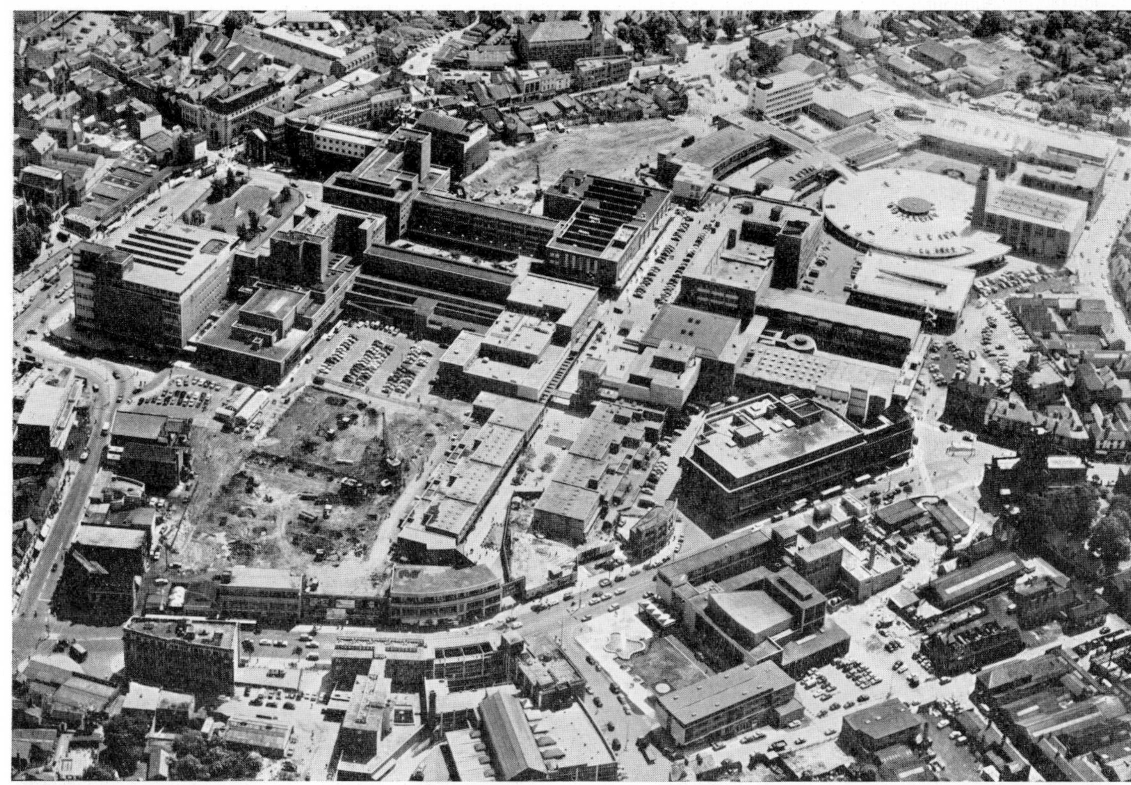

24

25

24. Air view, 1959

This photograph is taken from the north-west. At bottom right is the new Belgrade civic theatre, facing on to a new Place. Above it is the northern arm of the shopping precinct which was converted back from a roadway by Arthur Ling, and includes a ballroom. The original precinct runs across the upper centre of the photograph with Broadgate at left. Above the lower precinct to the right is the new circular market with roof-top car parking, and with a multi-storey garage adjacent. The roofs of the south precinct, market, and garage are all connected by road bridges. At lower left the foundations of a new multi-storey garage can be seen – this is now completed, as is a similar garage on the empty site in the upper centre of the photograph.

25. Air view, 1959

This view, taken from the west, shows the shopping precinct in the foreground with Broadgate above it.

26

27

28

28. Part of the Civic area, 1962

At the bottom of the photograph is the newly restored roof of the ancient St Mary's Guildhall, and above it the rear of the Council House (Coventry's Town Hall). Above and left are municipal offices, centre is the Police Headquarters, and upper right is the Government telephone building. These follow the original concept of having Civic and Government precincts.

29

29. The upper precinct

A view taken from below the upper-level walkway, with staircase on the right, looking east across the first part of the pedestrian shopping precinct. In the background, left, is the Leofric Hotel, on the right are municipally built and rented offices, while between them is the distant spire of the old Cathedral.

---

26. Air view, 1961

A more recent progress photograph which shows the new Cathedral almost completed and illustrates how carefully its architect, Sir Basil Spence, has related the new to the ruins of the old. At upper right can be seen a newly completed multi-storey garage.

27. Broadgate from the Cathedral spire, 1962

In the foreground are the roofs of temporary shops erected shortly after the war. In the centre is the Broadgate roundabout with the Godiva statue, presented to the City by a private citizen. Immediately above it is the main entrance to the shopping precinct, with the Leofric Hotel on the right, and Messrs Owen Owens store adjoining it, while to the left is the first block of shops and offices which were built by the Corporation and let to private interests. Adjoining this building is a restaurant which has been set over Hertford Street where it enters Broadgate. It abuts on to the National Provincial Bank, a survivor of the blitz.

30. The lower precinct

The lower precinct was enclosed by buildings of more modest scale than those of the upper precinct, and was more sensitively designed. In accordance with the original concept, its upper-level walkway came straight off at ground level from the upper precinct. Built out into the middle of it is a pleasant glass-walled café. Below the upper level walkway in the background is a large ceramic mural designed by Gordon Cullen.

30

31. Shelton Square

At the southern end of the shopping precinct the pedestrian way broadens out into a handsome square, which was designed as a collaborative venture between the City Council and a private firm of developers. The staircase leads up to the upper-level walkway.

31

32. The Locarno Ballroom

In the heart of the shopping precinct is the Locarno Ballroom, designed to keep the precinct alive in the evenings. An ingenious feature, and one only possible with comprehensive development, is the siting of some of its lifts (elevators) right out in the pedestrian way.

32

33. Multi-storey parking garage

Around the shopping precinct there are three multi-storey parking garages, of simple and economical construction (£220 per car space in 1961). This one is in the south-east corner.

33

34. The retail market

The retail market adjoins the shopping precinct and has brought into use an old factory building which can be seen reconditioned in the background, In the foreground is the ramp up to the roof car park, and on the right is a multi-storey parking garage.

34

35. The City Architectural and Planning Department

A night view in the square formed by municipal offices. Most of the ground floor of the Department is a glass partition containing a changing exhibition of models and photographs of proposals and achievements, open to all citizens for comment and criticism. A large number of materials have been used in the floorscape of the square, partly to add interest and partly for the benefit of the architects, who can see a large range of building materials in use.

35

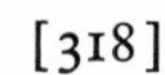

36

36. The Belgrade Theatre

The new civically owned and operated theatre faces a small new square off Corporation Street. It owes its name to the sympathy of the citizens of the Yugoslav capital for the bombed city of Coventry.

7

Rotterdam

Amsterdam for long held the lead as Holland's major seaport (also, incidentally, as Europe's finest planned city). It was always, however, apparent that Rotterdam, once it could solve the problem of the silting up of the River Maas and its connection with the sea, was much more strategically placed at the mouth of one of Europe's great waterways to be the principal exchange point between ocean-going traffic and the vast industrial market of the Ruhr. Rotterdam's great opportunity came in the 1870's, when a deep waterway to the sea was completed. The docks and harbour were thus the main sphere of development, but many heavy and light industries sprang up as well, and these, coupled with extensive tenement housing for the great influx of workers, rapidly turned Rotterdam into a congested industrial city. Although she did not emulate Amsterdam's fine lead in planned urban expansion, a number of well laid out suburbs were in fact developed. Since Holland was then experiencing an architectural renaissance, it was only natural that a fair number of significant modern buildings should be built in its vigorous new seaport. Thus, before 1939, the *Van Nelle* Factory set a very fine example of large-scale industrial buildings, while in the *Bergpolder* project an intelligent use was made of reinforced concrete and of good siting for multi-storeyed flats. In the centre, too, were the finely designed but somewhat mannered *Bijenkorf* store by Dudok, the *Erasmus Huis* office tower by the same architect, and the *Stock Exchange* by J. F. Staal—completed just before the outbreak of war.

It was this thriving, pushing, developing seaport of about 600,000 people that Hitler selected for his first 'blitz' or terror raid, the technique that was designed to shock a whole country into submission, and so eloquently forecast by H. G. Wells a few years before. In May 1940, the centre of Rotterdam was obliterated, and an area of some 645 acres was laid waste. This was equivalent to the total area of the City of London or the combined acreage of Hyde Park and Kensington Gardens. Approximately 11,000 buildings were destroyed, including 2,393 shops and department stores, 1,887 workshops, factories and warehouses, 1,483 offices, 69 schools, 21 churches, 4 railway stations, 184 garages, 26 hotels and 24,978 homes. Although the official death-roll was put at only 1900, the scale of tragedy and misery may be gauged by the fact that 78,000 people were rendered homeless.

When the war ended, both city and docks were in ruins, and a less phlegmatic and determined people than the Dutch might well have blenched at the prospect of Rotterdam ever recovering from a disaster of such magnitude. But the Dutch in general and the Rotterdammers in particular were quite clear what was at stake—it was nothing short of national survival. They set to work on the docks with such a will that by 1949 they had not only rebuilt and re-equipped them with the most up-to-date cargo-handling equipment in Europe, but had greatly enlarged them as well. The programme of harbour extension seems to get more ambitious every year. A new oil refinery has recently been completed, and now work is well advanced on a great new harbour at the mouth of the Maas for the 100,000-ton tanker market. All this port activity has already brought a planned new town into existence to the south of the river, and has greatly expanded an old town on the north at Vlaardingen, besides creating several new neighbourhoods both on the north and south. It also seems likely to create considerable location problems for more large communities in the near future.

Let us now consider the city centre. As with Coventry, where we continued to plan, but with new conditions, almost while the ground was still warm from the conflagration, the Rotterdammers were quickly off the mark. Four days after the great raid the Municipality instructed the City Architect, Mr W. G. Witteveen, to prepare a plan, and within three weeks he produced his first outline scheme. This scheme was based largely on the old city pattern, but proposed a considerable number of new streets, street widenings, and the opening up of public spaces in front of existing and proposed public buildings. Though it looked backwards rather than forwards for its theoretical inspiration, it did enable a number of urgently required buildings, such as the Rotterdamsche Bank and a temporary City Theatre, to be started on adequate sites.

Parallel with this civic enterprise, the Government made a compulsory purchase order by military ordinance over most of the blitzed land, and developed a special procedure for fixing and approving reconstruction plans for the damaged or destroyed parts. Planning studies continued during the war, under the leadership of Mr Van Traa, the outstanding new head of the Town Planning and Reconstruction Department. Much of this work had to be done in secret during the Nazi occupation, but in May 1946 the second plan, known as the *Basic Scheme for the Reconstruction of the City of Rotterdam*, was approved by the City Council and, not long afterwards, was endorsed by the Government. The central Government in Holland, which has always been much more active as a planning agency than its British counterpart, had passed an Order in Council (No. F.67) in May 1945 which for the greater part legalized the reconstruction procedure, which had come into force during the occupation. A National Board of High Commissioners for Reconstruction had been set up and had been empowered to issue acquisition directives to the Burgomaster (or Lord Mayor). The change of ownership took effect with the directive. All properties were entered in a reconstruction register which became a guarantee for the owners. Land values were taken at 1940 values, but compensation was not paid at the time, and the owners had the right to another piece of land of the same value. In order to obtain war damage compensation owners had to rebuild, and an allowance was made for betterment on improved sites.

For road traffic a system of three east-west and three-north-south main roads with rectangular crossings was designed to pick up and distribute all traffic. Between these main roads (with a width of 200-300 feet) large precinctual areas were formed which were made accessible by secondary roads. Much as we had gone about the job in Coventry, the Rotterdam Authorities decided to have their main shopping centre roughly where it had been before on either side of the *Coolsingel*, as the historic main street is called, but (and this came at a late stage in negotiations between planners, architects and shopkeepers) to have the western part mainly as a pedestrian precinct. They, too, believed that careful land-use zoning and good communications, although essential, were only facets of the total task of reconstruction and that the most vital job was a comprehensive three dimensional appreciation of the future city centre. For this reason (as with both Coventry and London), large scale models were made, and the various groups of buildings were worked out in collaboration with the individual architects.

The core of the city is still the Coolsingel, the equivalent of London's Piccadilly or Chicago's State Street. Three large public buildings facing this street, namely the *Town Hall*, the *General Post Office*, and the brand new and very capably designed *Stock Exchange*, survived the blitz, so here replanning was restricted to widening both street and pavements. The other main street to be treated in this conventional manner was the *Hoogstraat*, which runs at right angles to the Coolsingel, and which had much more of the intimate character of Bond Street. This was rebuilt to the same width and in my opinion may suffer from traffic congestion in consequence, although rear service-roads take the goods vehicles, and through traffic will normally use the main roads.

THE HOOGSTRAAT. From the 'place' where it joins the Coolsingel, the street begins with a group of multiple stores, including the excellent *Huf Store* by Messrs van den Broek and Bakema. Continuing eastwards, across the Delftse Vaart Canal, there are on the south side conventional, but well-designed blocks of offices and flats with ground-floor shops, by Messrs Bakker and Vermeer & Herwaarden; but on the north side there is a terrace of two-storey shops with four-storey blocks of showrooms, flats and offices running back at right angles (in the form so often discussed but not so far built in this country). It gives a most interesting street pattern, and also forms a good background to the *Cathedral*, which lies immediately to the north. The scheme was designed by Messrs Merkelbach and Elling.

Another example of blocks running back at right angles may be seen if one returns to the canal and looks northwards. Here there is a perspective of a series of blocks of office and commercial buildings, designed by Messrs Van Tijen & Maaskant and Dudok.

The really exciting shopping innovation was the *Lijnbaan*, the now well-known pedestrian shopping centre, which (if one excepts Coventry's pioneer conception and the American out-of-town centres) is something new, and is one of those imaginative experiments which has really 'come off'. The shops were restricted to two storeys in height, and the basic architectural design is simple, modular in construction, and economical to the point of crudeness; but a lively atmosphere is obtained by the numerous incidental details such as light covered ways, flower boxes, sculptures, and the excellent standard of display in the shops themselves.

The Precinct is of cruciform shape and consists of two pedestrian ways, the *Lijnbaan*, which is 59 feet wide, and the *Korte Lijnbaan*, 39 feet wide—the area occupied is

450,000 square feet and shop frontage widths were determined by the constructional module of 3 feet 3 inches, giving frontages of 21 feet 8 inches, 28 feet 10 inches, 43 feet 4 inches or 57 feet 8 inches. There are at present 66 shops with a total frontage of 3,300 feet. The final stage was held up through the presence, on the site, of a pre-war hospital, which lay across the site of the southward extension of the Korte Lijnbaan.

The method by which the Lijnbaan came into being is extremely interesting. In the first master plans the area was shown as zoned for shopping, and conventional streets were indicated. At an early stage, however, Mr Van Traa initiated negotiations between the shopkeepers and their architects, Professor Van den Broek and Bakema, and as a result he persuaded them that it would be better to have a comprehensively designed pedestrian centre. The shopkeepers formed themselves into an association, the Lijnbaan Shopping Promenade Association, and this now looks after advertising, lighting and furnishing in the precinct. From the point of view of historic continuity it is interesting that the name Lijnbaan comes from the covered rope-walk which was built on the same site in 1667. The precinct also includes two cinemas and a number of restaurants and cafés, while rising just behind the shops is a group of high blocks of flats. These are well designed, and finished in excellent materials, a reminder of how important it is that the new architecture, which so often looks so good inside, requires high-quality materials externally to make the simple forms satisfying to the critical eye.

Where the Lijnbaan opens out on to the Binnenweg are two large new buildings, both designed by the architectural firm of Van den Broek and Bakema. One is a furniture store completed in 1953, and the other, although one architectural unit, consists of three separate shops—a department store, a ladies outfitter and a shoe shop.

Near by, and also adjoining the Lijnbaan, where it crosses the v. Oldenbarnevelt, is the new *Bijenkorf* store, which has a total floor space of 387,504 square feet, and has the famous Gabo constructivist sculpture standing in front of it.

Other striking new experiments have been tried out in the blitzed central area. There is the *Groothandelsgebouw*, for instance, just near the new station. It is a portmanteau word for a portmanteau building, for its enormous concrete egg-crate façade encloses some five acres, with nine floors of some 230 warehouses, showrooms, offices, banks and shops; and one can drive into it at basement, ground or first floor level. In addition it has restaurants, canteens and bars, employs 5,000 people, and has parking for 400 vehicles. Then there are a number of flatted factories in which the smaller industrialists can hire factory space. Most notable is that on the *Goudse singel* which is a three-sided six-storey square with a large one-storey area in the middle; services include shops, showrooms and offices. Not far away is a new kind of multiple store, called the *Twaalf Provincien*, where small traders were to have been able to hire shopping space around a great concourse on several levels. Unfortunately this experiment was completed in advance of surrounding development and had to be closed after a very brief career. The planners have been careful with the siting of high tower buildings, and so far the two post-war examples are excellently placed on the *Leuvehaven* harbour, and both, in addition to fitting in well as parts of the overall urban design, get splendid views from their windows across the river. Incidentally, one of the planning ideas was to open up the city centre to the river, and this involved a controversial proposal to demolish the old Bijenkorf store which lay squarely across the southern end of the Coolsingel. In my view there was still enough left of what was one of Europe's finest pre-war stores to make it economically worth keeping, and the roundabout which will now take its place could have been realigned without too much difficulty.

Two other aspects of this remarkable reconstruction must be mentioned.

The communication services have been vastly improved; there is now one main railway station instead of two, and the new roads are generous in their width, with over/under crossings in addition to roundabouts—actually the Rotterdammers may eventually regret that they did not have more multi-level crossings, although admittedly excavation costs in Holland are very high owing to the condition of the sub-soil. More exceptional than new roads, though, and more than a new central heliport, which exists but about which there may have to be second thoughts owing to the noise problem, is the district heating scheme. Although this involves at least one rather unsightly power station in a central position, it is a tremendous boon as a municipal service.

Lastly, urban decoration. From an aesthetic point of view one hopes the trams will eventually go and take their ugly wirescape with them, but apart from this blemish a major effort has been made to adorn the new city with sculpture. At the top end of the Coolsingel is a great circular fountain donated by a shipping firm, that makes a good centre-piece to a traffic roundabout, while to the south there are a number of other civic embellishments. Opposite the *Town Hall*, where a paved place leads into the Lijnbaan, is a life-sized bronze realist group of sculpture, symbolizing the resistance movement. Near by in an adjacent office building is a mosaic mural, while further on, in front of the new Bijenkorf store, is what is probably the first really large-scale constructivist sculpture by Gabo. It is all in smooth shining metal, and after having been used to seeing such objects on tables in Art Exhibitions, it almost gives one the feeling of coming across an enormously magnified drop of water. Then down by the harbour are two more experimental pieces—the Zadkine bronze, a striking piece of expressionism, in which it is possible not only to recognize a human form with its heart torn out, but to feel very much what the artist was trying to convey about the city's destruction. By the harbour, too, is the naval monument by Carasso, which takes the form of a tall aluminium fin, symbolizing the bow of a great ship.

For good measure, there is the Henry Moore bas-relief in brick which is placed right across the north wall of the new *Bouwcentrum* (the Dutch word for Building Centre). It is not, I think, very successful and not nearly so good as his much smaller reclining figure in a balcony high up behind the smooth travertine façade of the new Bijenkorf store.

Much still remains to be done in Rotterdam, and part of what has been done is a little on the conventional side and occasionally even dull, but the total effect is inspiring. Here at last is one blitzed city which started on the right foot; which bought all its land first, and then (as Lord Reith once advised British blitzed cities to do) planned boldly and comprehensively. It is clear too that the City Council, the planners and most of the architects believe firmly in both modern architecture and modern planning.

Most important in this great experiment of city rebuilding are the lessons one can learn from it. A few may be mentioned, although without assessing their relative importance. First has been the determination of all the Rotterdammers to remodel their city as an up-to-date functional machine, as the new docks show so clearly; secondly, to rebuild it as an important national shopping centre with ample opportunities for the smaller as well as the larger shopkeepers; and third to create it as a place to enjoy living in; hence the new cultural facilities both built and planned, the well-designed flats in the centre surrounded with the bright city lights; the well laid out neighbourhoods on the outskirts, and the new parks, the excellent townscaping, and attention to public sculpture and well-designed street furniture.

Other lessons of particular importance in this book are that the comprehensive city reconstruction had to be made possible both legally and financially by the central government; that there was a continuity of design planning running right through in time. When one compares the first post-blitz plan with the present reality one sees what great strides have been made; but always there was an overall design, a design both flexible and capable of extensive modifications and improvements as time went on.

With the advantage of hindsight we can see that the widening of such conventional one-level streets as the Coolsingel was a mistake, that they should have avoided roundabouts in the road plan, that they should have designed the Lijnbaan and its adjacent blocks of flats as one unit so that the large area of flat surface of the shop roofs could be used for additional recreational space; and I am sure that the planners and architects often say as we did in London 'if only we could do it again . . .'. In spite of these and other defects the reconstruction of Rotterdam remains one of the best examples of its kind in the world. More recently, a new underground rail system has been constructed, principally to connect Rotterdam South with the reconstructed city centre, but it provides one move level of communication that does not interfere with the aboveground environment, as did the old elevated rail systems of Liverpool, New York, and Chicago.

1

7 ROTTERDAM

1. The Zadkine Statue

Symbolizing the destruction of the city centre in 1940, this magnificent expressionist statue stands at the entrance to the city from the river. It compares interestingly with the Phoenix stone carved by Trevor Tennant in the Coventry precinct.

2

2. The Port

An air view of one of the world's greatest seaports. With superb confidence the Dutch took advantage of the appalling destruction of the war to reconstruct the Port of Rotterdam with the finest modern equipment and facilities. It can berth and handle 167 sea-going vessels at the quayside, and another 85 on anchor buoys and dolphins. Since the war major new oil refineries have been developed down river, while a great new port (Europort) is being constructed at the river mouth.

3. Rotterdam, 1560

In this plan Rotterdam is a modest medieval river port, surrounded by a town wall and canal moat. There are as many canals as roads, and the one acting as the western moat was later filled in to become Rotterdam's main street, known as the Coolsingel. At this time the city had a population of 7,000 living in 1,731 houses. The herring fishery was the main economic activity, although it had also been a weaving centre for English wool for many years.

4. Rotterdam, 1649

Rotterdam was now an important seaport, although still difficult of access owing to the shoals in the river Maas. In spite of the English Navigation Act of 1651 a trade connection of great importance existed with London, to which Rotterdam shipped fish, dairy products, grains, salt, wines, and many other commodities. At this time there were many Scotsmen in Rotterdam, the principal import being Scottish coal.

5. Rotterdam, 1796

During the Napoleonic Wars Rotterdam's trade suffered disastrously, especially in consequence of the Continental System. After the end of hostilities the population began to increase rapidly, from 60,000 in 1816 to 72,000 in 1830. It was many years, however, before the city regained its prosperity. The introduction of Free Trade, the abolition of the Rhine shipping dues, and the repeal of the Navigation Act all helped.

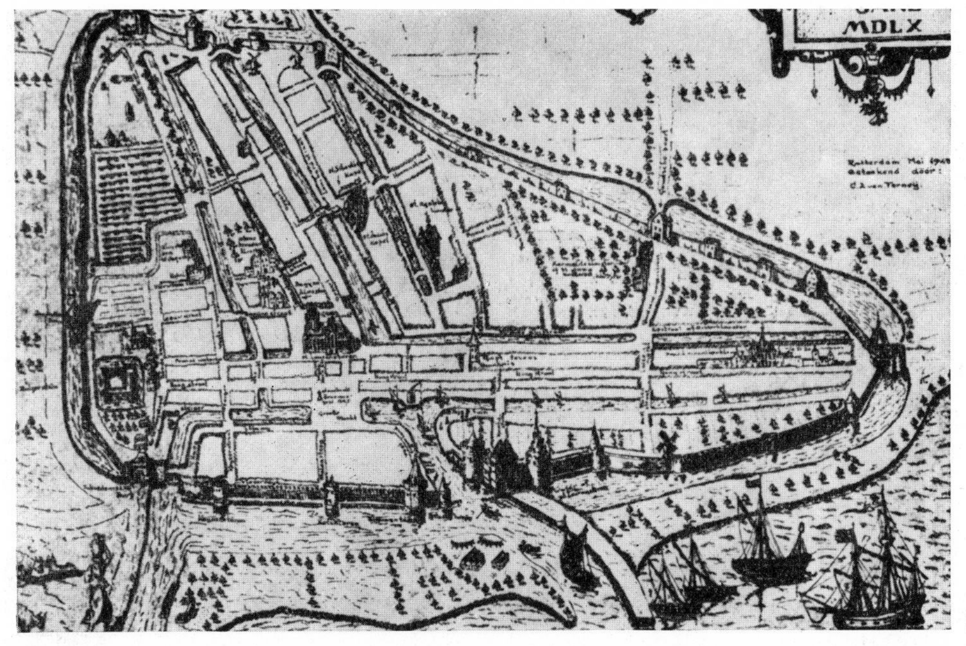

3

4

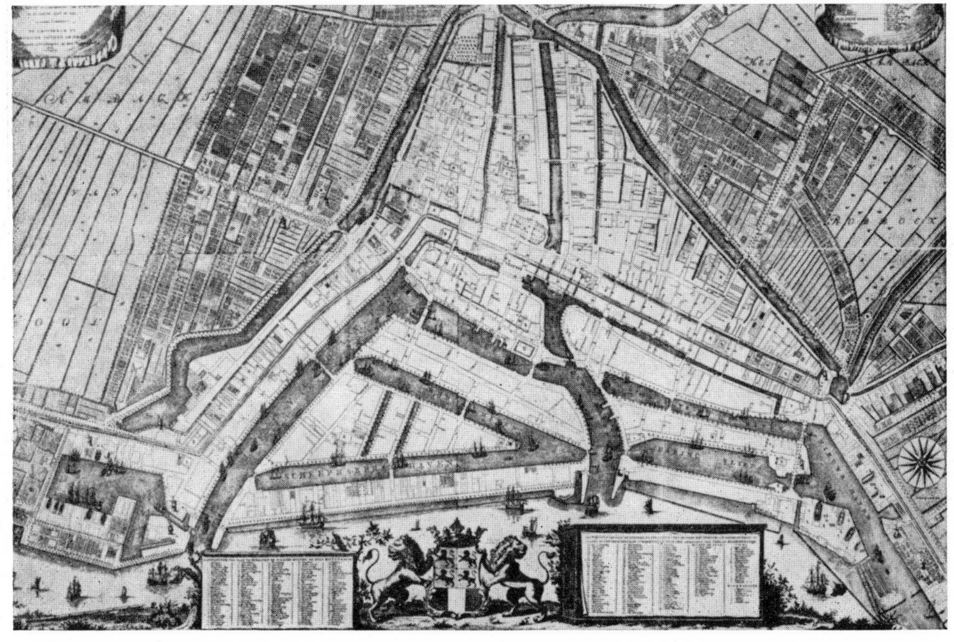

5

6. Rotterdam, 1887

During the nineteenth century the city developed rapidly. In 1825 a canal was cut across the island of Voorne which shortened the distance to the sea, while a series of docks and shipyards were built in 1854. After a great deal of study a new canal was cut between 1866 and 1868 giving direct access to the sea through the Hook of Holland. This still failed to give the depth required, and after a great deal of dredging the Rotterdam Waterway was completed in 1896; but one may say that by 1887 the foundations of Rotterdam as a world port had been laid.

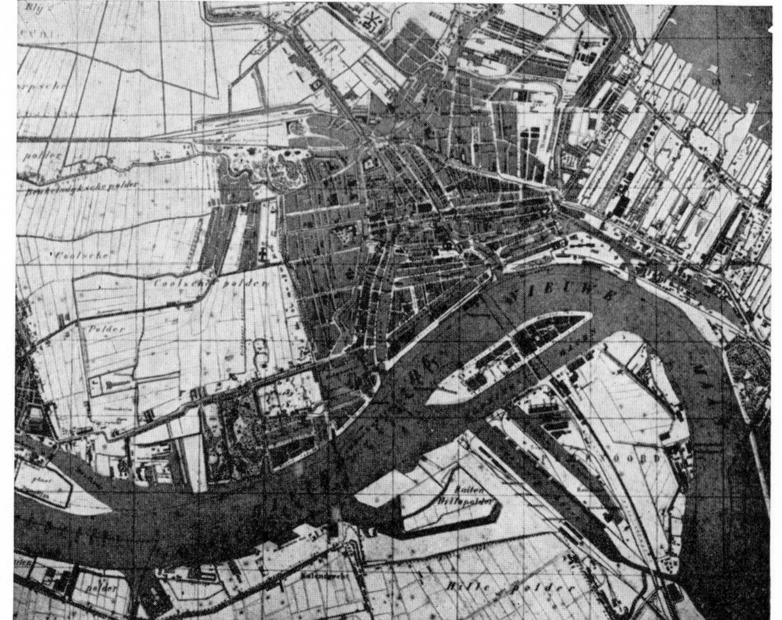

6

7

7. A pre-war scene

This is a fairly typical view of pre-war Rotterdam. Many of the former merchants' houses have been converted or have been rebuilt as business premises. The old street pattern has been retained but the bulk of building has been increased. Apart from the Dutch tradition of cleanliness and urban order, Rotterdam was rapidly becoming a typical big city problem case, where private land ownership, the cost of land, and the lack of planning legislation all combined to prevent the emergence of a new urban form. In the left background is the great church of St Lawrence, with the City Hall Tower behind it.

8

8. The destroyed central area

This air view is taken looking south-east over the area devastated by the bombing in 1940. In one day the whole core of a great commercial city had been laid in ruins, leaving only isolated urban fragments. In the centre foreground can be seen the Town Hall, the Post Office and the Stock Exchange, which all survived, facing on to the Coolsingel. The Coolsingel was Rotterdam's Piccadilly or State Street. Above the Town Hall may be seen the great church. At middle right is Dudok's famous Bijenkorf store, about half of which survived, but was demolished when the new Bijenkorf was completed between the Coolsingel and the Lijnbaan.

9. The scale of destruction (*overleaf*)

A photograph taken from the top of the spire of the ruined great church (recently rebuilt) in the centre of the city. The view is looking south, with the River Maas in the background. In the holocaust of May 14th, 1940, some 11,000 buildings were destroyed, including 24,978 dwellings, 2,393 shops, 1,483 offices, 1,212 factories and workshops, 675 warehouses, 526 restaurants and public houses, 256 boarding houses, 184 garages, 69 schools, 26 hotels, 21 churches, 12 cinemas, 6 large meeting halls, 4 hospitals, 4 railway stations, 2 theatres, and 2 museums. The death-roll was estimated at 1900, while 78,000 people were rendered homeless. In considering the opportunities for comprehensive replanning which this disaster gave, it is important to remember the vast scale of the human tragedy.

9

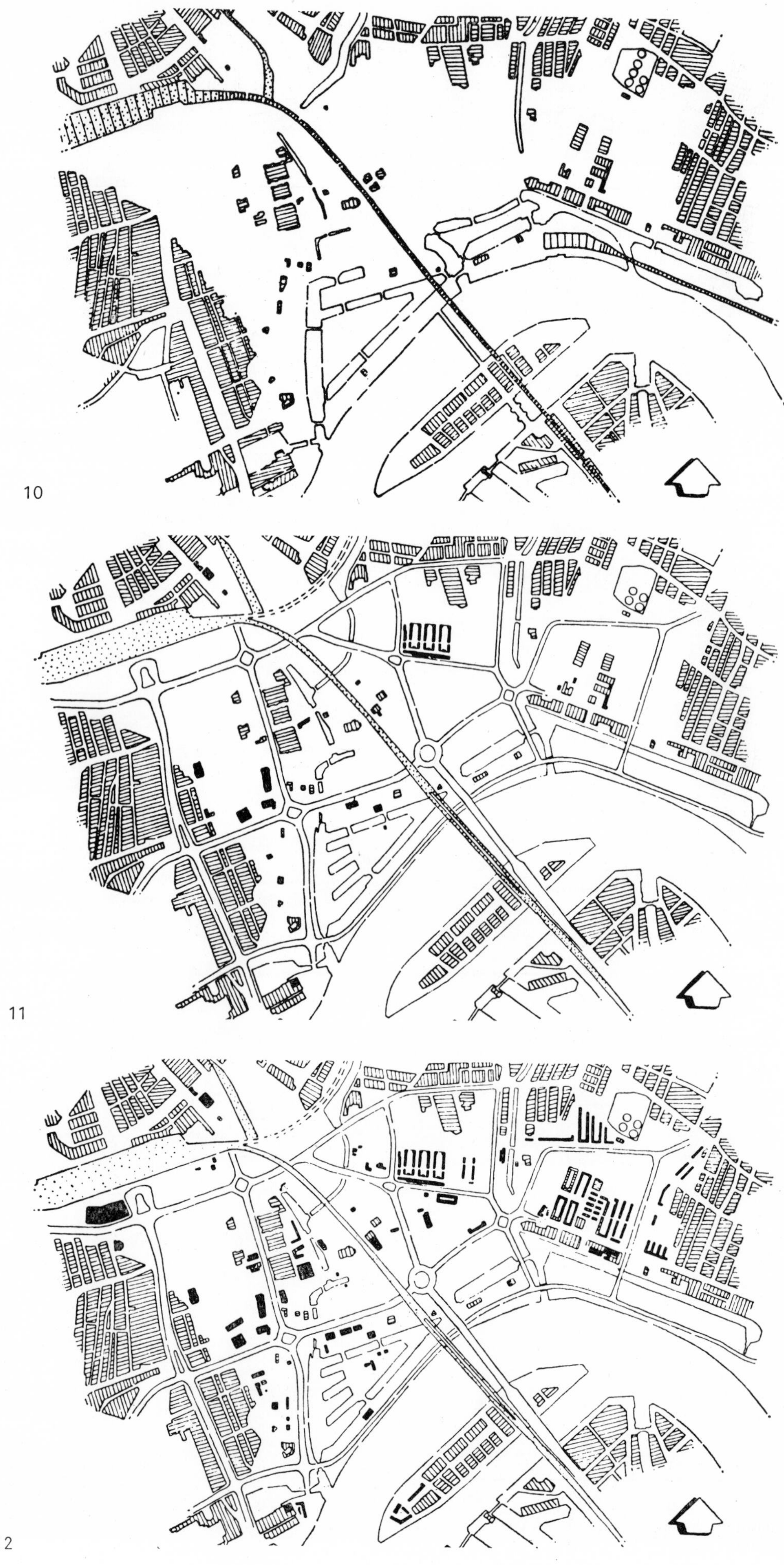

10

11

12

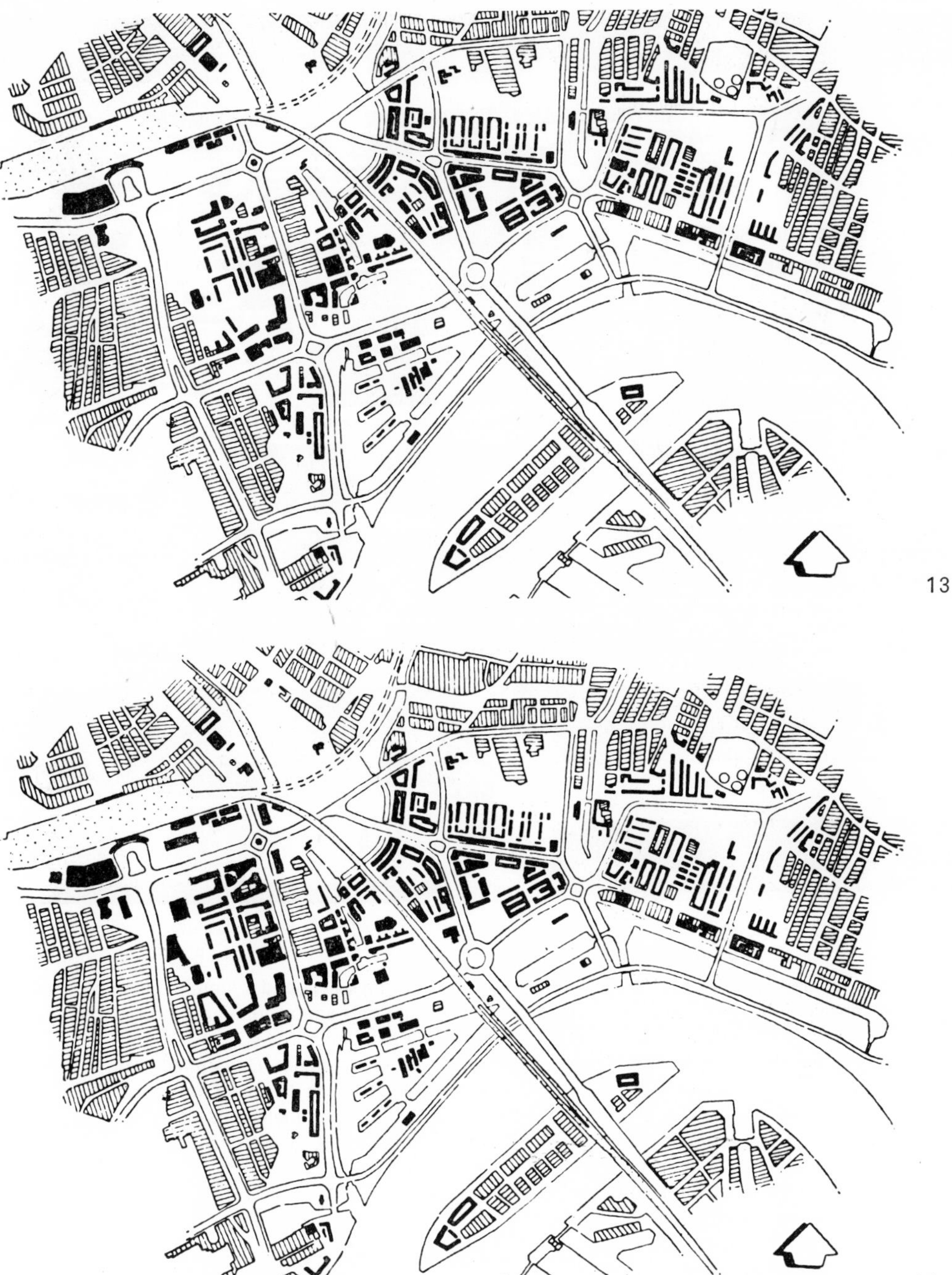

13

14

10, 11, 12, 13, 14. Reconstruction plans

1940: almost the entire centre of the city has been cleared by the bombing. Running diagonally across the centre is the railway line on viaduct, and to the left of it may be seen the three large public buildings still intact, the Town Hall, the Central Post Office, and the Stock Exchange.

1945: rebuilding has begun on the basis of the plan prepared shortly after the bombing. New buildings are shown in black, and include a group of apartments (upper centre), a bank and two stores, to the west of the Coolsingel.

1950: by this time rebuilding is in progress in various parts of the central area, and has not been concentrated in one place. More large stores have been built near the Coolsingel, new municipal offices near the Town Hall, a flatted factory just across the way from the 1945 apartments (seen as a black rectangle with a hollow centre), and a great new multi-purpose building known as the Groothandelsgebouw, seen as a large black shape at upper left. Immediately to its south is the first stage of the Bouwcentrum (Building Centre).

1955: the bulk of central area rebuilding has been completed. A large area of somewhat conventional high-density apartment building has been built to the north-east of the railway viaduct, and included in this is another experimental multi-purpose building known as the Twaalf Provincien. Immediately to the west of the viaduct is the great medieval church of St Lawrence, whose reconstruction is now complete, and to the south of it is the Old Hoogstraat, again rather conventionally rebuilt with shops with apartments over them. The great new achievement is the excellent pedestrian shopping centre known as the Lijnbaan, with two large squares of apartment buildings immediately to the west.

1964: redevelopment is now mainly a problem of filling the missing elements of the comprehensive urban design. One major new civic building, the new concert hall, is nearing completion to the west of the Lijnbaan. The space to the south is being laid out as a square with a garage beneath it. Another important new building is a hotel at the junction of the Coolsingel and the Weena. Below the Coolsingel a new underground railway is being built, while the obsolete roundabouts are in the process of being redesigned.

15

15. The first model

After the war the City Planning Director Mr Van Traa, drew up a Basic Comprehensive Scheme for Reconstruction. This scheme was revised in 1955 and a first model was made for the central area, which was used extensively for considering three-dimensional proposals before approval was given. To judge them Mr Van Traa chaired a committee composed of four other representatives of the Planning and Reconstruction Department and four private architects. Running up the left-hand side of the photograph is the Coolsingel, which now forms part of a major road framework, and unfortunately separates the Town Hall, Post Office and Stock Exchange (or Bourse) at far left, from the Lijnbaan area, centre. This cruciform shopping centre is entirely pedestrian. Between it and the Coolsingel are commercial offices and the famous new Bijenkorf store, while on the other side are high blocks of flats enclosing town squares. At far right a new concert hall was proposed. Nearly all the buildings shown on the model have since been built.

16. The second model

As the scheme developed a more detailed model was built. These models and accompanying drawings are on permanent exhibition in a spacious room of the Town Planning and Reconstruction Department. This view from the north-west shows a revised design for the concert hall, which is now complete, and on its right a recently built hotel. In the centre of the photograph are the residential squares.

17. The Lijnbaan

In the left foreground are a new cinema (left) and a theatre. Above the cinema is a restaurant standing at the crossing of the Lijnbaan. On the right are the high flats, with somewhat unsatisfactory balcony access, while at the southern end the Lijnbaan is temporarily blocked by a hospital, since demolished when the new one was completed. At the upper left is the Bijenkorf store.

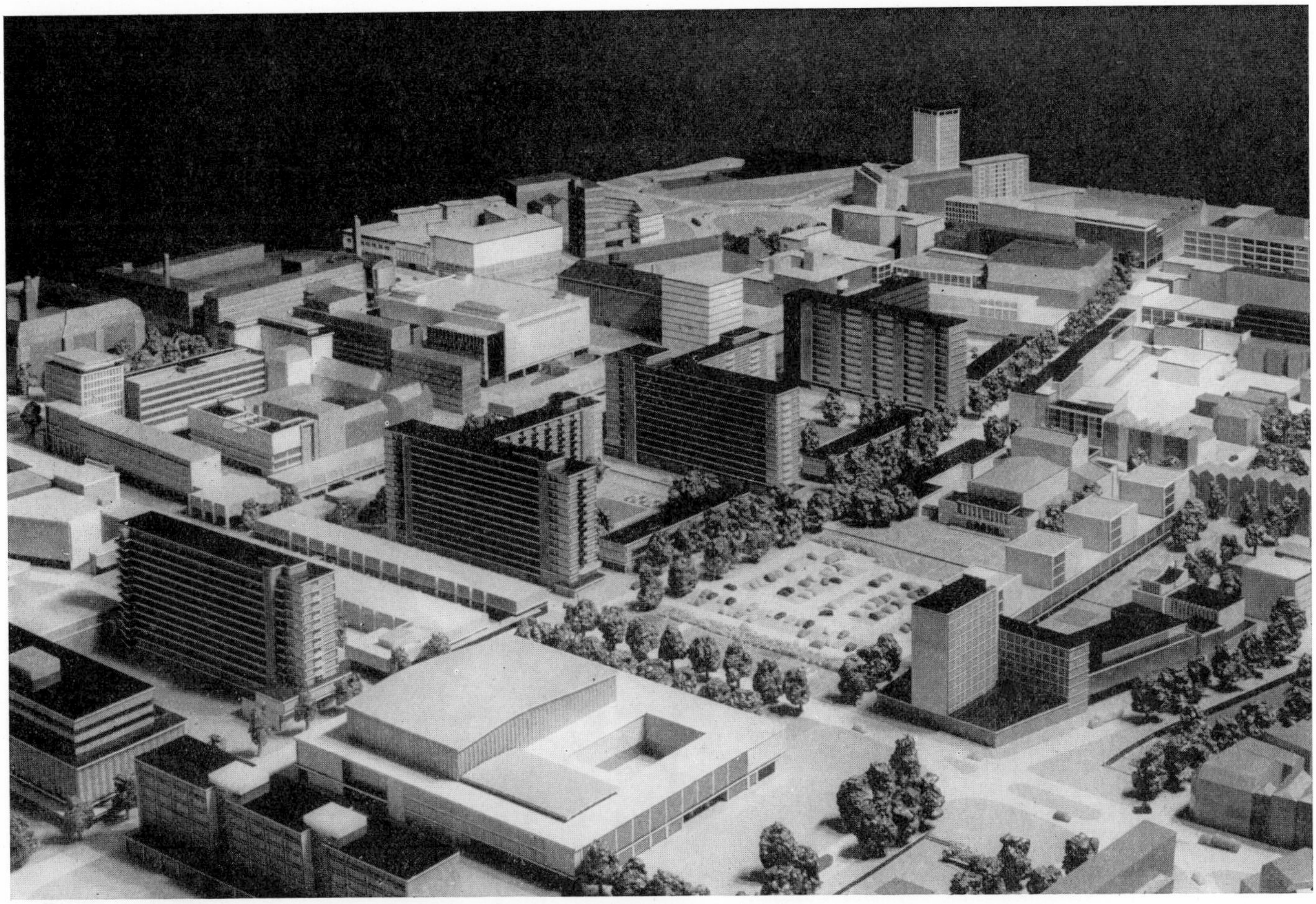

16

17

18. The Coolsingel and Lijnbaan from the south-east
Running obliquely across the foreground is the Coolsingel. At bottom centre is the Beursplein, with the Stock Exchange immediately to its right. In the centre is the new Bijenkorf store, and behind it is the Lijnbaan pedestrian shopping centre, consisting of small but rather expensive shops. At the far right-hand end of the Lijnbaan are a theatre and a cinema, while behind it are high blocks of apartments.

19. A general view
This air view is taken from the south-west of the central area and shows clearly the new scale of buildings and roads. In the centre foreground is the Euromast television tower, with its superb viewing restaurant. To its left is the Parkhaven, full of inland barge traffic: to its right the Het Park. Above it is a major traffic intersection with the road coming from the Maas Tunnel (below the centre of the photograph) proceeding at lower level towards the old town, which stands in strong contrast to the vast new municipal hospital immediately in front of it. Beyond and to the right of the hospital is the new Lever Building, and to the right again are the buildings of the E 55 Exhibition. Beyond them is the Boyman's Museum, while in the right background is the newly reconstructed city centre.

18

19

20

20. The Lijnbaan

A photograph taken from the meeting-place of the two pedestrian walkways. The whole shopping centre was designed as one building group by Messrs Van den Broek and Bakema, who used a pre-cast reinforced concrete structural grid based on a 1·1 metre module. It is this which gives such an interesting rhythm throughout the scheme. Rising up in the background are the high apartment blocks. At the right of the photograph is an attractive and playful sculpture, one of a number which adorn the shopping centre, and which, thanks to the centre being restricted to pedestrians, can be enjoyed in safety.

21

21. The Coolsingel

This is Rotterdam's most famous street. Once a canal on the western side of the old town, it was filled in, and as the town moved west it became the focus of urban activity. Along it were built the Town Hall, whose tower may be seen in the background; the central Post Office, a corner of which, with mansard roof, projects out near the tower; and the Stock Exchange, which was newly rebuilt just before the war, and may be seen clearly in the photograph in front of the Town Hall tower. All three buildings were more or less undamaged in the devastation, as was the Erasmushuis' office tower, designed by Dudok, and seen in the right foreground. With these undamaged and very permanent buildings remaining, together with a few on the other side of the street, the Rotterdam planners decided to leave the street as it was, although considerably widening the pavements, and designing an orderly control to guide the form of new buildings. Three of these can be seen in the photograph. On the left is a new bank, built almost immediately after the war – very ponderous, but with a wide paved forecourt on which are located attractive kiosk-shops. Behind it is the famous new Bijenkorf multiple store. On the right, behind the Erasmushuis (so called after the nearby statue of the great Dutch philosopher) is a new drapery store. The Coolsingel itself is kept as a main central area distributing road in the new plan. As can be seen, its great width, which includes two tramlines in the centre, forms an effective barrier to pedestrians, and separates the central area activities on either side of it. Perhaps only the drastic and expensive method of sinking would have enabled the centre to achieve cohesion, but this has been rendered impossible by the construction of an underground railway beneath it.

22

22. The K.L.M. building

Housing the main airline terminal, this office building completes the group of buildings on the east side of the Coolsingel. Its height is carefully related to the Town Hall, which is adjacent to it on the south, and may be seen on the right of the photograph.

23. The Town Hall Place

Immediately in front of the Town Hall, from which this photograph was taken is a broad open space which leads in to the Lijnbaan, seen in the background. It is faced on both sides by office buildings and banks. In the centre of this Place is a large group of realist sculpture commemorating the wartime resistance movement, while mosaics and sculpture adorn the walls of surrounding buildings. In fact civic adornment is one of the most stimulating things about the new Rotterdam.

23

24. The Lijnbaan

In the foreground the main axis of the pedestrian shopping way stretches away to the north. The light covered canopies can be seen clearly running either side of the way. To the west of the Lijnbaan the high apartment blocks rise up. From this view one can see that an opportunity was lost of using the flat roofs of the shops as a broad terrace.

24

25. The Lijnbaan

This view is taken at ground level about half-way up the main axis and looking north. Trees, flowers, and a small open air café all enliven the scene, while the careful detailing of the lamp standards, ground pattern, and canopy fascias are typical of the high standards that prevail almost everywhere in the Netherlands.

25

26

26. The Binnenwej

The Binnenwej was an old Rotterdam street now completely transformed visually but retained as a traffic access way. The Lijnbaan is planned to terminate on the Place here formed by setting back the large new stores. On the left is a design completed in 1951 by Messrs Van den Broek and Bakema, in which they persuaded three shop owners to collaborate in the erection of one large building with a total shopping floor space of 78,000 square feet. The same firm was responsible for the furniture store with 53,000 square feet of shopping floor space, which closes the eastern end of the Place designed and opened in 1953. Behind it may be seen the pre-war Erasmushuis designed by Dudok.

27

27. The Bijenkorf store

One of the most famous of pre-war contemporary designs was the fine Bijenkorf store designed by Dudok at the south end of the Coolsingel. Unfortunately it was half destroyed by the bombing, and this, together with a decision to make a large traffic roundabout at this point, caused the planners to propose resiting it further up the Coolsingel. As part of the articulation of the street, the planners suggested that part of it be brought forward as a feature. The architect, Marcel Breuer, wished to keep the form simple and rectangular, and suggested that a large sculpture might fulfil this requirement. This was accepted, and the well-known constructionist sculptor Naum Gabo was commissioned. The Bijenkorf and its sculpture is seen in this photograph from the large covered entrance of the Stock Exchange. The Store has a shopping floor space of 129,168 square feet and was completed in 1957.

28

28. The Beursplein

The Beursplein or Stock Exchange Place was formed in the new plan by opening up the space at the junction of the Coolsingel and the ancient Hoogstraat to the south side of the Stock Exchange, whose slender tower is in the centre of the photograph. The Coolsingel runs across the photograph and is being crossed by a dense crowd of pedestrians. In the background, closing the east side of the Beursplein, is Messrs Vroom and Dreesman's store, which was first built in the early 1950s with three storeys, and recently redesigned to give it an extra shopping floor.

29

30

29. The Maastoren flats

The proximity of water gives excellent opportunities in the siting of high buildings, both in terms of the views from them and of the reflections they create. Here the Maastoren tower block of flats is excellently sited, and contains basement car parking, offices on the lower floors, flats and a restaurant on the roof. It was designed by H. Bakker.

30. Flats in the city centre

As part of the wise policy of supplying living areas in the city centre, these flats provide a high standard of space and design. The tall blocks overlook spacious and carefully landscaped squares which have low three-storey blocks on their west side, in order not to obstruct sunlight. The latter have shops on the ground floor, which somewhat inconsistently (since the Lijnbaan is around the corner) face on to a road.

31

31. St Laurenskerk

The great church of St Lawrence, the only medieval building left in Rotterdam, was extensively damaged during the war, but restoration in now complete. On its south side Messrs Merkelbach and Elling designed a low group of buildings with shops facing the Hoogstraat on the far side and transverse blocks of flats projecting from them. These are seen in the centre of the photograph.

32

32. The Hoogstraat

In the new plan the ancient Hoogstraat was retained as a traditional shopping street, an understandable but incorrect decision, in my opinion. A number of interesting buildings have, however, been built along it, one of which is seen on the right, designed by Merkelbach and Elling. Its northern side faces St Laurenskerk, whose tower may be seen above it. Building heights were kept low, and the building form consisted of two-storey shops facing the Hoogstraat, with four transverse blocks of flats.

33

33. The Hoogstraat

This photograph is taken looking south west at the crossing of the Hoogstraat over the Delftse Vaart Canal, whose retaining wall is seen in the foreground. On the left is a large mosaic mural, which is part of the Galeries Modernes Store, while on the right is the HUF store designed by Messrs. Van den Broek and Bakema. In striking contrast to the Bijenkorf store at the western end of the Hoogstraat the HUF store is clad almost entirely with glass. It was completed in 1955.

34

35

36

37

36. The Groothandelsgebouw

This great collective building is located immediately to the west of the Central Station Place. It occupies a site of some 5 acres, with a floor space of 1·3 million square feet. It houses offices, showrooms, canteens, shops and the warehouses of 150 wholesalers. It has basement car parking for 400 cars and lorries, which can enter the building at three levels and serve directly some 30 per cent of the storage accommodation. Ancillary accommodation includes large meeting-halls, six skittle alleys, a post office and a bank, and it employs approximately 3,500 people. It was designed by the famous architectural pioneer Van Tijen.

37. The Groothandelsgebouw

A close up view of the great wholesalers' building, showing the three levels of vehicular access. This building is a valuable example of the trend of urban building where what would once have been a town of small buildings is grouped into one large complex. It illustrates clearly that the roads have become an integral part of the architecture.

---

34. The new Central Station

The new Central Station was at the core of a difficult planning problem—that of bringing thousands of people right into the heart of the city and enabling them thence to do a short journey by foot, bus, tram, or taxi to local destinations. The problem has perhaps been best solved at Grand Central Station in New York, which uses a series of levels to deal with the problem, with the long-haul passenger services coming in below ground level. In the case of Rotterdam, everything (except the new underground railway) is on the same level, and the consequent difficulties are obvious. From the platforms the passengers enter a spacious waiting-hall, but from there pour into a large Station Place in which pedestrians, bicycles (and there are thousands in Rotterdam), taxis, buses, and trams all mill about to mutual detriment. From an urban design aspect the planners wished to see a large imposing view enclosing the north side of the Place, and in order to achieve this economically the Hall has a curved ceiling with the apex facing the Place, while the office windows, like Mendelsohn's famous Potsdam Observatory, are two to a floor.

35. The Central Station Place

This is one of the least satisfactory parts of the new city centre. The new Central Railway Station is at the top of the photograph, with the multi-purpose Groothandelsgebouw warehouse building on the left. In the foreground is a traffic intersection with a narrow underpass for through traffic. The whole Place is a muddle of trams, vehicles, and people, and one hopes that it will be redesigned in the future.

38. The Twaalf Provincien

This is another large collective building, designed by H. Bakker, and located at the eastern end of the Hoogstraat. It was completed in 1955 and consists of 28 shops, totalling nearly 13,000 square feet, 30 maisonettes, and a cinema. The shops are all entered from a series of internal galleries.

38

39. The Rijn Hotel

Hotels are an essential component of the centre of cities, but they are expensive to build and it is difficult to make them pay. The Rijn Hotel was the first, although a second is being built to the north of the Lijnbaan. This one forms part of the larger building complex with the Y.M.C.A. building and is situated on the far side of the car park to the west of the Lijnbaan.

39

40. The Leuvehaven

An air view taken in 1955 of one of the oldest docks in the city. One of the important ideas of the new plan was to open up the central area to this part of the harbour. At the head of the Leuvehaven is the famous Zadkine statue set on a broad terrace. Seen above it is Dudok's war-damaged Bijenkorf store which was demolished to make way for a traffic roundabout. At top right is the Stock Exchange.

41. The Leuvehaven

At the north-western end of the Leuvehaven, the main inland waterway harbour, is a broad terrace visible from the city centre. On it is the magnificent expressionist statue by Zadkine, commemorating Rotterdam's destruction. Facing the western side of the Leuvehaven is a long terrace of five- and six-storey flats, with two carefully sited high towers among them. The slender tower to the left of the statue is the memorial to merchant seamen by Carasso

40

41

42

43

44

42. Approach to the Maas Tunnel

This is an interesting pre-war example of attempts made in Rotterdam to deal with the traffic problem. Not far from the northern entrance to the under-river tunnel the main road entered a densely built-up area. To deal with this problem the road was put in open cut in order to get down to the level of the tunnel entrance. In doing so an interesting possibility of treatment for traffic roads in urban areas was created. So long as no attempt is made to connect the lower to the upper road the space required can be kept to a reasonably modest width. The combination of motorway and access roads can be very disruptive to the urban pattern.

43. The Maas Tunnel

Like the road tunnels under the Mersey and the Hudson rivers, this example could be used extensively in urban areas where large building complexes make it possible economically to put the roads at a lower level. Additional problems of lighting and ventilation are, however, created.

44. A riverfront model

Typical of the bold three-dimensional designing of the City Planning Office, this model illustrates the treatment proposed for a broad sweep of the north bank of the Maas river. It consists mainly of high-density residential development in the form of high blocks of flats, sited so as to take advantage of the fine view across the river, which at this point is alive with all kinds of shipping.

45

45. The Bijenkorf store

A close up view of the fine new multiple store facing the Coolsingel. The building is almost entirely encased with honey coloured travertine marble. The large openings are restaurant windows, and in the left hand one is a superb Henry Moore sculpture. Apart from columns the whole ground floor consists of shop windows. In the foreground is the enormous constructivist sculpture by Naum Gabo. Most of Gabo's previous designs were of table-top scale, but this monumental work had to be built in a shipyard. It feels as though a bubble of water had been distended to the size of a balloon.

The City of the Twenty-first Century

Planners and architects, as the chief designers of our physical environment, should never forget that the most important thing about a city or town is the people. The city is essentially a stage for diverse human activity, and a physical environment reflects, often in a subtle way, the character and qualities of its inhabitants. Later it may condition them, but in the first place somebody must pay the piper to call some tune. The urban designer, in endeavouring to project a vision that is not just his own subjective idea of tomorrow but is something that will provide for the varied physical and emotional needs of all the citizens, needs some kind of brief in terms of a human specification, not perhaps in terms of 'what do people want?' as they tend to like what they know. The public generally tend to see possibilities of a new environment in the limited terms of curing the deficiencies of their present one; and the urban designer has the difficult task of suggesting what they did not know they could have. But there are a number of fairly obvious things on which generally an acceptance may be secured.

Here, then, are some ideas for a human specification expressed in elementary form —a sort of Atlantic Charter in urban terms.

First, we want urban *cleanliness*, so we can say we need *Hygienic Cities*.

Second, we all want *longevity*, so we will want *Safe Cities*.

Third, we want *efficiency*, hence we shall expect *Functional Cities*.

Fourth, we want a sense of *continuity*, which means Geddesian conservative surgery and selective preservation, so that we shall need *Continuous Cities*.

Fifth, we want to lead *well-tempered* lives, and this implies the need for *Balanced Cities*.

Sixth, we want above all to be *civilized* and therefore we shall need *Beautiful Cities*, cities as collective works of art.

Let us carry this somewhat rudimentary list a stage further and fill in more fully the specification against each main item.

HYGIENIC CITIES. The problem of collective hygiene was largely solved in the nineteenth century. As a counter-attack on disease in the rapidly growing urban agglomerations, the municipalities of the time were forced by public fear to take action, and thanks to Chadwick, Shaftsbury, and other reformers, nearly every city was equipped by the twentieth century with main drainage, paved roads with cambers, falls, and gullies to remove surface water, a clean water supply, and a municipal rubbish-removal service. All this involved a complicated technical organization, and the whole corpus of activity became confused in the municipal mind with town planning.

Today we still have some way to go in collective hygiene. There is still too much litter in our cities, a minor but unsightly disease that can only be cured by public education (and adequate facilities for depositing the litter). There is also too much atmospheric pollution; this is caused partly by the domestic coal fire, partly by industrial smoke, and partly by the exhaust fumes of the motor vehicle. Basically, only official regulations can cure this, and the startling results of determined action, by Pittsburgh, for instance, should be an example for all industrial cities.

SAFE CITIES. Thanks to the development of an organized and efficient police force, we no longer have the highwayman of old. We do have however, as a major source of personal danger, a new highwayman in the form of the careless driver.

The solution to this essentially twentieth-century problem is not easily accepted by the car-driving public, but must be faced if we are to rid cities of a new and intolerable scourge. We must accept drastic controls on the motor vehicle. The railways after all began by using the general highways and gradually were contained within specialized limits. In like manner we need new controls for the motor vehicle. Coming into the cities we need rigidly controlled motorways, which need not be so different from the old railway, with its viaducts, embankments, and fenced in curtilage. Coming into the city they may be above or below the normal ground level, depending on the facts of geography, but once they reach the central area they must, unless there are very exceptional circumstances, go down, or else the pedestrian urban level must go up. Since going down may well be very expensive in excavation costs, it will often be easier to raise the pedestrian level up a floor to form large-scale upper-level decks. In the case of residential areas outside the central ones it is essential that some layout technique such as the 'Radburn' method be adopted. This means that there must be no through roads within neighbourhoods; there must be pedestrian shopping centres, and there must be no need for children under five and old people to cross a major traffic road, except under very rare circumstances.

FUNCTIONAL CITIES. Everyone will expect tomorrow's cities to be efficient if nothing else, since we have all lived with increasing impatience in inefficient cities for the last hundred years. They must be made efficient, too, not only for the needs of today but, in so far as we can forecast and plan them, for those of tomorrow. In this sense everyone is a planner, and certainly every person or group in a responsible organizational position, be it the organizing of a factory, an office, a shop, on the one hand or a rail, bus or a transport system on the other. The urban designer's problem is to dovetail all these individual planning operations into an efficient synthesis, both in strategic or city-wide terms, tactically within the main zones of the city.

First, then, we need to reassess some of the familiar techniques of planning. Zoning areas for special purposes is technique number one, and used intelligently it is of fundamental importance. It must however, be used flexibly, be backed by considerable statistical analysis, and be closely correlated with programming planning and three-dimensional design. The *Handbook on the Redevelopment of Central Areas* dealt with this technique of planning excellently, and is a model of clear thinking in this respect. Together with the subsequent Development Plan regulations, we now have at least one acceptable technique for creating the functional city.

One needs, therefore, a clear but flexible zoning pattern with a well-balanced proportion of zones for various purposes.

The Heart of the City. The heart or central area of the city one sees functionally as a great meeting or 'getting together' place, for cultural, business, government, and entertainment purposes. It is not suited to large-scale work-places nor is it meant for general residential purposes; but it must really function as a meeting-place, and this means pedestrian spaces of all kinds—large, small, covered, open—but all, like the Piazza of St Mark, with the emphasis on the 'there'; and the core must not be overcrowded and congested, and in fact no longer needs to be, as Mumford has brought out so well in *The Culture of Cities.*

Work. Work-places for commercial and industrial purposes today need space above all. They tend to be of large scale, complex in character, and need to expand both horizontally and vertically: they also have space-eating and somewhat dangerous (for old people and children) problems of communications, of getting the raw materials in and the finished products out. Therefore the larger scale commercial and industrial enterprises need to be provided with special zones of their own, although this does not of course rule out small-scale workshops being closely associated with residential areas.

Residential Areas. In order to say anything about living in the city one must define the 'who' before describing the 'where' and the 'how'. Shakespeare set this out well in the seven stages of man, and these could form a useful breakdown of community types in order to make proposals.

'First the infant, mewling and pewking in its mother's arms' . . . . 'Mewling' raises immediately problems of noise and its insulation by mass or space. And so we can say broadly (and we cannot be too precise in matters of human living), that infants and children will normally be brought up in families, and that the families-with-children group will have certain common needs. Around their dwellings, whether they be houses or flats, or better still houses *and* flats, they will need space for various social purposes—space for the parents to get to work, to shop, to circulate; safe space for the children to play in and the old people to walk in; space for private and community gardens, and so on. All this involves specialized areas for family living in the big city, providing houses for large families and flats for small ones, and various degrees of specialized dwelling types for old people, etc. These areas of residential building may be laid out as squares, terraces, and many other forms which in their turn may be grouped into neighbourhoods, providing within their area a large area of safe space, round-the-corner-shops, and other family social facilities. In turn a group of neighbourhoods may form a community or district, with its shopping centre, workshops, and wide range of social facilities. All this points broadly to the rightness of the residential proposals put forward in the Greater and County of London Plans in so far as they apply to large cities, both in regard to types of residential unit and to densities, although both require more research. Human communities are of course made up of a more complex pattern than only families-with-children. In a large city there are families with grown-up children, married couples without children, single people of all ages, people on the move, and so forth. It is natural that many of these wish to live as near to the heart of the city, or at least of community cores, as possible, and here a plan must provide a considerable amount of residential space in or near these central areas.

Open Spaces. Last of the major land uses in the large city is that of open space; of parks and parkways and playing fields and gardens and squares and playgrounds and all the innumerable kinds of urban space not covered by or immediately attached to buildings. In a small city or a town, open space may best be provided around the periphery, but in a large urban area this is not possible. Here again one can only speak in general terms. Much research remains to be done on open space standards, and this is a study in itself. The pattern one sees is that of communities around the heart of the city (and the shape of both heart and communities may vary greatly), surrounded and separated from each other by green park land wherein many kinds of recreational activity will take place. Here is great opportunity for landscape designers, with community needs as diverse as a football match and a real setting for a *Midsummer Night's Dream.* Through, or better still over and under, these green spaces will go the main arteries of communication; and their landscaping must be so designed so as not to interfere with the enjoyment of the parks and so as to afford splendid and exciting views of the city seen with the fast moving eye. An example that comes to mind here is the Schuylkill Parkway leading into Philadelphia.

One of the most important and necessary elements in town planning is the provision of trees. Trees of as wide a variety as possible within the capabilities of climate and soil, trees in parks, trees in squares, trees in streets, trees almost, but not quite, everywhere, so that from the air the predominant urban pattern is of islands and archipelagoes of building set in a sea of rich green texture.

CONTINUOUS CITIES. One of the very difficult concepts about cities is continuity. A city should have a quality of immortality, a life force of continuous regeneration. Throughout any large city there is a constant process of change taking place, a process of building and rebuilding. At certain times, especially in periods of high cultural activity, the architectural environment may be of considerable quality, and it is clearly necessary to preserve and adapt for use such building groups for as long a period as possible.

This means that planning proposals need to embody bold decisions of replacement and conservation, decisions which may be easy to make concerning worn out tumble down slum areas, but more difficult when finely designed streets and squares and terraces and buildings have been allowed to fall into decay. The preservation of an individual building may have comparatively little urban design significance compared with complete areas or 'amenity groups' as the London County Council described them. But the rehabilitation of large groups of buildings costs money, and they may well be in many ownerships. Nevertheless it is an extremely important problem in urban design and has been resolved successfully in a number of different places. The city of Warsaw, for instance, rebuilt a replica of a completely destroyed historic square. Philadelphia succeeded in making its run-down eighteenth-century Society Hill a status address so that a number of private developers rehabilitated the excellently designed but sadly decayed dwellings. The London County Council did this as a public responsibility on its Brandon Estate in South London and again on the Trinity Almshouses in Stepney.

In a more superficial but extremely attractive way the British Civic Trust has spent a good deal of effort and money in persuading the occupiers of whole squares and streets (in Norwich, Kingston, Windsor, Haddington, to name a few) to refurbish and repaint their houses and shops to a co-ordinated scheme, in the hands of skilled architects. Urban continuity may, therefore, demand creative preservation (even if the building groups are of comparatively recent date) for reasons of good design or historical significance.

It may on the other hand demand demolition so that the continuity of effort and social purpose may be maintained—continuity of a way of life or of an improving standard of living. Clearly it is a problem demanding high skill in expert advice and civilized judgment from community leaders.

WELL-BALLANCED CITIES. The creation of the balanced city, aimed at the leading of well-tempered lives for its citizens, is a subtle and difficult problem, as so much depends on their broad cultural background. One is, too, not dealing with the needs of one particular person or family at any stage of their lives, but large numbers of people in all walks of life and at all stages of their lives. One must therefore try to postulate those human activities which aim towards an advance in civilization, which sharpen the intellects, broaden the minds, invigorate the bodies, and tend generally towards harmony and well-being.

In planning terms this means avoiding over-concentration on any one type of activity in the city. Extreme cases of this may be seen in some industrial towns where everything except the space needs of work and dwellings have been omitted. The balanced city is very much a regional and indeed national problem, since diversity of employment and other activities are often concerned with larger than local urban decisions. Suffice it to say that every large city needs a rich diversity of activity, and hence of opportunity leading to endless possibilities of fulfilment of personality—that vital human need which seems today so much neglected.

CIVILIZED CITIES. The Concise Oxford Dictionary defines the word *civilized* as 'to bring out of barbarism, enlighten, refine'. Clearly some cities have a long way to go. The planner must hope for a high level of thinking and doing in all walks of life. He must assure a sharpening of sensibility throughout the citizens and particularly a sharpening and developing awareness of the visual sense leading to a widely possessed vertical visual faculty. Where large areas of the city are still in a worn-out and muddled condition, such a group faculty cannot be expected to exist, but where a determined attack is being made on these social evils the planners have a great opportunity. As they plan, so they must inform—information and an exchange of ideas that must begin with the schools, training colleges, and spread through the community wherever organized societies and groups exist. In this way the people as a whole should begin to want what the planners want to give them, and the planners can show them what they did not know they could have.

The civilized city thus postulates, first, a determined economic and social effort on the part of its citizens to get rid of squalor, overcrowding and urban blight; second, a wish by the citizens at large to lead civilized lives; third, the planners and the architects can then respond in terms of environmental design. The overall planning strategy of space and time having been decided, the planner can then select areas of comprehensive development, areas of rehabilitation, areas of preservation, and even areas to be left alone. Within these areas well shaped sites for fine building, and building groups and urban spaces must be laid out, and expressed with visionary but practical ideas. Particularly important today is the treatment of roads in relation to the city as a whole. They are having much the same effect as the introduction of the railways in the nineteenth century, and useful parallels can still be drawn between road and rail. Wherever possible the railways were isolated within their own territory, and also separated by different levels from the rest of the urban area. In some cases they went underground as they approached central areas, and in others they were planned as totally subterraneous affairs. We have still to learn how to take advantage of the mobility of the motor vehicle and yet keep it under proper control.

The planner as urban designer cannot rest even when all these major tasks have been dealt with. He must persuade the numerous developers in detail to see that their street lamps, pillar boxes, railings, walls, telephone boxes, road signs are all well designed individually and well sited in the urban scene. The tasks vary greatly and demand infinite patience and endless faith. How, one may ask, is all this to be accomplished? There is of course no one panacea, one sovereign cure, but there are a number of fruitful ways which have been shown by experience to be effective.

First, the Government must believe in planning and must be prepared to support good planning programmes with the financial and legal means of implementation.

Second, the civic representatives of the citizens must be planning conscious, and hold in the forefront of their objectives the necessity of achieving a civilized environment. In some cities this may mean some changes in the municipal Committee structure, and in most cases a greater knowledge among Councillors of what good planning and good design can do for a city.

Third, the technical experts must be of the right quality and quantity, collaboratively minded and socially conscious, and aware that this is one of the great tasks of our time.

These attitudes must be developed along with the giving of university education itself. I have for many years been putting forward proposals for a new kind of higher educational institution for the environmental designers, for those responsible for the design and for the execution of buildings, for the design and co-ordination of cities and towns, and the design of their landscapes, and the planning of urban and other regions. These ideas were developed during the war, and came basically from such pioneers as Professor Walter Gropius and the Bauhaus. They have been published elsewhere and have not been discussed in this book. Assuming, however, new thinking in the educational field, aiming at more integration, understanding and collaboration between the experts, how should they be organized to do the job?

I suggest that the three urban examples described in this book offer useful prototypes. In the case of Coventry, there is a City Architectural and Planning Department under the overall direction of a Chief and Deputy. This Department is responsible for all planning and municipal architectural work in the city. It has a large programme of housing, schools, and other building projects which have to be integrated into overall planning schemes. These schemes, which consist either of comprehensive redevelopment areas for slum and worn out inner areas or new neighbourhoods on the urban periphery, are supplemented by the special and highly intricate urban design problems of the central area. There are also the overall planning problems involved in the Development (or Master) Plan. For all these tasks a combined operations Department of the kind which exists in Coventry would appear to be an excellent solution—providing it has outstanding leadership and enthusiasm throughout its members, has the full co-operation of the other municipal Departments, and wise policy making decisions made by the various Committees which such a Department serves.

The large city of Rotterdam has a separate Planning Department with a number of specialized Divisions, one of which concentrates on the reconstruction of the central area; close liaison was maintained with the Housing Department and with other technical agencies both in and outside the City Council, and the inspired Planning Director had the closest support from an enlightened City Council.

The metropolis of London has a very complicated local government organization which has been the subject of a number of official Commissions and Reports. Four years ago (1961) a Royal Commission appointed by the Government submitted proposals for reorganization. When the London County Council was formed in 1888 it included within its area almost the entire built-up area. Since then a vast expansion has taken place, and the most important problem today has been of creating a new form of regional government for London's Region. All this is however outside the scope of this book. The London County Council, in dealing with the problems raised by post war reconstruction had an Architect's Department which co-ordinated architectural planning duties (housing was temporarily transferred to another Department just after the war, but was returned in 1951).

Again great leadership and the devoted enthusiasm of many men and women over a period of years enabled much to be done. In the case of a great metropolis there is clearly a necessity for a Regional Planning Department with co-ordinating duties over the whole urban region. In the case of a complex country like Britain it may well be that two parallel bodies are necessary—one to co-ordinate Governmental action within a specific area and the other to co-ordinate all local and non-Governmental activities, to draw up the main strategic planning proposals, set the overall planning standards and see that physical development is correlated throughout the region. Below this level would be a number of city and town authorities, for which Coventry may well be considered a prototype.

Obviously there is scope here for a great deal of study, study which must go far beyond architecture and planning, deep into the roots of Government and local Government. In this book I have tried to restrict the story to the urban design problems of cities and have illustrated a number of contemporary solutions. Nobody today can feel truly happy about urban conditions today, and the sooner we realize that we are still only groping with the vast but highly complex possibilities of our civilization the sooner will we create adequate tools to fulfil the task of creating an harmonious environment for tomorrow.

1

1. The University of Edinburgh
The newly completed Hume Tower, which is part of a comprehensive plan for the University of Edinburgh (see nos. 24–28).

9 WORK IN PROGRESS

In cities all over the world a continuous process of urban renewal is taking place, much of it unplanned, and some planned in two dimensions but not in three. Here and there, where conditions have been favourable, building is taking place according to a comprehensive plan, and in this section a few examples are illustrated. No attempt has been made to present a representative selection either nationally or internationally, but each example illustrates a positive attempt to build or re-build cities within a practical context.

2

3

2. New York: site of the United Nations Building

In American terms this project would now be looked on as part of architectural history, but it represents an important stage in planning history. If the Rockefeller Centre may be said to have started a more intelligent type of central area redevelopment for Manhattan, the United Nations Building carried it much further. Before rebuilding, the site consisted of an indiscriminate muddle of industrial and commercial buildings, as is evident in this photograph. In the background is Welfare Island and the Freeborough Bridge, the latter one of the many impressive structures which make New York such a spectacular city for the visitor.

3. New York: United Nations Building

The United Nations Building took the ideas developed in the Ministry of Education Building in Rio to a further stage, and on a larger scale. It is located on the east side of Manhattan and stands as an oasis of intelligent development in a sea of urban muddle. It has a site of some 31 acres, and has its accommodation in three main groups, the General Assembly, the Conference Area, and the Secretariat. The first is the light coloured building with the dome, the second the rectangular building in the foreground, and the third is the office tower. There is car-parking space for over 1,760 cars at the lower levels, and there are large areas of upper level terracing for pedestrians. The main East River Drive highway is taken at a lower level along the waterside, and may be seen in the foreground. Compared with most of Manhattan it is a splendid example of urban redevelopment. It represents however, only the first stage of the redevelopment of this part of the city. It is hoped that all the urban renewal projects now on the drawing-boards in various parts of the world will be realized as successfully as this one.

4. Brazilia

Strictly speaking, this is not an example of urban rebuilding, but, like Chandigarh in India or Islamabad in Pakistan, is an outstanding example of comprehensively planned development. Brazilia is noteworthy for many reasons: first, it is part of a national policy of development, away from the coastline and in to the interior, in order to open up Brazil's vast empty hinterland; second, by removing the capital functions from Rio de Janeiro, it was intended to reduce the severe congestion in that city; third, the plan was chosen as a result of a competition. It was won by the doyen of Brazilian architects, Lucio Costa, three of whose preliminary diagrams are shown here. The first shows the basic cruciform frame of the plan: The second shows how it was related to the site, and how Costa swung the cross axis in a gentle curve; while the third shows how the main governmental building groups were arranged in the vertical axis, with the residential groups on the horizontal axis. The execution of this great urban vision has been largely in the hands of Oscar Niemeyer, the most brilliant of a highly imaginative school of young contemporary Brazilian architects.

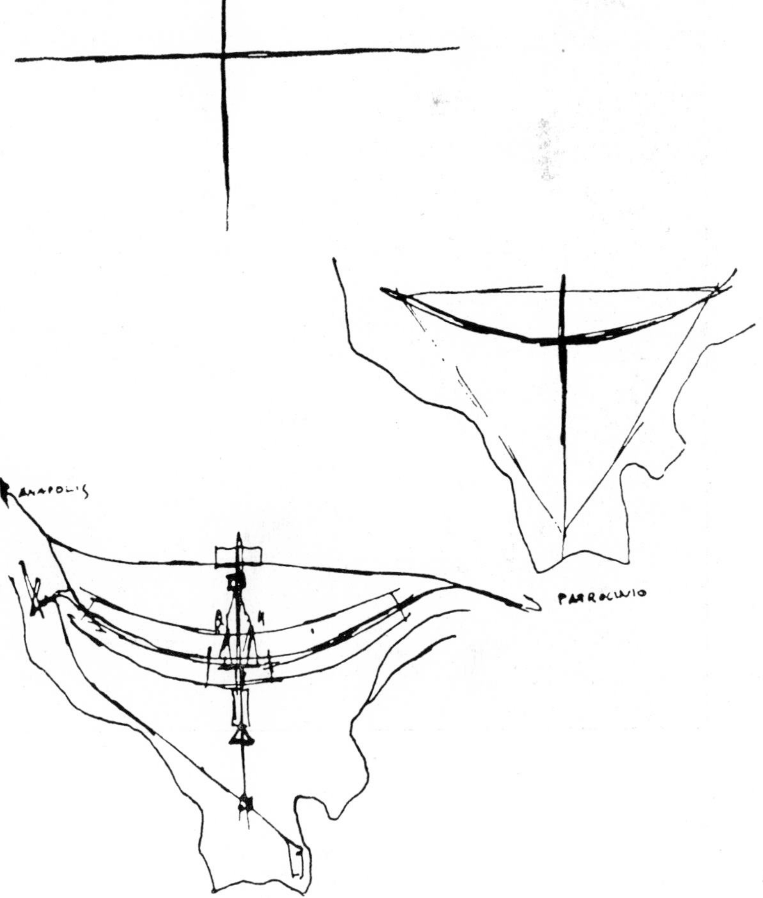

4

5

5. Brazilia : residential super-block

The basic residential unit is the super-block, four of which make a neighbourhood unit. Each super-block is of 240 metres square and is fringed with trees, and has a primary school and kindergarten, while each neighbourhood unit has a cinema, shops, a church and a garden school

6

6. Brazilia: principal crossing

In the centre of the photograph is the main crossing of road communications with the bus station below. In the foreground is the new theatre, designed by Brazilia's chief architect, Oscar Niemeyer. Beyond is a group of commercial office towers.

7 

7. Brazilia: governmental centre

The centre is known as the Plaza of the Three Powers, and consists of the National Congress, the Senate, and the House of Representatives. The twin towers of the National Congress, the highest building in Brazilia, overlook the senate (left), and the House of Representatives (right). The architect, Oscar Niemeyer, has been a strong protagonist of pure form in architecture, and has disciplined the design of these great public buildings to forms of basic simplicity.

8. Philadelphia: Market East Plaza, 1962

Philadelphia is one of the most planned and best planned of all large American cities, thanks both to enlightened citizens and an outstanding team of planners led by Mr Edward Bacon. Within a carefully worked out Master Plan a number of very interesting projects have been completed, are in progress, or are contemplated in the near future. Determined efforts are being made to redevelop the central area (which almost coincides with William Penn's original plan for the city of 1662.) The first scheme was Penn Centre, which after many difficulties, is now complete. On the opposite side of the City Hall from this scheme is projected another development known as Market East Plaza. It is five blocks long and one wide, and consists of a major bus terminal, a parking garage for 2,500 cars, 3 levels of pedestrian shopping space, commercial office development, and a raised pedestrian walkway, which will ultimately connect Penn Square with Independence Mall. The lower level below ground will have a subway station, and will connect through to the existing low-level plaza in Penn Center The drawing. shows the subway station with the three shopping levels and the multi-storeyed parking garage on the right. In the background are office buildings. The project was designed in the City Planning Commission Department. The team leader was Mr W. von Moltke.

8

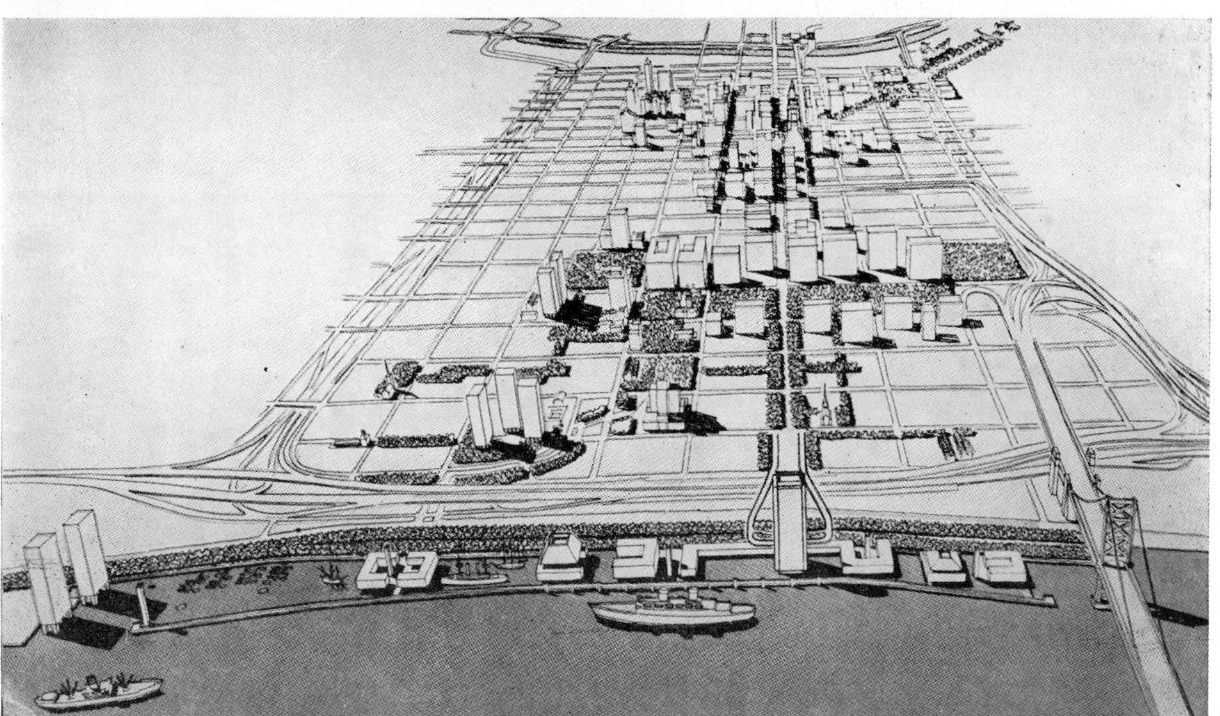

9

9. Philadelphia: City Centre

The drawing shows the area of the city originally laid out by William Penn, between the Delaware and Schuylkill Rivers. In the foreground is a boat basin, part of which is used as an historic ship museum. Behind it is a motorway, which is part of the inner rectangular motorway system which bounds the urban core. Beyond on the left are the three recently completed residential towers of the Society Hill scheme designed by I. M. Pei, and leading back towards the City Hall in the distance is the proposed tree-lined avenue of Market Street. In front of the City Hall is the Market East Plaza, which is not yet built, and behind it is Penn Centre, the first stage of central urban redevelopment to be completed.

10. Philadelphia: Penn Centre

This scheme had a chequered history, and, like the South Bank in London, underwent considerable modifications on its way to realization. The completed scheme consists of four densely sited commercial office blocks, two of which are seen in the foreground of the photograph. West of them is the Transportation Centre, which includes a bus terminal and maintenance depot, as well as a parking garage for 1,000 cars, and a railway station. Between the office buildings are ground and lower level pedestrian spaces, with 150 shops and parking for 2,000 cars.

11. San Francisco: Golden Gateway Redevelopment Project, 1960

This was a site of nearly 50 acres of rundown urban land lying between the docks and the central area (central business district) of the city. The City Planning Department advocated its comprehensive redevelopment, and carried out a market analysis of redevelopment potential jointly with the Real Estate Research Corporation. The San Francisco Redevelopment Agency then acquired the land and had a sketch plan of possible development prepared. Subsequently a limited competition was held, the conditions giving a definite accommodation brief to competitors, who consisted of developer/architect teams. The competition was won by Perini-San Francisco Associated, as developers, with Messrs Wurster, Bernardi, and Emmons, De Mars and Reay as architects and planners. This is, of course, a famous team: Dean Wurster is one of the pioneers of the modern movement in America, De Mars has been responsible for some of the finest low-cost housing schemes in the country, while Donald Reay was formerly Chief Architect and Planner of Stevenage New Town in Britain. Their scheme consists of five towers of twenty-two storeys, and three slab buildings of almost equal height. Fundamental to the scheme is the separation of pedestrians and vehicles, with broad pedestrian decks on the roofs of the extensive garaging.

10

11

12

12. Stockholm: Haymarket scheme

This famous multi-level scheme began with a competition many years ago, but the present proposals are based on an original study by Paul Hedqvist, developed by the former City Architect, Sven Markelius, and brought to reality under the guidance of the present City Planning Director, Goran Sidenbladh. The photograph shows the completed scheme, from the upper terrace level over the shops. The group of five office towers rises on the left. The scheme is noted for the careful attention to detail which is characteristic of so many Swedish projects.

13

13. Stockholm: Haymarket scheme

A view in the shopping precinct, showing the pedestrian bridge joining the upper-level terraces (the railing on the upper right of the photograph is that shown on the left of no. 12). Below the precinct are three floors of car parking, and servicing for shops.

14

14. Stockholm: Haymarket scheme

A photograph of the 1952-53 model of the central business area from the east. The five office towers of the Haymarket Scheme can be seen on the upper right of the model.

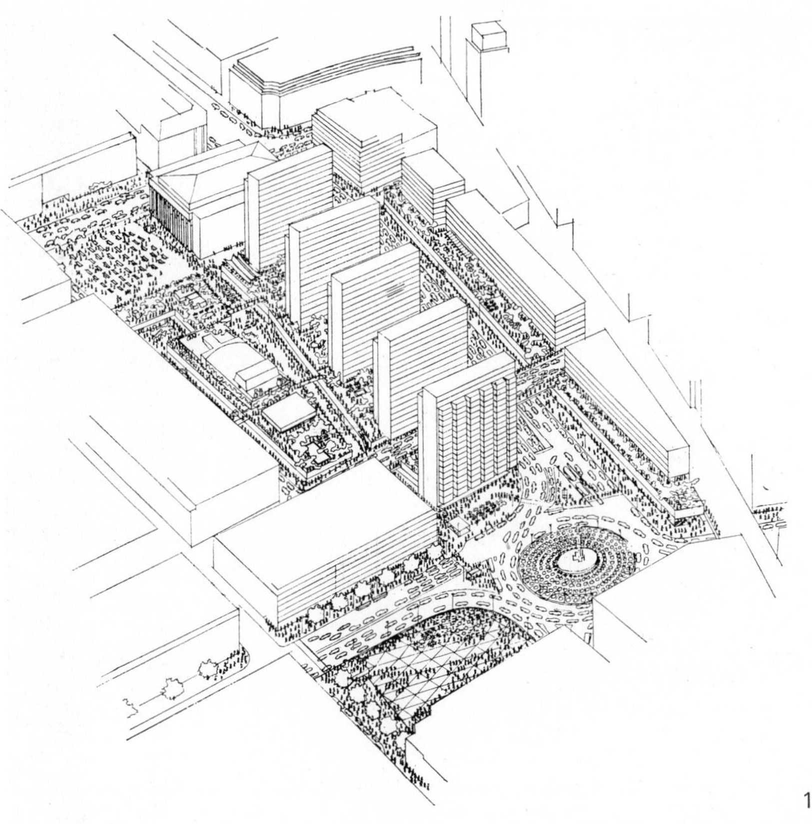

15. Stockholm: Haymarket Scheme

A bird's-eye drawing of the scheme when it was still in the project stage, showing its relationship to surrounding development. In the foreground is a traffic roundabout, now under construction, with a similar piazza under street level, and at the far end is the existing Concert Hall, with its open-air market.

15

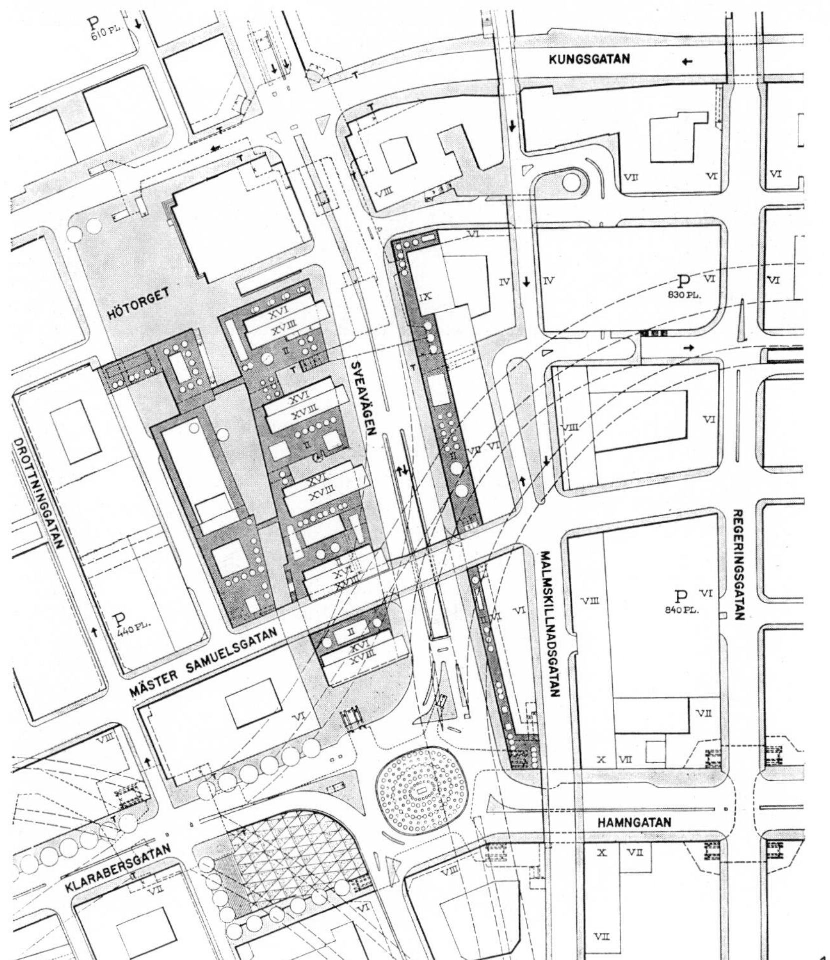

16. Stockholm: Haymarket Scheme

The plan shows the ground-level traffic system, with the pedestrian areas at ground level lightly shaded. Upper-level terraces above the shops are in a darker zone. T indicates entrances to the underground railway, the route of which is shown by dotted lines. P means a large car-parking structure above ground level.

16

17 

17. Salford: the site

Salford is a nineteenth-century industrial town, and is part of the Manchester conurbation. It suffered severely both from unplanned industrial development in the nineteenth century and from urban blight and decay in the twentieth. One of its worst slum areas was that known as the Ellor Street Area, which is seen at the top left hand of the air photograph, with a large part of the slums recently cleared away. The adjacent main road is also to be widened. The City Engineer and Planning Officer is Mr T. W. McWilliam.

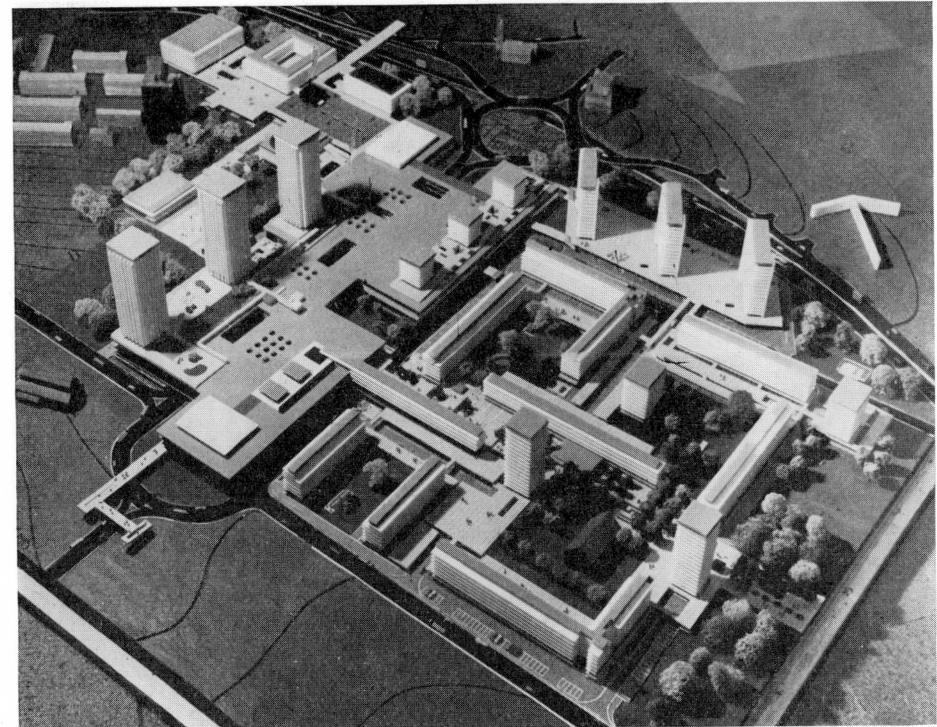

18

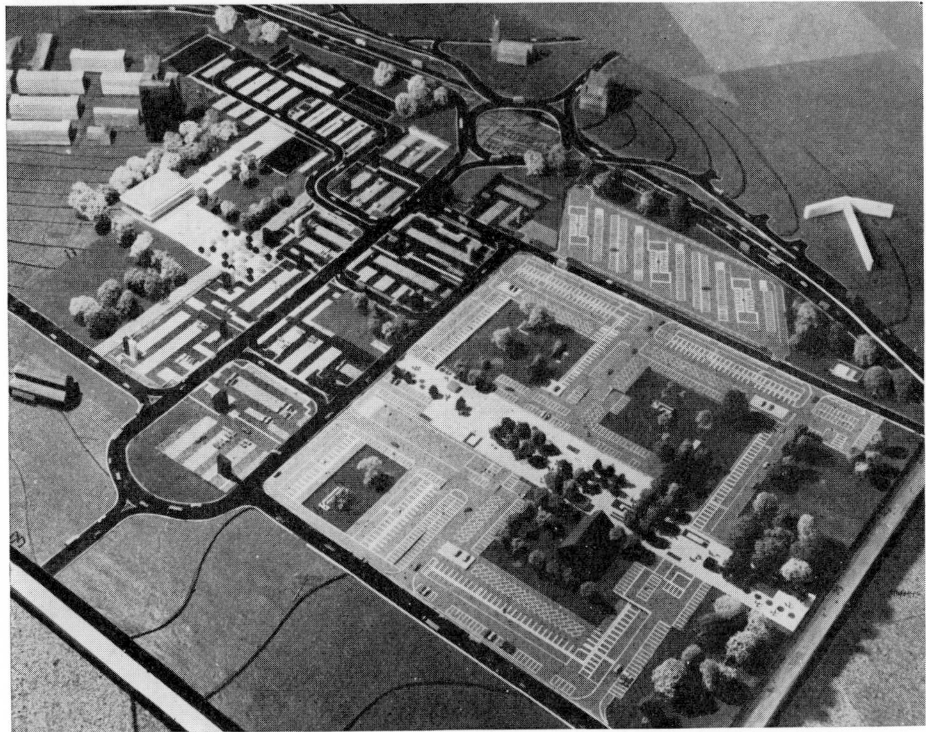

19

18. Salford: Town Centre

Salford is at present an almost unidentifiable part of the Manchester conurbation. One of the main problems was to give it identity as a city within the region, with its own urban nucleus. The photograph shows a model of the entirely new central area, designed for an approximate population of 200,000. At the top of the model is one of the new radial motorways of the region with a two-level intersection which brings traffic into the new centre. The whole of the new shopping centre will be under cover. It has approximately 400,000 sq. ft. of shopping sales area, and garaging for 2,100 cars. Above it will rise office buildings and tall towers of upper income apartments. At top left is the Civic Centre, also set on a raised podium which is joined to that of the Shopping Centre, with garaging at the lower level. To the right of the Shopping Centre, and also connected to it at the upper pedestrian level, are a number of residential squares all resting on decks, below which are garages.

19. Salford: Shopping Centre

The model with all the buildings removed to show the ground-floor garaging. Almost the whole ground-floor level is given over to vehicle access, servicing, bus station, and garaging. The whole scheme was designed under the direction of Sir Robert Matthew and Percy Johnson-Marshall as Planning Consultants.

20

21

20. Salford: residential area.

On the left are the residential squares adjacent to the town centre (density 185 persons per acre) and in the centre the main residential area (155 persons per acre) which is designed with four-storey maisonettes (duplexes) for medium sized families and tall point blocks for small families. In this area garages are grouped around a cul-de-sac, while between the housing is a large area of green safe space, for pedestrian use only. Over 1,000 trees are to be moved into the area as soon as building operations permit.

21. Salford: progress

One of the most exciting aspects of the Salford comprehensive plan is the rapidity with which it is being converted into reality. The comprehensive plan was submitted in 1962, and redevelopment began, in accordance with the plan, almost at once. The first buildings were three seventeen-storey blocks of flats to house some of the families being displaced by clearance, and the photograph is taken from the top of one of them. In the foreground is an old school, due for replacement in the plan. In the background the first of five seventeen-storey tower blocks is nearing completion.

22

23

22. Cumbernauld New Town

Like Brazilia, Cumbernauld is not strictly an example of redevelopment, but may be said to represent a large number of relevant planning ideas actually being carried into practice. The photograph is a model of the whole town as it will look on completion. Situated on the ridge of a hill, fifteen miles north east of Glasgow, it was designed as part of the Clyde Valley Plan to take population overspill from Glasgow's extremely congested inner areas. Unlike the earlier British New Towns, such as Stevenage and Harlow, Cumbernauld is much more compact, and concentrates its shopping and commercial development in the main town centre, which is based on the principle of milti-level vertical separation of pedestrians and vehicles. The Chief Architect and Planning Officer was L. Hugh Wilson, now succeeded by Dudley Leaker.

23. Cumbernauld New Town

A progress photograph taken in 1964, showing the residential development along the southern slopes of the ridge, and the town centre beginning to take shape beyond. In the background are the northern residential groups.

24

24. The University of Edinburgh

The model shows the Comprehensive Plan of 1962 for the redevelopment of the whole 125 acres of the University area over a twenty-year period. Certain historic and other prominent buildings are to be retained in the area. The main planning principles are to raise all pedestrian activity to the upper level throughout the area with pedestrian bridges over the one-way road system below. Lower levels of all new buildings will largely be occupied by car parking. An important feature is the redevelopment of the existing corridor-street type of shopping centre with a new shopping precinct, to be equipped with hotel, restaurant, and multi-purpose hall. Above the shopping precinct will rise blocks of apartments and offices. The shopping precinct is seen at upper centre of the photograph to the left of the Old College building (with the dome) by Robert Adam.
To the right of the latter building is the Royal Scottish Museum, and immediately above the Museum is the proposed Students' Union, with the existing McEwan Hall and Medical buildings at upper right. At the top are proposed buildings for the Faculties of Arts and Social Science and the University Library. In preparing this Comprehensive Plan I tried to preserve the spirit of an historic and ancient city.

25

26

25. The University of Edinburgh
A sketch of the proposed new University Quadrangle. On the left is the existing McEwan Hall, now given a setting which befits its scale and purpose. Around the other two sides will be the proposed buildings of the new University Students' Union, now being designed by Messrs Morris and Steedman. This is an example of a large pedestrian space recovered from an urban muddle by comprehensive redevelopment.

26. The University of Edinburgh
This sketch, by Alexander Bell, shows a view looking along one of the terraces of the new Shopping Precinct. In the background the historic University dome rises above the scene, while below the traffic moves along, uninterrupted by pedestrians ,cross turning traffic, or traffic lights.

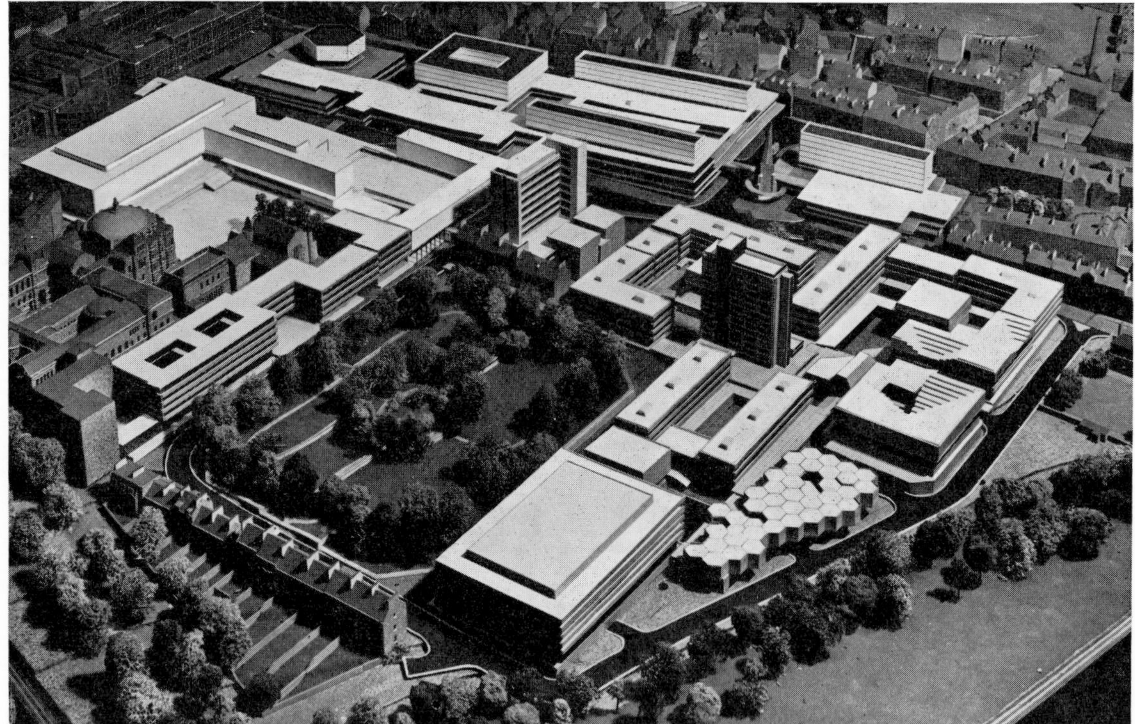

27

28

27. The University of Edinburgh
The photograph shows part of a large working model made in sections so as to illustrate the stage-by-stage redevelopment of the whole area. The stage illustrated shows design studies for the main western group of University buildings as they may look when completed. Behind this is the shopping centre which will be connected to the other new buildings by upper-level bridges.

28. The University of Edinburgh
This progress photograph, taken in 1965, shows the two completed buildings—the Hume Tower on the right and the First Year Science block on the left. In the foreground, sites have been cleared for the new Library and for the Faculties of Arts and Social Science.

INDEX

C

INDEX

INDEX

D

INDEX

INDEX

Q

R

T

ACKNOWLEDGEMENTS

Every effort has been made by the publishers to trace the copyright ownership of the illustrations used in this book. In some cases this has not proved possible and we would welcome the opportunity to include any omissions in future editions. We are grateful to the many organizations and individuals listed below who have cooperated so readily in giving their permission to reproduce photographs, maps, and diagrams. The first figure of the reference refers to the chapter number; those figures after the oblique refer to the plate numbers within that particular chapter.

Acacia Card Co., 2/21, 24. Acrapole, from *Brazilia*, 9/4, 7. Stephens Adamson, 3/57, 58, 59. Aero-Camera, 2/40; 7/18, 40. Aerofilms, 1/45, 48; 2/17, 32, 54; 5/19, 20, 22, 26, 35, 36, 39, 40, 64, 65, 75, 96, 117, 118, 123, 124, 130; 6/22, 24, 25, 26; 9/3. Airviews (M/c) Ltd., 9/17. American Society of Mechanical Engineers, 3/17, 64. Architects Journal, 3/52-5; 5/125. Architectural & Building News, 5/88. Architectural Design, 3/47; 5/104; 9/8-10. Architectural Press, from *The Modern Flat* (Yorke), 2/35-7. Arkitektur, 9/12, 13. Artemis Verlag, from *Oeuvre complète de Corbusier*, 3/29. Baubehörde, 4/21, 22. Boissevain & Osmond, 5/106. Boston Center Architects—The Architects Collaborative Inc., 3/44. British Museum, 1/27. Cameo Greeting Cards Inc., 2/65. Campbell's Press Studios Ltd., 5/53. Cas Oorthuys, 7/43. Central Aerophoto Co. Ltd., 6/2. Central Press Photos Ltd., 5/24. Chicago Area Transportation Study, 4/20. City of Detroit, Public Relations Department, 1/61; 2/77. Coventry Corporation, 6/7, 16-19, 21, 29-31, 33, 35, 36. Corporation of Coventry and *Coventry Evening Telegraph*, 1/41-3. Corporation of London, Guildhall Library, 5/97. Corporation of the City of London, 5/114, 115. D. P. Crease, 9/5, 6. Cumbernauld Development Corporation, 9/22, 23. Doeser Fotos, 7/1. Downtown Lower Manhattan Ass. Inc., 4/18. Echte Foto, 7/7, 22, 39. Editions de France, Marseille, 2/45. Editions de l'architecture d'aujourd'hui, 2/27. Eugen Rentsch Verlag: *The New Architecture* (Roth), 2/22, 23. Faber & Faber Ltd., 3/20, 21. Fairchild Aerial Surveys Inc., 2/1. Fox Photos, 5/139; 6/23. Maxwell Fry, 3/40-2, 48-51. Erno Goldfinger, 5/4. Greater London Council, 1/55; 2/19, 47-53, 55-61; 4/17; 5/3, 5-17, 21-3, 25, 27-32, 34, 38, 41-52, 54-63, 66-9, 71-4, 76, 77, 80-6, 91-5, 99-103, 105, 108, 109, 111-13, 116, 119, 121, 140-5. Greater London Council Library, 5/78, 79, 131-8. Harvard University Press, from *Space, Time and Architecture* (Giedion), 3/27, 35, 36. Hattrell & Partners, 6/20. H.M.S.O. (Crown Copyright) 4/2-16; 5/2, 18. Lord Holford, 5/126-9. Horizon Press, N.Y., from *The Living City* (Frank Lloyd Wright), 3/43. Hulton Picture Library, 5/122. Indian Air Survey & Transport Ltd., 1/57; 3/8. Kadleigh, Horsburgh and Whitfield, 5/110. Walter Kerr, 3/61. K.L.M., 2/6; 7/2, 8, 17, 35. Lockwood Survey Corporation Ltd. (Canada), 1/60. National Graphical Association, 1/24. Los Angeles Chamber of Commerce, 1/67; 2/68. Eric Lyons, 2/62. Fred Millet, 6/32. National Film Library, 3/39. Netherlands Information Service, 2/16, 38; 7/9, 36. Penguin Books Ltd., from *Building Modern Sweden* (Bertil Hulten), 2/66, 70. Phoenix Chamber of Commerce, 1/62. Photoflight Ltd., 1/4. 'Publicam', 2/14; 7/30. Gerald Ratto, 9/11. Real-Photo Cie. des Arts Photomécaniques, 1/19. Renes, Arnhem, 7/34. R.I.B.A., 2/28; 3/15, 25, 26. Rotterdam Town Planning & Reconstruction Dept., 2/39, 41-3; 7/3-6, 10-16, 19-21, 23-33, 41, 44. Bank of Scotland, 1/46. Salford Corporation, 9/18-21. San Francisco Chamber of Commerce, 1/64; 2/4. Saul Steinberg, from *The Passport* (Steinberg), 1/54, 2/3, 10. Sport and General Press Agency Ltd., 5/37, 70. Stadsingeniørens Direktorat, Copenhagen, 4/19. Stockholm City Planning Dept., 9/14-16. Syndication International, 4/1; 5/1. Thames & Hudson Ltd., from *The Heart of Our Cities* (Gruen), 3/45. Paul Théobald, from *The New City* (Hilberseimer) 1/51; 3/46. Thompson, Coventry, 2/15; 6/1, 34. *The Times*, 1/36; 5/87, 107. University of Edinburgh, 9/1, 24-8. U.S. Information Service, 1/58, 59, 65, 66; 2/12, 13, 18, 26, 31, 63, 64, 67, 69, 71-6; 3/24, 63. Vera Foto Grafia, 1/18. Vrij Van, 7/45. Warsaw Town Planning Office, 2/44. Ziff-Davies, 1/50, 52; 2/20.